MURDER...
by CATEGORY

a subject guide to
mystery fiction

by
TASHA MACKLER

The Scarecrow Press, Inc.
Metuchen, N.J., & London
1991

British Library Cataloguing-in-Publication data available

Library of Congress Cataloging-in-Publication Data

Mackler, Tasha.
  Murder . . . by category : a subject guide to mystery fiction / by Tasha Mackler.
     p. cm.
  Includes index.
  ISBN 0-8108-2463-9
  1. Detective and mystery stories, English—Bibliography.
2. Detective and mystery stories, American—Bibliography.
3. Detective and mystery stories, American—Indexes.
4. Detective and mystery stories, English—Indexes. I. Title.
Z2014.F4M34   1991
[PR830.D4]
016.823′087208—dc20   91-37638

Copyright © 1991 by Natalie J. Mackler
Manufactured in the United States of America
Printed on acid-free paper

With loving memories
I dedicate this book to
Bill Hayden
and
R. D. Brown

ACKNOWLEDGMENTS

To Janet M. Amos who gave so graciously of her time and talent that I could sit at the computer.

To Ashley McConnell for her valuable criticisms and enduring encouragement.

To my writing group who offered continual support.

And to Meredith Cary who said I could do it.

CONTENTS

Acknowledgments   v
Introduction   xi

A ... is for	Academics	1
	Accidents	12
	Advertising	15
	Africa	17
	Americans in England	18
	Anthropology and Archaeology	19
	Antiques	25
	Arson	31
	Art and the Artist	33
	Australia	48
B ... is for	Ball Games	52
	Bees	57
	Birdwatching	57
	Black Detectives	59
	Blackmail	62
	Bookstores	74
	Botany	76
C ... is for	Canada	79
	Cats	84
	Children	86
	Christmas	90
	Clergy	96
	Computer Crimes	100
	Cooks and Cooking	102
	Corruption	105
	Crossword Puzzles	107
D ... is for	Dance and Ballet	110

	Dogs	111
	Drugs	112
E ... is for	Economics	122
	Espionage, the Industrial Kind	124
F ... is for	Famous People	127
	Fashion	132
	Fathers	133
	Fraud	139
G ... is for	Gay	149
	Getting Away with Murder	153
H ... is for	Historical	162
	Holiday for Murder	165
	Hollywood	169
	Horses and Horse Racing	172
I ... is for	Imposter	177
	Incest	182
	Indians	184
	Infidelity	188
	Insurance	195
	Intrigue	198
J ... is for	Jealousy	211
	Jewels and Jewelry	215
	Journalism	221
K ... is for	Kidnapping	232
L ... is for	Lawyers	236
	Libraries	243
	Locked Room	245
M ... is for	Manuscripts	248
	Medical	253
	Medieval	258
	Missing Persons	262
	Mothers	271
	Music	275
	Mystery Games	279
	Mystery Writers	281
O ... is for	Old Crimes and Murders	287
	Orient	300
P ... is for	Pathologist	305
	Political	306
	Pornography	312

CONTENTS

	Prostitution	315
	Psychics, with a Touch of Magic	318
	Psychological	320
R . . . is for	Rape	328
	Real Estate	329
	Revenge	335
	Richard III	355
	Russia	356
S . . . is for	At Sea	358
	Serial Killers	360
	Sherlock Holmes	369
	Smuggling	371
	Social Issues	376
	Suicide or Murder?	378
T . . . is for	Television and Radio	384
	Theater	389
V . . . is for	On Vacation	395
	Vampires	399
	Victorian	400
W . . . is for	Where There's a Will	406
	Witches, Curses, and a Little Voodoo	418
	Witness Protection Program	424
	Writers and Their Conventions	426

British Women Mystery Writers   433
Female Detectives   435
Award Winners   442
Reference Books   453
Author Index   455

INTRODUCTION

OVER THE PAST FOURTEEN YEARS at my mystery bookstore—Murder Unlimited—I have listened to what my customers have said about what they like in murder fiction and have noted the questions they've asked me: "I'm interested in mysteries with a female detective." "What mystery stories do you have set in foreign countries?" "Something about art?" "Which ones have humor?" "Just the puzzle, please, a cozy. I don't like blood and gore." "Series characters are my favorites." This book is a response to their questions and requests.

Frequently mystery readers become intrigued with a particular author and want to read everything they can lay their hands on by that same writer. At other times, specific kinds of settings or something about the subject of a mystery story spurs the reader on to find others about the same topic or location.

For the first kind of reader, there are several good comprehensive bibliographies available that list mystery fiction by author (see "Reference Books" section). Usually a copy can be found at a bookstore specializing in mystery fiction, or at your favorite library.

The second kind of reader has a more difficult task. In general, the mystery fan must rely on the knowledge and memory of the local librarian or of bookstore personnel. Until very recently, there have been almost no books available listing current murder mysteries by subject.

There have been a few attempts over the years to fulfill the needs of the fans of category mysteries. But the attempts have been limited, mostly confined to newsletters or mimeographed sheets from someone who has researched a single topic. And, in general, these listings have not been annotated. In addition, the majority of the selections included in these listings are so old that it is almost impossible to locate them, except through an interlibrary loan system.

Murder . . . by Category introduces the reader to a selective compilation of annotated mysteries by subject matter. Each of the books listed is placed under the topics that reflect the main interest of the content of the book. A short annotation gives the reader an entrée into the story itself.

The first mystery story, *The Murders in the Rue Morgue*, by Edgar Allan Poe, published in 1841, was, after all, the first category mystery, belonging to the time-honored collection of "Locked Room" mysteries.

Because the customers that I see every day at Murder Unlimited tell me they find it particularly frustrating to come across an interesting listing, only to discover that the book has long been out of print, I have confined the entries to mystery stories that are readily available as recently-released hardcovers and paperbacks, or as titles kept on a publisher's backlist. These books can easily be located at your library or on the shelves of your frequently visited used-book store. I have designated 1985 as the starting year for the inclusion of a particular title, continuing to add new publications through early 1991. But I must confess to including a few older favorites.

Notations: The first date and publisher after a listing refer to the publication of the hardcover edition; the second date and publishing house indicate the book's release in paperback, keeping in mind that some paperbacks stay in print for many years. If the date is followed by the letters "PBO," that means the book is a paperback original, at least in this country. Books with series characters are noted by "1st," "2nd," etc. The notation "w/a" preceding an author's name means "writing as."

A number of books lend themselves to more than one category. Where this is the case, a second category will be enclosed in brackets at the end of the annotation, such as "[Art and the Artist]." The index will help you locate all of an author's mysteries included in this book.

At the end of the categories proper, there are several

INTRODUCTION

special listings. These are in answer to the most frequently asked questions by my customers. There are no annotations, and the authors are listed elsewhere.

British Women Mystery Writers:. The most frequent request I receive is for mysteries by British women. Long ago, I set up this special listing for my customers.

Female Detectives: Whether the detective is professional or amateur, mystery readers enjoy their heroines less sprinkled with blood and gore, and more apt to be dressed with a hint of romance. The majority of these entries have a touch of humor.

Awards: It is relatively easy to locate the award-winning mystery writers of a particular year. But what about the others who were nominated for an award? Not so easy. Thus, I have included these writers.

And finally, an author doesn't always write about the same subject, book after book. So, for your convenience, authors are indexed at the end of the book, serving as a source for cross-reference, enabling you to locate other mysteries by the same writer.

A . . . IS FOR

ACADEMICS

SOME OF OUR NEWER MYSTERY WRITERS *are university professors, from Western Washington State (R. D. Brown) to Colby College, Maine (Susan Kenny). With the dictum "write what you know about," is it any wonder that the murder rate in mystery fiction with a campus setting has increased over the last few years? And, according to the latest findings, the deadliest part of the campus is the English Department. These murderous practices are filtering down to the boarding school and the public school.*

ASIMOV, Isaac. *A Whiff Of Death.* 1958 Walker/ Fawcett 1987. They were all shocked when Ralph Newfeld died in the lab. He'd apparently confused his chemicals. Professor Lou Brade isn't convinced—Ralph had been a careful student. Lou scouts the campus for clues.

BARNARD, Robert. *Death Of An Old Goat.* [Australian]

BERNARD, Robert. *Deadly Meeting.* 1970 Norton/ Perennial 1988. The chairman of the English Department at Wilton University is poisoned at a convention. Professor Bill Stratton joins with the police to solve the mystery. Enter Dame Millicent, medieval scholar and writer of gothic novels.

BORTHWICK, J. S. *The Student Body.* 1986 St. Martin/ St. Martin 1987. Sarah Deane is filling a vacancy at Bowmouth College and Dr. Alex McKenzie is at the Medical School. At the height of the Winter Carnival, the body of a young woman is found strangled and frozen into an ice sculpture. 3rd.

BROWN, R. D. *Prime Suspect.* 1981 Tower/ PBO. In charge of Affirmative Action at Benson University, Susan Meredith is getting the message that someone doesn't like her. Detective Harry Bliss, investigating the accidents that have beset her, agrees.

CANDY, Edward. *Words For Murder Perhaps.* 1971 Doubleday/ Ballantine 1985. Gregory Roberts teaches an evening class: Crime Fiction, Past and Present. As several of his colleagues disappear, he seems the likely suspect. With each death is a quote from a British poet, someone with a literary mind. 3rd. [Revenge]

CARLSON, P. M. *Murder Is Academic.* 1985 Avon/ PBO. He was labeled the Triangle Murderer, and he's struck again. Jackie, a graduate student, is dead. Her roommates, Maggie Ryan and Mary Beth Nelson, stumble into trapping the killer, only to discover that Jackie's murderer is still on the loose. 2nd. [Rape]

CARLSON, P. M. *Murder Is Pathological.* 1986 Avon/ PBO. A lab experiment was destroyed. Then Norman, the maintenance man, was killed as he rode his bicycle. Maggie Ryan, after a glance at the statistics, and Nick O'Connor go back over the multimillion dollar experiment looking for clues, and the murderer. 3rd. [Medical]

CLARKE, Anna. *Last Judgment.* 1985 Doubleday/ Berkley 1989. World-famous novelist G. E. Goff is almost ninety, and people are lining up, waiting for him to die. Paula Glenning senses something very disturbing in his house. His stepdaughter, Mary, plays her own waiting game, until the night she stands up for herself. 1st. [Father]

CLEMEAU, Carol. *The Ariadne Clue.* 1982 Scribner/

Ballantine 1983. Artifacts for the Aegean Exhibition are missing. And so is Ariadne Pappas, graduate student. Professor Antonia Nielson delves into Ariadne's family and her work, discovering that a thesis can be deadly.

CRAIG, Philip R. *The Woman Who Walked Into The Sea.* 1991 Scribner. Retired policeman Jeff Jackson met Marjorie Summerharp who will be staying at a friend's cottage while working on a Shakespearian paper. In her seventies, she's an excellent swimmer. But Marjorie drowns. 2nd. [Anthropology]

CRIDER, Bill. *One Dead Dean.* 1988 Walker. The small, sedate Baptist College was in for culture shock. Dean Elmore wants to turn it into a diploma mill to fill the empty coffers. Someone bludgeons the dean at his desk, and English professor Carl Burns is looking for the motive. 1st. [Blackmail]

CRIDER, Bill. *Dying Voices.* 1989 St. Martin. English professor Carl Burns is in charge of the Edward Streeter Seminar, honoring Hartley Gorman College's famous colleague. But Streeter dies in his motel room before the papers about his works are even read. 2nd.

CROSS, Amanda. *The James Joyce Murder.* 1967 Macmillan/Ballantine 1987. Professor Kate Fansler is in the Berkshires with some other scholars. They are examining a collection of letters from James Joyce. When the obnoxious lady next door is killed, Kate's household is under suspicion. 2nd.

CROSS, Amanda. *The Theban Mysteries.* 1971 Knopf/Avon 1979. Kate Fansler returns to Theban, her alma mater, to conduct a senior seminar on *Antigone.* When the mother of one of the students is found dead of fright at the school, Kate throws herself into the mystery. 4th.

CROSS, Amanda. *The Question Of Max.* 1976 Knopf/ Ballantine 1987. As executor of the late novelist, Max Reston is making sure Cecily's papers are safe. He persuades Kate Fansler to go with him to the coast of Maine, to Cecily's house. There at the foot of a cliff is a body, one of Kate's students. 5th.

CROSS, Amanda. *Death In A Tenured Position.* 1981 Dutton/ Ballantine 1987. Janet Mandelbaum, first tenured woman in the English Department at Harvard, is in trouble . . . and soon dead of cyanide in the men's room. Kate Fansler, attending an institute, is determined to solve the riddle of her death. 6th. [Suicide]

CROSS, Amanda. *Sweet Death, Kind Death.* 1984 Dutton/ Ballantine 1987. Kate Fansler is asked to investigate the death of a woman professor at Clare College in New England. With the help of two biographies, Kate finally tracks down the murderers. 7th. [Suicide]

DEAN, S. F. X. *By Frequent Anguish.* 1982 Walker/ Tor 1986. Before Professor Neil Kelly can declare his love for his godchild, Priscilla, she's found dead in the library stacks. He must find the killer . . . and open old wounds. 1st. [Library]

DEAN, S. F. X. *Death And The Mad Heroine.* 1985 Walker/ Bantam 1987. Professor Neil Kelly returns to Old Hampton College and faces a former student. Dick Coltrane is tempted to find the culprit who ruined his sports career and Margaret Mary wants her father's name cleared. 4th. [Old Crime]

DELMAN, David. *Death Of A Nymph.* 1985 Doubleday. Lt. Jacob Horowitz is lecturing on the criminal mind when someone takes a shot at him. Then the president of the college is murdered. Jacob's wife, Sgt. Helen, pokes through the hallowed halls, investigating faculty and students alike. 6th.

ACADEMICS

DEXTER, Colin. *The Riddle Of The Third Mile.* 1984 St. Martin/ Bantam 1988. The dismembered corpse of Professor Browne-Smith was found in the Oxford Canal. Why was the note he left behind so carelessly misspelled? Inspector Morse will trip over a few more bodies before he finds the truth. 6th. [Revenge]

FISKE, Dorsey. *Academic Murder.* 1986 St. Martin/ Critic's Choice 1987. Garmoyle, Prye Librarian at Cambridge, has made a few enemies over the years. But no one expected him to be poisoned by arsenic in his port. Inspector Bunce wanders the unfamiliar campus to find the murderer. 1st.

FISKE, Dorsey. *Bound To Murder.* [Manuscripts]

GALBRAITH, Ruth. *A Convenient Death.* 1986 Paperjacks/ PBO. Convocation can be dull . . . but deadly dull? Audrey Benedict was not particularly popular. Is that a good reason to kill her? Grace Forrester, retired dean of women at Lockland University doesn't think so. [Canadian]

GEORGE, Elizabeth. *Well-Schooled In Murder.* 1990 Bantam/ Bantam 1991. A young boy is missing from Bredgar Chamber, an isolated boys' school founded by Henry VII. When his body is found beside the churchyard at Stoke Poges, Detective Inspector Thomas Lynley and Sergeant Barbara Havers take over a case that twists and turns toward the truth. 3rd. [Father]

GILL, B. M. *Death Drop.* 1980 Scribner/ Ballantine 1985. John Flemming flew back to England from Bombay. He'd gotten a call that David, his only child, was dead. At Morristone Grange, David's school, he's not satisfied that it was an accident. [Gay]

GOSLING, Paula. *Monkey Puzzle.* 1985 Doubleday. Most of the English Department hated Aiken Adamson, and now he is dead with his tongue cut out. Before Lt. Jack Stryker can solve the murder, the chairman has an ear removed and there is an attempt to blind Kate Trevorne, a young instructor.

GRIFFITHS, John. *Snake Charmer.* Jove 1989/ PBO. Philip Nolan, teacher at a private school in northern New Mexico, was climbing early one morning when he discovered the body of a young female student, dead at the bottom of a cliff. [Real Estate]

HARRIS, Charlaine. *A Secret Rage.* 1984 Houghton Mifflin/ Ballantine 1985. Nickie Callahan jumps at the chance to stay with her friend Mimi near Memphis and finish her studies at Houghton College. A rapist roams the campus and Nickie is his third victim. She's out for revenge. [Rape]

HAYNES, Conrad. *Bishop's Gambit Declined.* 1987 Bantam/ PBO. Harry Bishop, political science professor at John Jacob Astor College in Portland, Oregon, becomes involved in the death of one of his students, the editor of the college newspaper. Then his own life is threatened. 1st.

HAYNES, Conrad. *Perpetual Check.* 1988 Bantam/ PBO. Harry Bishop got a call the morning after the trustees' big party. One of them, Llewellyn, was dead, knifed and dumped in the downtown square. Another trustee is being held for murder. Harry and a young journalist, Tucker, follow the story to the end. 2nd. [Father]

HESS, Joan. *Strangled Prose.* 1986 St. Martin/ Ballantine 1987. Claire Malloy runs the Book Depot, a classy bookstore. Against her better judgment, she agrees to host a book-signing party for a torrid romance writer. When the party is over, the author is strangled and Claire is under suspicion. 1st. [Bookstores]

HILL, Reginald *An Advancement Of Learning.* 1985 Foul Play/ Signet 1986. They're moving the statue of Alison Girling at Holm Coultran College. As the hoist raises the bronze figure, bones and red hair fall free. Two more deaths occur before Dalziel and Pascoe solve the crimes. 3rd. [Old Crime]

HILL, Reginald, writing as Patrick Ruell. *Death Takes The Low Road.* 1987 Mysterious/ PBO. Deputy registrar William Blake Hazlett has disappeared. Caroline Nevis, an American student, is determined to find him, and her only clue is in Scotland. She finds that someone is hunting Bill and trying to stop her.

HULLAND, J. R. *An Educated Murder.* 1986 St. Martin. Kate Henderson, student at the Teacher Training College, discovers a headless body in the lily pond. Only later does she discover that the death of a friend two years before is part of the same parcel. [Old Crime]

JEVONS, Marshall. *The Fatal Equilibrium.* 1985 MIT Press/Ballantine 1986. A young man, turned down by Harvard's Promotion and Tenure Committee, is found dead the next morning . . . suicide. His girlfriend is arrested when committee members start to die. Professor Spearman is suspicious. 2nd. [Economics]

JORDAN, Cathleen. *A Carol In The Dark.* [Christmas]

KELMAN, Judith. *When Shadows Fall.* 1987 Berkley/ PBO. For her own peace of mind, Sarah Spooner traveled to Cromwell University to find out why her son killed himself. It was with horror that she discovered something more deadly. [Suicide]

KELVIN, Ned. *Pegged For Murder.* 1988 Paperjacks/ PBO. The dean of Arts and Sciences was dead, shot to death. He left behind a message in a cribbage hand. It's up to

Professor Ned Kelvin, his friend and cribbage partner, to decipher the cryptic testament.

KENNEY, Susan. *Graves In Academe.* 1985 Viking/ Penguin 1986. Roz Howard signs on to teach a course in English literature at Canterbury College after the scheduled professor dies in a freak accident. Soon other accidents happen, and the deaths follow her course outline. 2nd.

KLASS, David. *Night Of The Tyger.* 1990 St. Martin. Alyssa was researching ancient Carthage at Yale's Sterling Library late one evening. She was found dead on the 12th floor. English professor Kevin Randall burst into the police investigation. Two years ago, his wife Anne died in the same way. [Children]

LAKE, M. D. *Amends For Murder.* 1989 Avon/ PBO. Campus cop Peggy O'Neill answers a call from an irate professor: the frat houses are whooping it up and he can't work. When Peggy checks with him, she discovers someone got there first and smashed his skull with a hammer. 1st. [Drugs]

LANGTON, Jane. *The Memorial Hall Murders.* 1978 Harper & Row/ Penguin 1986. Homer and Mary Kelly are at Harvard. After the rose windows explode at Memorial Hall from a bomb blast, a faculty member is missing. Homer searches through the debris for the answer. 3rd.

LANSBURY, Coral. *Felicity.* 1987 Dutton/ Ivy 1988. Prestigious Pequod College has a problem: there's a rapist on the loose, plaguing the coeds. Where and when will he strike again? Art professor Felicity Norman does her part to stop him. [Rape]

LARSEN, Gaylord. *An Uneducated Death.* 1983 Regal/ Ballantine 1986. Geology professor Ralph Pangbourne was dead, though he wasn't mourned by many.

Henry Garrett, retired CIA, noses around to find the murderer.

LARSEN, Gaylord. *The 180-Degree Murder.* 1987 Ballantine/ PBO. Psychology professor Alexander Hacchi, Trinity University, committed suicide. Then a student was found stabbed. Hacchi's replacement, Jason Bradley, is looking into the circumstances. What he finds distresses him. [Suicide]

LeCLAIRE, Anne D. *Every Mother's Son.* 1987 Bantam/ PBO. They came from Annapolis to tell Kate Tyler that her son had killed himself, and she hadn't even had a chance to read his last letter. Now the letter is missing, and she's headed south to prove he was murdered. [Suicide]

LUPICA, Mike. *Extra Credit.* 1988 Villard/ Ballantine 1990. Julie Samson walked into Washington Square Park and shot herself. When TV reporter Peter Finley is persuaded to investigate, he discovers that there is a lot going on behind the hallowed university walls. 2nd. [Revenge]

MacLEOD, Charlotte. *Rest You Merry.* [Christmas]

MacLEOD, Charlotte. *The Luck Runs Out.* 1979 Doubleday/ Avon 1981. It looked like a student prank gone wrong. The horseshoes at Balaclava College had been turned upside down, and the blacksmith was found dead in the pigs' mash feeder. Professor Shandy is finding too many clues. 2nd. [Smuggling]

MATERA, Lia. *Where Lawyers Fear To Tread.* [Lawyer]

McCORMICK, Claire. *Résumé For Murder.* 1982 Walker/ Walker 1986. John Waltz, professional recruiter, is at Witherspoon College, in the heart of Amish country, where people are kind and friendly. But a body in the administration building leads to another side of town life. 1st.

McINERNY, Ralph. *The Search Committee.* 1991 Atheneum. The Chancellor at Fort Elbow Campus is arrested for DWI on his way home from a massage parlor. Two people who vie for his job are poisoned, one after the other. Professor Matthew Rogerson is on the lookout for a killer. 3rd.

MICHAELS, Barbara. *Search The Shadows.* [Father]

PENN, John. *Mortal Term.* 1985 Scribner/ Bantam 1986. This was to be a bad term for Headmaster Hugh Roystone. He had a new, young wife to introduce around. Superintendent George Thorne is on hand when the female student who accused Hugh of assault is found murdered. 2nd. [Jealousy]

RESNICOW, Herbert. *The Seventh Crossword.* [Crossword Puzzles]

RESNICOW, Herbert. *The Crossword Hunt.* [Crossword Puzzles]

ROBINSON, Robert. *Landscape With Dead Dons.* 1956 Rinehart/ Penguin 1983. There is a tragedy at Oxford. Someone has destroyed *Paradise Lost.* As an unknown Chaucer poem surfaces, the Vice-Chancellor is murdered on the roof with a fruit knife. Inspector Autumn is about to get an education. [Manuscript]

SILVER, Victoria. *Death Of A Harvard Freshman.* 1984 Bantam/ PBO. Lauren Adler used to stare at him in her Russian seminar. Then he was dead, floating in the Charles River. With her friend Michael Hunt she comes to a frightening conclusion: the murderer is someone in the seminar. 1st.

SILVER, Victoria. *Death Of A Radcliffe Roommate.* 1986 Bantam/ PBO. Lauren Adler is looking for a roommate. One of her choices is found strangled with her own harp string. Laura enlists Michael Hunt's help as they look for another roommate who got an "A" in murder. 2nd.

SKOM, Edith. *The Mark Twain Murders.* [Manuscript]

SPRINKLE, Patricia Houck. *Murder At Markham.* 1988 St. Martin. After her husband died, Sheila Travis joined the staff of Chicago's Markham Institute, training ground for diplomats. A young woman is found dead in the basement, rolled up in an Oriental rug. With Aunt Mary, Sheila investigates. 1st.

TAYLOR, Elizabeth Atwood. *Murder At Vassar.* 1987 St. Martin/ Ivy 1988. PI Maggie Elliott is at a reunion at Vassar. A wealthy old lady has just been murdered and her niece, Pudgie, is arrested. But Pudgie's classmates insist she's innocent. Maggie is hired to investigate. 2nd. [Where There's A Will]

TOWNSEND, Guy M. *To Prove A Villain.* [Richard III]

WALLACE, Patricia. *Deadly Grounds.* Zebra 1989/ PBO. Nicole Halpern left the school library headed for the dorm. On the path she found the body of her friend Melissa. With her father out of town, Nicole calls her friend P.I. Sydney Bryant. And the investigation begins. 1st. [Drugs]

WALTCH, Lilla M. *The Third Victim.* 1987 Dodd, Mead. Lisa Davis eased open the door to Professor Silverman's office and found him staring at the ceiling, sightless and dead. Soon there is another death. Lisa is following some hints to student unrest back in l968 to solve the crime. [Old Crime]

WENDER, Theodora. *Knight Must Fall.* 1985 Avon/ PBO. President Knight of Turnbull College is found floating in the swimming pool. He wasn't popular, but he'd already planned to resign. Professor Glad Gold's life is threatened before she and Police Chief Alden Chase find the murderer. 1st.

WENDER, Theodora. *Murder Gets A Degree.* 1986 Avon/ PBO. Arson destroys one of the oldest houses in Wading River, along with the crazy owner Adah Storm. Soon Professor Glad Gold and Police Chief Alden Chase are caught up in the crime and the danger. 2nd. [Holiday]

WILLIAMS, David. *Treasure In Oxford.* [Art]

WRIGHT, Eric. *The Night The Gods Smiled.* [Canadian]

YAFFE, James. *A Nice Murder For Mom.* 1988 St. Martin/ Worldwide 1990. As an investigator for the Public Defender's Office, Dave had always talked his cases over with Mom. Now living in Colorado, he has the murder of a college professor on his hands. Mom shows up and starts to put the pieces together. [Mother]

ACCIDENTS

Thousands of murders must masquerade as accidents every year: the sudden fall from the top of the stairs, a body floating in the swimming pool, the ingestion of a mistaken drug. It takes the suspicious sleuth to investigate the incidents and ferret out the truth, bringing the culprit to justice. Or maybe it really was an accident.

ALLEGRETTO, Michael. *Death On The Rocks.* [Blackmail]

BABSON, Marian. *Untimely Guest.* 1987 St. Martin. Birdie had just been turned out of the convent and was headed home. At the same time, her sister Dee-Dee came home with her fiancé. Unfortunately, her ex-husband was still under the same roof. Within days, Dee-Dee was dead at the foot of the stairs. [Jealousy]

BANKS, Joan. *Death Claims.* 1988 Charter/ PBO. Lora Montgomery was taking a routine accident-insurance claims phone call. Suddenly the woman caller screamed, then a man picked up the phone. Lora quickly hung up. But the man knew who she was and he was coming to get her. [Insurance]

BARNARD, Robert. *The Skeleton In The Grass.* 1988 Scribner/ Dell 1989. Sarah Causeley went to work for the Hallam family as governess in 1936. The family was deeply committed to the principle of peace as Hitler marshaled his forces. There's conflict with the villagers, until the night of the murder.

BLOCK, Lawrence. *The Burglar Who Studied Spinoza.* [Bookstore]

CAUDWELL, Sarah. *The Shortest Way To Hades.* 1985 Scribner/ Penguin 1986. Camille Galloway petitioned the court to alter a trust on a £5 million estate to save on taxes. Suddenly her cousin Deidre wants a goodly sum to sign the petition. But then Deidre has a deadly fall. 2nd. [Lawyer]

DOBSON, Margaret. *Primrose.* [Bookstore]

DOWNING, Warwick. *A Clear Case Of Murder.* [Lawyer]

GREENLEAF, Stephen. *Impact.* [Lawyer]

HALL, Adam. *Bishop In Check.* HarperCollins 1991/PBO. On a rainy country road outside London, Hugo Bishop's car is sideswiped. Bishop watches as the other car plunges into a ravine. David Brain is dead. A terrible accident. The two women in Brain's life arrive to complicate the picture. 1st. [Getting Away With Murder]

HORANSKY, Ruby. *Dead Ahead.* [Fraud]

KEATING, H. R. F., w/a Evelyn Hervey. *The Man Of Gold.* 1985 Doubleday/ Berkley 1989. Governess Harriet Unwin is caring for the motherless twins of Richard Partington in the home of his miserly father. When the old man dies, Richard is accused of the crime. Harriet bones up on poisons to clear him. 2nd. [Historical]

KEATING, H. R. F. *Under A Monsoon Cloud.* 1986 Viking/ Penguin 1987. The chief inspector threw the inkwell across the room. Unfortunately it struck and killed a deficient policeman. Ghote, the only witness, works quietly to cover up the incident. When the inspector commits suicide, Ghote is left with his own career in jeopardy. 22nd.

LEMARCHAND, Elizabeth. *The Wheel Turns.* [Revenge]

MICHAELS, Barbara. *The Grey Beginnings.* 1984 Congdon & Weed/Tor 1985. Kathy Morandini made the trip to Florence after her husband died in a terrible auto accident. She wanted to see the contessa, his grandmother. Kathy wasn't very welcome, but the contessa's great-grandson, a disturbed young boy, attracted her attention. In a short time she discovered they were both in danger. [Where There's A Will]

RADLEY, Sheila. *Fate Worse Than Death.* [Missing Person]

SMITH, Joan. *Don't Leave Me This Way.* 1990 Scribner. Loretta Lawson answered the phone on Christmas Eve and discovered Sandra, a woman she hardly liked at all, needed a favor, a place to stay for a few days. But on New Year's Eve, Sandra vanished, only to turn up dead in a car accident. 3rd. [Jealousy]

SPRINKLE, Patricia Houck. *Murder In The Charleston Manner.* 1990 St. Martin. Aunt Mary enlists Sheila

Travis to run over to Charleston for a few days. Dolly and her family have been plagued by accidents. Sheila has to delve into the history of the town and its prominent families for hidden answers. 2nd. [Where There's A Will]

ADVERTISING

The break-neck world of advertising, with its glitz and glitter, seems made for murder. The pace, the politics, and the backstabbing provide motives galore. Our newer entrants in the field forsake the coasts and move to the midwest, a location just as deadly.

BARTHELME, Peter. *Push, Meet Shove.* 1987 St. Martin. Wellamation Oil hired Beaumont for a big ad campaign, the biggest he'd ever had. Except now that the bills are rolling in, the oil tycoon claims he never hired Beaumont. The play turns deadly. 1st. [Drugs]

CRESPI, Trella. *The Trouble With A Small Raise.* Zebra 1991/ PBO. All Simona Griffo wanted that Monday morning was to arrive at the advertising office early and hit her boss up for a raise. Instead, Fred was dead on his office floor. Simona was assigned to help the police interview all the suspects. 1st. [Revenge]

GORMAN, Edward. *New, Improved Murder.* 1985 St. Martin/ Ballantine 1986. Jack Dwyer, ex-cop and PI, answers a call from Jane Branigan, an ex-lover. He finds her in shock, holding a gun. Before Jane's charged with murder, Jack explores the advertising business . . . and blackmail. 2nd. [Blackmail]

GORMAN, Edward. *Rough Cut.* 1985 St. Martin/ Ballantine 1986. Michael Ketchum went to have it out with his partner Dennis, and found him stabbed to death. Then Michael was knocked out. One by one, the people in his advertising firm are implicated in fraud and death. It's a rush for information and survival.

GOULART, Ron. *Even The Butler Was Poor.* 1990 Walker. H. J. Movitz, romance cover artist, agreed to meet her ex-boy friend at the shopping mall. After all, he owed her $5,000. But he collapsed dead at the foot of the escalator, his dying words a clue to her money. 1st. [Blackmail]

McMULLEN, Mary. *Stranglehold.* 1951 Harper & Row/Jove 1988. Eve Fitzsimmons couldn't look at the nude body of the strangled woman in the conference room at the ad agency. Instead she stared down at the skaters in Rockefeller Center. The staff had all worked late that night, making each of them a suspect. [Blackmail]

ORENSTEIN, Frank. *A Candidate For Murder.* 1987 St. Martin. It's not the kind of job advertising executive Ev Franklin wants: pollster for a presidential candidate. Then someone starts a smear campaign against the candidate, and a young girl dies. 3rd. [Political]

ORENSTEIN, Frank. *Paradise Of Death.* 1988 St. Martin. Ev Franklin's advertising agency was having its annual meeting on San Seho. After the opening meeting, the president of the Olds Media Group was found dead. A few days later there's a plane crash and a second murder. 4th. [Revenge]

ROBERTS, Les. *Pepper Pike.* 1988 St. Martin. Advertising hotshot Richard Amber hired PI Milan Jacovich as his bodyguard. But Richard has disappeared. Now his wife wants Milan to find him. Milan's search digs into Cleveland's society. [Missing Person]

SAYERS, Dorothy L. *Murder Must Advertise.* 1933 Harper & Row/Perennial 1986. Pym's Publicity, an ad agency, has a valued reputation. So when Victor Dean dies in a fall from the stairs, it's considered an accident. Lord Peter Wimsey goes undercover to prove otherwise. 8th. [Drugs]

AFRICA

The works of Elspeth Huxley aside, most mysteries set in Africa are the product of the visitor to the Dark Continent. A few mysteries with a South African setting full of atmosphere and culture, have developed almost a cult following. Both the visitor and the resident give us a picture of this relatively unknown continent.

FRANCIS, Dick. *Smokescreen.* 1972 Harper & Row/ Pocket 1978. Edward Lincoln was doing Nerissa a favor. He'd go out to Africa and find out why her horses were running so poorly. Link barely makes it out alive. [Horses]

HUXLEY, Elspeth. *Murder On Safari.* 1989 Viking/ Perennial 1982. Lady Baradale insisted on taking her collection of valuable jewelry on safari. When the jewels were stolen, Superintendent Vachell was notified at once. The next day, Lady Baradale was shot. 2nd. [Jewels]

HUXLEY, Elspeth. *The African Poison Murders.* 1987 Viking/ Perennial 1981. CID Officer Vachell went up to the Wests' ranch in Africa. There seemed to be some trouble with the Wests' neighbors, the Munsons. Then the killings start, and Vachell is on the trail of a specific poison. 3rd. [Jealousy]

KAYE, M. M. *Death In Zanzibar.* 1983 St. Martin/ St. Martin 1984. Dany Ashton flew to Zanzibar to visit her mother, now married to wealthy Tyson Frost. Her quiet vacation turned into murder and more. [Intrigue]

McCLURE, James. *The Artful Egg.* 1984 Pantheon/Vintage 1985. Naomi Stride is a prizewinning writer whose books are banned in South Africa where she lives. One morning the postman finds her dead. Lt. Tromp Kramer and Zulu Sgt. Mickey Zondi have to find the killer. 7th.

ROBERTS, Nora. *Hot Ice.* [Jewels]

WAUGH, Hillary. *Murder On Safari.* [Birdwatching]

WESTLAKE, Donald. *Kahawa.* 1982 Viking/ Tor 1984. This was to be the biggest rip-off of all. Lew Brady and his cohorts were going to steal a trainload of coffee, right out from under the nose of Idi Amin. The caper would have its share of dangers, of course. [Intrigue]

AMERICANS IN ENGLAND

The urge to travel must be firmly recorded in our genes, for we move about the globe with increasing frequency, despite any dangers. The tiny British Isles, and especially England, have become stuffed to the bursting point with travelers from their former colony who manage to find themselves embroiled in mystery and murder.

BABSON, Marian. *Death Swap.* [Witness Protection]

BABSON, Marian. *Murder On A Mystery Tour.* 1987 Walker/ Bantam 1988. Reggie and Midge, trying to keep the stately home solvent, developed a country inn. Midge's old schoolmate wanted to use it for a series of "mystery tours" for Americans. But the games become real. [Mystery Games]

BOROWITZ, Albert. *The Jack The Ripper Walking Tour Murder.* 1986 St. Martin. Paul Prye is in London for the Centennial Jack the Ripper Walking Tour. When

Margaret, also on the tour, is found dead, and there is another death, he wonders if a new Jack the Ripper is on the loose.

CLARKE, Anna. *Last Seen In London.* 1987 Doubleday/ Charter 1990. Cathy, an American student at the university, asks Professor Paula Glenning for help. She has a neighbor who reminds her of a spider. But when the old lady is found dead in the bathtub, Cathy discovers the woman is her unknown grandmother. [Father]

MICHAELS, Barbara. *Wait For What Will Come.* [Witches]

ANTHROPOLOGY AND ARCHAEOLOGY

There is something novel about anthropology and archaeology for the professional and amateur alike. Digging up old bones, investigating different cultures, and collecting artifacts intrigue us all. And here in the Southwest, where every third person is a part-time anthropologist, we're still enchanted with every new Tony Hillerman or the current Elizabeth Peters set along the Nile.

ARNOLD, Margot. *The Cape Cod Caper.* 1988 Foul Play/ PBO. Penny Spring returned to the States to see her publisher. An urgent call took her to Cape Cod. Zeb had found a fresh body in an old Indian grave. He's attacked and left for dead. Tobias asks a few questions in Italy and flies to the Cape for the finish. 2nd.

BANNISTER, Jo. *The Mason Codex.* 1988 Doubleday. Welsh teacher Annie Meredith has just discovered she has a brother. But it comes too late—he's just been found dead, locked in a truck at the Mexican border. Annie heads for Mexico—she wants the truth about her brother's death. [Smuggling]

BLACKSTOCK, Charity. *The Foggy, Foggy Dew.* 1958 London House/ Ballantine 1986. Anthropologist Andrew Mallory is in England. At a party, he hears a message in the very language of the island where he's been researching. The young woman with him pretends to understand the words. She has to die. [Christmas]

CRAIG, Philip R. *The Woman Who Walked Into The Sea.* [Academic]

ELKINS, Aaron J. *The Dark Place.* 1983 Walker/ Popular 1986. Gideon Oliver, forensic consultant, is in the middle of an interesting puzzle. The body of a hiker, missing for eight years, is found in the Olympic National Forest, killed by a prehistoric spear. And then there's Julie . . . 2nd.

ELKINS, Aaron J. *Murder In The Queen's Armes.* 1985 Walker/ Bantam 1987. Gideon and Julie are on their honeymoon in Wessex, England. So, of course, Gideon plays busman's holiday and visits a nearby dig run by an old classmate. It's not long before bodies start to appear. 3rd.

ELKINS, Aaron J. *Old Bones.* [Imposter]

ELKINS, Aaron J. *Curses!.* 1989 Mysterious/ Mysterious 1990. Dr. Abe Goldstein asked Gideon Oliver to go with him to check out a skeleton found at a reopened Mayan site on the Yucatan peninsula. Shortly after Gideon arrived, the translation of a set of hieroglyphs revealed an ancient series of curses. 5th. [Old Crime]

ELKINS, Aaron J. *Icy Clutches.* 1990 Mysterious. M. Audey Tremaine had gathered a small group at Glacier Bay Lodge to finish his book on the avalanche that buried three members of the research party thirty years earlier. When old bones surface from the glacier, Gideon Oliver is on the scene. 6th. [Imposter]

ANTHROPOLOGY AND ARCHAEOLOGY 21

FISH, Robert L. *The Gold Of Troy.* [Antiques]

GRANT-ADAMSON, Lesley. *Death On Widow's Walk.* 1985 Scribner. Gossip columnist Rain Morgan is on holiday in England's West Country. Instead of relaxation, she becomes involved when a body is found in the ruins of the local castle where Robin Woodley, archaeologist, is on a dig. 1st.

HESS, Joan, w/a Joan Hadley. *The Night-Blooming Cereus.* [Intrigue]

HILLERMAN, Tony. *The Blessing Way.* [Indians]

HILLERMAN, Tony. *People Of Darkness.* [Indians]

HILLERMAN, Tony. *The Dark Wind.* [Indians]

HILLERMAN, Tony. *Skinwalkers.* [Indians]

HILLERMAN, Tony. *A Thief Of Time.* [Indians]

HILLERMAN, Tony. *Talking God.* [Indians]

KNIGHT, Kathryn Lasky. *Trace Elements.* 1986 Norton/ Pocket 1987. Tom Jacobs died in the Nevada desert, of a rattlesnake bite. As Calista adjusts to widowhood, another death occurs—another rattlesnake. And the artifacts in the Peabody Museum are being replaced. 1st.

KUNETKA, James W. *Shadow Man.* 1988 Warner/Warner 1988. On a trip to the Tsankawi ruins outside of Los Alamos, David Parker and his family stumble over the body of a scientist. At his feet are tribal prayer sticks. The local police see a ritual slaying; the FBI is concerned about national secrets. [Intrigue]

LEVI, Peter. *Grave Witness.* 1985 St. Martin. Ben Jonson, archaeologist, is called down from Oxford and asked, by Ralph Iggleby, to examine some pieces of Greek pottery. Then Iggleby is murdered and there is a hint of salted grave goods in a burial mound. 1st.

MANN, Jessica. *Faith, Hope & Homicide.* 1991 St. Martin. Louise Dench returned from a Brazilian expedition very ill. She died soon after. Called to investigate, Tamara Hoyland discovered Alastair was also in Brazil, and that Robert Waugh, Louise's husband, had died in the jungle, a victim of witchcraft. 3rd. [Medical]

McCRUMB, Sharyn. *Lovely In Her Bones.* [Indians]

McCRUMB, Sharyn. *Paying The Piper.* 1988 Ballantine/ PBO. Elizabeth MacPherson is part of the group studying megalithic monuments on a small Scottish island. Their quarters are damp and their tempers are high. One of the crew dies, another has a fall. Elizabeth is afraid no one will leave the island alive. 4th. [Imposter]

MELVILLE, James. *The Bogus Buddha.* [Oriental]

MEREDITH, D. R. *The Sheriff And The Folsom Man Murders.* 1986 Walker/ Avon 1987. Raul, Sheriff Charles Matthews's deputy, is accused of murdering his cousin, archaeologist Enrique Armijo. The murder weapon, an atlatl, was in Raul's room. Charles hastens to Clayton, New Mexico, to clear his friend. 3rd.

MICHAELS, Barbara. *The Sea King's Daughter.* [Father]

MOODY, Susan. *Penny Royal.* [Black Detective]

MOORE, Barbara. *The Wolf Whispered Death.* [Indians]

PAINE, Michael. *Cities Of The Dead.* 1988 Charter/ PBO. Egyptologist Howard Carter has lost his job as inspector of monuments. There was a hint he might get it

ANTHROPOLOGY AND ARCHAEOLOGY

back if he cleared up the mystery of the mummies. At Wadi Natrun, he discovered the truth. [Witches]

PETERS, Elizabeth. *The Jackal's Head.* 1968 Meredith/Tor 1988. Althea Tomlinson has returned to Luxor, Egypt, at the request of an Arab man. He has some information that might clear her father's name. He'd been accused of faking antiquities. The Arab is dead, and Althea has some new enemies.

PETERS, Elizabeth. *The Camelot Caper.* 1969 Meredith/Tor 1988. Jessica Tregarth was invited to visit her grandfather in Cornwall. She was instructed to bring the ring her father had taken to America. Once in England, Jessica is followed and attacked. Will she get to see her grandfather?

PETERS, Elizabeth. *The Dead Sea Cipher.* 1970 Dodd, Mead/Tor 1988. Dinah is touring the Middle East. At her Beirut hotel, she hears an argument in the next room. The man is found dead, and now Dinah is searching for a strange treasure. Someone is also on her trail.

PETERS, Elizabeth. *The Seventh Sinner.* 1972 Dodd, Mead/ Mysterious 1986. Jean Suttman has a fellowship in Rome. After she finds Albert dead in a room beneath the church, she has a series of accidents, each more deadly. It takes Jacqueline Kirby's watchful eye to keep Jean alive. 1st.

PETERS, Elizabeth. *The Crocodile On The Sandbank.* 1975 Dodd, Mead/ Mysterious 1988. Amelia Peabody inherited her father's fortune and left for Egypt to fulfill her passion. Her companion is attacked by a mummy, and Amelia enlists archaeologist Radcliffe Emerson to decipher the plot. 1st. [Victorian]

PETERS, Elizabeth. *The Curse Of The Pharaohs.* 1981 Dodd, Mead/ Mysterious 1988. Now married, Amelia and

Radcliffe leave for Egypt. Lady Baskerville wants them to finish excavating the tomb her husband had been working on. Lord Baskerville's death had been attributed to a curse. 2nd. [Victorian]

PETERS, Elizabeth. *The Copenhagen Connection.* 1982 Congdon & Weed/ Critic's Choice 1987. When a stack of luggage disabled the secretary of Nobel Prize winner Margaret Rosenberg, Elizabeth Jones was enlisted to fill the post. Later Margaret disappeared in Copenhagen. The only ransom asked for was Margaret's bathrobe. [Kidnapping]

PETERS, Elizabeth. *Silhouette In Scarlet.* 1983 Congdon & Weed/Critic's Choice 1987. Sir John Smythe, thief and cheat, sent Vicky Bliss a ticket to Stockholm. Her head said "no," but her heart said "go." On the island where Gustaf Jonssan lives, his fields might be a treasure hunter's dream. 3rd.

PETERS, Elizabeth. *The Mummy Case.* 1985 Congdon & Weed/Tor 1986. Amelia and Radcliffe are in Egypt again with their son Ramses. While waiting to excavate the Black Pyramid, Amelia comes face to face with the Master Criminal. 3rd. [Victorian]

PETERS, Elizabeth. *Lion In The Valley.* 1986 Atheneum/ Tor 1987. Off to Egypt for another season, Amelia is sure that this time she'll have her own pyramid to dig. In between digging, she rescues damsels in distress. And she has a startling encounter with the Master Criminal. 4th. [Victorian]

PETERS, Elizabeth. *Trojan Gold.* [Antiques]

PETERS, Elizabeth. *The Deeds Of The Disturber.* 1988 Atheneum/ Warner 1989. Amelia and Radcliffe return to England. They're just in time to get caught up in the "curse of the mummy" that plagues the British Museum. Confounding the mystery is the addition of two more children to the Emerson household. 5th. [Victorian]

PRICE, Anthony. *The Labyrinth Makers.* [Antiques]

SHUMAN, M. K. *The Maya Stone Murders.* 1989 St. Martin. Dr. Thorpe was worried about his display of Mayan artifacts at Tulane. Someone was smuggling artifacts *in*—fake ones. PI Micah Dunn was trying to find out who was trying to make a fool out of Dr. Thorpe. Then one artifact becomes important. 1st. [Smuggling]

ZANNOS, Susan. *Trust The Liar.* 1988 Walker. No one listened to Brandon when he said his friend was missing. Then a classmate was knifed . . . in the same way that Carrie Pritchard's husband had been killed, just weeks before. Carrie and Brandon want to find the killer. 1st. [Smuggling]

ANTIQUES

Which of us has not, at one time or another, poked through a secondhand store for just the right sought-after item or hoped, against all odds, that we would stumble across that lost, unknown treasure? Follow Lovejoy (Jonathan Gash) or Tim Simpson (John Malcolm) down dusty aisles, at remote estate sales, and on wild-goose chases . . . where what they find is more apt to be murder.

BABSON, Marian. *A Trail Of Ashes.* [Arson]

COCKRELL, Amanda. *The Moonshine Blade.* 1988 Bantam/PBO. Steven Cullen lost control of his car in an ice storm and died in the crash, just two weeks after his wedding. He left behind a sword collection. His widow, Mary Rose, discovered that someone was after one of the swords: the Moonshine Blade.

COLLINS, Max Allan. *The Baby Blue Rip-Off.* 1983 Walker/ Tor 1987. Mallory's delivering Hot Supper Service to some old ladies in Port City. One woman dies—murdered—and her possessions are stolen. Soon there's a rash of break-ins on the outskirts of town. Mallory wants the criminals. 1st.

DUNLAP, Susan. *An Equal Opportunity Death.* [Revenge]

FISH, Robert L. *The Gold Of Troy.* 1980 Doubleday/ Berkley 1984. The Schliemann treasure has finally surfaced, and major museums around the world have received notice of an imminent auction. Dr. Ruth McVeigh of the Metropolitan wants it. So does Dr. Gregor Koopak of the Hermitage. [Anthropology]

FLYNN, Lucine Hansz. *Antique And Deadly.* 1988 Walker. Susan Beckett tried to forget the scandal. Hank, her father, an expert on eighteeneth-century American furniture, had misappraised a Chippendale highboy. Uncle Jim's death brings back an ugly reminder. Now she's out to find the truth. 1st.

GASH, Jonathan. *The Judas Pair.* 1977 Harper & Row/ Penguin 1988. Mr. Field had a specific mission. He wanted Lovejoy to get him the Judas Pair, the legendary dueling flintlock pistols. Eric died and the pistols vanished. Lovejoy's life is threatened and his cottage burned. He'll have to duel to stay alive. 1st.

GASH, Jonathan. *Gold By Gemini.* 1978 Harper & Row/ Penguin 1988. Some British-Roman coins disappeared from a local museum. On the Isle of Man with the beautiful Nicole, Lovejoy has to find the coins in order to survive. 2nd.

GASH, Jonathan *Spend Game.* 1981 Ticknor & Fields/ Penguin 1982. One rainy night, Lovejoy and Sue, his current lady friend, see a car forced off the road, the driver thrown against a tree. Leckie is dead. He'd been a fellow antique dealer and army buddy. Lovejoy wants the killer. 4th.

GASH, Jonathan. *The Vatican Rip.* 1982 Ticknor & Fields/ Penguin 1988. Mr. Arcellano has a tough job for Lovejoy. There is a family heirloom he wants recovered. It just so happens that the Chippendale table belongs to the pope and is in the Vatican. How is Lovejoy going to manipulate this adventure? 5th.

GASH, Jonathan. *The Gondola Scam.* 1984 St. Martin/ Penguin 1985. A millionaire and antique collector hires Lovejoy to "rescue" all the art treasures in Venice before the whole city vanishes into the sea. Now fakes and forgeries are flooding the sinking city. 8th.

GASH, Jonathan. *Pearlhanger.* 1985 St. Martin/ Penguin 1986. Donna Vernon hires Lovejoy to find her husband, Sidney, an antique dealer scouting the countryside. As they follow his trail, Lovejoy becomes suspicious. But not before he's arrested for Sidney's murder. 9th. [Missing Person]

GASH, Jonathan. *The Tartan Sell.* 1986 St. Martin/ Penguin 1987. On a foggy night, Lovejoy waits for a truck to deliver a fake bureau. But the bureau is missing and the driver is dead. As Lovejoy noses around, he discovers that the bureau was real. He heads for Scotland and the solution. 10th.

GASH, Jonathan. *Moonspender.* 1987 St. Martin/ Penguin 1988. The "moonspenders" are at work; they are antiques poachers using metal detectors. They are out to loot Britain's national treasures by digging up ancient buried artifacts. Lovejoy wants them stopped. 11th.

GASH, Jonathan. *Jade Woman.* 1989 St. Martin/ Penguin 1990. Lovejoy flees East Anglia with the bailiff's men about to foreclose on everything. Janie helps him get to Hong Kong. He wakes to find his traveler's checks and passport stolen. And then he gazes on the Jade Woman. 12th. [Oriental]

GILMAN, Dorothy. *The Tightrope Walker.* 1979 Doubleday/ Fawcett 1986. Amelia Jones bought the Ebbtide Shop to find some stability. Tucked into a hurdy-gurdy is a note: "They're going to kill me soon. . . ." Intensely curious about the writer of the note, Amelia travels to Maine, and danger. [Old Crime]

HARDWICK, Mollie. *Uneaseful Death.* 1988 St. Martin. Antique dealer Doran Fairweather drove down to Caxton Manor in Kent for her first Antiques Roadshow. She tripped over a body just as a snowstorm cut the houseful of experts off from the rest of the world. Undaunted, Doran carries out her own investigation. 3rd.

HILL, Reginald. *A Fairly Dangerous Thing.* 1986 Signet/ PBO. Village English teacher Joseph Askern is captivated by Averingerette, a stately home. A ring of professional thieves is also interested in the estate, and any inside information Joe possesses. They set him up—for a break-in.

MacGREGOR, Rob. *Crystal Skull.* Ballantine 1991/ PBO. About to display a rare crystal skull at the museum, curator Paul Lofter had a chore for PI Nicholas Pierce: find out who has the twin to the skull. As they talk, a man bursts in, shoots Paul and steals the skull.

MacLEOD, Charlotte. *Wrack And Rune.* 1982 Doubleday/ Avon 1983. Strange things were happening at the Horsefall Farm, all blamed on the Viking rune stone and its curse. When the body was found in the quicklime, the owners called Professor Peter Shandy at once. 3rd. [Witches]

MacLEOD, Charlotte, w/a Alisa Craig. *The Terrible Tide.* 1983 Doubleday/ Avon 1987. Holly Howe is recuperating from an accident at her brother's home in New Brunswick. She goes to Cliff House to help take care of old Mrs. Parlett. As soon as she moves in, things really do go bump in the night. [Canadian]

MacLEOD, Charlotte. *The Bilbao Looking Glass.* 1983 Doubleday/ Avon 1984. Sarah Kelling and Max Bittersohn are at Ireson's Landing for the summer. They've hardly unpacked when they find a valuable looking glass in the front hall. The next morning Alice B. is found murdered. Was it robbery? 4th. [Blackmail]

MacLEOD, Charlotte. *Vane Pursuit.* 1989 Mysterious/ Mysterious 1990. Someone is stealing priceless antique Praxiteles Lumpkin weathervanes in Balaclava County. As Helen Shandy sets off to photograph some of the last existing vanes, she runs into trouble. 7th. [Corruption]

MALCOLM, John. *Gothic Pursuit.* 1987 Scribner/ Ballantine 1988. The Art Fund is going to purchase a nineteenth-century bookcase crafted by Richard Norman Shaw. Alf Brown knows where to find one. Then Alf is dead in his shop. Before Tim Simpson can track the bookcase down, another man is murdered. 5th.

MICHAELS, Barbara. *Shattered Silk.* 1986 Atheneum/ Berkley 1988. Karen was back at her aunt's house in Georgetown. Deciding to open a shop specializing in antique clothing, she contacts friends with full attics. Her house is broken into, an attempt is made to run her down, and she faces a gun. [Old Crime]

MULLER, Marcia. *The Cheshire Cat's Eye.* [Old Crime]

OLIPHANT, B. J. *The Unexpected Corpse.* Fawcett 1990/ PBO. Uncle January and his young wife were killed by a London van. Claris brought their ashes back to the

Colorado ranch for burial. But there were three boxes of ashes to inter. Soon there's a fourth box, and cousin Shirley McClintock dives in to investigate. 2nd. [Infidelity]

OLIVER, Anthony. *The Pew Group.* 1980 Doubleday/ Fawcett 1985. Doreen becomes a widow when her husband trips and falls down a flight of stairs. Then a rare and priceless ceramic figurine is stolen from her antique shop. Her mother, Lizzie Thomas, and retired detective John Webber track it down. 1st.

OLIVER, Anthony. *The Property Of A Lady.* 1983 Doubleday/ Fawcett 1985. Shy Margaret, recently orphaned, picked up an ailing hitchhiker and took him home. But Lizzie Thomas is getting bad feelings about the situation. With John Webber, she starts probing into the young man's past. 2nd.

PAUL, Barbara. *First Gravedigger.* 1980 Doubleday/ Bantam 1987. Earl Sommers, agent for Speer Gallery, isn't a very nice man. He wants the gallery *and* Speer's wife. He discovers an antique chair worth a lot of money and starts to figure out how to get rid of Speer.

PETERS, Elizabeth. *Trojan Gold.* 1987 Atheneum/ Tor 1988. At the museum in Munich, Vicky Bliss received a picture of a woman draped in the Gold of Troy, missing since World War II. Managing to contact John Smythe, art forger, thief, and lover, she heads for the Bavarian Alps and the treasure. 4th. [Anthropology]

PRICE, Anthony. *The Labyrinth Makers.* 1986 Mysterious/ PBO. They were draining the lake in Lincolnshire; in it was a downed bomber that had smuggled something out of Berlin in 1945. Dr. David Audley is on hand, and so are the Soviets. David's about to find the treasure. 1st.

SALE, Medora. *Murder In A Good Cause.* [Canadian]

STEED, Neville. *Tinplate.* 1987 St. Martin/ St. Martin 1988. It was a simple trip: drive to the south of France, appraise and purchase eleven antique tinplate toys, return to England, and turn them over to the purchaser. But at the border, Peter discovers the toys have been replaced with plastic ones. 1st.

STEED, Neville. *Die-Cast.* [Revenge]

TAPPLY, William G. *The Spotted Cats.* 1991 Delacorte. Jeff Newton summoned Brady Coyne to his Cape Cod home for the weekend. But before Jeff could tell Brady why he wanted his legal services, Jeff was severely struck on the head and his seven gold Mayan jaguars were stolen. 10th. [Insurance]

TYLER, Alison. *Chase The Wind.* [Intrigue]

WOODS, Sherryl. *Stolen Moments.* [Journalism]

ARSON

When the cave dwellers discovered fire, it probably never crossed their minds that such a life-giving force could be turned to utter destruction. There is fire for profit and fire to cover up robbery or murder.

BABSON, Marian. *A Trail Of Ashes.* 1985 Walker/ Walker 1986. Celia arranged for her recently-widowed sister to come to New Hampshire for the summer, on a house swap, to help Rosemary forget. But Edgemarsh Lake is being beset by a rash of fires, and suddenly Rosemary is in the middle of one. [Antiques]

BARNARD, Robert. *A City Of Strangers.* [Children]

COLBERT, James. *Skinny Man.* 1991 Atheneum. A New Orleans cop needs a favor from Skinny. A warehouse was torched and a man died in the fire. A blonde who lives in Skinny's apartment complex might have some answers. Skinny doesn't have anything else to do at the moment. 2nd. [Real Estate]

CRAIG, M. S. *Flash Point.* 1987 Dodd, Mead. Ash Parker was badly injured, but he told his foster son, Luke Adams, not to come. Luke comes to the Sierra country anyway, just in time to help put out a forest fire. Fire and death are all around. Then Luke is charged with the murder of Ash. [Fraud]

DeBROSSE, Jim. *The Serpentine Wall.* 1988 St. Martin. Porno king Al Greenburg died in a boat fire, a pure case of arson. Rick Decker, reporter on the *Cincinnati Eagle,* was surprised when the fire chief called it an accident. Decker's about to do his own private investigation. [Journalism]

EARLY, Jack. *Razzamatazz.* 1985 Franklin Watts/ Paperjacks 1988. It was happening all over again: the murdered bodies. Colin Maguire could never forget the unsolved killings of his wife and children. Here in Seaview, New York, a killer is loose, and an old crime is going to be avenged. [Revenge]

HELGERSON, Joel. *Slow Burn.* 1987 Bantam/ PBO. The old woman hired ex-fireman-turned-PI, Chet Johnston, to find out who murdered her son. Q.T. had died in a fire at the fire station. Chet turns up a strange mixture of blackmail and murder, including the death of his own wife, five years ago. 1st. [Old Crime]

HUEBNER, Frederick D. *Judgement By Fire.* 1988 Fawcett/ PBO. Hugh Prokop's Seattle marine supply warehouse burned down, leaving a dead body and a safe full of cash. Arrested for arson and murder, he hires lawyer Matt Riordan to prove him innocent. The case gets more complicated. 3rd. [Lawyer]

LIVINGSTON, Jack. *Die Again, Macready.* 1984 St. Martin/ Signet 1985. The cops said that Arnold Pelfry committed suicide. PI Joe Binney doesn't believe it. Actor Bill Macready hires Joe to find the quarter million dollars Pelfry had stolen from him. 2nd. [Suicide]

LOGUE, John. *Flawless Execution.* [Ball Games]

PENTECOST, Hugh. *Death By Fire.* 1986 Dodd, Mead. Peaceful Lakeville is shattered by arson. First a dairy barn, then the town hall, where a charred body is found the next day. Uncle George gets some help from an adversary from out of his past and his nephew Joey. 5th. [Imposter]

PULVER, Mary Monica. *Ashes To Ashes.* 1988 St. Martin. Crazy Dave's TV and Appliance store in Charter, Illinois, burned down. Sgt. Dave Brichter is positive it's arson. There's a lot of talk about the Mafia, but the final chase shows that it's just homegrown crime. 3rd.

TURNBULL, Peter. *Two Way Cut.* 1988 St. Martin. The beheaded body was discovered in a vacant lot. It had been washed and dressed in a clean suit of clothing. Inspector Donohue and the officers of Glascow's P Division are looking for a Chinese woman. 5th. [Holiday]

WILHELM, Kate. *The Dark Room.* [Witches]

WRIGHT, Eric. *Smoke Detector.* 1984 Scribner/ Signet 1986. An antique shop is burned and its owner dies in the fire. A lot of people wanted him dead, and Inspector Charlie Salter has to sift the ashes of the past to find the one person who did the job. 2nd. [Canadian]

ART AND THE ARTIST

Art theft and art forgery have been popular topics in mysteries for a long time. And the notion of a long-lost painting surfacing, all covered with dust and grime, has kept us turning the pages. New on the scene is the specialty of art restoration, another perfect framework for murder. And we mustn't neglect the artist as victim or villain.

ALBERT, Marvin. *The Last Smile.* 1988 Fawcett/ PBO. Pete Sawyer's partner has been shot and wounded in Paris. The case he's been working on now belongs to Pete. An Etruscan tomb filled with artifacts is up for sale. Susan Kape wants it, but she insists that each piece be authenticated first. 5th.

ALEXANDER, Gary. *Kiet And The Golden Peacock.* 1989 St. Martin. It's just a few days before the annual Savhanakip Festival in the Southeast Asian country of Luong, and the Golden Peacock has been stolen. Police Superintendent Bamsan Kiet has to recover this national treasure. 3rd. [Holiday]

BANKS, Oliver. *The Caravaggio Obsession.* 1984 Little, Brown/ Signet 1984. Just before he's murdered, Jake Sloane, New York City art dealer, brags to Amos Hatcher about a shipment of old masters he plans to put up for auction. Amos's investigation leads him to Rome and a young man obsessed with a single artist. 2nd.

BLOCK, Lawrence. *The Burglar Who Painted Like Mondrian.* [Bookstore]

BORTHWICK, J. S. *The Down East Murders.* 1985 St. Martin/ Critic's Choice 1987. Sarah Deane is working at a museum in Maine for the summer. There have been a series of art thefts up and down the coast. Soon there's a murder, and Sarah and Alex McKenzie are in the middle. 2nd.

BOYER, Rick. *The Daisy Duck.* [Drugs]

ART AND THE ARTIST 35

BRAUN, Lilian Jackson. *The Cat Who Saw Red.* [Cats]

BRETT, John. *Who'd Hire Brett?* 1980 St. Martin/ Bantam 1989. It was four o'clock in the morning when John Brett got the phone call. Edie Wilson's Guinean Mud Dancer had been stolen and she wanted John to steal it back. Then her husband was murdered and the primitive art was missing again. [Drugs]

BRILL, Toni. *Date With A Dead Doctor.* [Mystery Writer]

BURLEY, W. J. *Wycliffe And The Winsor Blue.* 1987 Doubleday/ Avon 1988. When Edwin Garland, painter, died while working on a canvas in his studio, it was no surprise. He was almost eighty. However, four days later, his son Francis was murdered. Now Superintendent Wycliffe gets interested. 12th.

CAUDWELL, Sarah. *Thus Was Adonis Murdered.* 1981 Scribner/ Penguin 1987. Julia Larwood, bright but in need of a keeper, is off to Venice on holiday. Soon she's being questioned about the murder of the man she spent the afternoon with. Hilary Tamar and friends endeavor to solve the crime . . . from London. 1st. [Lawyers]

CAVANDISH, Faith. *Silent Portrait.* [Where There's A Will]

CHARLES, Hampton. *Miss Seeton At The Helm.* [At Sea]

CLOTHIER, Peter. *Chiaroscuro.* 1985 St. Martin/ Signet 1987. Jacob Molnar, a dropout from the hype of the art world, is plunged back into the mainstream by evidence of a multimillion-dollar art scam and murder.

CLOTHIER, Peter. *Down-Dirty.* 1987 Atheneum. Artist Wil Garretson is slowly burning out. Then Sally Horan, an ex-student, comes running to him, scared.

Her lover has just been murdered. Wil protects her and uncovers an art scam.

COKER, Carolyn. *The Other David.* 1984 Dodd, Mead/Signet 1985. Andrea Perkins is spending a year in a museum in Florence as an art restorer. An elderly priest hands her a painting; it's a gift. Is it the lost David by Michelangelo? Someone else wants to know. 1st.

COKER, Carolyn. *The Vines Of Ferrara.* 1986 Dodd, Mead. At the castle of Ferrara, bridal home of Lucrezia Borgia, Andrea Perkins is restoring a fresco. Then a maid, the chef, and a guest all die after drinking wine bottled twenty years ago. Is this Lucrezia's hand, reaching out from the past? 2nd.

COKER, Carolyn. *The Hand Of The Lion.* 1987 Dodd, Mead. Andrea Perkins is shocked when a Renaissance drawing is stolen and smuggled out of Florence. Later, in Venice, she's embroiled in a similar scam. This time lives are in danger, including Andrea's. 3rd.

COKER, Carolyn. *The Balmoral Nude.* 1990 St. Martin. In London, art restorer Andrea Perkins meets her old beau, Clayton Foley. Married to a wealthy British woman, Foley wants Andrea to restore some old Victorian drawings by an artist who was hanged for murder. 4th. [Infidelity]

COLLINS, Eliza G. C. *Going, Going, Gone.* 1986 Scribner/ Signet 1987. Helen Greene had owned the painting once and was forced to sell it to continue the gallery her father had founded. Now the landscape is up for auction; Helen wants it back. Someone else is bidding against her.

DAVIS, Kenn. *Melting Point.* [Black Detective]

DAVIS, Kenn. *As October Dies.* 1987 Fawcett/ PBO. There are three paintings missing from a private museum and Jordan Kooby, the curator, has been fired. Although the paintings are returned, Kooby dies. Carver Bascombe is ferreting out the truth when he becomes the next target. 4th. [Black Detective]

DeANDREA, William, w/a Phillip DeGrave. *Unholy Moses.* 1985 Doubleday/ Paperjacks 1988. The cream of the New York City art world was at the gallery. When the masterpiece was unveiled, a body hung from the easel. Sgt. Terry Webb takes charge, but her cartoonist husband, Glenn, has the information she needs.

DEAVER, Jeffery Wilds. *Always A Thief.* 1988 Paperjacks/ PBO. Joseph Packer was a successful gallery owner. But by night he was an even more successful art thief. Then a millionaire he delivered a painting to is murdered.

DOBSON, Margaret. *Nightcap.* 1987 Dell/ PBO. Janet Bailey and Phillip took a vacation to Hawaii. When the artist Anton Goodnight was strangled, Janet was framed for the murder. As danger overtakes them, an old enemy surfaces. 4th. [Vacation]

DOBYNS, Stephen. *Saratoga Bestiary.* 1988 Viking/ Penguin 1990. Super Bowl Sunday was a day to remember: Charlie Bradshaw got the job of recovering the stolen painting of Man o' War from the Racing Museum. Then the gambling party was robbed and a small grocer was murdered. Charlie's feeling too old for it all. 5th. [Pornography]

ELKINS, Aaron J. *A Deceptive Clarity.* 1987 Walker. Chris Norgen, art curator from San Francisco, is on loan in Germany to hang a showing of recovered art from World War II. Just before Peter, his boss, is found dead, he's told Chris that one of the paintings is a fake. Chris has to find out which one. 1st.

ENGEL, Howard. *A Victim Must Be Found.* [Canadian]

FOLLETT, Ken. *The Modigliani Scandal.* 1985 Morrow/ Signet 1985. On the track of a lost Modigliani, Dee Sleign and her boyfriend stay one step ahead of two others, hot on their heels. Meanwhile, an even bigger art scam is taking place in the London art world.

FRANCIS, Dick. *In The Frame.* [Australia]

FRIEDMAN, Mickey. *Magic Mirror.* 1988 Viking/ Penguin 1989. Georgia Lee Maxwell left Florida for Paris and a job writing "Paris Patter" for a New York City magazine. At the Musée Bellefroide she ends up on the floor as two men kill a guard and steal the Magic Mirror once used by Nostradamus. She wants the story badly. 1st. [Journalism]

FROST, Joan Van Every. *Portrait In Black.* 1985 Fawcett/ PBO. Crystal Perry does portraits . . . of pets, for the well-to-do of Santa Barbara. The owners are receiving extortion letters: pay up or your pet dies. When a horse is murdered, who else could be guilty but Crystal? [Blackmail]

GOSLING, Paula. *The Woman In Red.* 1984 Doubleday/ Popular 1986. After an indiscretion, Charles Llewellyn is sent off to a post in Alicante, Spain. One night he gets called out to check on a countryman charged with murder. What starts out looking like art forgery turns into something more deadly. [Drugs]

GRAY, Malcolm, w/a Ian Stuart. *Pictures In The Dark.* 1986 Doubleday. Clive Fordham heard the plane crash in the nearby woods and saw it explode in flames. Derek, the pilot, was very dead . . . and he was a crook. Clive joins with Reekha Graham, the pilot's estranged wife, for a murderous solution.

HARDWICK, Mollie. *The Dreaming Damozel.* 1991 St. Martin. A little tight for money, Doran Fairweather decides to expand her antiques business to include

Pre-Raphaelite paintings. Then two murders occur and each victim resembles a model used by Rossetti in his late period. 6th. [Drugs]

HOVING, Thomas. *Masterpiece.* 1986 Simon & Schuster/ Berkley 1988. Velázquez had painted the *Marchesa*, his lover, in the seventeenth century. Its owner has just died, and the masterpiece is about to go on the auction block. Olivia Cartright of the Metropolitan wants it. Up against some tough competition, she gets more than she dreamed.

HUNSBURGER, H. Edward. *Death Signs.* 1987 Walker. Mattie Shayne taught deaf children and free-lanced as interpreter for the Medical School. One night a man signed a message and died. Lt. Ryder asks Mattie to continue to help on the investigation. It almost means her life. 1st.

INNES, Michael. *Picture Of Guilt.* 1969 Dodd, Mead/ Perennial 1988. Retired Chief Commissioner Sir John Appleby has a long memory. He manages to put together a pattern of art losses over the years and comes up with a lucrative art swindle. With his son, he devises a plan to catch the thieves. 23rd.

JEFFRIES, Roderic. *Too Clever By Half.* 1990 St. Martin. Art expert Justin Burnett was found shot to death in his home in Mallorca, a suicide note and gun nearby. His sister Phillipa refuses to believe her brother would kill himself. Soon Inspector Alverez has another suspicious death. 9th. [Suicide]

KENNEALY, Jerry. *Polo's Wild Card.* 1990 St. Martin. Lionel Martel hosted a charity ball at his father's house, while his father was out of the country. By the end of the evening Lionel had been hit over the head and some valuable paintings were missing. Charles Martel flew back to hire Nick Polo to recover the art work, without the police. 5th. [Father]

KRENTZ, Jayne Ann. *Gift Of Gold.* 1988 Popular/ PBO. Restaurant owner Verity Ames hired him as a dishwasher. She didn't know that Jonas Quarrel had followed her from Mexico. Nor did she know that Jonas had powers that might get them both killed. 1st. [Revenge]

KRENTZ, Jayne Ann. *Gift Of Fire.* 1988 Popular/ PBO. Verity Ames and her dishwasher-lover, Jonas Quarrel, are hired to locate a lost medieval treasure off the coast of Washington State. Their relationship is sorely tested. 2nd.

LEE, Elsie. *Sinister Abbey.* 1988 Zebra/ PBO. She's won the Catlin Prize for the best fabric design, and Danica Hughes is off to France to do research. Strange men disappear, attaché cases vanish, and danger dogs her every step.

LLEWELLYN, Caroline. *The Masks Of Rome.* 1988 Scribner/ Ivy 1989. Kate Roy, art restorer, is in Rome at the home of the Torreleones working on several canvases. While looking around, she discovers one of the masters is a forgery. And it looks like it might be just the tip of a Roman iceberg.

LORENS, M. K. *Deception Island.* [Mystery Writer]

MacLEOD, Charlotte. *The Palace Guard.* 1981 Doubleday/ Avon 1982. Max Bittersohn invited Sarah Kelling to one of the Sunday concerts at Madame Wilkin's palazzo. As the music played, a guard went flying over the balustrade and landed in the hyacinths. 3rd.

MacLEOD, Charlotte. *The Plain Old Man.* 1985 Doubleday/ Avon 1986. Sarah Kelling Bittersohn agreed to help her Aunt Emma on a production of Gilbert and Sullivan. A valuable painting is suddenly missing from the wall at Aunt Emma's, and out of the assembled cast comes a murderer. 6th. [Theater]

ART AND THE ARTIST

MALCOLM, John. *A Back Room In Sommers Town.* 1985 Scribner/ Ballantine 1986. Tim Simpson, art advisor, was invited to view some early 1900s British art. Hours later the art dealer was dead and the paintings had vanished. In São Paulo, Tim finds a lead and almost loses his life. 1st.

MALCOLM, John. *The Godwin Sideboard.* 1985 Scribner/ Ballantine 1986. Tim Simpson asked Peter, antique dealer, to keep an eye out for a sideboard. A phone call and Tim is on the run, right into Peter's body. Without a clue, Tim decides to retrace Peter's trip the day he was murdered. 2nd.

MALCOLM, John. *The Gwen John Sculpture.* 1986 Scribner/ Ballantine 1987. Tim Simpson received a letter from France, a hint about an unknown Rodin. By the time he crosses the Channel, the elderly Madame Boiteau has been attacked. It seems someone else knows about the sculpture. 3rd.

MALCOLM, John. *Whistler In The Dark.* 1987 Scribner/ Ballantine 1988. Tim Simpson doesn't know what to make of the phone call about a Whistler painting going on the market. Before he gets a chance to view the painting, the owner is dead. Tim has to look for both the killer and the art work. 4th.

MALCOLM, John. *Mortal Ruin.* 1988 Scribner. Tim Simpson lands at O'Hare and is beset by thugs who want his briefcase. He's in Chicago about some old gold shares, involving Winston Churchill's uncle, and a missing portrait of the Jerome sisters. 6th.

MALCOLM, John. *The Wrong Impression.* 1990 Scribner. Chief Inspector Nobby Roberts is in intensive care. He's in a coma, suffering from broken bones and two bullet wounds. Nobby was working on a drug case. Tim Simpson is tracking down an unknown Pissarro and he suspects he's following Nobby's path. 7th. [Drugs]

MANN, Jessica. *A Kind Of Healthy Grave.* 1988 St. Martin. Tamara Hoyland is preparing a series for the BBC and is researching Dame Viola, leader of *Watchwomen.* Dame Viola lives with her brother Basil, headmaster of St. Uny's School. A hornets' nest is about to be overturned. 1st. [Incest]

MARSH, Ngaio. *Clutch Of Constables.* [At Sea]

MARSHALL, William. *Head First.* 1986 Holt/ Mysterious 1988. It was a routine patrol, but the Chinese coffin floating in Hong Bay was out of place and the corpse had no head. The Harbor Police found others, and each body was missing a different part. Inspector Harry Feiffer wants to clear up the mystery. 12th. [Oriental]

MASON, Clifford. *The Case Of The Ashanti Gold.* 1985 St. Martin. PI Joe Cinquez's brother told him he was involved with some "guy from Africa." Once the deal went through Phil would be set for life. After Phil is murdered, Joe receives a package in the mail—a golden stool. 1st. [Black Detective]

McCORMICK, Claire. *Murder In Cowboy Bronze.* [Indians]

MULLER, Marcia. *The Tree Of Death.* 1983 Walker/ Signet 1987. The Museum of Mexican Art is about to reopen in its new location and Elena Oliverez, curator, is preparing the press preview. Under the smashed Tree of Life is the body of the director, and Elena is a suspect. 1st.

MULLER, Marcia. *Cavalier In White.* 1986 St. Martin/ Worldwide 1988. Joanna Stark, fleeing her partnership in an art security firm in San Francisco after the death of her husband, is living quietly in Sonoma. A famous Hals painting is stolen, and old friends are involved. She feels she has to help. 1st.

MULLER, Marcia. *There Hangs The Knife.* 1988 St. Martin/ Worldwide 1989. This time Joanna Stark was going to get her man. She's had a false Brueghel painted, set up a gallery in London to handle it, and waited for the trap to ensnare Parducci. But she's just discovered a double-cross. 2nd. [Revenge]

MULLER, Marcia, and Bill Pronzini. *Beyond The Grave.* 1986 Walker. Elena Oliverez purchased a small marriage coffer at auction for the museum. Locked away in it is the report of John Quincannon, a PI from San Francisco. The papers are dated 1894. Quincannon had been hired to locate a lost treasure. Elena follows his old leads. 3rd. [Old Crime]

MURRAY, William. *The Hard Knocker's Luck.* 1985 Viking/ Penguin 1986. Shifty Anderson, horseplaying magician, met Allyson when she shoplifted a purse from a department store in Santa Monica. When he saw her again at the races, he had no idea he was about to get involved in the art world. 2nd. [Horses]

O'HAGAN, Joan. *Death And The Madonna.* 1987 Doubleday. The art lecture tour took the group to the hills outside Rome, to an old Benedictine monastery. Strange things start to happen. There is something wrong with a car, and a Japanese man is found dead. All this for the love of art!

OLIVER, Anthony. *The Elberg Collection.* 1985 Doubleday/ Fawcett 1986. On vacation in the south of France, master potter David Walton and his wife died in flames. Their daughter, Jessica Elberg, wants to know what happened. Lizzie Thomas and John Webber set out to find the answer. 3rd.

OLIVER, Anthony. *Cover-Up.* 1987 Doubleday/Fawcett 1988. Antique dealer John Greenwood stopped at a country house to look at some possible purchases. He died of a heart attack and the £ 20,000 he was carrying vanished. Lizzie and John make a startling discovery. 4th.

PAGE, Martin. *The Man Who Stole The Mona Lisa.* 1984 Pantheon/ Pantheon 1985. Hired by J. P. Morgan in 1909 to steal the Mona Lisa, Adam Worth bides his time. Attending his own funeral two years later, he is about to begin the caper.

PUTRE, John Walter. *Death Among the Angels.* [Fraud]

RANDISI, Robert J. *No Exit From Brooklyn.* 1987 St. Martin/Tor 1989. Jodi Hayworth "borrowed" a statue from her stepfather's collection and hocked it. Then she hired PI Dick Delvecchio to find it. One man is already dead. There may be others. [Getting Away With Murder]

RESNICOW, Herbert. *The Gold Frame.* 1984 St. Martin/ Avon 1986. With raised eyebrows, Norma Gold goes along with her husband, Alex, as he works out a complex problem. The museum has unearthed a painting that may be a Vermeer, and the director has just been killed with an oyster knife. 3rd.

RUSSELL, Alan. *No Sign Of Murder.* 1990 Walker. Tommy Walters hired San Francisco PI Stuart Winters to find his daughter. Anita was taking a year off from school. She's been missing for six months and the police have found no leads. Anita, deaf since birth, has a collection of very strange friends. 1st. [Revenge]

SHAW, Patricia. *Never Paint A Stranger.* 1989 Tor. Her grandfather had told her that the inheritance smuggled out of Russia during the revolution was to be hers. Hanna Anders is in Basel, Switzerland, to paint . . . and to claim the treasure, whatever it is. Someone is on her trail. 1st. [Where There's A Will]

SHERWOOD, John. *Green Trigger Fingers.* [Botany]

SHERWOOD, John. *Menacing Groves.* 1989 Scribner/ Ballantine 1990. Celia Grant was surprised to see a young couple she knew on her flight to Italy. They were using a different name and looked like they had money. She said nothing till the murder happened. Now she has to speak up. 5th.

SKLEPOWICH, Edward. *Death In a Serene City.* [Old Crime]

SMITH, Evelyn. *Miss Melville Returns.* 1987 Fine/ Fawcett 1988. Retired now from being a free-lance assassin, Susan Melville is painting again. At the opening of the De Marnay Gallery, an artist collapses, and Susan learns the next day that he's dead. On the other end of a gun, this time she turns sleuth. 2nd. [Drugs]

SMITH, Joan. *The Polka Dot Nude.* [Writers]

SMITH, Joan. *A Brush With Death.* Jove 1990/ PBO. Insurance investigator John Weiss is in Montreal to visit Cassie Newton, student at McGill. John searches the studio of Yves Latour, a known art forger, discovering ten van Gogh canvases. Within hours, Latour is murdered. [Canadian]

THOMPSON, Gene. *A Cup Of Death.* 1987 Random House/ Ballantine 1989. Paul Van Damm, archaeologist, had just returned from Greece with his new young wife. Apparently surprised by a burglar, he's been killed. His old friend, Dade Cooley, is going to defend the accused murderer, convinced he's innocent. 3rd. [Lawyer]

THOMSON, June. *Portrait Of Lilith.* 1983 Doubleday. Max Gifford is at the end of his career as a painter. Then Eustace Quinn proposes a major exhibition at his London gallery. Quinn proposes something else and ends up dead. Inspector Rudd follows a worn trail to find the killer. 9th.

TRAVIS, Elizabeth. *Under The Influence.* [Jealousy]

UCCILLO, Linda. *Death Of A Renaissance Man.* 1986 St. Martin. On a beautiful spring afternoon, Nikki Andrews was lolling in bed waiting for Joe Savanah to return. But Joe was lying on the pavement in the alley, dead. Has one of his ex-wives or mistresses done him in?

WALLACE, Robert. *To Catch A Forger.* 1989 St. Martin. Essington Holt wasn't doing well as an art dealer in Sydney. So when Aunt Eloise sent him tickets and expense money he flew to the South of France. Aunt Eloise is convinced that her six small monotypes have been replaced with fakes. 1st.

WALLACE, Robert. *An Axe To Grind.* [Political]

WATSON, Clarissa. *The Fourth Stage Of Gainsborough Brown.* 1977 McKay/ Ballantine 1986. Persis Willum suspected that the drowning of artist Gainsborough Brown was no accident. As an artist herself, she knew the picture wasn't right. She soon discovers artists who don't paint and unmarried widows. 1st.

WATSON, Clarissa. *The Bishop In The Back Seat.* 1980 Atheneum/ Ballantine 1986. Persis agreed to help out while art treasures, on loan from the community, were hung for the opening of the new Waldheim Museum. Then the biggest prize of all, a Rembrandt, was stolen by two deaf-mute nuns. 2nd.

WATSON, Clarissa. *Runaway.* 1985 Atheneum/ Ballantine 1986. On a runaway horse, Persis sails across a hedge and into a secret meeting in the yard of an empty house. When the owner of the house is found murdered in the south of France, Persis heads for Europe and a cache of gold. 3rd.

WATSON, Clarissa. *Somebody Killed The Messenger.* [Blackmail]

WATSON, Peter. *Landscape Of Lies.* 1989 Atheneum. Someone tried to steal a painting that had been in Isobel Sadler's family for centuries. At the gallery of Michael Whiting she's told that the oil is worth a hundred pounds. Then Michael discovers that the painting is a treasure map and the treasure could be worth millions. [Jewels]

WEINMAN, Irving. *Tailor's Dummy.* 1986 Atheneum/ Fawcett 1987. Horvay, the owner of a fancy New York City gallery, was found dead, and so was a jogger in Central Park. As Inspector Lenny Schwartz checks into Horvay's background, he finds his expenses exceed his income. Only a quick trip to Holland holds the answer. 1st.

WHITNEY, Phyllis A. *Poinciana.* 1981 Doubleday/ Fawcett 1981. In shock after the fiery death of her parents, Sharon Hollis had married Ross Logan, a friend of her mother's. In Florida, Ross died mysteriously. Feeling compelled to finish the book on netsuke that Ross had started, Sharon finds that the little carved figures lead her to trouble.

WILCOX, Collin. *Bernhardt's Edge.* 1988 Tor/ Tor 1991. Betty Giles is missing and her boss wants her found, so he hires PI Alan Bernhardt. As soon as he finds her, Betty's lover Nick is murdered and she's on the run again. Bernhardt is sure he's been set up to finger Nick. He's going to check it out. 1st.

WILLIAMS, David. *Treasure In Roubles.* 1987 St. Martin/ Avon 1988. Mark Treasure is in Russia with the Baroque Art Circle. As they tour the Hermitage, a Raphael canvas is stolen. The next night at the Kirov Opera a man dies from a balcony fall. Mark joins forces with the Soviet police. 6th. [Imposter]

WILLIAMS, David. *Treasure In Oxford.* 1988 St. Martin. Mark Treasure is at Oxford for the annual governor's meeting of the Moneybuckle Architectural Endowment. The members are excited about some Constable sketches a local dealer has for sale. The dealer dies, the culprit is in jail, and Treasure suspects another. 12th. [Academic]

WILLIAMS, Philip Lee. *Slow Dance In Autumn.* 1988 Peachtree. Sherrill wants PI Hank Prince to find her husband, Tony. He'd dashed in, grabbed some clothes, and left. Hank discovers that others want Tony, too. He's got something they all want. 1st.

WRIGHT, L. R. *Sleep While I Sing.* [Canadian]

AUSTRALIA

The land of the dingo and Christmas in the summer is becoming another locale for mayhem and murder. Arthur Upfield gave us a panoramic view of small towns and the outback. Now Peter Corris invites us to join him on the mean streets of Sydney and other places that his investigations lead.

BARNARD, Robert. *Death Of An Old Goat.* 1977 Walker/ Penguin 1987. Boring as Professor Belville-Smith was, he was still invited to Australia to lecture on Jane Austen. The next morning he was still in his motel room with his throat cut. Inspector Royle, a novice at murder crimes, was reluctant to follow the clues. [Academic]

CORRIS, Peter. *The Dying Trade.* 1986 Fawcett/ PBO. Sidney PI Cliff Hardy is hired by a wealthy young man to find out who is harassing his twin sister, maybe even driving her to suicide. A little digging and Cliff has almost too many trails to follow. 1st. [Incest]

CORRIS, Peter. *White Meat.* 1986 Fawcett/ PBO. Ted Tarleton, a very rich bookie, hires PI Cliff Hardy.

Tarleton's daughter is missing and he wants her found. Hardy practically has to step over dead bodies and dodge bullets before he returns Noni to her father. 2nd. [Missing Person]

CORRIS, Peter. *The Marvelous Boy.* 1986 Fawcett/ PBO. Lady Catherine Chatterton is growing old. She's not interested in her daughter Bettina inheriting her estate. Instead, she wants PI Cliff Hardy to find her missing grandson, the grandson she's just learned about. 3rd. [Missing Person]

CORRIS, Peter. *The Empty Beach.* 1987 Fawcett/ PBO. Two years ago John Singer, pinball machine mogul, vanished on Bondi Beach. His widow, Marion, has heard that John was recently seen on the other side of town. She wants Cliff Hardy to find him. 4th. [Missing Person]

CORRIS, Peter. *Make Me Rich.* 1987 Fawcett/ PBO. Paul Gutherie's stepson is missing; he's gotten in with a bad crowd. Cliff Hardy needs to find him. He learns the boy's been in contact with his real father. But that's only the beginning of the sinister subplot. 5th. [Missing Person]

CORRIS, Peter. *Heroin Annie.* 1987 Fawcett/ PBO. A collection of ten short stories featuring PI Cliff Hardy as he wends his way through crime in Sidney.

CORRIS, Peter. *Deal Me Out.* 1988 Fawcett/ PBO. Cliff Hardy is doing a favor for a friend. Reeves, owner of a car rental agency, has had five of his cars stolen. The man on the security videotape was Cliff's friend Bill Mountain, TV writer. Cliff's investigation hits seamy Sydney. 6th.

CORRIS, Peter. *The Big Drop.* 1988 Fawcett/ PBO. A second collection of Cliff Hardy short stories set in Australia.

CORRIS, Peter. *The January Zone.* 1989 Fawcett/ PBO. Peter January, Minister of the Crown, hired Cliff Hardy as a security consultant just before a bomb ripped through January's office. Then Karen is missing and Cliff has another task. 8th. [Political]

FERRARS, E. X. *Come To Be Killed.* 1987 Doubleday. Rachel Gardiner flew to Australia to visit her brother. He failed to meet her at the airport, and his lodgings were empty. Then one night Rachel is roused from a suicide attempt that she'd never planned. [Drugs]

FRANCIS, Dick. *In The Frame.* 1976 Harper & Row/ Pocket 1978. When several houses in the country burn, the only clue is that the owners purchased art in Australia. To help out his cousin, Charles Todd heads for Melbourne looking for an art lover who likes fine wine. [Art]

THOMPSON, Estelle. *A Toast To Cousin Julian.* 1987 Walker. Trisha Kent is summoned to Queensland: something about a share in the family business her aunt left her. The family is in absolute turmoil, and cousin Julian has disappeared. Soon there's a murder, then things get worse. [Smuggling]

UPFIELD, Arthur W. *No Footprints In The Dust.* 1944 Doubleday/ Collier 1986. On a lonely road in the middle of the outback, the pilot of a small plane swept low and killed the man in the police car. Sent out to investigate, Napoleon Bonaparte is drawn into the strange tangle of a family. 8th.

UPFIELD, Arthur W. *An Author Bites The Dust.* 1948 Doubleday/ Collier 1987. Mervyn Blake was hosting a group of writers. The next morning he's found dead inside his writing room at the bottom of the garden. Inspector Napoleon Bonaparte is sent to Yarrabo to look into the mysterious death. 11th. [Writers]

UPFIELD, Arthur W. *The Bachelors Of Broken Hill.* 1950 Doubleday/ Collier 1986. Two elderly gentlemen have died of cyanide poisoning in Broken Hill. Inspector Napoleon Bonaparte discovers that the men died in public places; a woman was seen nearby. Bony is soon faced with more bodies. 14th. [Psychological]

UPFIELD, Arthur W. *Death Of A Lake.* 1954 Doubleday/ Collier 1986. He'd just won £12,500 in the lottery. He went for a swim in Lake Otway one night and never returned. An intense drought is drying up the lake. A group of people are watching the water level drop, watching for Ray Gillen and his money. Inspector Bonaparte watches, too. 18th.

B . . . IS FOR

BALL GAMES

*A**NY MANNER OF BALL GAME can be the setting for a murder story. In some of the earlier mysteries, the games included such sedate activities as tennis and golf, where the settings were tangential to the mystery. Currently, the games are more vigorous, and it may be that the game itself is the crucial element in the murder.*

CARR, John Dickson. *The Problem Of The Wire Cage.* 1939 Harper & Row/ Zebra 1987. Frank Dorrance was strangled in the middle of a clay tennis court. The only footprints were his. It seems an impossible task to figure out how Frank was killed until Dr. Gideon Fell fills in the who and why. 11th. [Where There's A Will]

CHARLES, Hampton. *Advantage Miss Seeton.* Berkley 1990/ PBO. Off on a summer outing, Miss Seeton is at a tennis match, cheering on Britain's up-and-coming star. But Trish Thumper's father, the stern judge, has been receiving threatening letters, and his daughter is to be the target. 7th. [Kidnapping]

CHRISTIE, Agatha. *The Murder On The Links.* 1923 Dodd, Mead/ Pocket 1987. Monsieur Renauld summoned Hercule Poirot, but Poirot arrived too late. Renauld was already dead on the golf course. Poirot has a list of suspects: Renauld's wife, his mistress, and his estranged son. 2nd.

CORK, Barry. *Unnatural Hazard.* 1990 Scribner. Chas MacLiven, friend of Inspector Angus Straun, has turned his castle into a hotel and hopes the golf tournament on the Scottish island will generate some publicity for him. But the body of a guest at the bottom of the oubliette won't do his business much good. 2nd. [Revenge]

CORK, Barry. *Laid Dead.* 1991 Scribner. Inspector Angus Straun's ex-wife wants his help. She's concerned that her new boy friend is about to be canned. Instead, Dirk's golf partner and friend is accidently killed: he got in the way of a golf swing. But Angus isn't quite satisfied. 3rd. [Real Estate]

DEFORD, Frank. *The Spy In Deuce Court.* 1986 Putnam/ Ivy 1988. Sports journalist Ronnie Ratajczak was hired by the CIA to pose as a spy, so the real spy could work undercover. The tennis tour gets a little deadly as people start dying and someone takes a shot at Ronnie. [Intrigue]

ELKINS, Charlotte & Aaron J. *A Wicked Slice.* 1989 St. Martin/ Fawcett 1990. Taking some practice shots at Carmel Point, Lee Ofsted hit a wicked slice and trudged down to the lake to retrieve her ball. What she retrieved was the body of star golfer Kate O'Brien. By the next day, Lee is the star suspect. [Fraud]

ENGLEMAN, Paul. *Dead In Center Field.* 1983 Ballantine/ PBO. In the middle of a doubleheader, Rita Delancey rang PI Mark Renzler's doorbell. A man had photos of her and wanted $5,000. Next the owner of the New York Gents wanted Mark to protect his superstar, Marvin Wallace, from threats on his life. 1st. [Blackmail]

EVERSON, David. *Suicide Squeeze.* 1991 St. Martin. Pitcher Dewey Farmer is trying to make a come-back with the Chicago Cubs. PI Robert Miles was hired to look into some death threats against him when Dewey's ball player brother was murdered. And now the senator's daughter is missing. 5th. [Mother]

GELLER, Michael. *Major League Murder.* 1988 St. Martin. Jefferson Davis was accused of doctoring baseballs. His friend, a bookie, hires PI Slots Resnick to clear Davis of the charge. Unfortunately, Slots hates Davis. But this was going to be murder. 2nd.

GORDON, Alison. *The Dead Pull Hitter.* 1989 St. Martin/ Onyx 1991. The Toronto Titans look as though they are about to take their first pennant. But the designated hitter misses a game. Someone used his skull for batting practice. Kate Henry, sportswriter, is looking for a big story. [Journalism]

IRVINE, Robert. *Gone To Glory.* 1990 St. Martin. Prissy Dalton was murdered and her brother, ex-Salt Lake City Bee's best shortstop, Pepper Dalton, is being charged with her death. For the money, the police say. PI Moroni Traveler was hired to clear Pepper and he discovers some strange truths. 3rd. [Where There's A Will]

KATZ, Michael J. *Murder Off The Glass.* 1987 Walker/ Pocket 1988. Just before the end of the third quarter, the lights went out in the stadium. When electricity was restored, Lester Beldon was dead and Andy Sussman, his co-sportscaster, was the only suspect. Andy calls on PI Murray Glick. 1st. [Drugs]

LOGUE, John. *Follow The Leader.* 1983 Ballantine/ PBO. Sports reporter John Morris was covering the U.S. Open. But a killer was eliminating the golf pros as fast as they could tee off. Three men were dead and a suspect was in jail. Morris was uneasy, and with good reason. 1st. [Journalism]

LOGUE, John. *Replay: Murder.* 1983 Ballantine/ PBO. The greatest football team that the South had ever produced had just lost its star quarterback. He was found murdered in his hotel room. Then the manager was found in the whirlpool. Harry, the coach, was next. Sports reporter John Morris wants the killer. 2nd. [Journalism]

LOGUE, John. *Flawless Execution.* 1986 Ballantine/ PBO. Sportscaster George Hoagland had few friends in his profession. But when the press box went up in flames on prime-time TV, and Hoagland with it, there were some raised eyebrows. 3rd. [Journalism]

MILES, Keith. *Bullet Hole.* 1986 Harper & Row/ Fawcett 1988. Alan Saxon's chances of winning the British Open look better than ever, until a young girl is strangled in his motor home. Being prime suspect doesn't do much for his game; neither does getting shot at. 1st.

PARKER, Robert B. *Mortal Stakes.* 1975 Houghton Mifflin/ Dell 1987. Spenser was hired to check out Marty Rabb. He was the Boston Red Sox star pitcher, but there was a rumor he might be shading a game. It didn't take Spenser too long to discover the real problem. 3rd. [Prostitution]

REED, J. D., and Christine Reed. *Exposure.* 1987 Soho/ Ivy 1988. Sports photographer Paul McGuire is on assignment: get some shots of Goddet, star soccer player. What he gets is pictures of the corpse. One by one the players are dying. Paul wants the killer stopped.

RICHARDSON, Robert. *Bellringer Street.* [Gay]

RISENHOOVER, C. C. *Murder At The Final Four.* 1987 McLennon/ Knightsbridge 1990. Star basketball player "Tater" Jones was found dead in his apartment off campus and Coach Knopf wants Professor Brian Stratford to handle it. Stratford, ex-CIA agent, ends up with three more murders to investigate. 2nd. [Drugs]

ROSEN, Richard. *Strike Three, You're Dead.* 1984 Walker/ Signet 1986. They found relief pitcher Rudy Furth at the bottom of the whirlpool. There were hints of Rudy's impropriety. Harvey Blissberg, his ex-roommate, knowing Rudy was clean, lets himself be persuaded into playing detective and scouting out the truth. 1st.

ROSEN, Richard. *Fadeaway.* 1986 Harper & Row/ Signet 1987. When the Boston Celtics forward disappears, PI Harvey Blissberg is hired to locate him. The trail leads Harvey back in time, to another city, to an old crime. 2nd. [Old Crime]

STANSBERRY, Dominic. *The Spoiler.* 1987 Atlantic/ Dell 1990. Regina Amanti wanted to spill the beans over a drink with reporter Frank Lofton. Her secrets turned dangerous and one of the minor league baseball players was dead. Lofton didn't know if he'd live to see his story printed. [Journalism]

TAPPLY, William G. *Follow The Sharks.* 1985 Scribner/ Ballantine 1987. Eddie Donagan was the fastest-rising pitcher for the Red Sox twelve years ago. Now he sells running shoes at the mall. His ten-year-old son E.J. has been kidnapped, and Eddie turns to Brady Coyne for help. 3rd. [Blackmail]

THOREAU, David. *The Good Book.* Pocket 1988/ PBO. Charles Randolf, owner of the NFL Marlins, was dead of a heart attack. The team now belongs to his second wife. His son Kurt is suspicious and asks PI Jimmy Lujack to nose around. Kurt is killed in a fire and the pace quickens. [Holiday]

UPTON, Robert. *Dead On A Stick.* 1986 Viking/ Penguin 1987. When Lyle Boone dropped dead at the Palm Isle Golf Club, Amos McGuffin was hired to investigate. It would be a great vacation for Amos. But there were more deaths, and the very posh club members had secrets to hide. 3rd. [Jealousy]

VALIN, Jonathan. *Life's Work.* 1986 Delacorte/ Dell 1987. The Cougars' guard, Billy Parks, disappeared just four weeks before the season's opening. The league hired Harry Stoner to bring him back. Harry finds the field strewn with bodies and mayhem. 6th. [Drugs]

BEES

You saw the movies as a child: bees everywhere, waiting for the chance to sting to death any victim in their way. The same theme makes our skins crawl a bit as we read. We can almost hear the buzzing of the wings; we tense, ready to flee the attack of the horde of insects.

DRUMMOND, John Keith. *Thy Sting, Oh Death.* 1985 St. Martin. Matilda Worthing, retired court reporter, thought it strange that bees were swarming in November. A few hours later, her neighbor Rudolf Besserman is stung. And he's allergic to bee stings. When he dies, Mattie moves to investigate. 1st. [Where There's A Will]

LANGTON, Jane. *Natural Enemy.* [Real Estate]

WILHELM, Kate. *Sweet, Sweet Poison.* 1990 St. Martin. Loud and likable Al and Sylvie Zukal won the lottery and moved to an expensive house in Spender's Ferry. They didn't fit in very well and someone poisoned their dog. Charles and Constance start looking for a neighbor who doesn't want them in town. 3rd. [Psychological]

BIRDWATCHING

A country sort of pastime, pleasant and laid back—that's the picture birdwatching conjures up. There is the feel of the early morning, fresh crisp air, the excitement of the unusual bird spotted.

The competition of being the first to locate the rarely sighted species makes the juices flow. However, the thick ground fog and misty wetlands are the perfect cover for a murder.

BORTHWICK, J. S. *The Case Of The Hook-Billed Kites.* 1982 St. Martin/ Penguin 1983. Sarah Deane, graduate student from Boston, is birdwatching in Texas at a refuge along the Rio Grande. Her friend Philip is found dead in the marsh. Alex McKenzie steps in to help Sarah find the murderer. 1st. [Drugs]

CLEEVES, Ann. *A Bird In The Hand.* 1988 Ballantine/PBO. Tom French, birdwatcher, got up early one morning and walked into the fog. His body was found face down in the reeds. Birdwatching enthusiasts George Palmer-Jones and his wife Molly are asked to investigate. It's like stalking a rare bird. 1st.

CLEEVES, Ann. *Come Death And High Water.* 1988 Ballantine/ PBO. The executive committee was at the observatory for a weekend of birdwatching. Just after Charlie Todd announced he was going to sell the island, he turned up dead. George and Molly Palmer-Jones want a better motive. 2nd. [Real Estate]

KALLEN, Lucille. *C. B. Greenfield: The Piano Bird.* [Real Estate]

VAN GIESON, Judith. *Raptor.* 1990 Harper & Row/Pocket 1991. When Neil Hamel's aunt died she discovered that Aunt Jane had booked a birdwatching trip to Fire Pond, Montana. The prize was a glimpse of the rare gyrfalcon. Soon Neil finds herself on the endangered list. 2nd. [Lawyer]

WAUGH, Hillary. *Murder On Safari.* 1987 Dodd, Mead/ Worldwide 1989. The birdwatching safari was just starting out in Kenya when Phineas Cartwright was poisoned. Colonel Dagger joins the local police. The safari moves on, the killings continue. None of the pieces fits. [Africa]

BLACK DETECTIVES

He may not have been the first black detective, but Pharoah Love is probably the most unique. His creator, George Baxt, made him gay and black, and misspelled his name. By comparison, in some mysteries being black is an important part of the story, adding color with insights into culture. In others, it is incidental to the plot and has no relevance to the solution. And then we have Penny Wanawake!

BALL, John. *The Cool Cottontail.* 1966 Harper & Row/ Perennial 1985. Dr. Roussel was found floating naked in the pool at the Sun Valley Lodge, a nudist camp. Only he wasn't one of the guests. Virgil Tibbs walks quietly among the nude to solve this assignment. 2nd. [Revenge]

BALL, John. *Singapore.* [Oriental]

BAXT, George. *A Queer Kind Of Death.* [Getting Away With Murder]

DAVIS, Kenn. *Melting Point.* 1986 Fawcett/ PBO. Eleven-year-old Amber has a bullet in her shoulder and she wants Carver Bascombe to find her father, Tom Ferrik, the sculptor. That's only the first step in unraveling a long chain of mysteries and double-crossing partners. 2nd. [Art]

DAVIS, Kenn. *Nijinsky Is Dead.* 1987 Fawcett/ PBO. Joel Burck, San Francisco ballet star, hires Carver Bascombe to find out who is trying to kill him. As Bascombe tiptoes around the ballet company, Burck's male lover is killed. Suddenly Bascombe has information about Burck he'd rather not have. 3rd. [Gay]

DAVIS, Kenn. *As October Dies.* [Art]

HAYWOOD, Gar Anthony. *Fear Of The Dark.* 1988 St. Martin/ Penguin 1990. When a white kid guns down two black men, it starts to look like a race war. But when a gunman is killed, PI Aaron Gunner has to ask some different questions. 1st. [Blackmail]

HAYWOOD, Gar Anthony. *Not Long For This World.* 1990 St. Martin. Darryl Lovejoy gave up a career in advertising to return to the streets of Los Angeles. He set out to try to save the teen youth gangs. Instead, he was assassinated. PI Aaron Gunner is combing the Black community for his killer. 2nd. [Children]

HILARY, Richard. *Snake In The Grasses.* 1987 Bantam/ PBO. Walter Epps, a respectable civil servant, is found dead wearing a Batman cape and mask, lewd photos strewn on his desk. His widow wants PI Ezell Barnes to find his murderer. Barnes turns up a nifty scam as well. 1st. [Drugs]

HILARY, Richard. *Pieces Of Cream.* 1987 Bantam/ PBO. Showgirl Muff Anglaise wants PI Ezell Barnes to help her collect her ex-boyfriend's insurance. He's been killed while committing a felony. In Atlantic City, that's a small problem. Before it's over, Ezell gets to con the con men. 2nd. [Real Estate]

HILARY, Richard. *Pillow Of The Community.* 1988 Bantam/ PBO. PI Ezell Barnes finds a baby in an orange laundry basket. After he gathers his neighbors together to help care for the little girl, he sets out to find the father. He finds two of them, and murder. 3rd. [Jealousy]

KENYON, Michael. *A Healthy Way To Die.* [Revenge]

MASON, Clifford. *The Case Of The Ashanti Gold.* [Art]

MOODY, Susan. *Penny Black.* 1986 Fawcett/ PBO. Penny Wanawake's friend was found stabbed to death in a bathroom at LAX, and she's determined to find the killer. Her search leads her to Washington, D.C., some interesting suspects, and a tiny orchid. 2nd. [Botany]

MOODY, Susan. *Penny Dreadful.* 1986 Fawcett/ PBO. Max Maunciple, beside being a schoolmaster, made his living writing true crime novels . . . about his friends. He'd made a few enemies that way. When he died of an overdose of alcohol, Penny Wanawake smelled murder. 2nd. [Mystery Writer]

MOODY, Susan. *Penny Post.* 1986 Fawcett/ PBO. Kendal Sartain invites Penny Wanawake down to Ingleford Manor. Someone's trying to kill him and he wants her to find out who it is. She isn't able to save Kendal, but she's determined to find his killer. 4th. [Revenge]

MOODY, Susan. *Penny Royal.* 1987 Fawcett/ PBO. Archaeologist Bruno Ferlinghetti disappeared from his home near Naples with a pair of valuable gold statuettes from an archaeological site. Penny Wanawake isn't convinced he's a thief, but first she has to find him. 5th. [Anthropology]

MOODY, Susan. *Penny Pinching.* Fawcett 1989/ PBO. There on the deck at her father's beach house in Big Sur was a body. And the young woman looked just like Penny. Before she can discover whether she herself was the intended victim, her father is kidnapped. 6th. [Incest]

PHILLIPS, Mike. *The Late Candidate.* 1990 St. Martin. Ashton Edward, controversial politician, was found stabbed to death. Journalist Sam Dean is working on a retrospective of his friend's life, an inquiry that will dig and dig until he finds the truth about Ashton's murder. 2nd. [Fraud]

VALENTINE, Paul W. *Crime Scene At "O" Street.* 1989 Scribner. Franklin Kandinsky was murdered in his D.C. apartment. Homicide Detectives Hudlow and Johnson have been assigned the case. It goes from routine to strange as they follow leads across state lines and into dark caverns. [Intrigue]

BLACKMAIL

Nasty, mean, and insidious, blackmail often leads to murder. The most vicious form of blackmail shows itself in the small-town and village mysteries, where neighbor suspects neighbor. A tangle of suspicion reigns and tension mounts.

ALBERT, Marvin. *Back In The Real World.* 1986 Fawcett/ PBO. Pete Sawyer stops by a friend's house one night and finds a dead man and woman, and neither one belongs there. Frank Crowley, owner of the house, is suspected of the killings, and Pete's out to find the real murderer. 2nd. [Fashion]

ALBERT, Marvin. *Long Teeth.* 1987 Fawcett/ PBO. Karl Malo's third wife has been kidnapped on the road to Nice. Pete Sawyer's been hired to carry the seven-million-franc ransom and rescue Jacqueline. It goes smoothly, too smoothly. Malo wants to know if either of his children is involved. 4th. [Kidnapping]

ALDYNE, Nathan. *Vermilion.* [Gay]

ALLEGRETTO, Michael. *Death On The Rocks.* 1987 Scribner/ Paperjacks 1988. Phillip Townsend died in a car crash in the mountains outside of Denver. His wife hired PI Jake Lomax to prove it was murder. Jake quietly discovers the strong smell of blackmail. 1st. [Accident]

BARNES, Linda. *Bitter Finish.* [Espionage]

BAYER, William. *Blind Side.* [Journalism]

BEATON, M. C. *Death Of A Cad.* [Fraud]

BECK, K. K. *Murder In A Mummy Case.* [Journalism]

BLOCK, Lawrence. *Burglars Can't Be Choosers.* 1977 Random House/ Pocket 1983. It was to be a simple job. Break into an empty apartment and find a blue box. Then, the cops burst in and find a dead body in the bedroom. Bernie Rhodenbarr has to find a killer or go to jail. 1st. [Theater]

BORGENICHT, Miriam. *Still Life.* 1986 St. Martin/ Worldwide 1989. Margaret Berringer's brother David is wheelchair bound. He talks about killing Sandy Fleming, the man responsible for his paralysis. When Sandy is found dead, Margaret has to use all her efforts to keep David out of prison.

BREAN, Herbert. *The Traces Of Brillhart.* 1960 Harper & Row/ International Polygonics 1988. Songwriter Brill Brillhart was reported murdered. Since he was such a heel, few people were very upset. But why are the gossip columnists reporting his activities all over Manhattan? Magazine writer William Deacon may find the answer. 1st.

CARLSON, P. M. *Murder Unrenovated.* 1988 Bantam/ PBO. Maggie Ryan and her husband, Nick O'Conner, are house hunting. In the basement apartment of the New York City brownstone is Julia. She has a vested interest in discouraging any potential sale. As Maggie looks over the house she discovers a body. To buy the house, she has to discover the murderer. 4th.

CHANDLER, Raymond & Robert B. Parker. *Poodle Springs.* 1989 Putnam/ Berkley 1990. Philip Marlowe was in a very strange situation; he'd just gotten married and moved to Poodle Springs. Anxious to get back to work, he's hired by Lipshultz to find Les Valentine. It seems Les left a $100,000 IOU that could be deadly. [Father]

CHASE, Elaine Raco. *Dangerous Places.* 1987 Bantam/PBO. Nikki Holden, journalist, wants a story: an interview with Ignace, the hotshot jai alai player. So she cottons up to his girlfriend, Marcy, only to discover that PI Roman Cantrell is watching Marcy. All of a sudden, Miami becomes deadly, and Nikki and Roman join forces to solve three murders. 1st. [Journalism]

CLARKE, T. E. B. *Murder At Buckingham Palace.* 1981 St. Martin/ St. Martin 1987. Alice Gill, the young housemaid at Buckingham Palace, has the gall to be murdered just before George V's Silver Jubilee. Detective Sergeant Harry Bennett is upstairs and downstairs looking for the killer.

CONANT, Susan. *A New Leash On Death.* [Dogs]

COYNE, P. J. *Manuscript For Murder.* [Writer]

CRIDER, Bill. *One Dead Dean.* [Academic]

DENHAM, Bertie. *Foxhunt.* [Intrigue]

DEWHURST, Eileen. *A Nice Little Business.* 1987 Doubleday. Cathy, wife of Scotland Yard Detective Inspector Neil Carter, meets a charming old woman on the bus. Later, when she calls at the home, she finds Mrs. Willoughby very dead. Neil goes outside the law for justice. 5th.

DEXTER, Colin. *The Dead Of Jericho.* 1981 St. Martin/ Bantam 1988. Inspector Morse had met Anne Scott at a party and had been attracted. But she was married. Now, six months later, she's dead. He feels drawn into the investigation of her death. 3rd. [Imposter]

EBERHART, Mignon G. *The Patient In Cabin C.* [At Sea]

ECCLES, Marjorie. *Death Of A Good Woman.* [Writers]

ENGEL, Howard. *Murder Sees The Light.* [Canadian]

ENGLEMAN, Paul. *Dead In Center Field.* [Ball Games]

ESTLEMAN, Loren D. *Motor City Blues.* [Political]

FROST, Joan Van Every. *Portrait In Black.* [Art]

FULTON, Eileen. *Take One For Murder.* [Television]

FULTON, Eileen. *Dying For Stardom.* [Television]

GARDNER, Erle Stanley w/a A. A. Fair. *Bedrooms Have Windows.* [Suicide]

GAULT, William Campbell. *Death In Donegal Bay.* 1984 Walker/ Charter 1987. Brock Callahan retired from the PI business. When a con man tried to hire him, he referred him to his young friend Corey. Then Brock got worried. He dove in to help out, finding crime, corruption, lies, and murder. 10th.

GAULT, William Campbell. *The Dead Seed.* 1985 Walker/ Charter 1987. Retirement gnawed at Brock Callahan. An old movie star moved in next door. Next day, the star had vanished and someone was watching the house. Now there's a body on the beach. 11th.

GIELGUD, Val. *Through A Glass Darkly.* 1963 Scribner/ Perennial 1986. Simon Hargest, an executive with Gargantuan TV, took his own life. Someone in CID wants Inspector Pellew to investigate the circumstances of the man's death. At first, there's hardly any information about Hargest. Then Pellew finds a clue. 3rd. [Television]

GIROUX, E. X. *A Death For A Darling.* [On Vacation]

GIROUX, E. X. *A Death For A Dancer.* 1985 St. Martin/ Ballantine 1986. Barrister Robert Forsythe and his secretary Miss Sanderson are off to the country house of the Dancers. The body of a young woman has been found in the family crypt. 3rd. [Imposter]

GORMAN, Edward. *New, Improved Murder.* [Advertising]

GOULART, Ron. *Even The Butler Was Poor.* [Advertising]

GRAFTON, Sue. *"C" Is For Corpse.* 1986 Holt/ Bantam 1987. Bobby Callahan, recovering from a serious auto accident, hires Kinsey Millhone to find out who forced him off the road. Only a few days into the case, Bobby dies in another car accident. Keeping her agreement, Kinsey vows to find his killer. 3rd.

GRAHAM, Caroline. *The Killings At Badger's Drift.* [Incest]

GRAHAM, Caroline. *Death Of A Hollow Man.* [Theater]

GRANGER, Ann. *Say It With Poison.* [Television]

GREENAN, Russell H. *A Can Of Worms.* 1987 Bantam/ PBO. Magda Gilman's husband has been murdered, and several people are very uneasy. Two different cops are asking questions about the case, and at the showdown only one of them will live. [Incest]

GREENLEAF, Stephen. *Grave Error.* 1979 Dial/ Ballantine 1984. Jacqueline Nelson wants John Marshall Tanner to find out if her husband is being blackmailed. She also wants to know where he went the week he was missing. A murder speeds up Tanner's investigation. 4th. [Old Crime]

HALLERAN, Tucker. *A Cool, Clear Death.* 1984 St. Martin/ St. Martin 1986. Ex–NFL player turned PI, Cam

MacCardle was hired by his old Vietnam buddy, lawyer Dick Ellis. Cam's needed to prove that Ellis's client didn't kill his wife. Cam digs into Laura's past and what comes up isn't particularly clean. 1st. [Gay]

HARRISON, Ray. *A Season For Death.* [Victorian]

HARRISON, Ray. *Harvest Of Death.* [Victorian]

HART, Roy. *A Fox In The Night.* 1988 St. Martin. Inspector Roper suspects murder when Hannah Blezzard's body is washed up on the early tide. At her home, he finds no personal papers, no evidence of relatives, and what appears to be a blackmail letter. 3rd.

HAYWOOD, Gar Anthony. *Fear Of The Dark.* [Black Detective]

HEALY, Jeremiah. *The Staked Goat.* [Imposter]

HENDRICKS, Michael. *Friends In High Places.* [Manuscript]

HESS, Joan, w/a Joan Hadley. *The Deadly Ackee.* 1988 St. Martin/ Ballantine 1990. Theo's niece, Dorrie, and her friends have arranged for spring break on Jamaica. Theo was conned into being their chaperone. Soon one of the young women is missing and there's a dead body in the swimming pool. Theo and Dorrie put their heads together. 2nd.

HESS, Joan. *A Really Cute Corpse.* 1988 St. Martin. Eighteen girls are competing for Queen of the Miss Thurberfest Beauty Pageant, and Claire Malloy is drafted as the director. When someone takes a shot at last year's queen, a young senator insists the bullet was meant for him. 4th. [Political]

JEFFERS, H. Paul. *The Rag Doll Murder.* [Fashion]

JOHNSTON, Velda. *The Girl On The Beach.* [Old Crime]

KAMINSKY, Stuart. *Lieberman's Folly.* [Old Crime]

KEATING, H. R. F., w/a Evelyn Hervey. *Into The Valley Of Death.* [Victorian]

KEATING, H. R. F. *The Body In The Billiard Room.* 1987 Viking/ Penguin 1988. At the bastion of the Brits, the Ooty Club, the body of a servant was found on the billiard table where snooker was invented. Inspector Ghote is sent from Bombay to the hill country to clear up the matter. 17th.

KELLEY, Patrick A. *Sleightly Lethal.* [Psychic]

KENNEALY, Jerry. *Polo Solo.* 1987 St. Martin/ St. Martin 1988. San Francisco Mayor Barbara Martin went to her country place for the weekend. She was overpowered, drugged, and filmed. They are asking a lot of money for the videos. PI Nick Polo is to carry the cash . . . and get rid of the filmmakers. 1st.

LINDSEY, David L. *Heat From Another Sun.* 1984 Harper & Row/Pocket 1987. Cameraman Wayne Powell was found stabbed to death in the darkroom of a Houston ad agency. Homicide detective Stuart Hayden discovered that the agency had recently been bought by a man reputed to befriend the darkest side of human nature. 2nd. [Psychological]

LIVINGSTON, Jack. *The Nightmare File.* 1986 St. Martin/ Onyx 1987. Gene Liston was working on a story about some Southeast Asian tribesmen who died in their sleep during a nightmare. He died, scared to death. His wife asks deaf PI Joe Binney for help. But Gene's files are missing . . . 3rd.

LOCHTE, Dick. *Sleeping Dogs.* 1985 Arbor House/ Warner 1986. For PI Leo G. Bloodworth in Southern California, it started out as a case of dognapping and ended with bank fraud, blackmail, and murder.

LYONS, Arthur. *Fast Fade.* [Missing Person]

MACHIN, Meredith Land. *Outrageous Fortune.* 1985 St. Martin/ Signet 1986. Kate Downing's husband died in Vietnam and she put her life back together. For ten years she's worked for a Chicago financier. He's been missing for a week when Kate discovers that her husband is alive.

MacLEOD, Charlotte. *The Bilbao Looking Glass.* [Antiques]

MARON, Margaret. *Death In Blue Folders.* 1985 Doubleday. After Clayton Gladwell was murdered in his office, the killer looted the place. Lt. Sigrid Harald, NYPD, is going through his personal cases: the blue folders. It all adds up to blackmail. But who? 3rd. [Imposter]

MATHIS, Edward. *See No Evil.* Berkley 1990/ PBO. There has been a rash of murders in the Dallas-Ft. Worth area. Detective Hamilton Pope can see no pattern in the killings, but the weapon is the same, a sharp hooked knife. [Serial Killers]

MAXWELL, A. E. *The Frog And The Scorpion.* 1986 Doubleday/Bantam 1987. Shakpour, an Iranian, is an illegal alien. So is the rest of his large family. A blackmailer has discovered the secret, and Fiddler is hired to find a way to protect them all. 2nd.

McBAIN, Ed. *The House That Jack Built.* [Lawyer]

McCAHERY, James R. *Grave Undertaking.* [Where There's a Will]

McCONNELL, Frank. *Blood Lake.* 1987 Walker/ Penguin 1988. Ex-nun Bridget O'Toole, owner of O'Toole Investigations, sends Harry Garnish off to Blood Lake to keep an eye on Mr. Howard's wife, suspected of being unfaithful. Soon Cheryl Howard is found floating in the lake, and Harry's work is just beginning. 2nd.

McGOWN, Jill. *An Evil Hour.* 1986 St. Martin. Member of Parliament Gerald Culver dies at a small hotel in Amblesea. By the time PI Harry Lambert arrives, the murderer is ready to strike again. The only connection seems to be Annie Maddox, who runs the Wellington Hotel.

McMULLEN, Mary. *Funny, Jonas, You Don't Look Dead.* 1976 Doubleday/Jove 1988. It was another late night call from her ex-husband Jonas, bragging about his latest racket. Then Millie Lester heard him being murdered. She took the next train to Philadelphia; she had to find out for herself. [Infidelity]

McMULLEN, Mary. *Stranglehold.* [Advertising]

MOFFAT, Gwen. *Snare.* 1988 St. Martin. Famous mystery writer Miss Melinda Pink packed up her typewriter and moved to the quiet Scottish village of Sgoradale to finish her book. She lands right in the middle of blackmail and murder. 11th. [Mystery Writer]

MORGAN, D. Miller. *Money Leads To Murder.* 1987 Dodd, Mead. Widowed Daisy Marlow, PI, is hired to locate a missing show girl in Las Vegas, where old beau, Sam Milo, is the police captain. They both become embroiled in murder, money and blackmail. [Jealousy]

MURRAY, Lynne. *Termination Interview.* 1988 St. Martin. Working as a temp, Ingrid Hunter runs into an old friend, Miranda. Miranda's the personnel director for a prestigious law firm. When Miranda dies from a fall out a window, Ingrid discovers that she'd been keeping her own personnel files.

NOEL, Atanielle Annyn. *Murder On Usher's Planet.* 1987 Avon/ PBO. A letter of diplomatic importance has fallen into the wrong hands. Gwen Gray and her cousin Garamond were hired to infiltrate the castle of Lord Usher and get it back. In a house full of eccentrics, murder strikes.

O'CALLAGHAN, Maxine. *Hit & Run.* [Jewelry]

PARKER, Robert B. *The Widening Gyre.* [Political]

PAUL, Barbara. *The Renewable Virgin.* 1985 Scribner/ Bantam 1986. Actress Kelly Ingram sent her writer friend home with his headache. The next day Rudy was dead, poisoned with the medication she'd handed him. Detective Marion Larch, NYPD, is on the case. She and Kelly start looking into Rudy's past.

PAYNE, Laurence. *Knight Fall.* [Theater]

PENN, John. *A Will To Kill.* 1984 Scribner/ Bantam 1986. Peter Derwent has worked so hard to keep Broadfields solvent. When he took a shortcut through the woods headed for home, he wasn't expecting to be shot down in the rainstorm. A puzzle for Detective Superintendent George Thorne. 1st.

PERRY, Anne. *Callander Square.* [Victorian]

PHILBRICK, W. R. *Ice For The Eskimo.* [Kidnapping]

PHILLIPS, R. A. *Gun Play.* [Smuggling]

PICKARD, Nancy. *No Body.* [Fraud]

PICKARD, Nancy. *Dead Crazy.* [Social Issues]

PRATHER, Richard S. *The Kubla Khan Caper.* [Imposter]

PULVER, Mary Monica. *Murder At The War.* [Holiday]

RAY, Robert J. *Murdock For Hire.* 1987 St. Martin/ Penguin 1988. Mr. Hennessy died of a heart attack and his widow wants his coin collection; it's missing. When Matt Murdock starts poking around, he discovers that's only the tip of a very messy iceberg. 2nd.

RESNICOW, Herbert. *Murder Across And Down.* [Crossword Puzzles]

REYNOLDS, William J. *The Nebraska Quotient.* 1984 St. Martin/ Ballantine 1986. Morris Capel, Nebraska's ex-PI partner, died on his living room floor. He left a few strips of color negatives: nude photos of the senator's daughter. Nebraska returns the negatives and ends up in a mess. 1st. [Revenge]

RICE, Craig. *My Kingdom For A Hearse.* [Lawyer]

ROBERTS, Gillian. *Caught Dead In Philadelphia.* 1987 Scribner/ Ballantine 1988. Amanda Pepper, English teacher, has an early morning visitor, Liza, the drama teacher. When Amanda returns home, Liza is dead on her hearth. C. K. Mackenzie, a city cop, joins with Amanda to solve the crime. 1st.

SANGSTER, Jimmy. *Blackball.* [Father]

SAWYER, Corinne Holt. *The J. Alfred Prufrock Murders.* 1988 Fine/ Fawcett 1989. The California retirement center of Camden-Sur-Mer was usually quiet, until Sweetie was found dead on the beach. Her friends Angela, Nan, Caledonia and Stella set out to play detective. Then another woman is murdered and Detective Martinez arrives to give them a hand. 1st. [Pornography]

SHANNON, Dell. *Mark For Murder.* [Serial Killer]

SQUIRE, Elizabeth Daniels. *Kill The Messenger.* [Journalism]

STRUNK, Frank C. *Jordon's Wager.* [Fraud]

TAIBO, Paco Ignacio III. *An Easy Thing.* 1989 Viking/ Penguin 1990. Mexico City PI Hector Shayne met an old man in a bar. He dropped a bag of coins on the table and told Hector he wanted him to find Emiliano Zapata who had not died at Chinameca. [Famous People]

TAPPLY, William G. *Follow The Sharks.* [Ball Games]

TRENCH, Jason. *The Hammer.* 1989 Doubleday. When his regular visit to his prostitute turns into blackmail, Harry Denman's anger gets him into trouble. The woman dies accidently and the serial killer, the Hammer, is blamed for her death. [Serial Killers]

TRUMAN, Margaret. *Murder In The Supreme Court.* [Lawyer]

WATSON, Clarissa. *Somebody Killed The Messenger.* 1988 Atheneum. Much-married Seraphine Bracely is sending a canvas from Amsterdam for the charity exhibit at Gull Harbor. The messenger vanishes and later the canvas arrives, only to provoke gasps and fear among these rich viewers. Persis Willum flies to Europe for the answer. 5th. [Art]

WENTWORTH, Patricia. *Wicked Uncle.* 1947 Lippincott/ Warner 1986. Gregory Porlock invited a group of people to Mill House for the weekend. Then their host is found with a knife in his back. Frank Abbott and Maud Silver begin to uncover evidence of blackmail. 11th. [Where There's A Will]

WENTWORTH, Patricia. *Through The Wall.* [Where There's A Will]

WHALLEY, Peter. *Robbers.* 1986 Walker/ Avon 1989. When Clifford Humphries died of a major coronary, he left Cornet Private Investigation Agency to his mistress Yvonne Robinson. She makes Harry Summers a partner. Harry's first case is an old friend, clutching a blackmail note and pleading for help. 1st. [Old Crime]

WHEAT, Carolyn. *Where Nobody Dies.* 1986 St. Martin/ Bantam 1988. Linda Richie had just won custody of her daughter when she was found murdered. Her ex-husband is charged with the crime. Cass Jameson, Linda's lawyer, discovers reasons for others to want Linda dead. 2nd. [Lawyer]

BOOKSTORES

What better setting for a murder than a bookstore preferably one that deals in used books. And what better characters than book dealers. Dust motes whirling in the sunbeams, stacks of books that momentarily threaten to slither to the floor in a jumble, and the Irish setter that sneaks out from behind the counter to con a willing customer into rubbing her belly—all contribute to the atmosphere.

BLOCK, Lawrence. *The Burglar In The Closet.* 1978 Random House/ Pocket 1981. Bernie Rhodenbarr broke into Crystal's apartment as a favor to his friend Craig. He got locked in the closet, and when he came out Crystal was dead. Before long there's another body in his own apartment. Bernie has to clear himself. 2nd. [Jewels]

BLOCK, Lawrence. *The Burglar Who Liked To Quote Kipling.* 1979 Random House/ Pocket 1982. Bernie Rhodenbarr delivered a rare book to Madeleine's apartment. She drugged Bernie, then someone else arrived, shot Madeleine and put the gun in Bernie's hand. He has to clear himself of this murder, too. 3rd. [Manuscript]

BLOCK, Lawrence. *The Burglar Who Studied Spinoza.* 1980 Random House/ Pocket 1982. The burglary ended in death. Not only had the Calcannon house been robbed, but Wanda was dead. Bernie's fence died shortly afterward. It's another case of Bernie having to clear his own name. 4th. [Accident]

BLOCK, Lawrence. *The Burglar Who Painted Like Mondrian.* 1983 Arbor House/ Pocket 1986. Someone set out to frame Bernie Rhodenbarr. He was hired to put a price on a private library. After he'd left and his fingerprints were all over the apartment, the owner was murdered and a painting stolen. 5th. [Art]

BREEN, Jon L. *Touch Of The Past.* [Mystery Writer]

DOBSON, Margaret. *Touchstone.* [Jewels]

DOBSON, Margaret. *Primrose.* 1987 Dell/ PBO. Jane Bailey wasn't tending her bookstore today. Instead, she was exploring a strange accident. Her old friend Glenn had died when he was crushed beneath his own classic Camaro. Just then Phillip Decker walked back into her life, and into the hospital. 2nd. [Accident]

DOBSON, Margaret. *Soothsayer.* 1987 Dell/ PBO. Jane Bailey left the confines of her bookstore to help Phillip find Howard Springer. He's a thirty-eight-year-old momma's boy who took a hike. His mother's convinced he's still alive. Jane and Phillip are in deep woods. 3rd. [Missing Person]

HART, Carolyn. *Death On Demand.* 1987 Bantam/ PBO. Uncle Ambrose left Annie Laurance his bookstore, Death on Demand, along with the Sunday Night Regulars, a get-together for mystery writers. This Sunday, things were different. Elliot Morgan was dead, the target of a dart in the dark. 1st. [Mystery Writers]

HART, Carolyn. *Design For Murder.* 1988 Bantam/ PBO. When Annie planned the Mystery Night for the

Historical Society, she hadn't expected to find a body in the backyard pond. Corrine Webster was dead and not too many people seemed upset about it. But Annie was the one accused of murder. 2nd. [Mystery Games]

HART, Carolyn. *Something Wicked.* 1988 Bantam/ PBO. The Broward Rock Players are putting on a benefit performance. But there seems to be a prankster in their midst playing a lot of dirty tricks, ending with murder. Annie and her fiancé Max are forced to play detective. 3rd. [Theater]

HESS, Joan. *Strangled Prose.* [Academic]

LEWIS, Roy Hartley. *Miracles Take A Little Longer.* [Journalism]

SIMONSON, Sheila. *Larkspur.* 1990 St. Martin. Lark Dailey, owner of Larkspur Bookstore, receives an invitation to a "literary weekend" from well-known poet Dai Llewellyn. When Dai is poisoned with larkspur, Lark is a suspect. 1st. [Psychological]

WARGA, Wayne. *Hardcover.* [Manuscript]

WREN, M. K. *Curiosity Didn't Kill The Cat.* [Imposter]

BOTANY

Formal gardens, hundreds of years in the growing, are often the murder scene in English mysteries. Genteel plants, fragrant and daintily blossomed, can be the vehicle of death for the unwary victim. Is the ardent gardener an unsuspecting suspect, victim, or determined murderer?

BLACK, Lionel. *Death Has Green Fingers.* 1971 Walker/ Penguin 1982. Ashworth was a village that took pride in its roses. Nick Bell, in a remarkable feat, had produced a new variety, a blue rose. When he was murdered, the roses vanished. Kate Theobald camps in the village to get the story. 2nd. [Journalism]

HILL, Reginald. *Dead Heads.* 1983 Macmillan/ Signet 1985. The Perfecta Porcelain company is losing its top officers, one by one, by death. It leaves lots of room for Patrick Alderman, accountant and horticulturist. Dalziel and Pascoe wonder if "deadheading" a company is like pruning roses. 8th. [Getting Away With Murder]

MOODY, Susan. *Penny Black.* [Black Detective]

O'HAGAN, Joan. *Against The Grain.* 1988 Doubleday. Jack Duquesne got mad when the government refused to let him send a sample of his new wheat to the world grain bank. Then he meets Irina, and he's on the run to the world conference in Rome. [Intrigue]

RATHBONE, Julian. *Greenfinger.* 1987 Viking/ Penguin 1988. There's a new strain of maize being developed in Central America. Called Zdt., the maize could well cost Greenfinger, Inc., a lot of money. A massive plot is instituted to wipe it out. But nobody is prepared for Esther Sommers Carter, the wife of the U.N.'s agricultural economist. [Economics]

SHERWOOD, John. *Green Trigger Fingers.* 1984 Scribner/ Ballantine 1987. Widowed Celia Grant moved to Westfield and opened a nursery and gardening service. The town buzzed with the recent murders of the Emersons. Then Celia discovers a body buried in another garden. She turns sleuth. 1st. [Art]

SHERWOOD, John. *A Botanist At Bay.* 1985 Scribner/ Ballantine 1986. Off to New Zealand for the birth of her daughter's first child, Celia Grant, horticulturist, is sidetracked into looking for Uncle Bertie. But "misplanted" plants point the way to murder. 2nd.

SHERWOOD, John. *The Mantrap Garden.* 1986 Scribner/ Ballantine 1987. The Monk's Mead Gardens have come on hard times, along with a few episodes of destruction. Celia Grant is asked to join the board of trustees to help repair the damage. No one told her about the body in the garden. 3rd.

SHERWOOD, John. *Flowers Of Evil.* 1987 Scribner/ Ballantine 1990. The owner of the old rectory, Richard Galliant, was starting to act strange, especially whenever he made a public appearance. It's suspected that he's being poisoned, and Celia Grant is plowing through her reference books. 4th.

SHERWOOD, John. *The Sunflower Plot.* 1991 Scribner. Celia Grant is in financial difficulty. Her only hope is to land a contract designing a fake Elizabethan garden at Clintbury Park. Soon Celia is recruited by the police to spy on Victor Stratton's household. 7th. [Kidnapping]

WHITNEY, Phyllis A. *Dream Of Orchids.* 1985 Doubleday/ Fawcett 1985. Laurel York is summoned to Key West to meet Clifton York, the father who deserted her as a child. His wife has just died mysteriously, and he's withdrawn. Amid orchids are answers.

C... IS FOR

CANADA

THE PAST FEW YEARS have seen a flowering of mysteries from north of the border. The settings stretch from the Maritime Provinces (Charlotte MacLeod) to Vancouver Island (Phyllis A. Whitney), with some choice locations in between.

CHUDLEY, Ron. *Freeze Frame.* [Drugs]

DAWSON, David Laing. *Last Rights.* 1990 St. Martin. Henry Thornton's roommates at Shelburn Villa Nursing Home seemed to be dying at a faster than expected rate. Over a beer, he enlists the aid of Dixie Brown, his flirtatious fellow resident. They set out to investigate and both get marked for murder. [Medical]

ENGEL, Howard. *The Suicide Murders.* [Suicide]

ENGEL, Howard. *Murder Sees The Light.* 1985 St. Martin/ Penguin 1986. A Toronto lawyer wants PI Benny Cooperman to locate TV evangelist Norbert E. Patten. Below the surface there's murder and blackmail... and a woman. 4th. [Blackmail]

ENGEL, Howard. *A City Called July.* 1986 St. Martin/ Penguin 1988. Larry Geller had been entrusted with money from the members of the congregation; he was to invest it. Larry is missing and Rabbi Tepperman wants PI Benny Cooperman to find him, and the money. 5th. [Fraud]

ENGEL, Howard. *A Victim Must Be Found.* 1988 St. Martin/Penguin 1989. PI Benny Cooperman has another job. Pambos Kiriakis wants him to find the list of people who have valuable art on loan from the late Arthur Tallon's collection. Then Pambos dies, and someone else wants the list. 6th. [Art]

GALBRAITH, Ruth. *A Convenient Death.* [Academic]

GODFREY, Ellen. *Murder Behind Locked Doors.* 1988 St. Martin. Headhunter Jean Tregar is looking for a vice president for a small data processing company. She learns that the former jobholder died in the locked computer room. Evidence implicating a company officer almost costs her her life. [Locked Room]

GOUGH, Laurence. *The Goldfish Bowl.* 1988 St. Martin/Penguin 1990. A serial killer is stalking the rain-swept streets of Vancouver. As detectives Jack Willow and Claire Parker follow empty leads, a pattern begins to develop. But to make matters worse, the killer seems to be always one step ahead of them. 1st. [Serial Killers]

GOUGH, Laurence. *Silent Knives.* [Prostitution]

GOUGH, Laurence. *Hot Shots.* 1990 Viking. The Vancouver police found a blood-spattered car but no body. Detectives Willow and Parker are pacing the beach and dragging the bay for the corpse. Meantime, a shipment of heroin has been jettisoned into English Bay by nervous couriers. 3rd. [Drugs]

MacLEOD, Charlotte, w/a Alisa Craig. *A Pint Of Murder.* 1980 Doubleday/ Avon 1988. Aunt Aggie collapsed on the kitchen floor, dead from botulism—a bad jar of green beans. It takes RCMP Madoc Rhys and Janet Wadman to sort out the relatives searching for the missing fortune. 1st. [Cooks]

MacLEOD, Charlotte, w/a Alisa Craig. *The Grub-And-Stakers Move A Mountain.* 1981 Doubleday/ Avon 1987. A man was killed with a bow and arrow in the town's wildflower preserve, Enchanted Mountain. Dittany Henbitt almost loses her own life as she starts looking for a motive. 1st.

MacLEOD, Charlotte, w/a Alisa Craig. *The Terrible Tide.* [Antiques]

MacLEOD, Charlotte, w/a Alisa Craig. *The Grub-And-Stakers Quilt A Bee.* 1985 Doubleday/ Avon 1987. The Grub-and-Stakers inherit a museum, a run-down old house with no funds for the upkeep. Everyone in town wants to display their "treasures." They hire acrophobic Mr. Fairfield and his wife as curators. Then Mr. Fairfield falls to his death from the roof. 2nd. [Jewels]

MacLEOD, Charlotte, w/a Alisa Craig. *Murder Goes Mumming.* [Christmas]

MacLEOD, Charlotte, w/a Alisa Craig. *A Dismal Thing To Do.* [Smuggling]

MacLEOD, Charlotte, w/a Alisa Craig. *The Grub-And-Stakers Pinch A Poke.* 1988 Avon/ PBO. The Grub-and-Stakers are performing *The Shooting of Dan McGrew* in the Scottsbeck competition. But someone is trying to eliminate the leading man. Dittany Monk takes on the role of sleuth and starts poking into the goings-on in Lobelia Falls. 3rd. [Theater]

MacLEOD, Charlotte, w/a Alisa Craig. *The Grub-And-Stakers Spin A Yarn.* Avon 1990/ PBO. Too many things are happening all at once in Lobelia Falls. There are a couple of thugs, blood on Aunt Jane's floor and unknown cousins are due in from England. Then the local mincemeat magnate is murdered. Dittany and Osbert Monk gather up the forces. 4th. [Cooks And Cooking]

PHILLIPS, Edward. *Sunday's Child.* [Gay]

QUOGAN, Anthony. *The Fine Art Of Murder.* 1988 St. Martin. Playwright Matthew Prior accepts an invitation to teach a drama course and direct one of his own plays at a small college in Ontario. But his cast is dying one by one. He turns sleuth, fast. [Theater]

RITCHIE, Simon. *The Hollow Woman.* 1987 Scribner/ Signet 1988. One-armed PI Jantarro sees the case as pretty easy: deliver the quarter of a million dollars in ransom, and Helene and her son Hugo will be returned. But the charred bodies are found in the railyard, and Jantarro's reputation is on the line. [Kidnapping]

SALE, Medora. *Murder In Focus.* 1989 Scribner. Harriett Jeffries had just set up her photographic equipment in Ottawa when Inspector John Sanders bumped into her, literally. Soon Harriett would need the policeman; she'd taken a picture that someone would murder to get back. 2nd. [Political]

SALE, Medora. *Murder In A Good Cause.* 1990 Scribner. Photographer Harriett Jeffries crossed the room to bid her hostess goodnight. Actress Clara von Hohenkammer took a sip of her tea and dropped dead. Inspector John Sanders and Harriett interview a parcel of greedy relatives and not a few strange servants. 3rd. [Antiques]

SMITH, Joan. *A Brush With Death.* [Art]

WOOD, Ted. *Corkscrew.* [Pornography]

WOOD, Ted. *When The Killing Starts.* [Smuggling]

WOOD, Ted. *On The Inside.* 1990 Scribner. Reid Bennett has only been married three days but he's on assignment. Kennedy, of the Provincial Police Commission, wants him to go to the mining town of Elliot and check out rumors of corruption in the police department. 6th. [Smuggling]

WRIGHT, Eric. *The Night The Gods Smiled.* 1983 Scribner/Signet 1985. On the trip to Montreal, David Summers had been elated, calling it his lucky day. He treated his colleagues to dinner, then vanished. They found him dead in a seedy hotel room. Inspector Charlie Salter invades the academic halls. 1st. [Academic]

WRIGHT, Eric. *Smoke Detector.* [Arson]

WRIGHT, Eric. *The Man Who Changed His Name.* 1986 Scribner/Signet 1987. Inspector Charlie Salter almost didn't recognize his ex-wife. Gerry wants him to find out who killed her friend Nancy. It's been over two months since she died. Catching the murderer would make a nice Christmas present for Gerry. 4th. [Christmas]

WRIGHT, Eric. *A Body Surrounded By Water.* [On Vacation]

WRIGHT, Eric. *A Question Of Murder.* 1988 Scribner/Worldwide 1990. The royal princess was visiting Toronto and wanted to explore the Yorkville section of town. The police were out in force. A bomb exploded near the route of the princess. But Charlie Salter suspected it had nothing to do with the lady. 9th. [Insurance]

WRIGHT, Eric. *A Sensitive Case.* 1990 Scribner. Old-time cop Sergeant Mel Pickett, nearing retirement, joins Inspector Charlie Salter in Special Affairs. Their case is a sensitive one; a massage therapist has been murdered and her client list is very influential. 7th. [Infidelity]

WRIGHT, L. R. *The Suspect.* [Revenge]

WRIGHT, L. R. *Sleep While I Sing.* 1986 Viking/ Penguin 1987. She was hitching a ride on a rainy night on Vancouver Island. Now she was dead, propped against a tree, the blood washed from her face. Staff Sergeant Karl Alberg, RCMP, wants desperately to pin the murder on actor Roger Galbraith. 2nd. [Art]

CATS

Man's best friend may be a dog, but there is something satisfying about a cat wandering through a murder mystery. We watch silently as the feline gently paws a clue out of sight or manages to bring some hidden article to the detective's attention. A well-timed yowl could point to the solution.

ADAMSON, Lydia. *A Cat In The Manger.* Signet 1990/PBO. Out-of-work actress Alice Nestleton earned most of her income by cat-sitting. When she arrived at the Starobin's Long Island estate for a Christmas holiday job, she found Henry Starobin hanging from a clothes hook and the house demolished. 1st. [Horses]

BRAUN, Lilian Jackson. *The Cat Who Could Read Backwards.* 1966 Dutton/ Jove 1986. Jim Qwilleran is assigned to human interest stories about artists for the *Daily Fluxion*. Before he can write his first column, three people are dead and he's inherited Koko, the cat who could read backwards. 1st. [Journalism]

BRAUN, Lilian Jackson. *The Cat Who Ate Danish Modern.* 1967 Dutton/ Jove 1986. Jim Qwilleran's assignment is interior design. When murder and a missing collection of jade hits the papers, Jim and Koko have to do some fast footwork. Yum Yum comes to join the family. 2nd. [Insurance]

BRAUN, Lilian Jackson. *The Cat Who Turned Off And On.* 1968 Dutton/ Jove 1986. Writing on Junktown at

Christmas, Jim Qwilleran hopes to win a writing contest. As his research starts, he finds a place to live, a ghost, and a couple of fatal accidents. Or were they accidents? Koko and Yum Yum will find out. 3rd. [Christmas]

BRAUN, Lilian Jackson. *The Cat Who Saw Red.* 1986 Jove/PBO. Jim Qwilleran moves to a house tainted with an old suicide. He discovers a former girlfriend there with her husband. She vanishes and Jim is convinced she's dead. Koko and Yum Yum help as much as they can. 4th. [Art]

BRAUN, Lilian Jackson. *The Cat Who Played Brahms.* 1987 Jove/ PBO. On vacation, Jim Qwilleran stays at the cottage of his "Aunt" Fannie. She's found dead, the cottage is broken into, and things come up missing. What will Koko and Yum Yum discover on this case? 5th. [Smuggling]

BRAUN, Lilian Jackson. *The Cat Who Played Post Office.* 1987 Jove/ PBO. Living in Pickax, after inheriting from his "Aunt" Fannie, Jim Qwilleran discovers that the former maid is missing. Daisy's mother dies and it looks like Jim is next. But not if Koko and Yum Yum have anything to say about it. 6th. [Suicide]

BRAUN, Lilian Jackson. *The Cat Who Had Fourteen Tales.* 1988 Jove/ PBO. A collection of short stories featuring the Siamese cats Yum Yum and Koko and their owner Jim Qwilleran.

BRAUN, Lilian Jackson. *The Cat Who Knew Shakespeare.* 1988 Jove/ PBO. It started with the car accident that killed the editor of the local paper. Jim Qwilleran and the cats smell murder. Then the newspaper burns down and Junior breaks a leg. It's almost too much for our feline sleuths. 7th. [Journalism]

BRAUN, Lilian Jackson. *The Cat Who Sniffed Glue.* 1988 Putnam/ Jove 1989. Pickax is shattered at the deaths of wealthy Harley Finch and his bride Belle. As Qwilleran digs into Harley's history, things seem strained. Then there's an attack on his life. And what is Koko doing with those old books? 8th. [Imposter]

PAPAZOGLOU, Orania. *Sweet, Savage Death.* [Writers]

CHILDREN

Childhood isn't always the pleasurable time that we like to think it is. For some, it is a pretty dismal experience. Nor are all children so innocent as we would believe them to be. Fiction reflects reality all too often.

BARNARD, Robert. *A City Of Strangers.* 1990 Scribner. Jack Phelan has won the pools and is looking to move into a middle-class enclave called "The Hollies." But Jack, and most of his family, are thoroughly unpleasant people. The neighbors are outraged: some set out to stop the move. [Arson]

BARTH, Richard. *Blood Doesn't Tell.* 1989 St. Martin/Fawcett 1990. Widow Margaret Binton volunteers to be a foster mother while baby Eric awaits adoption. But Margaret manages to get involved with the organization in charge of placing the baby. Then someone tries to bribe Margaret into giving Eric to them. 5th. [Fraud]

BRETT, Simon. *What Bloody Man Is That?* [Theater]

BRINGLE, Mary. *The Man In The Moss-Colored Trousers.* [Intrigue]

BUNN, Thomas. *Worse Than Death.* [Kidnapping]

CARLSON, P. M. *Murder Misread.* 1990 Doubleday. Maggie Ryan is back on campus working for Educational Psychology. But Dr. Chandler, professor emeritus, is found shot to death on the edge of campus, an apparent suicide. However, the gun is in the right hand of a lefthanded man. 7th. [Suicide]

CHASE, Samantha. *Postmark.* Tudor 1988/ PBO. The quiet town of Potomac, Maryland, had become a nightmare for Johanna Hamilton. Little girls were disappearing and they looked a lot like her daughter Kirsten. Then the letters started, the letters with the strange postmarks. [Psychological]

CREWS, Lary. *Kill Cue.* [Pornography]

DIBDIN, Michael. *Tryst.* [Psychological]

DORNER, Marjorie. *Nightmare.* 1987 McGraw-Hill. Linda Hammond's daughter was the victim of a child molester. He's out on bail and harasses Linda and her daughter. Linda starts to make some plans of her own. [Revenge]

GEORGE, Elizabeth. *A Great Deliverance.* 1988 Bantam/ Bantam 1989. Inspector Lynley and Sergeant Havers are on a strange case. There is a dead dog and a beheaded man in a barn in Yorkshire. The daughter, Roberta, has confessed to the murders. But what information does the old priest have about the crime? 1st. [Incest]

GILL, B. M. *Nursery Crimes.* 1987 Scribner/ Ballantine 1988. She was just six the first time, when Willie drowned in the fish pond. For her own protection, her parents sent Zanny off to Convent School. Now the nightmare was starting all over again, and a man sat on death row. [Psychological]

HANDLER, David. *The Man Who Died Laughing.* [Writers]

HAYWOOD, Gar Anthony. *Not Long For This World.* [Black Detective]

HESS, Joan. *Madness In Maggody.* [Real Estate]

HILTON, John Buxton. *The Innocent At Home.* 1987 St. Martin. Henry Gower, schoolmaster at St. Botolph's, has been accused of carrying the demonstrations of his sex education classes much too far with four young schoolgirls. When Henry's body is found, Inspector Kenworthy questions the girls. 15th.

HOLLAND, Isabelle. *Bump In The Night.* [Missing Person]

KELLERMAN, Jonathan. *Blood Test.* 1986 Atheneum/ Signet 1987. Child psychologist Alex Delaware was called in by a worried colleague. A sick child's parents were hesitant about chemotherapy, and the Touches, a religious sect, supported the parents. How can Alex help the child? 2nd. [Drugs]

KENDALL, Jack. *Playing For Keeps.* Avon 1988/ PBO. Arnold "Zip" Zipke is worried. Winnamuk Cove, a quiet village, has just had the fourth murder of a teenager. Zip, working at the Youth Employment Office, knew them all. He's trying to find something that links the youngsters together. [Serial Killers]

KITTREDGE, Mary. *Fatal Diagnosis.* [Medical]

KLASS, David. *Night Of The Tyger.* [Academic]

LAIKEN, Deirdre S. *Death Among Strangers.* 1987 Macmillan/ Avon 1988. They found the body in the cemetery, a young girl brutally murdered. The small town was fearful. Lt. George Murphy is the cop in charge. He has to stop the killer before Elizabeth becomes his next victim. [Psychological]

MARON, Margaret. *Death Of A Butterfly.* 1984 Doubleday/ Bantam 1991. Julie Redmond lay dead on her kitchen floor, her head bashed in. NYPD Lt. Sigrid Harald is checking the husband, Karl, and his girlfriend. But the case takes several unexpected turns. 2nd.

MARON, Margaret. *Baby Doll Games.* [Theater]

O'DONNELL, Lillian. *The Other Side Of The Door.* 1987 Putnam/ Fawcett 1988. Teacher Alyssa Hanrest was attacked at her school and nearly killed. To Detective Gary Reissig, it seemed clear her assailant was Roy Easlick, a man sent to prison on Alyssa's testimony. Roy has just been paroled. 12th. [Revenge]

PENTECOST, Hugh. *The Fourteenth Dilemna.* [Intrigue]

RAUCH, Constance. *A Deep Disturbance.* 1990 St. Martin. Madeleine Rafferty took her two young children and fled to upstate New York. Her husband had been taking not very nice pictures of his daughters. But Gil knows where she is and the children have disappeared. [Getting Away With Murder]

RAY, Robert J. *Merry Christmas, Murdock.* [Christmas]

RENDELL, Ruth. *Talking To Strange Men.* [Psychological]

RISENHOOVER, C. C. *Matt McCall.* [Journalism]

SCHOLEFIELD. A. T. *Dirty Weekend.* 1990 St. Martin. On a cold Easter weekend in London, a young man emerges from under Hungerford Bridge where the homeless sleep. Left behind is the body of a TV personality, and the young man has blood on his hands. 1st. [Fraud]

SHUBIN, Seymour. *Never Quite Dead Enough.* [Mystery Writer]

STORY, William L. *Final Thesis.* [Prostitution]

WHITNEY, Phyllis A. *Feathers On The Moon.* [Kidnapping]

WILCOX, Collin. *Night Games.* 1986 Mysterious/ Mysterious 1987. Katherine Haney came home one night to find her third husband dead at the foot of the stairs and a dagger at his side. A break-in has ended in murder. The pieces don't fit together for San Francisco PD's Lt. Frank Hastings. 13th. [Incest]

YORKE, Margaret. *No Medals For The Major.* [Missing Person]

CHRISTMAS

The country manor house, a hint of snow in the air, the cozy fire in the library, and the clink of sherry glasses being passed around by the proper manservant are visions conjured up just before the murder occurs at Christmastime.

Christmas is by far the most popular holiday setting for the arrival of a corpse at the festivities—our favorite unexpected guest.

ASIMOV, Isaac, Charles G. Waugh and Martin Harry Greenberg, eds. *The Twelve Frights Of Christmas.* 1986 Avon/ PBO. An extra gift of a baker's dozen of horror tales to scare you right into the Christmas spirit.

BABSON, Marian. *The Twelve Deaths Of Christmas.* 1979 Walker/ Dell 1985. As the Christmas season approaches, there are a number of strange, impulsive murders. The murderer uses whatever weapon is handy. Superintendent Knowles has a heavy task as the bodies pile up and the holiday comes closer.

BLACKSTOCK, Charity. *The Foggy, Foggy Dew.* [Anthropology]

BRAUN, Lilian Jackson. *The Cat Who Turned Off And On.* [Cats]

BURLEY, W. J. *Wycliffe And The Quiet Virgin.* 1986 Doubleday/ Avon 1988. The "Virgin" of the local Christmas pageant, the sexy teen Francine, has vanished. Then her mother turns up dead. Superintendent Wycliffe and his wife, visiting Cornwall for the holidays, uncover too many secrets, too fast. 13th. [Old Crime]

CHRISTIE, Agatha. *A Holiday For Murder.* 1939 Dodd, Mead/ Bantam 1985. Simeon Lee gathered his family around him for the holidays. On Christmas Eve, he announced that he'd changed his will. Within hours, he was dead. Hercule Poirot has the knack of seeing things as they really are. 17th. [Locked Room]

COHEN, Charles. *Silver Lining.* 1989 Dutton/ Dell 1989. House husband Nicky Silver wandered into Carol Beth's dress shop in the wealthy Chicago suburb to buy his wife Alice a special Christmas present. Instead, he found co-owner Carol in the dressing room hanged by a rhinestone belt. 1st. [Infidelity]

CONSTANTINE, K. C. *Upon Some Midnights Clear.* 1985 Godine/ Penguin 1987. It was just a mugging. But it was almost Christmas and it was all the money Mrs. Gabin had for the holidays. Mario Balzic, Rockport's Police Chief, has the culprit in jail. Still, something doesn't fit. 7th. [Fraud]

CRAMER, Kathryn, and David G. Hartwell. *Christmas Ghosts.* 1987 Arbor House/ Dell 1988. Seventeen short stories to scare you into merry Christmas—a haunting volume. [Witches]

DeANDREA, William L. *Killed On The Ice.* [Revenge]

DRUMMOND, John Keith. *'Tis The Season To Be Dying.* 1988 St. Martin. Aunt Eulalia was spreading Christmas cheer at the Andersons' when the general took a turn for the worse. Matilda Worthing, her niece, is summoned to find out who spiked his orange juice. 2nd. [Where There's A Will]

GODFREY, Thomas, ed. *Murder For Christmas.* 1982 Mysterious/ Mysterious 1987. A collection of short stories set at Christmas.

GODFREY, Thomas, ed. *Murder For Christmas, Vol. 2.* 1982 Mysterious/ Mysterious 1988. The second collection of short stories to make your Christmas merry.

GRANT, Charles L., w/a Geoffrey Marsh. *The Fangs Of The Hooded Demon.* 1988 Tor/ Tor 1989. Lincoln Blackthorne is hunting for the Fangs of the Hooded Demon, a relic with enormous powers, recently smuggled into the U.S. The carved rubies are capable of bringing the dead to life. This will be Linc's most exciting Christmas. 4th.

GRANT-ADAMSON, Lesley. *Too Many Questions.* 1991 St. Martin. PI Laura Flynn did some investigative work for fashion designer Kate Mullery. Then, just before Christmas, Kate's body was found in the Thames. It's also coming up on the twentieth anniversary of the disappearance of Laura's father, Joe Flyn. 1st. [Father]

HALL, Robert Lee. *Ben Franklin And A Case Of: Christmas Murder.* [Historical]

HILL, Reginald, w/a Patrick Ruell. *Red Christmas.* 1974 Hawthorn/ Mysterious 1987. It was to be a Dickensian Christmas at Dingley Dell, with everyone in costume. Arabella Allen was looking forward to it. Somehow blood spots on the snow and a peephole in her bedroom made her uneasy. And then, things weren't what they seemed.

HOLLAND, Isabelle. *A Fatal Advent.* [Clergy]

CHRISTMAS

JORDAN, Cathleen. *A Carol In The Dark.* 1984 Walker/Dell 1986. It was just before Christmas when visiting professor Tom Donahue was found frozen to death on campus. Dr. William Gray and the police suspect foul play. There are leads to a mysterious society and a missing treasure. [Academic]

KERRIGAN, Philip. *Dead Ground.* 1985 St. Martin/ Avon 1987. They met at Waterloo Station, getting together for Christmas. After the bomb exploded, Michael Sayers had lost both his sister and his fiancée. He'd also had a good look at the face of a man, a man he'd never forget. [Revenge]

MacLEOD, Charlotte. *Rest You Merry.* 1978 Doubleday/ Avon 1979. The Balaclava Agricultural College did Christmas up in a big way. The "Illuminations" brought visitors from all around. But the body on Professor Shandy's living room floor wasn't part of the festivities. 1st. [Academic]

MacLEOD, Charlotte, w/a Alisa Craig. *Murder Goes Mumming.* 1981 Doubleday/ Avon 1989. Madoc Rhys and Janet Wadman are spending Christmas at the isolated mansion of Graylings. It is after the roast goose that Granny is found dead. With this family of jokers, Madoc and Janet have to pull their own prank to get a confession. 2nd. [Canadian]

MacLEOD, Charlotte. *The Convivial Codfish.* 1984 Doubleday/ Avon 1985. Someone stole the Great Chain of the Convivial Codfish from around Uncle Jem's neck, and an accident put him in the hospital. With a lot of coaxing from Sarah, Max agreed to take the Christmas private train ride, only to end up helping with the casualties. 5th. [Revenge]

MARSH, Ngaio. *Tied Up In Tinsel.* 1972 Little, Brown/ Jove 1978. Troy Alleyn was doing a portrait for Hillary at his country estate. She's staying for the holidays in a house where all the servants are convicted murderers. Death haunts the Christmas pageant and it's up to her husband Inspector Alleyn to find the murderer. 27th.

McBAIN, Ed. *Eight Black Horses.* 1985 Arbor House/ Avon 1986. The Deaf Man was back in town and sending messages to the 87th Precinct. Detectives Carella, Kling, and Meyer were struggling to sort out the clues that would tell them where the Deaf Man would strike next. 37th.

McCLINTICK, Malcolm. *Death Of An Old Flame.* [Infidelity]

McGOWN, Jill. *Murder At The Old Vicarage.* 1988 St. Martin. It's Christmas in the small village, and the vicar is in a turmoil. George Wheeler has fallen for Eleanor, a young widow who has just moved to the area. Then his daughter Joanna comes home, followed by her husband. Now Joanna's husband is dead. Inspector Lloyd and Judy have to find his killer. 2nd. [Mother]

MULLER, Marcia. *There's Nothing To Be Afraid Of.* 1985 St. Martin/ Mysterious 1990. It's just before Christmas and frightening things are happening at the Globe Hotel where Vietnamese families are living. Sharon McCone is hired to get to the bottom of the problem. 7th.

PARIS, Ann. *Arrowheart.* 1988 Pocket/ PBO. Marnie Pynchon, living in Paris, is invited for a Christmas house party by her famous Uncle Batel, whom she's never met. At the Villa Montrouge strange things start happening, guests disappear and the villa becomes something vicious . . .

PETERS, Ellis. *The Raven In The Foregate.* 1986 Morrow/ Ballantine 1988. Ailnoth is recommended for the parish of Holy Cross, known as the Foregate. He so alienates his flock that few are sorry when he is found in the millpond on Christmas morning. The suspect is a friend of Brother Cadfael. 12th. [Medieval]

PETERSON, Keith. *The Scarred Man.* [Old Crime]

PULVER, Mary Monica. *Original Sin.* 1991 Walker. Kori Brichter and her retired policeman husband Peter have planned a Christmas house party. A special guest is Evelyn Biggins, a cousin who left Tretower fifty years ago. But within hours of her arrival, she's found dead on the library floor. 4th. [Old Crime]

RAY, Robert J. *Merry Christmas, Murdock.* 1989 Delacorte/ Dell 1990. Heather Blasingame was badly injured in a hit-and-run at Newport Beach shopping mall. Her senator mother wants PI Matt Murdock to investigate the accident. Then Matt meets another teen. Cindy is looking for her father. 4th. [Children]

ROOSEVELT, Elliott. *The White House Pantry Murder.* [Famous People]

TAYLOR, Elizabeth Atwood. *The Cable Car Murder.* [Where There's A Will]

UNDERWOOD, Michael. *Hand Of Fate.* [Getting Away With Murder]

WAUGH, Carol-Lynn Rossel, Martin Harry Greenberg, and Isaac Asimov, eds. *The Twelve Crimes Of Christmas.* 1981 Avon/ PBO. Twelve Christmas tales to make the holidays brighter.

WINGFIELD, R. D. *Frost At Christmas.* 1984 Paperjacks/ PBO. Bumbling Inspector Jack Frost goes looking for a missing child who doesn't make it home from the vicarage. He stumbles into the leftovers of an old crime and ends up in the hospital. 1st. [Old Crime]

WRIGHT, Eric. *The Man Who Changed His Name.* [Canadian]

CLERGY

The clergy has access to almost any situation, making them the ideal characters to investigate all manner of crime. Mystery writers, with a fond remembrance of Father Brown, have felt free to use the clergy as sleuth, victim, or villain, to the delight of generations of readers.

AIRD, Catherine. *The Religious Body.* 1966 Doubleday/ Bantam 1985. At the Convent of St. Anselm, Sister Gertrude is making morning rounds, waking the rest of the nuns. Sister Anne's room is empty. She's found dead in the cellar. Inspector Sloan and Constable Crosby have to figure out who would murder a cloistered nun. 1st.

BLOCK, Lawrence. *The Sins Of The Father.* 1982 Jove/PBO. He wanted Matt Scudder to find out who killed his daughter. She was a hooker, and the man picked up for the murder had hanged himself in jail. As for NYPD, the case was closed. What Matt discovers turns him sour. 2nd. [Gay]

BOUCHER, Anthony. *Nine Times Nine.* 1940 Duell/ International Polygonics 1986. The ancient family curse falls upon Wolfe Harrigan. Matt Duncan looked toward the study window and saw a man in a yellow robe. Moments later, the study door was locked, there was no man, and Wolfe Harrigan was dead on the floor. It takes Sister Ursula to paint the picture. 1st. [Locked Room]

CAMPBELL, Robert. *The Cat's Meow.* 1988 NAL/ Signet 1990. The cemetery at old St. Patrick's Church has been sold to an oil company; they plan to erect a gas station. Then Jimmy Flannery hears about signs of satan worship and cats howling at night. 4th. [Real Estate]

DUNLAP, Susan. *Pious Deception.* 1989 Villard/ Fawcett 1991. Fired medical examiner Kiernan O'Shaugnessy took a private investigation job in Arizona. Bishop Dowd wants her to look into the strange death of a young priest. He was found hanging on the altar in a compromising position. 1st. [Where There's A Will]

ESTLEMAN, Loren D. *Peeper.* 1989 Bantam/ Bantam 1990. Hooker Lyla Dane phoned PI Ralph Poteet in the apartment below her. She needs his help. There's a dead monsignor in her bed. Pocketing a few pictures, Ralph wonders if the local bishop would be good for a few hundred dollars. [Political]

GRANGER, Bill, w/a Joe Gash. *Priestly Murders.* 1984 Holt/Penguin 1985. As the priest gave Holy Communion in the Chicago church, a man in a police uniform and helmet shot him to death. Sgt. Terry Flynn heads up the team investigating the murder. They learn enough to set a trap in the confessional and get their killer. 1st. [Revenge]

GREELEY, Andrew M. *Happy Are The Meek.* [Witches]

GREELEY, Andrew M. *Happy Are The Clean Of Heart.* 1986 Warner/ PBO. Lisa Malone, famous singer, was in a deep coma, victim of a mysterious attack. Her dear friend, Father Blackie Ryan, is desperate to find her assailant before there's another crime. 2nd. [Jealousy]

GREELEY, Andrew M. *Happy Are Those Who Thirst For Justice.* 1987 Mysterious/ Warner 1988. Fionna Downs plotted her rich grandmother's death. But when the plan turns to reality, she knows she didn't do it. Father Blackie Ryan has to hurry on this case; someone in his family is on the killer's list. 3rd.

HADDAM, Jane. *Precious Blood.* Bantam 1991/ PBO. Cheryl Cass, destitute and dying, returned to Colchester after twenty years. Soon after contacting Father

Andrew and several old classmates, she was found dead in an alley. Gregor Demarkian is summoned by the church to clear up the murder. 2nd. [Holiday For Murder].

HOLLAND, Isabelle. *A Lover Scorned.* 1986 Doubleday/ Fawcett 1987. Ida Blake was found dead in Central Park. Reverend Claire Aldington, trying to locate Ida's friends, discovers that the dead woman was more than a friend to Claire's fiancé. 3rd.

HOLLAND, Isabelle. *A Fatal Advent.* 1989 Doubleday/ Fawcett 1990. A boy's choir from England will join St. Anselm's for Advent. And the former dean of St. Paul's is a Christmas guest. But the dean is found dead in the parish house and suspicion points to Reverend Claire Aldington's husband. 4th. [Christmas]

KEMELMAN, Harry. *Someday The Rabbi Will Leave.* [Corruption]

KIENZLE, William X. *Death Bed.* [Medical]

KIENZLE, William X. *Eminence.* 1989 Andrews, McMeel & Parker/ Ballantine 1990. A group of four religious brothers have formed a makeshift monastery called St. Stephen's. The brothers are supposed to be able to perform miracles. Sent to investigate, Father Koesler finds that things are not as they seem. 11th. [Fraud]

McINERNY, Ralph. *Basket Case.* [Infidelity]

McINERNY, Ralph. *Abracadaver.* [Where There's A Will]

MITCHELL, Kay. *A Lively Form Of Death.* [Infidelity]

NORDAN, Robert. *All Dressed Up To Die.* Fawcett 1989/ PBO. Theda Hendrick had been missing for several days when a farmer found her strangled body in his cornfield. Widow Mavis Lashley, one of the few visitors at the Hendrick house, agrees to tell Ruth Anne about her mother's death. [Mother]

O'MARIE, Sister Carol Anne. *A Novena For Murder.* 1984 Scribner/ Dell 1986. It was just a minor San Francisco quake, but when Sister Mary Helen goes out to check for possible injuries at Mount St. Francis College, she discovers Professor Villanueva's skull damaged by a bronze figurine. Now she's up to her wimple in murder. 1st.

O'MARIE, Sister Carol Anne. *Advent Of Dying.* 1986 Delacorte/ Dell 1987. Sister Mary Helen had a secretary, Suzanne, who was quiet and efficient. When she's found dead in her apartment, the sister calls Inspector Kate Murphy. Suzanne's privacy must be invaded to solve her murder. 2nd.

O'MARIE, Sister Carol Anne. *The Missing Madonna.* 1988 Delacorte/ Dell 1989. The medal that Erma always wore was found dangling from her bedsprings in her empty apartment. The landlord told Sister Mary Helen that Erma was off visiting relatives. Sister Mary Helen wasn't satisfied. 3rd.

PHILBIN, Tom. *Death Sentence.* Fawcett 1990/ PBO. Precinct Siberia has its usual share of problems. A religious fanatic is bombing abortion clinics and Detective Barbara Babalino is combing the dark streets to find a rapist who is attacking young couples. 7th. [Rape]

QUILL, Monica. *The Veil Of Ignorance.* 1988 St. Martin. Lydia Hopkins, convicted of killing both her husband and her daughter, was released from jail on a technicality. Almost at once, she appears at the Order of Martha and Mary seeking refuge. Sister Mary Teresa wants to find the real murderer. 6th.

REYNOLDS, John Lawrence. *The Man Who Murdered God.* 1989 Viking/ Penguin 1990. As Father Thomas opened up the church that morning, a young man entered and blasted him with a 12-gauge shotgun. As Boston homicide detective Joe McGuire investigates, another priest dies. [Rape]

SPICER, Michael. *Cotswold Murder.* 1990 St. Martin. Lady Jane Hildreth met a young woman on the train; she confessed that she had killed someone, then vanished. A few day later, Jane has to go to Chipping Campden to identify the woman's body . . . and find out who murdered her. 2nd. [Political]

STEWART, Gary. *The Tenth Virgin.* [Missing Person]

TELUSHKIN, Joseph. *The Unorthodox Murder Of Rabbi Wahl.* [Old Crime]

TELUSHKIN, Joseph. *The Final Analysis Of Dr. Stark.* [Old Crime]

WESTLAKE, Donald E. *Good Behavior.* [Kidnapping]

WILCOX, Collin. *The Pariah.* [Serial Killer]

ZUBRO, Mark Richard. *The Only Good Priest.* [Gay]

COMPUTER CRIMES

The nightly news carries more and more information about the extensive use of the computer in all manner of crimes, from planting a virus to tapping into bank transactions. It's no wonder, then, that computer crime finds a ready place in the mystery story and is a category that is sure to grow.

CAMP, John. *The Fool's Run.* 1989 Holt/ Signet 1990. Kidd would rather be painting or fishing. But he happened to be a computer genius. And someone was paying him to foul up Whitemark Aviation. Seems they'd stolen some sensitive plans from a rival company. 1st.

DEAN, S. F. X. *Such Pretty Toys.* 1982 Walker/ Tor 1986. Neil Kelly postpones his sabbatical when an old love is blinded in an explosion and her husband is killed. He travels to Santa Fe and finds the CIA and the FBI on his heels. 2nd. [Holiday]

GILLESPIE, Robert R. *Print-Out.* 1983 Dodd, Mead/ Paperjacks 1986. Retired business consultant Robert Simmons has discovered a secret computer file. The printout shows that the bankrupt company is having million-dollar transactions. Before long he's on the run for his life. [Drugs]

GRANT, Linda. *Blind Trust.* 1990 Scribner. First Central Savings hired Catherine Sayler to check on a security problem. James Mendoza, who knew the system's weakness, has disappeared. Catherine has to find him before the bank loses money. 2nd. [Fraud]

HANSON, Dirk. *The Incursion.* 1987 Little, Brown/ Avon 1988. SEEK was a vast computer network, the nerve center of the U.S. If data was destroyed, chaos would result. Now someone has broken into SEEK. Peter Cassidy has the spotlight—he has to clear his name or go under.

JANCE, J. A. *Dismissed With Prejudice.* Avon 1989/ PBO. Tadeo Kurobashi, president of MicroBridge, was found dead, suicide by hara-kiri. But his friend George is convinced it's not suicide. He tells homicide detective J. P. Beaumont that Tadeo would have paid more attention to details. 7th. [Oriental]

McGILL, E. J. *Immaculate In Black.* [Imposter]

STERN, Richard Martin. *Tangled Murders.* [Indian]

WHITE, Ned. *The Very Bad Thing.* 1990 Viking/ Penguin 1991. A software company out on Route 128 hired PI Dred Balcazar to find out who the hacker is that's planted a virus in it's system. How could a simple meeting at the staid Boston Athenaeum lead to a corpse or two? 1st. [Getting Away With Murder]

WINDNER, Robert. *No Admission.* 1989 Viking/ Penguin 1990. Erica Sanders, journalist, has been asking around about a computer fraud at the bank. It could be the scoop of her lifetime. When Erica suddenly disappears, her brother Eric is caught up in a transatlantic mystery. [Intrigue]

COOKS AND COOKING

The kitchen is the laboratory of murder, containing all the ingredients and utensils to shorten a life or two. The dinner table may be the execution chamber, with the victim falling dead into the soup or salad. And snacking really can be dangerous to your health.

BARNES, Linda. *Cities Of The Dead.* 1986 St. Martin/ Fawcett 1987. Spraggue, PI turned actor, rushes south where his aunt's cook, Dora, has been charged with murder. She's accused of stabbing a man at the annual gathering of the Great Chefs of New Orleans. 4th. [Old Crime]

BOND, Michael. *Monsieur Pamplemousse.* 1985 Beaufort/ Fawcett 1986. Monsieur Pamplemousse and his dog Pomme Frites are at the restaurant La Langoustine in France. The main dish turns out to be the replica of a head. As other disasters occur, he has to figure out how to save his own neck. 1st. [Insurance]

BOND, Michael. *Monsieur Pamplemousse And The Secret Mission.* 1986 Beaufort/ Fawcett 1987. The director of

Le Guide wants Pamplemousse quietly to investigate Hôtel du Paradis. Something strange seems to be happening to some of the patrons. 2nd. [Dog]

BOND, Michael. *Monsieur Pamplemousse On The Spot.* 1986 Beaufort/ Fawcett 1988. Pamplemousse stops at Les Cinq Parfaits. He discovers that the Soufflé Surprise has been taken off the menu and the dessert chef is missing. He sets out to save the chef, and saves France. 3rd. [On Vacation]

CANNELL, Dorothy. *The Thin Woman.* 1984 St. Martin/ Penguin 1987. Ellie Simons dreaded the weekend Uncle Merlin had arranged in the country. So she rented Ben to be her fiancé. Merlin died and left Merlin's Court to Ellie and Ben, if they met four conditions, one of which was to find the hidden treasure. But that's not all. 1st. [Imposter]

DAVIDSON, Diane Mott. *Catering To Nobody.* 1990 St. Martin. When Goldy Bear set out to cater the food after Laura Smiley's funeral, she didn't expect her ex-father-in-law to collapse, rat poison in his coffee. When the police closed down Goldy's catering business, she has to find the poisoner or starve. 1st. [Medical]

DUNLAP, Susan. *The Last Annual Slugfest.* [Revenge]

LAURENCE, Janet. *A Tasty Way To Die.* 1991 Doubleday. The Wooden Spoon Catering Service had just celebrated its first birthday. A few days later, Claire died from poisoned mushrooms and it looks like Eve might have been the intended victim. Dorina Lisle, helping out, decides to investigate. 2nd. [Where There's A Will]

LYONS, Nan, and Ivan Lyons. *The President Is Coming To Lunch.* 1988 Doubleday. The hottest restaurant in Manhattan is Libby's. After avoiding Libby's for twenty years, the president has made a reservation for lunch. Amid the Secret Service preparations, Libby strains to keep the secret they share. [Mother]

MacLEOD, Charlotte, w/a Alisa Craig. *A Pint Of Murder.* [Canadian]

MacLEOD, Charlotte, w/a Alisa Craig. *The Grub-And-Stakers Spin A Yarn.* [Canadian]

RICH, Virginia. *The Cooking School Murders.* 1982 Dutton/ Ballantine 1986. Mrs. Potter had agreed to give some cooking lessons at Dorrance High School. The menu wasn't deadly, but someone stabbed Jackie with Mrs. Potter's knife. Two more deaths occur before she has the last piece of the mystery. 1st. [Jealousy]

RICH, Virginia. *The Baked Bean Supper Murders.* 1983 Dutton/Ballantine 1984. The highlight of the social season at Northcutt Harbor was the Baked Bean Supper. Shortly after, people started dying from accidents and strange natural causes. Mrs. Potter senses she might be next, unless she can stop the killer. 2nd.

RICH, Virginia. *The Nantucket Diet Murders.* 1985 Delacorte/ Dell 1986. When Mrs. Potter returns to Nantucket for a reunion with Les Girls, she's startled that they are all so thin. The new man in town, Count Tony Ferency, has them on a diet. But it seems to be a deadly one. 3rd. [Jealousy]

WAUGH, Carol-Lynn Rossel, Martin H. Greenberg, and Isaac Asimov, eds. *Murder On The Menu.* 1984 Avon/ PBO. Sixteen short stories about food, the people who cook it, and the fine art of dining . . . and detecting.

WOODS, Sherryl. *Reckless.* Popular 1989/ PBO. Chef Maurice was giving a cooking demonstration when he keeled over in his chocolate soufflé. Reporter Amanda

Roberts, besides taking notes, teams up with ex-homicide cop Joe Donelli to capture a murderer. 1st. [Journalism]

CORRUPTION

Sometimes it seems that, for some, corruption has become a way of life. We find it in government, in business, and in unexpected places, too. And there are strange kinds of corruption, most insidious, that involve our most cherished values.

ALLINGHAM, Margery. *The Black Dudley Murder.* 1929 Doubleday/ Avon 1988. They'd all been invited to Black Dudley Manor for the weekend. As part of the weekend activities, there was to be the Black Dudley ritual involving a dagger that had been in the family for hundreds of years. Albert Campion will be needed before the weekend is over. 1st.

BISHOP, Paul. *Sand Against The Tide.* [Drugs]

COLLINS, Michael, w/a Mark Sadler. *Deadly Innocents.* 1986 Walker/ Worldwide 1988. Paul Scott, security investigator, waited for his four o'clock client. They found him in the cleaning closet. A cry for help from his young wife leads to false identities and the power of the rich. 6th. [Drugs]

DeNOUX, O'Neil. *The Big Kiss.* [Serial Killer]

DOYLE, James T. *Epitaph For A Lover.* [Fraud]

EARLY, Jack. *A Creative Kind Of Killer.* 1984 Franklin Watts/Ballantine 1985. Jennie Baker is found dead in a store window, and her young brother is missing. Hired by their Uncle Charles Horton to find Patrick, Fortune Fannelli explores the Greenwich Village art scene and the underworld. [Drugs]

KELLY, Susan. *Until Proven Innocent.* 1990 Villard. Ex-cop Dalton Craig has accused Lt. Jack Lingeman of destroying evidence that would have cleared a man of a murder charge years earlier. Liz Conners wants to get to the bottom of the story when she discovers that Dalton is the step-brother of Jack's late wife. 4th. [Revenge]

KEMELMAN, Harry. *Someday The Rabbi Will Leave.* 1985 Morrow/ Fawcett 1986. A man was killed in a hit-and-run accident late at night in Barnard's Crossing. That is the beginning of a confusing situation for Rabbi Small, leading to potential corruption and blackmail. 8th. [Clergy]

MacLEOD, Charlotte. *Vane Pursuit.* [Antiques]

PARKER, Robert B. *Taming A Sea Horse.* [Prostitution]

PATTI, Paul. *Silhouettes.* [Witness Protection Program]

PEDNEAU, Dave. *Dead Witness.* 1987 Avon/ PBO. A black man was killed and the Trans Am kept right on going. Rock County Prosecutor Josh De Burke wants to know why the hit-and-run has never been solved. When someone tries to get him, Josh just asks more questions. [Political]

PETIEVICH, Gerald. *Shakedown.* 1988 Simon & Schuster/ Pocket 1989. FBI agent John Novak may be disillusioned but he has tenacity plus. As he follows shakedown artist Eddie Sands, the path leads to higher and higher levels of Las Vegas crime.

PRONZINI, Bill. *Jackpot.* [Suicide]

ROBB, T. N. *Private Eye.* [Political]

THOMAS, Ross. *The Fools In Town Are On Our Side.* 1970 Morrow/ Mysterious 1987. Dismissed from Section

Two, a secret intelligence agency, unemployed and clutching his severance check, Lucifer Dye lounges in San Francisco. He's approached by a man who cleans up corrupt cities.

VAN DE WETERING, Janwillem. *Hard Rain.* [Suicide]

WEINMAN, Irving. *Virgil's Ghost.* 1990 Fawcett/ Fawcett 1991. Lenny Schwartz has quit NYPD and become a PI. His first case is a sad one. Mr. and Mrs. Conrad Hayes want him to investigate the murder of their son. He was found in the river and the medical examiner said he had AIDS. 3rd. [Medical]

WHEAT, Carolyn. *Dead Man's Thoughts.* 1983 St. Martin/ Dell 1984. Cassandra Jameson, attorney for Legal Aid, finds her lover, Nathan, murdered in his apartment. Whoever killed him went to a lot of work to make it look like a gay killing. Cassie knows better. 1st. [Lawyer]

WOLK, Michael. *The Big Picture.* [Political]

WOODRELL, Daniel. *Under The Bright Lights.* 1986 Holt/ Avon 1988. Cajun County Detective Rene Shade was investigating the murder of Alvin Rankin. He was soon locked into the sleazy world of shady politicians and more murder. 1st.

CROSSWORD PUZZLES

For the ultimate in pleasure: you have to solve the crossword puzzle in order to solve the crime. All the clues are planted deeply in either across *or* down.

MOYES, Patricia. *A Six-Letter Word For Death.* 1983 Holt/ Owl 1986. Henry Tibbett receives a crossword puzzle in the mail. It contains the names of people he knew who had died. On the Isle of Wight, he and Emily join a mystery writers' weekend for the last clue. 13th. [Mystery Writers]

RENDELL, Ruth. *One Across, Two Down.* 1971 Doubleday/ Bantam 1987. Stanley Manning had reached the end of his rope. He was sick of his wife, Vera, and his mother-in-law, Maud. If he could do the crossword puzzle in the *Daily Telegraph* in twenty minutes, he was smart enough to commit the perfect murder. 7th. [Psychological]

RESNICOW, Herbert. *Murder Across And Down.* 1985 Ballantine/ PBO. Harvey Brundige fell dead over his trout at dinner at the Cruciverbal Club. As the Fiftieth Anniversary celebration continues, Giles Sullivan and Isabel Mackintosh work to fit the clues into the right spaces. 1st. [Blackmail]

RESNICOW, Herbert. *The Seventh Crossword.* 1985 Ballantine/ PBO. A project at Windham University is just about over when the director threatens to close it down. The tenure of six professors will be left in doubt. When Humboldt is stabbed, Giles Sullivan scrambles to figure out who killed him. 2nd. [Academic]

RESNICOW, Herbert. *The Crossword Code.* 1986 Ballantine/ PBO. Giles Sullivan and Isabel Mackintosh have been summoned to Washington, D.C., to solve the Crossword Code. An unknown person has been using the daily puzzles to send messages to a Russian agent. And then comes a very strange murder. 3rd. [Holiday]

RESNICOW, Herbert. *The Crossword Legacy.* 1987 Ballantine/ PBO. At the Cruciverbal Club, Cornelius Van Broek's survivors are struggling to solve a series of crossword puzzles, under the watchful eye of Giles Sullivan. The one who wins will inherit the fortune. 4th.

RESNICOW, Herbert. *The Crossword Hunt.* 1987 Ballantine/ PBO. Abraham Hardwick is endowing an institute at Windham University in Vermont. The candidates to head the program have to solve a crossword puzzle. When Hardwick dies, Giles Sullivan suspects one of the contenders. 5th. [Academic]

D ... IS FOR

DANCE AND BALLET

THE STAGE IS DIMMED, the music muted. A shot rings out, and the lead dancer crashes to the planks, dead. Not a likely setting for murder, is it? It is in the mystery story. And the murder occurs at the most dramatic moment, to wreak the most horror on the audience. And thus, the gentle art of the dance turns to mayhem.

BRAHMS, Caryl, and S. J. Simon. *Murder à La Stroganoff.* 1938 Doubleday/ International Polygonics 1985. Adam Quill was on vacation in La Bazouche, where two competing casinos planned a ballet performance, starring the same ballerina, on the same night. There were diamonds and a murder or two. 2nd. [On Vacation]

MITCHELL, Gladys. *The Death-Cap Dancers.* 1981 St. Martin/ Paperjacks 1986. A member of the Yorkshire folk-dance troupe was found murdered, with bits of poisoned mushrooms pushed into her wounds. Hermoine Lestrange calls on her aunt, Dame Beatrice, to help figure it out. 60th.

MURPHY, Haughton. *Murder Takes A Partner.* 1987 Simon & Schuster/ Fawcett 1988. While Reuben Frost was chairing the director's meeting of the NatBallet, Clifton Holt was being stabbed at the stage door. The drug addict who killed him had too many crisp new bills hidden away. Reuben and the police have to do a lot of fancy footwork. 2nd.

RESNICOW, Herbert. *The Gold Deadline.* 1984 St. Martin/ Avon 1985. While Norma and Alexander Gold sat in Max Baron's box, watching the Boguslov Ballet, death sat in the next box. Nasty Viktor Boguslov had a knife stuck into him and he never uttered a sound. His companion was Jeffrey, Baron's son. 2nd. [Gay]

VIDAL, Gore, w/a Edgar Box. *Death in the Fifth Position.* 1952 Random House/ Vintage 1979. As the public relations man for a ballet company, Peter Sargeant finds his job complicated when a dancer is killed onstage.

DOGS

And, since the dog is man's best friend, of course it shows up in the mystery story, although not so often as one would expect. As a favorite companion, a dog becomes very important in one of the mysteries.

BARNARD, Robert. *Fête Fatale.* 1985 Scribner/ Dell 1987. Veterinarian Marcus Kitteridge was found dead on Castle Walk in the Yorkshire village. He'd been killed just as the fete was ending. His widow, Helen, will find no rest without an answer.

BOND, Michael. *Monsieur Pamplemousse And The Secret Mission.* [Cooks]

CONANT, Susan. *A New Leash On Death.* Diamond 1990/ PBO. Dr. Stanton, DVM, was strangled at the obedience trials with his malamute Rowdy's leash. Holly Winter, columnist for *Dog's Life,* took Rowdy home. Soon the dog joined her in digging up clues to his master's murder. 1st. [Blackmail]

MOORE, Barbara. *The Doberman Wore Black.* 1983 St. Martin/Dell 1984. The first time veterinarian Gordon

Christy saw the Doberman it was in the backseat of the MG that almost forced him off the road. Now the dog is keeping the police at bay, and there's a body staining the condo carpet. 1st.

MOORE, Barbara. *The Wolf Whispered Death.* [Indian]

DRUGS

One of the curses of our generation is the availability of drugs. Like corruption, drugs invade every facet of our lives. It's interesting to note that as early as 1933 Dorothy Sayers used this topic in one of her mysteries. The size of the category is a comment on the times.

ALBERT, Marvin. *Get Off At Babylon.* 1987 Fawcett/ PBO. Seated in a sidewalk café in Nice, Pete Sawyer watched a young woman flee from an apartment building just before the police arrived. A few days later, her father hires Pete to locate his daughter. Can he find Odile before she's in deadly trouble? 2nd.

ALDYNE, Nathan. *Cobalt.* [Gay]

ALEXANDER, Gary. *Kiet And The Opium War.* 1990 St. Martin. While Chief of Police Bamsan Kiet shakes his head at the creeping Westernization of Luong, he and Captain Binh launch an all-out attack against the flourishing opium trade. 4th.

BANK, Lawrence Henry. *17 Farrington Way.* 1987 Ashley/ Paperjacks 1988. Ron Henderson's neighbor is killed in his own home, and a child hooker confesses to the murder. Ron feels obligated to help Veronica, the widow, and finds himself enmeshed in more crime than he wants to handle.

BARNES, Linda. *Blood Will Have Blood.* [Theater]

BARTH, Richard. *The Rag Bag Clan.* 1978 Dial/ Avon 1979. Margaret Binton serves coffee to the needy at the Flora K. Bliss Center. When one of the bag ladies is murdered and another whispers that she just found $1,000 in the garbage, Margaret agrees to go undercover for the police. 1st.

BARTH, Richard. *Deadly Climate.* [On Vacation]

BARTHELME, Peter. *Push, Meet Shove.* [Advertising]

BAXT, George. *A Parade Of Cockeyed Creatures.* [Missing Person]

BAXT, George. *The Dorothy Parker Murder Case.* [Famous People]

BIEDERMAN, Marcia. *Post No Bonds.* [Television]

BISHOP, Paul. *Sand Against The Tide.* 1990 Tor. Calico Jack Walker has retired from LAPD and has his own charter fishing boat, the Thieftaker. But when his boat is highjacked and his son is gunned down, Calico and his friend Tina are caught up in a three-continent drug ring. 2nd. [Corruption]

BLACKSTOCK, Charity. *Dewey Death.* [Library]

BORTHWICK, J. S. *The Case Of The Hook-Billed Kites* [Birdwatching]

BOYER, Rick. *The Daisy Duck.* 1986 Houghton Mifflin/ Ivy 1988. At a New Year's Eve party, Doc Adams is cornered by a Vietnam vet friend. The problem is that the friend has one key to a safety deposit box and a missing buddy has the other. In the box is a gold Hindu statue. 3rd. [Art]

BRETT, John. *Who'd Hire Brett?* [Art]

BURKE, James Lee. *A Morning For Flamingos.* 1990 Little, Brown. Transporting two prisoners to death row, Dave Robicheaux is brutally wounded and his partner is killed. Dave agrees to go undercover for the DEA in New Orleans, the last place his attacker Boggs was seen. Dave wants revenge. 4th. [Revenge]

BURNS, Rex. *Ground Money.* 1986 Viking/ Penguin 1987. Tommy Sanchez worries about his two sons. He wants Gabe Wager to poke around and find out what's going on. Tommy is killed: the raft that Gabe and his girlfried Jo are on is shot up. Jo dies. Gabe wants blood. 7th. [Father]

CHUDLEY, Ron. *Freeze Frame.* 1987 Paperjacks/ PBO. TV star Stephen Corsten is in Toronto visiting his almost-brother. Next morning Max is dead, an interrupted burglary. Steve doesn't want Max's death to be just another unsolved crime. [Canadian]

COLLINS, Max Allan. *A Shroud For Aquarius.* 1985 Walker/ Tor 1988. They'd grown up together, were close. Now Ginny is dead, shot in the head, a suicide. Mallory isn't buying the verdict. He checks into her life since he'd last seen her, and he remembers her dream: a millionaire before age thirty. 4th. [Mystery Writer]

COLLINS, Michael, w/a Mark Sadler. *Deadly Innocents.* [Corruption]

COOK, Bruce. *Mexican Standoff.* [Father]

CREWS, Lary. *Extreme Close-Up.* [Television]

D'AMATO, Barbara. *Hardball.* [Journalism]

DAVIS, Maggie. *Miami Midnight.* Bantam 1989/ PBO. Gabrielle Collier is on a rescue mission. She's out to save her mother from the bottle and a ruined mansion. She's quickly involved with handsome James

Santo Marin, drug running and the strange Santeria religion.

DOBYNS, Stephen. *Saratoga Long Shot.* 1986 Atheneum/Penguin 1987. Charlie Bradshaw's girlfriend from the tenth grade needed a favor, again. She's worked hard to keep her son out of trouble. This time he's involved with a big-time drug deal. Charlie has to go to New York City to find him. 4th.

DOLD, Gaylord. *Hot Summer Cold Murder.* [Missing Person]

DOYLE, James T. *Deadly Resurrection.* [Old Crime]

DUNCAN, W. Glen. *Rafferty's Rules.* [Revenge]

DUNCAN, W. Glen. *Rafferty: Last Seen Alive.* 1987 Fawcett/PBO. At Lake Texoma for a week, Rafferty starts out flirting with cute Cindy. When she's found murdered, he becomes a suspect. To clear himself, he has to find the killer. He turns over buckets of dirt in the process. 2nd. [On Vacation]

DUNLAP, Susan. *The Bohemian Connection.* [Missing Person]

EARLY, Jack. *A Creative Kind Of Killer.* [Corruption]

FERRARS, E. X. *Come And Be Killed.* [Australia]

GILLESPIE, Robert B. *Print-Out.* [Computer Crime]

GOSLING, Paula. *The Woman In Red.* [Art]

GOUGH, Laurence. *Hot Shots.* [Canadian]

GRINDAL, Richard. *Over The Sea To Die.* [Suicide]

GRISSOM, Ken. *Drop-Off.* 1988 St. Martin. Salvage diver John Rodrigue would make a couple thousand just by towing an abandoned boat out from Galveston and sinking it. But he's quickly caught up with a big-time drug dealer and death. 1st. [Journalism]

HAIBLUM, Isidore. *Murder In Yiddish.* 1988 St. Martin. PI Jim Shaw is on a stakeout when he hears a scream. An elderly woman has been hurt in what looks like a burglary attempt. When she dies, Jim is the suspect. His only clue is a letter written in Yiddish.

HALL, Parnell. *Detective.* 1987 Fine/ Onyx 1988. PI Stanley Hastings didn't want the job, but when the client turned up dead, he felt compelled to prove something. So he took on the Big Boys from Miami and New York. 1st.

HANSEN, Joseph. *Obedience.* [Oriental]

HARDWICK, Mollie. *The Dreaming Damozel.* [Art]

HAVILL, Steven F. *Heartshot.* 1991 St. Martin. The car hit speeds of a hundred miles an hour before it crashed, leaving five teenagers dead and a cache of $150,000 in cocaine. Posada County, New Mexico, undersheriff Bill Gastner wants the mastermind behind the operation. [Revenge]

HESS, Joan. *Mischief In Maggody.* 1988 St. Martin. When Police Chief Arly Hanks returned from vacation, she was faced with more problems than a small-town cop should have. A psychic had moved in, some hippies had opened a health food store, and the local prostitute and moonshiner had disappeared. 2nd.

HILARY, Richard. *Snake In The Grasses.* [Black Detective]

HILL, Reginald. *Exit Lines.* 1984 Macmillan/ Signet 1986. When Dalziel and Pascoe set out to investigate the deaths of three elderly men, they're looking for some kind of connection. Then another case takes all their attention. 9th.

HILLERMAN, Tony. *The Dark Wind.* [Indians]

HOLT, Samuel. *I Know A Trick Worth Two Of That.* 1986 Tor/ Tor 1988. Samuel Holt agreed to hide his ex-cop friend Douglas at his Greenwich Village house. He'd forgotten that he'd planned a dinner party. At the party, Douglas died, and Sam's friends were all suspects. One by one he checked them off his guest list. 2nd.

JANCE, J. A. *Taking The Fifth.* 1987 Avon/ PBO. An early morning phone call took J. P. Beaumont, Seattle PD, to a corpse by the railroad tracks. When cocaine is found in the house where he lived, the dead man is suspected of having been a pusher. Beaumont finds the spotlight shining elsewhere. 4th.

JANCE, J. A. *Minor In Possession.* [Mother]

JANESCHUTZ, Trish, aka T. J. MacGregor. *In Shadow.* [Psychological]

KANTNER, Rob. *Made In Detroit.* Bantam 1990/ PBO. PI Ben Perkins was just leaving the Under New Management when a car outside blew up, killing his close friend Paul Reardon. The police find a tape made by Paul's bride accusing Ben of having an affair with her. Ben gets charged with murder. 5th. [Revenge]

KATZ, Michael J. *Murder Off The Glass.* [Ball Games]

KELLERMAN, Jonathan. *Blood Test.* [Children]

KENYON, Michael. *Peckover Holds The Baby.* 1988 Doubleday/ Avon 1988. Peckover of Scotland Yard is sent to the jungles of Belize to hunt for cocaine king Vivian White. White has kidnapped his own baby from his father's estate and is on the run. 6th. [Kidnapping]

KOHLER, Vincent. *Rainy North Woods.* [Journalism]

LAKE, M. D. *Amends For Murder.* [Academic]

MacLEOD, Charlotte. *The Recycled Citizen.* 1988 Mysterious/ Mysterious 1989. Uncle Dolph and Aunt Mary are holding an auction to benefit the Senior Citizens Recycling Center. Before the big night, a man is dead and Max and Sarah have to save Uncle Dolph from jail. P.S.: It's a boy! 7th.

MALCOLM, John. *The Wrong Impression.* [Art]

MATHIS, Edward. *Another Path, Another Dragon.* 1988 Scribner/ Ballantine 1990. Wade Mannion of Jerico Falls, Texas, needs PI Dan Roman's help. His nephew Stephen and Stephen's girlfriend have been murdered and left under an Indian blanket. It looks like a drug case, but something else is smoldering. 4th. [Revenge]

McBAIN, Ed. *Jack & The Beanstalk.* [Lawyer]

McBAIN, Ed. *Cinderella.* 1986 Holt/ Mysterious 1987. PI Otto Samalson had been shot in his car on U.S. 41. He'd been doing a job for lawyer Matthew Hope. Now Matt wants to find his killer. His only clue has to come from Otto's office. 6th. [Lawyer]

McCALL, Wendell. *Dead Aim.* 1988 St. Martin/ Dell 1990. Ex-musician Chris Klick usually works at tracking down musicians who are owed money. But Nicole Russell wants him to find her husband and $50,000. Why did Paul take the dog if he was going to leave his wife and disappear?

O'BRIEN, Meg. *Salmon In The Soup.* [Journalism]

PAGE, Katherine Hall. *The Body In The Kelp.* [On Vacation]

PARKER, Robert B. *Pale Kings And Princes.* 1987 Delacorte/ Dell 1988. A young reporter is killed investigating the cocaine business in Wheaton. The newspaper hires Spenser to smoke out the killer. When the police chief is murdered, Spenser's getting a line on the dead reporter. Time to call in Hawk. 14th.

PETERSON, Audrey. *The Nocturne Murder.* [Music]

PULVER, Mary Monica. *The Unforgiving Minutes.* [Old Crime]

RISENHOOVER, C. C. *Murder At The Final Four.* [Ball Games]

SALVO, Gillian. *Death Comes Staccato.* [Music]

SAYERS, Dorothy L. *Murder Must Advertise.* [Advertising]

SINGER, Shelley. *Full House.* 1986 St. Martin/ Worldwide 1988. A group of people are building an ark on a vacant lot in Oakland. They hire Jake Samson to find their missing leader, Noah, together with a woman named Marjorie. Jake enlists Rosie's help when Marjorie is found murdered. 3rd.

SMITH, Evelyn. *Miss Melville Returns.* [Art]

STERN, Richard Martin. *Interloper.* [Indian]

STUART, Anne. *Escape Out Of Darkness.* [Witness Protection]

TAPPLY, William G. *The Vulgar Boatman.* 1988 Scribner/ Ballantine 1989. Tom Baron desperately needs Brady Coyne's help. His son Buddy is missing and Buddy's girlfriend has been murdered. But there's something else going on beneath the surface of quiet Windsor Harbor, something very dirty. 9th. [Lawyer]

TONE, Teona. *Full Cry.* [Historical]

TUCKER, John Bartholomew. *He's Dead, She's Dead: Details At Eleven.* [Television]

VALIN, Jonathan. *Life's Work.* [Ball Games]

VALIN, Jonathan. *Fire Lake.* 1987 Delacorte/ Dell 1989. Someone registered at the motel under Stoner's name and took an overdose of tranquilizers. He's Harry's old college roommate Lonnie. Then Lonnie's corpse disappears, and Harry has to work fast or be left with a load of guilt. 7th.

VAN DE WETERING, Janwillem. *Outsider In Amsterdam.* [Suicide]

VAN DE WETERING, Janwillem. *The Rattle-Rat.* [Medical]

WALLACE, Carol McD. *Waking Dream.* [Writer]

WALLACE, Patricia. *Deadly Grounds.* [Academic]

WARD, Donald. *Death Takes The Stage.* [Gay]

WEBSTER, Noah. *Witchline.* [Insurance]

WEEKS, Dolores. *The Cape Murders.* [Infidelity]

WOLK, Michael. *The Beast On Broadway.* 1988 Signet/ PBO. John Sugarnam came to New York City to visit his brother. All in an afternoon, his wallet's stolen, he watches a drug deal take place, and someone gets murdered. And that's only the start.

WOLZIEN, Valerie. *Murder At The PTA Luncheon.* 1988 St. Martin/ Fawcett 1990. Jan Ick took the last canapé from the tray and died from cyanide. Two months later Paula Parker added sweetener to her iced tea and died the same way. Now PTA president Susan Henshaw and State Police Officer Brett Fortesque have their heads together. 1st.

WOODS, Sheryl. *Body And Soul.* [Journalism]

ZIMMELMAN, Lue. *Honolulu Red.* [Jewels]

E . . . IS FOR

ECONOMICS

MONEY MAY NOT BE the root of all evil, but it sure can be the cause of a lot of crime. Now that we have computers that move money around at a rapid rate, Wall Street will never be the same.

BABSON, Marian. *There Must Be Some Mistake.* [Fraud]

BEINHART, Larry. *No One Rides For Free.* 1986 Morrow/ Avon 1987. Tony Cassella, New York City PI, has a lush job: to locate Edgar Wood, who's spilling his guts to the SEC, and find out what he's telling the Feds. What Tony doesn't know is that there's a contract out on his own life and he's going to have to run to survive. [Fraud]

BERRY, Carole. *The Year Of The Monkey.* 1988 St. Martin/ Dell 1990. Bonnie Indermill lands a job with Creative Financial Ventures and locks on to respectability. Then the CEO Ashley Gardner is murdered with a large clay flowerpot right after the Christmas party and Eddie Fong disappears. 2nd.

BROD, D. C. *Murder In The Store.* 1989 Walker. Quint McCauley, head of security at Hauser's department store, is asked to take a private assignment: letters are threatening his wife. Reporting on the case one morning, Quint watches Hauser keel over dead, cyanide in his vitamins. 1st. [Real Estate]

EVERSY, Robert. *The Bottom Line Is Murder.* 1988 Viking/

Penguin 1989. Leslie Carlisle hired free-lance corporate investigator Paul Marston to find out why her husband went down in a plane crash in Topanga Canyon. Did it have something to do with the company? It sure did, and then some. 1st.

GUTHRIE, Al. *Grave Murder.* Zebra 1990/ PBO. When they moved to the quiet town of Sarahville, Mac and Abby McKenzie wanted just that—quiet. At the local Historical Society meeting, Jerome Bedford left to keep an appointment and was found dead in the morning. Mac has to go back to work. 2nd. [Old Crime]

JEVONS, Marshall. *The Fatal Equilibrium.* [Academic]

LATHEN, Emma. *Something In The Air.* 1988 Simon & Schuster/ Pocket 1989. The Sloan Guaranty Trust has been approached to provide funds for the expansion of Sparrow Flyways. John Putnam Thatcher is in on the discussions. Then one of the pilots ends up in Boston Harbor with his head bashed in. The talk changes to murder. 20th. [Old Crime]

LLEWELLYN, Sam. *Blood Orange.* [At Sea]

MURPHY, Haughton. *Murder For Lunch.* 1986 Simon & Schuster/ Fawcett 1987. A confidential letter to Graham Donovan, member of a Wall Street firm, has been made public. When Donovan collapses at lunch, a retired partner, Reuben Frost, is drafted to help clean out his office. That was a mistake. 1st.

NEEL, Janet. *Death Of A Partner.* [Missing Person]

PALMER, Stuart. *The Penguin Pool Murder.* 1931 Bretano/ Bantam 1986. Schoolteacher Hildegarde Withers was at the New York Aquarium with her students to see the Galapagos penguins. There floating in the pool is a Wall Street broker. And Hildegarde's ruby hat pin was the murder weapon. 1st. [Revenge]

RATHBONE, Julian. *Greenfinger.* [Botany]

ROBINETT, Stephen. *Final Option.* Avon 1990/ PBO. Wall Street "whiz kid" Horton Queller was missing. Jerry Jetter, staff writer for *Global Capitalism* is given the assignment of following up several new leads. His trail winds up in deception and murder. 1st. [Missing Person]

SANDERS, Lawrence. *The Timothy Files.* 1987 Putnam/ Berkley 1988. At Haldering & Co., Wall Street Investigators, they've just gotten word that Ed Griffon is dead. He was pushed under a subway car. Timothy Cane gets Ed's assignment; he'll follow it to the bitter end. And that's just the first case. 1st. [Fraud]

TAPPLY, William G. *A Void In Hearts.* [Lawyer]

WEBSTER, Noah. *A Flight From Paris.* 1987 Doubleday. Blackthorn, a man with an unsavory reputation, has been filled with barbiturates and ended up in a fatal crash. Jonathan Gaunt, resident troubleshooter in Scotland, is assigned to probe the death. He's soon involved in a multi-million dollar hill. 9th. [Real Estate]

ESPIONAGE, THE INDUSTRIAL KIND

As our technology gets more sophisticated, as there is a push to be the first on the market with the best, and as research becomes more costly, the atmosphere is ripe for industrial espionage. The scale ranges from local competition to international theft.

BARNES, Linda. *Bitter Finish.* 1983 St. Martin/ Fawcett 1985. Kate Holloway, Napa Valley wine producer, is having problems. She's just been arrested for murder. She calls on an old lover, Michael Spraggue, a PI turned actor, who comes on stage in the middle and plays it out till the end. 2nd. [Blackmail]

BLAKE, Nicholas. *Murder With Malice.* 1940 Harper & Row/ Carroll & Graf 1987. Someone is playing pranks at holiday Camp of Wonderland, and Nigel Strangeways is asked to investigate. Then a murder occurs. Nigel pulls all the loose ends together at the Mad Hatter's tea party. 6th.

BURNS, Rex. *Suicide Season.* [Real Estate]

CAMPBELL, Robert. *Plugged Nickel.* 1988 Pocket/ PBO. At 4:20 a.m., on the California Zephyr, someone pulled the emergency brakes. Railroad detective Jake Hatch rushed to investigate and found half a body, then another half. But they don't match. His only clue is a plugged nickel. 1st.

FRANCIS, Dick. *Proof.* 1985 Putnam/ Fawcett 1987. Jimmy, secretary to Jack Hawthorn, has a serious question for the wine merchant Tony Beach. He wants to know if Tony can tell one malt from another. It seems that one of the horse owners has a restaurant, and what comes out of the bottle doesn't match the label.

GRANT, Linda. *Random Access Murder.* 1988 Avon/ PBO. Peter Harman was on the run; the police wanted him for murder. A piece of his shirt had been clutched in the woman's hand when Peter found the body. PI Catherine Sayler has to clear her boyfriend and find the motive for the killing. 1st.

KENNEALY, Jerry. *Polo, Anyone?* 1988 St. Martin/ St. Martin 1988. From a crooked poker game, PI Nick Polo is plunged into murder and missing papers. Someone wants to make a lot of money, but Nick keeps getting in the way. 2nd.

MURPHY, Haughton. *Murder & Acquisitions.* 1988 Simon & Schuster/Fawcett 1989. Flemming Anderson, of Anderson Foods, was worried about a hostile takeover of his company; then he's found dead in the hot tub in Greenwich, CT. Retired lawyer Reuben Frost checks everyone's alibi, then checks them all over again. 3rd. [Father]

PYLE, A. M. *Trouble Making Toys.* 1985 Walker/ Signet 1986. The call came in to Homicide Detective Cesar Franck. Irving Golden of Golden Time Toy Co. was dead in his office. He'd just found out that Whizbang was beating him to the punch in the production of a new doll. Franck plays dolls. 1st.

TONE, Teona. *Lady On The Line.* [Historical]

F . . . IS FOR

FAMOUS PEOPLE

THE LAST FEW YEARS have shown an abundance of famous people as characters, sleuths, and even victims in murder mysteries. We get to have another look at some of the people who have become important to us as heroes and heroines. And even some of the infamous are included.

ALEXANDER, Lawrence. *The Big Stick.* 1986 Doubleday/ Paperjacks 1988. Newly appointed as police commissioner, Teddy Roosevelt roams New York City's back streets. He's hunting for a robber who's stolen a painting from the Frick mansion. The man has also committed other crimes involving the rich and the famous. 1st. [Historical]

ALEXANDER, Lawrence. *Speak Softly.* 1987 Doubleday/ Paperjacks 1988. New York City Police Commissioner Teddy Roosevelt has a series of murders on his hands. Each one bears the signature of organized crime. Teddy's cousin Franklin, enrolled at Groton, has become involved. Teddy has to work fast. 2nd. [Historical]

ALLEN, Steve. *Murder In Manhattan.* 1990 Zebra/ Zebra 1991. Steve Allen has been offered a cameo part in a movie being filmed in Manhattan. He's going to play Superman; after all, he does resemble Clark Kent. Suddenly there's an unscripted murder and the corpse lands in his outstretched arms. 3rd.

BAXT, George. *The Dorothy Parker Murder Case.* 1984 St. Martin/ International Polygonics 1986. Ilona Mercury, a Ziegfeld beauty, is found dead in George S. Kaufman's hideaway. And, since Dorothy Parker is between suicide attempts, she's drawn into a mystery that fits into a novel by Fitzgerald. 1st. [Drugs]

BAXT, George. *The Alfred Hitchcock Murder Case.* 1986 St. Martin/ International Polygonics 1987. Several murders occurred while Alfred Hitchcock was on location in Munich in 1925. Now, in London in 1936, those killings come back to haunt Alfred and his wife Alma. This time Hitchcock wants everything tied up nicely. [Intrigue]

BAXT, George. *The Tallulah Bankhead Murder Case.* 1987 St. Martin/ International Polygonics 1988. At the height of the House Un-American Activities Committee's hearings, a series of deaths occurs in New York City. They seem to revolve around Tallulah Bankhead. Together with Detective Jacob Singer, she gets to play sleuth. 2nd. [Revenge]

BLOCH, Robert, and Andre Norton. *The Jekyll Legacy.* 1990 Tor. Dr. Jekyll's long-lost niece, Hester Jekyll, has inherited his fortune and the secrets to his laboratory. Because she's suspected of murdering her uncle, the police are stalking her. But so is someone else. [Victorian]

BROWN, R. D. *Villa Head.* [Political]

BUCKLEY, William F., Jr. *Mongoose, R.I.P.* [Intrigue]

DOZOIS, Gardner, and Susan Casper, eds. *Ripper!* 1988 Tor/ PBO. Jack the Ripper was the first mass-murderer to gain notoriety. Here is a collection of short stories about a man who will not die.

HALL, Robert Lee. *Murder At San Simeon.* 1988 St. Martin. The famous and the hardly-ever-heard-of were gathered at William Randolph Hearst's famous San Simeon. In the middle of a rainstorm, the dwarf is found shot to death in Hearst's private elevator. Is Hearst next? [Revenge]

HALL, Robert Lee. *Benjamin Franklin Takes The Case.* 1988 St. Martin. It's 1757 and Benjamin Franklin is in London when an old friend is murdered by an American Indian. As Franklin traverses the dark byways of the city, he's involved in stolen goods, more murder, and he finds a son. 1st. [Historical]

KAMINSKY, Stuart. *The Fala Factor.* 1984 St. Martin/ Mysterious 1988. Eleanor Roosevelt stops at Toby Peters' office. The dog in the White House is behaving strangely and she thinks the real Fala has been kidnapped and brought to Los Angeles. Toby promises to help. 9th. [Hollywood]

KAMINSKY, Stuart M. *Smart Moves.* 1987 St. Martin. Toby Peters is in New York City during World War II to help Albert Einstein. It looks as though members of the fifth column are trying to discredit Einstein and prove he's a traitor. 12th. [Intrigue]

KAMINSKY, Stuart. *Think Fast, Mr. Peters.* 1988 St. Martin. It was a distress call from his office mate Sheldon Minck: his wife Mildred has run away with Peter Lorre. At the filming of a rooftop scene, a look-alike Lorre is shot and killed. Suddenly other Lorre imitators are attacked. Toby has to find Mildred. 13th. [Old Crime]

KAMINSKY, Stuart. *Buried Caesars.* 1989 Mysterious/ Mysterious 1990. General Douglas MacArthur is planning to run for president. But when one of his aides runs off with the campaign funds and some of the general's papers, MacArthur calls in Toby Peters. And to help Peters is Dashiell Hammett. 14th. [Political]

LARSEN, Gaylord. *Dorothy And Agatha.* 1991 Dutton. Dorothy L. Sayers returned from London to find her husband out and a dead man in her dining room. Such a nuisance as she's in the middle of producing her first play. Despite Dorothy's protests, Agatha Christie is determined to solve the mystery. [Revenge]

PAUL, Barbara. *A Chorus Of Detectives* 1987 St. Martin/ Signet 1988. During a performance of *Samson and Delilah,* a female chorister is killed by a falling urn. This is just the first attack on the chorus. Enrico Caruso and Geraldine Farrar are scampering around backstage to find a killer. 3rd. [Music]

ROOSEVELT, Elliott. *Murder And The First Lady.* 1984 St. Martin/ Avon 1985. Philip Garter, a minor staff member at the White House, has been poisoned at the apartment of the First Lady's secretary. Eleanor is convinced that Pamela is innocent. When more deaths occur, the case becomes complicated with diamonds and an emerald or two. 1st. [Jewels]

ROOSEVELT, Elliott. *The Hyde Park Murder.* 1985 St. Martin/ Avon 1986. When Alfred Hannah was indicted for securities fraud, Eleanor Roosevelt got a hurried call from her friend Adrianna. She was in love with Hannah's son, and her father had forbidden her to see him. Eleanor agrees to help, but she can't prevent Alfred's death. 2nd. [Fraud]

ROOSEVELT, Elliott. *Murder At Hobcaw Barony.* 1986 St. Martin/ Avon 1987. What was to be a peaceful respite at Bernard Baruch's North Carolina estate explodes into the death of a movie producer. Once more Eleanor Roosevelt delves into everyone's relationship to the dead man. 3rd. [Getting Away With Murder]

ROOSEVELT, Elliott. *The White House Pantry Murder.* 1987 St. Martin/ Avon 1988. It's Christmas 1941 at the White House, a grim holiday in the early days of

World War II. Winston Churchill is visiting and security is tight. But there in the pantry refrigerator is the body of a man. The First Lady has another crime to solve. 4th. [Christmas]

ROOSEVELT, Elliott. *Murder At The Palace.* 1988 St. Martin/ Avon 1989. Sir Anthony Brooke-Hastings invited some people in for drinks, but none of them could be called a friend. As they waited in his rooms at Buckingham Palace, he was dead in the next room. Eleanor, visiting there, sleuths again. 5th. [Manuscript]

ROOSEVELT, Elliott. *Murder In The Blue Room.* 1990 St. Martin/ Avon 1991. 1942: Soviet Minister Molotov is at the White House urging President Roosevelt to open a Second Front. After a small state dinner, Emily Ryan, from the press office, is found dead in the Blue Room. The First Lady has another investigation on her hands. 8th. [Infidelity]

SMITH, Terrence Lore. *Yours Truly, From Hell.* [Psychic]

SWAIM, Don. *The H. L. Mencken Murder Case.* 1988 St. Martin. It's 1948, and Howard is running his father's Fourth Avenue used-book store. His friend Lenny puts him on to a rare manuscript. To be sure it's worth money, Howard checks it out with an old friend of his father, H. L. Mencken. [Manuscript]

TAIBO, Paco Ignacio III. *An Easy Thing.* [Blackmail]

TUCKER, Bartholomew. *The Man Who Looked Like Howard Cosell.* 1988 St. Martin. TV agent Harry Baker, sitting in the Oak Room, caught a glimpse of Howard Cosell, or someone who looked like him. Within minutes, the Plaza men's room has a dead body. Now an old army buddy wants Harry for a CIA project. [Intrigue]

FASHION

The fashion industry can be as cutthroat as any other. Timing of the introduction of new styles and fabrics is important to the economics of any fashion house. There is competition to get the very top models. The subject is pattern perfect for a murder.

ALBERT, Marvin. *Back In The Real World.* [Blackmail]

ASHFORD, Jane. *Mirage.* 1986 Fawcett/ PBO. Geri Tyrrel, famous model, had just landed the new J.G. Cosmetics line when accidents began to happen. At a shoot in London one of the lights crashed, and, later, the brake line in her car was cut. Who was out to get her?

BABSON, Marian. *Death In Fashion.* 1985 Walker/ Bantam 1987. Decemo Designers are about to show their collection during London Fashion Week when they are suddenly plagued by "accidents." The flowers turn out to be funeral displays, there's salt in the cold cream . . . and murder. [Revenge]

CLARK, Mary Higgins. *While My Pretty One Sleeps.* 1989 Simon & Schuster/ Dell 1990. Gossip writer Ethel Lambston was found murdered in a remote part of New York. Neeve Kearney, boutique owner, is drawn into the mystery. She hadn't been able to deliver Ethel's last special order for dresses. [Old Crime]

FROST, Joan Van Every. *Silvershine.* 1987 Fawcett/ PBO. Blaise Cory is in Mexico, about to open a swimwear boutique in the Los Dorados Hotel. A strange silver coin turns up; a body soon follows. Blaise and writer Whitney Gower suddenly have to drop everything and find his young daughter. [Smuggling]

JEFFERS, H. Paul. *The Rag Doll Murder.* 1987 Ballantine/ PBO. Her sister, Jamey Flamingo, the famed model, has been strangled in her New York City apartment, and Evelyn wants PI Harry MacNeil to find the murderer. Although the young delivery boy is in custody, Harry pounds the streets of the garment district for different answers. 1st. [Blackmail]

MELVILLE, James. *Kimono For A Corpse.* 1988 St. Martin/ Fawcett 1989. Mode International is holding a series of fashion shows in Kobe, Japan. A chandelier falls, injuring Mr. Watanabe. Then a body is found in a dressing room. Superintendent Otani is on the case with Inspector Kimura. 9th. [Oriental]

FATHERS

As the saying goes: you can always be certain as to who your mother is, but it's a wise man who knows his own father. This can be an interesting theme in the mystery story, as is the issue of the father's not even knowing he has a child. And then there is the close relationship between father and child that provides strange complications.

ALBERT, Marvin. *Bimbo Heaven.* [Jewels]

ALLINGHAM, Margery. *The China Governess.* 1962 Doubleday/ Avon 1990. Timothy Kinnit wants to learn the truth about his parentage before he marries Julie. As Albert Campion traces his roots, he discovers an old scandal, and a present-day murder. 18th. [Imposter]

BARNARD, Robert. *Death Of A Mystery Writer.* [Mystery Writer]

BURNS, Rex. *Ground Money.* [Drugs]

CARR, John Dickson. *Scandal At Chimneys.* [Victorian]

CHANDLER, Raymond & Robert B. Parker. *Poodle Springs.* [Blackmail]

CLARKE, Anna. *Last Judgment.* [Academic]

CLARKE, Anna. *Last Seen In London.* [Americans In England]

CONSTANTINE, K. C. *The Rocksburg Railroad Murders.* 1972 Saturday Review/ Godine 1987. John Andrasko was waiting for the train to go to his night job, when he had his head bashed in. Police Chief Mario Baltic, on his first case, has to wade through past history to find the killer. 1st.

COOK, Bruce. *Mexican Standoff.* 1988 Franklin Watts/ St. Martin 1990. Paul Jarret and his girlfriend were run off the road and the car burned. The man arrested for the crime has skipped bail. Paul's father hires Chico Cervantes to cross the Mexican border and return the man to stand trial. [Drugs]

CORRINGTON, John William, and Joyce H. Corrington. *A Project Named Desire.* 1987 Viking/ Fawcett 1988. Rat Trap, New Orleans PD Homicide Captain, is just a step away from getting the goods on the local mob king. Then his witness is dead and a rock star collapses in the middle of a concert. Things from the past come back to haunt him. 2nd. [Imposter]

DEAN, S. F. X. *Nantucket Soap Opera.* [Television]

DOOLITTLE, Jerome. *Body Scissors.* [Political]

ENGER, L. L. *Comeback.* [Real Estate]

ESTLEMAN, Loren D. *Any Man's Death.* 1986 Mysterious/ Mysterious 1987. Ex-hit man Peter Macklin is trying to keep a TV evangelist alive. Reverend Sunsmith is leading a fight against legalizing gambling in Detroit. Peter's frightened, scared that his son holds the contract on the reverend. 3rd.

ESTLEMAN, Loren D. *Lady Yesterday.* [Missing Person]

FLINN, Denny Martin. *San Francisco Kills.* [Father]

FRANCIS, Dick. *Hot Money.* [Horses]

GEORGE, Elizabeth. *Well-Schooled In Murder.* [Academic]

GIRDNER, Jaqueline. *Adjusted To Death.* [Revenge]

GRANT-ADAMSON, Lesley. *Too Many Questions.* [Christmas]

GRAY, Caroline. *The Third Life.* 1988 St. Martin. Jolted from her life at the Swiss school, Julie Allen returned to London when her father was murdered. She was shocked to discover that her gentle dad had a second life, as a leader of organized crime. Then she discovers a third life.

GUNNING, Sally. *Hot Water.* Pocket 1990/ PBO. Odd job specialist Pete Bartholomew arrived at Edna Hitchcock's house to catalogue her books. He found her dead in the bathtub. Before long Pete is consoling Edna's daughter and digging into the background of her Aunt Lizzie. 1st.

HAYNES, Conrad. *Perpetual Check.* [Academic]

HOOPER, Kay. *Crime Of Passion.* [Incest]

KENNEALY, Jerry. *Polo's Wild Card.* [Art]

KIJEWSKI, Karen. *Katapult.* [Where There's A Will]

LINDSEY, David L. *In The Lake Of The Moon.* 1987 Atheneum/ Bantam 1990. Stuart Haydon, Houston police detective, has received a series of photographs; the last one spells out his own death. In order to stop the nightmare, Stuart has to look into his late father's life . . . and loves. 3rd. [Revenge]

LINSCOTT, Gillian. *A Whiff Of Sulphur.* [On Vacation]

LUCE, Carol Davis. *Night Stalker.* Zebra 1990/ PBO. Alexandra Carlson was just beginning to enjoy her own life in the mountains outside of Reno. Her paintings were selling well and she was starting to entertain. Then the phone calls started, she was sure someone had been inside her house, and someone knew too much about her childhood. [Revenge]

MARTIN, Lee. *Hal's Own Murder Case.* [Psychological]

McDONALD, Gregory. *Fletch, Too.* 1986 Warner/ Warner 1987. The minister has just pronounced them married when a strange man hands Fletch a letter from his father, the father he'd thought was dead. So it's off to Africa . . . and danger for the bride and groom. 8th. [Africa]

McDOWELL, Rider. *The Mercy Man.* 1987 St. Martin. Spanish Harlem PI Willy Diaz is just making it when a case comes along. A beautiful Latin woman disappears the same night that a priest is killed. All his employer Carmen cares about is finding her sister. One man stands in the way.

MICHAELS, Barbara. *Search The Shadows.* 1987 Atheneum/ Berkley 1988. At the time of her engagement, Haskell Maloney discovered that the man she thought was her father couldn't possibly be related to her. She packs up and heads for the Oriental Institute in Chicago to find him. [Academic]

MORTIMER, John. *Like Men Betrayed.* 1988 Viking/ Penguin 1990. Christopher Kennet, solicitor, is a man of routine. He dines always at the same club, and has had the same house and wife for many years. But that's all about to change. His son Kit lives in another world, and Kennet may have to join him.

MURPHY, Haughton. *Murder & Acquisitions.* [Espionage]

ORDE, A. J. *Death And The Dogwalker.* 1990 Doubleday. Jason Lynx was walking his dog in a Denver park when he discovered the body of Fred Foret under a tree. Fred's sister asks Jason to look into Fred's death. And that involves looking into Fred's whole family. 2nd. [Getting Away With Murder]

PARKER, Robert B. *Stardust.* [Television]

PERRY, Anne. *Cardington Crescent.* [Victorian]

PETERS, Ellis. *The Confession Of Brother Haluin.* [Medieval]

PETERSON, Keith. *The Trap Door.* [Journalism]

REYNOLDS, William J. *Moving Targets.* 1986 St. Martin/ Ballantine 1987. Local banker Jack Castelar was dead, and his daughter Kate was missing. The dead man's lawyer wants PI Nebraska on the case. Then there's another death. The police think they know the killer. Nebraska isn't so sure. 2nd. [Incest]

SANGSTER, Jimmy. *Blackball.* 1987 Holt. It all started when James Reed found a woman rifling a safe, in the nude. Then James gets charged with her rape. Out on bail, he has to find out just what's going on, and fight to stay alive. 2nd. [Blackmail]

SIMPSON, Dorothy. *Close Her Eyes.* [Missing Person]

SIMPSON, Dorothy. *Element Of Doubt.* [Infidelity]

SIMPSON, Dorothy. *Suspicious Death.* 1988 Scribner/ Bantam 1990. Marcia Salden drowned in the river Teale. Inspector Luke Thanet suspects she was pushed. He begins by filling in some gaps in the victim's past. 8th.

SMITH, Richard C. *A Secret Singing.* 1988 NAL/Signet

1989. Wealthy Brahmin Morton Streeter wants PI Mallory to investigate the young woman that her step-father Caleb Johnson has gotten involved with. Then Caleb dies, cyanide in his $2,000 scotch. And the woman in question has become his widow. 1st. [Fraud]

STEED, Neville. *Chipped.* 1989 St. Martin. A local private detective has disappeared. His charming assistant wants Peter Marklin to help her find him. With his fisherman friend Gus, Peter starts to snoop. He's soon in the middle of a very real fire. 3rd.

TAPPLY, William G. *The Dutch Blue Error.* 1984 Scribner/ Ballantine 1985. Oliver Hazard Perry Weston, wealthy recluse, has just received a letter offering to sell him the Dutch Blue Error, a rare stamp. He believed that he owned the only existing copy. He hires Brady Coyne to find out who had the "duplicate." 2nd. [Lawyer]

TAPPLY, William G. *Client Privilege.* 1990 Delacorte/ Dell 1991. Superior Court Judge Chester Y. Popowski has a task for Brady Coyne: meet a blackmailer at a local bar and tell him to buzz off. Brady does, only to discover, hours later, that the blackmailer is murdered. The police are asking Brady questions he can't answer. 9th. [Lawyer]

TAYLOR, Andrew. *Our Father's Lies.* 1985 Dodd, Mead/ Penguin 1986. Major Ted Dougal's goddaughter, Celia Prentisse, is convinced her historian father was murdered. It was the wrong brand of gin. Dougal enlists the help of his son William as the clues lead them back to World War II. 3rd. [Old Crime]

THACKERY, Ted, Jr. *Preacher.* [Real Estate]

THOMPSON, Gene. *Murder Mystery.* [Hollywood]

THOMSON, June. *No Flowers By Request.* 1987 Doubleday. David Hamilton had a charming wife, a fine house, and was successful at his law practice. Then one night someone broke into his house and shot him to death. Inspector Rudd found a flaw and the whole plot came tumbling down. 12th. [Infidelity]

WARD, E. C. *A Nice Little Beach Town.* [Real Estate]

WENTWORTH, Patricia. *The Alington Inheritance.* [Where There's A Will]

WESLEY, Carolyn. *King's Castle.* [Writer]

WILCOX, Collin. *Silent Witness.* [Where There's A Will]

WILCOX, Stephen. *The Dry White Tear.* [Revenge]

WILTZ, Chris. *The Killing Circle.* 1981 Macmillan/ Pinnacle 1985. Flemming bought some rare William Blakes and had them shipped to New Orleans to have the bindings tightened. Unable to contact the dealer, he hired Neal Rafferty to retrieve his books. Neal finds the dealer dead and the books missing. 1st. [Manuscripts]

WOODS, Sara. *Naked Villainy.* [Witches]

ZUBRO, Mark Richard. *A Simple Suburban Murder.* [Gay]

FRAUD

It's always seemed a paradox: if crooks put their effort into legitimate endeavors instead of fraudulent ones, we'd have more rich people and fewer people in prison. The imagination and planning that go into the scams and capers are frequently remarkable. Oh well, it does make for a good mystery story.

BABSON, Marian. *There Must Be Some Mistake.* 1987 St. Martin. Karen Randolph's husband is three days overdue from a trip to Brussels. Also missing are his secretary Grace and a quarter million pounds worth of bearer bonds. Grace is found drowned and the whole company of Harding Handicrafts is in a quandary. [Economics]

BARTH, Richard. *Blood Doesn't Tell.* [Children]

BEATON, M. C. *Death Of A Cad.* 1987 St. Martin/ Ivy 1988. Twelve selected guests were invited for the weekend to celebrate, at last, Priscilla's engagement to playwright Henry Withering. One of the guests is found dead and it looks like an accident. Hamish Macbeth, the village constable, does some digging to prove otherwise. 2nd. [Blackmail]

BECK, K. K. *The Body In The Volvo.* 1987 Walker/ Ivy 1989. Uncle Cosmo won big in the lottery just as his nephew was denied tenure. Cosmo turns over the Cosmo Car Center to Charles. Then a body is found welded into the trunk of a Volvo, and Charles is the suspect. Sylvia, the bookkeeper, adds the numbers up. [Psychological]

BEINHART, Larry. *No One Rides For Free.* [Economics]

BLOCK, Lawrence. *When The Sacred Ginmill Closes.* 1986 Arbor House/ Charter 1987. Matt Scudder was sitting in Morrissey's Bar on the Fourth of July when two men burst in with guns. They took the cash and the IRA contributions and left. 6th. [Holiday]

BURKE, James Lee. *Black Cherry Blues.* [Indians]

CANDY, Edward. *Which Doctor.* [Medical]

CARVIC, Heron. *Picture Miss Seeton.* 1968 Harper & Row/Berkley 1988. Art teacher Miss Emily Seeton leaves a performance of *Carmen* and bumps into a real-life stabbing. With a gentle prod from the police, she produces a drawing of the culprit. But he has her handbag and her address. Even as she ventures to her cottage in the country, new troubles brew. 1st.

CARVIC, Heron. *Witch Miss Seeton.* [Witches]

CARVIC, Heron. *Miss Seeton Sings.* 1973 Harper & Row/ Berkley 1988. Just before Miss Seeton boarded the wrong plane, headed for Genoa instead of Geneva, she noticed a man pick up someone else's briefcase. This was just the first lap in Miss Seeton's trek across Europe. 4th.

CONSTANTINE, K. C. *Upon Some Midnights Clear.* [Christmas]

COOPER, Natasha. *A Common Death.* [Writer]

CRAIG, M. S. *The Third Blonde.* 1985 Dodd, Mead/ Critic's Choice 1987. Angie Bramley watched her fellow post office worker walk through the snow storm, to spend her coffee break with Charles, her fiancé. She wasn't seen alive again. The next morning the snowplow found her body.

CRAIG, M. S. *Flash Point.* [Arson]

DALE, Celia. *Sheep's Clothing.* 1988 Doubleday. Ex–prison mates, Grace set herself and Janice up in a scam. Posing as social workers, they enticed the elderly to a drug-laced cup of tea. Then they robbed them. But Miss Frimwell died, and Detective Wally Simpson wants to turn in his badge. 14th.

DeANDREA, William. *Killed In The Ratings.* 1978 Harcourt Brace Jovanovich/ Avon 1979. Someone had monkeyed with the network's ratings and one man was already dead. Troubleshooter Matt Cobb has been attacked once. Tragedy strikes again, and it seems that everyone at the TV station is somehow involved. 1st. [Television]

DeANDREA, William. *Killed In The Act.* 1981 Doubleday/ Mysterious 1987. For the network's big celebration, it flew in stars from the Coast. Ken Shelby and Lenny Green, an old comedy pair, were to team up again after a long break. Matt Cobb, troubleshooter for the network, can't stop the murder. 2nd. [Television]

DeANDREA, William. *Killed On The Rocks.* [Television]

DEXTER, Colin. *The Silent World Of Nicholas Quinn.* 1977 St. Martin/ Bantam 1988. The almost deaf Nicholas Quinn was found in his apartment, dead from sherry laced with cyanide. Inspector Morse questions all the people he worked with at the Oxford Foreign Examinations Syndicate. 3rd.

DILLON, Eilís. *Sent To His Account.* [On Vacation]

DISNEY, Doris Miles. *Mrs. Meeker's Money.* 1961 Doubleday/ Zebra 1987. Mrs. Meeker had lots of money and she was willing to spend some of it to find the grandson of an old friend. The detective she'd hired was defrauding her. Postal Inspector Madden was called in. Before long, Mrs. Meeker is murdered.

DOLD, Gaylord. *Snake Eyes.* 1987 Ivy/ PBO. This time PI Mitch Roberts gets several jobs rolled into one. He's to find out who killed two of Jules Reynard's colts, get his wife to return home and behave herself, and prove that someone is skimming from his nightclub. The plot can only get dirtier. 2nd.

DOYLE, James T. *Epitaph For A Loser.* 1988 Walker. When Norm fled Tampa, he neglected to tell PI Paul Broder that his girlfriend was dead at his condo. With Norm also dead, Paul's ex-wife Margaret wants him to clear her brother's name of the murder. [Corruption]

DUNLAP, Susan. *Not Exactly A Brahmin.* 1985 St. Martin/ Paperjacks 1987. Wealthy Ralph Palmerston picked up his Cadillac from the garage, drove down Berkeley's steepest hill in a rainstorm, and died in the crash. Homicide Detective Jill Smith uncovers a strange pact by the Shareholders Five. 3rd. [Revenge]

DUNLAP, Susan. *Too Close To The Edge.* 1987 St. Martin/ Dell 1989. Wheelchair-bound Liz Goldenstern had spearheaded access for the handicapped. She's found drowned in a foot of water at the site of Marina Vista, a special-needs complex. As Jill Smith, Berkeley homicide cop, follows her leads, one of the suspects is murdered and Jill ends up in the hospital. 4th. [Real Estate]

ECCLES, Marjorie. *Cast A Cold Eye.* [Revenge]

ELKINS, Charlotte & Aaron. *A Wicked Slice.* [Ball Games]

ENGLE, Howard. *A City Called July.* [Canadian]

ESTLEMAN, Loren D. *Angel Eyes.* [Missing Person]

FISH, Robert L. *Brazilian Sleigh Ride.* [Imposter]

FRANCIS, Dick. *Bolt.* [Horses]

FRIEDMAN, Mickey. *The Fault Tree.* 1984 Dutton/ Ballantine 1985. Trying to save her sister from a guru, Marina went to India. She arrived to find that Catherine died in a house fire. Back in San Francisco, Marina is involved in the collapse of a ride at the amusement park. Suddenly messages start arriving from India. Could Catherine still be alive?

GARDNER, Erle Stanley. *The Case Of The Crooked Candle.* [Lawyer]

GILLIS, Jackson. *Chain Saw.* 1988 St. Martin/ St. Martin 1990. Louise Telford, owner of Telford Timber Mills, has just lost her only son, Myron. He died suddenly with no heirs. A young girl, Julie, turns up, claiming to be Myron's daughter. Louise is willing to spend some of her millions to have Jonas Duncan find the truth. 2nd.

GRANT, Linda. *Blind Trust.* [Computer Crimes]

HANDLER, David. *The Man Who Would Be F. Scott Fitzgerald* [Writer]

HARRISON, Ray. *Why Kill Arthur Potter?* [Victorian]

HILL, Reginald, w/a Patrick Ruell. *Death Of A Dormouse.* 1987 Mysterious/ Mysterious 1988. Trudi Adamson had been a well-cared for wife in Vienna. Just after her husband's transfer to Sheffield, he died in a car accident. Now Trudi has to face some tough questions. And she has some of her own to ask.

HORANSKY, Ruby. *Dead Ahead.* 1990 Scribner. It was Nikki Trakos's first homicide since she'd made detective. The corpse had a phone number in his wallet, the number of a stock broker whose boat had blown up off Rockaway a few days before. What's the connection? 1st. [Accident]

HOWATCH, Susan. *Call In The Night.* [Missing Person]

JEFFRIES, Roderic. *Relatively Dangerous.* [Imposter]

JERINA, Carol. *Sweet Jeopardy.* [Smuggling]

KELLEY, Patrick A. *Slightly Guilty.* [Psychic]

KIENZLE, William X. *Eminence.* [Clergy]

KIJEWSKI, Karen. *Katwalk.* 1989 St. Martin/ Avon 1990. Kat Colorado's friend Charity is in the middle of a divorce. Charity's husband says he lost the $200,000 gambling. Charity wants her share of the money and sends Kat to Las Vegas to find out what happened to the cash. 1st. [Real Estate]

KRAFT, Gabrielle. *Bullshot.* 1987 Pocket/ PBO. Los Angeles lawyer Jerry Zalman doesn't think much of his brother-in-law Phil, and sure enough, Phil's in trouble again. The man he gave ten grand to is missing and he wants Jerry to find him. Jerry finds him all right, frozen in a Frigidaire. 1st. [Lawyer]

LEONARD, Elmore. *Freaky Deaky.* [Rape]

LEWIS, Roy. *The Salamander Chill.* [Lawyer]

MacLEOD, Charlotte. *Something The Cat Dragged In.* [Political]

MATHIS, Edward. *September Song.* [Revenge]

McGOWN, Jill. *The Stalking Horse.* [Old Crime]

MEYERS, Annette. *Tender Death.* 1990 Bantam/ Bantam 1991. Les Wetzen and her older friend had just paid a visit to Evelyn Cunningham, wealthy socialite. As they left her building, Evelyn fell twenty floors to her death. A terrible accident for a confused old woman, said the police; Les thinks otherwise. 2nd.

MURRAY, William. *The Getaway Blues.* [Horse Racing]

NEEL, Janet. *Death's Bright Angel.* 1988 St. Martin/ Pocket 1991. Inspector John McLeish was investigating the apparent mugging and murder of Fireman. It led to the company he worked for. Francesca Wilson seems to be getting in his way. 1st.

NEEL, Janet. *Death On Site.* [On Vacation]

ORMEROD, Roger. *A Death To Remember.* [Getting Away With Murder]

PARETSKY, Sara. *Indemnity Only.* 1982 Dial/ Ballantine 1985. Chicago PI V. I. Warshawski was hired to find Peter Thayer's girlfriend. But Peter's dead in his campus apartment, and Anita's still missing. V.I. keeps digging, more bodies show up, and a criminal trail reaches into the past. 1st.

PARETSKY, Sara. *Deadlock.* 1984 Dial/ Ballantine 1986. Boom Boom is dead, drowned, an accident. His cousin, V. I. Warshawski, isn't convinced. She closely examines the last months of his life, and all the people in it. She finds her answers, but not without personal danger. 2nd.

PHILLIPS, Mike. *The Late Candidate.* [Black Detective]

PICKARD, Nancy. *No Body.* 1986 Scribner/ Pocket 1987. The Union Hill Cemetery was empty, none of the graves had bodies in them. Then when they opened John Rudolph's casket, just before interment, they found he'd been joined by his secretary. Jenny Cain was curious. Was fraud from a past century being repeated? 3rd. [Blackmail]

PRATHER, Richard S. *Shellshock.* [Missing Person]

PUTRE, John Walter. *Death Among The Angels.* 1991 Scribner. Diana Raney, Doll's old girl friend, is in trouble. She's in jail for murdering her lover, but she remembers nothing about the night he died. Doll flies to Florida to find the real killer. 2nd. [Art]

RAY, Robert J. *Dial "M" For Murdock.* [Insurance]

RESNICOW, Herbert. *The Dead Room.* [Locked Room]

RESNICOW, Herbert. *The Hot Place.* [Lawyer]

ROOSEVELT, Elliott. *The Hyde Park Murder.* [Famous People]

ROSS, Jonathan. *Daphne Dead And Done For.* [Missing Person]

SANDERS, Lawrence. *The Timothy Files.* [Economics]

SCHOLEFIELD, A. T. *Dirty Weekend.* [Children]

SHERBURNE, James. *Death's Pale Horse.* [Historical]

SHERBURNE, James. *Death's Gray Angel.* [Historical]

SMITH, Richard C. *A Secret Singing.* [Father]

STEVENS, Christian D. *Printer's Devil.* [Journalism]

STRUNK, Frank C. *Jordon's Wager.* 1991 Walker. Betsy Trotter's young body was found in a glen, her own private place. As Deputy Sheriff Berkley Jordon investigates, the company town of Buxton, Kentucky, becomes close-mouthed. [Blackmail]

WHITE, Terri. *Fault Lines.* 1988 Mysterious/ Mysterious 1989. Recovering from a heart attack, ex–New York City cop Bryan Murphy is in peaceful Topanga Canyon. An ex-con wants him to locate an old girlfriend. Before Kathryn is killed, Bryan discovers she's been involved with two other ex-cons who are out for the chance of their lifetime.

WILLIAMS, David. *Treasure Preserved.* 1983 St. Martin/ Avon 1987. Lady Bassett had been sniffing around in the Sydney Marsh Papers in the library looking for a way to stop the destruction of the Round House. When she was blown up by a gas leak in her cottage, Mark Treasure wants to know why she was murdered. 6th. [Real Estate]

WILLIAMS, David. *Divided Treasure.* 1988 St. Martin. Mark Treasure is on a trip to a Welsh seaside resort to gather some information about a pension fund scam at the candy factory. But George Evans is dead in a vat of his own candy, and bigger things are at stake. 11th. [Infidelity]

WILLIAMS, Philip Carlton. *Mission Bay Murder.* 1988 Paperjacks/ PBO. At company headquarters, attorney Michael Thompson uncovers embezzlement. He hires young PI Sheila Simmons to find additional evidence. Then Sheila is killed and Michael is on the hot seat for the crime. [Lawyer]

WOLFE, Susan. *The Last Billable Hour.* [Lawyer]

G . . . IS FOR

GAY

*O*NCE THE CLOSET OPENED, the theme of homosexuality became a more respectable topic for the murder mystery. Sometimes the stories are sensitive, sometimes judgmental. They are written by both men and women, about men and women, and the characters may be victim or detective, featured or incidental.

ALDYNE, Nathan. *Vermilion.* 1985 Ballantine/ PBO. Billie, a young hustler, was murdered one winter night in Boston's "Combat Zone." The cops are looking into it, but are asking all the wrong questions. Dan Valentine and Clarisse Lovelace are following any leads they can find. 1st. [Blackmail]

ALDYNE, Nathan. *Cobalt.* 1982 St. Martin/ Ballantine 1986. Daniel Valentine and Clarisse Lovelace are in Provincetown for the summer. After the first big party of the season, people start dropping like flies. Ann's dead in the swimming pool, Jeff died on the beach, and Terry got it on the street. Clarisse and Daniel are asking hard questions. 2nd. [Drugs]

ALDYNE, Nathan. *Slate.* 1984 Villard/ Ballantine 1985. Sweeney Drysdale II was shot to death in Clarisse's bedroom above the bar she and Dan run. As Dan and Clarisse question everyone who comes into Slate, the prospects seem dimmer. At the New Year's Eve bash, Clarisse gets her answers. 3rd. [Holiday]

ALDYNE, Nathan. *Canary.* 1986 Ballantine/ PBO. A number of gay men last seen at Slate, the bar Valentine and Clarisse run, turn up murdered. For business's sake, they have to run down the killer. 4th.

BAXT, George. *A Queer Kind Of Death.* [Black Detective]

BLOCK, Lawrence. *The Sins Of The Fathers.* [Clergy]

DAVIS, Kenn. *Nijinsky Is Dead.* [Black Detective]

ELBERT, Joyce. *Murder At A.A.* [Revenge]

FARRELL, Maud. *Skid.* [Medical]

FENNELLY, Tony. *The Glory Hole Murders.* 1985 Carroll & Graf/ Carroll & Graf 1986. There's been a particularly brutal murder at the Ramrod Club in New Orleans. Matt Sinclair, formerly of the DA's office, is being blackmailed to help with the investigation. Matt does so well that his own life is threatened. 1st.

FENNELLY, Tony. *The Closet Hanging.* 1987 Carroll & Graf/ Carroll & Graf 1988. As Matt Sinclair crossed Jackson Square, he had a seizure. He lost all account of where he'd been. When the body of Brad Rutledge was found hanged in Matt's house, he had to bustle to clear himself. 2nd. [Real Estate]

GILL, B. M. *Death Drop.* [Academic]

HALLERAN, Tucker. *A Cool, Clean Death.* [Blackmail]

HANSEN, Joseph. *Troublemaker.* [Insurance]

HANSEN, Joseph. *Nightwork.* 1984 Holt/ Owl 1985. Paul Myers died in a great truck fire off a mountain road outside Los Angeles. Death-claims insurance investigator Dave Brandstetter is asking the questions. When it's discovered that the truck was bombed, his field of inquiry widens. 7th. [Social Issues]

HANSEN, Joseph. *Steps Going Down.* [Where There's A Will]

HANSEN, Joseph. *The Little Dog Laughed.* [Political]

HANSEN, Joseph. *Early Graves.* 1987 Mysterious/ Mysterious 1988. They were all going to die anyway, they all had AIDS. Why, then, was someone hurrying them to their graves? When Dave Brandstetter finds a dead man on his patio, and the killing doesn't fit the pattern, he sets out to investigate the flaw. 9th. [Revenge]

MacDONALD, Patricia J. *No Way Home.* 1989 Delacorte/ Dell 1990. It was Founder's Day in the small Tennessee town and Michele Burdette was all dressed up, ready for the pageant. But Michele never came home. They found her body by the river and a family was torn to shreds. [Revenge]

McDERMID, Val. *Open And Shut.* 1991 St. Martin. Journalist Alison Maxwell was found strangled in her apartment by Jackie, her ex-lover. Jackie was found guilty of the crime and sent to prison. Lindsay Gordon, on her return to Scotland, is determined to find out the identity of the real killer. [Getting Away With Murder]

NABB, Magdalen. *The Marshal's Own Case.* 1990 Scribner/ Penguin 1991. They only found parts of the body of the young woman, then at autopsy discovered the corpse was a transsexual. Marshal Guarnaccia is in for a crash course on a side of Florence he little understands. 7th. [Psychological]

PERRY, Anne. *Bluegate Fields.* [Victorian]

PHILBIN, Tom. *Cop Killer.* Fawcett 1986/ PBO. A cop in Precinct Siberia has been killed. Detective Joe Lawless and his fellow NYPD officers wonder who's next as they look for the murderer. Meanwhile, Piccolo is chasing a ring selling babies. 3rd. [Kidnapping]

PHILLIPS, Edward. *Death Is Relative.* [Where There's A Will]

PHILLIPS, Edward. *Sunday's Child.* 1987 St. Martin. It was New Year's Eve and Geoffrey Chadwick was lonely. The young man he picked up in Montreal and took home was more interested in Geoffrey's wallet than his body. What was Geoffrey to do with his corpse? 1st. [Canadian]

PRONZINI, Bill. *Labyrinth.* [Smuggling]

RESNICOW, Herbert. *The Gold Deadline.* [Dance]

RICHARDSON, Robert. *Bellringer Street.* 1988 St. Martin. Playwright Agustus Maltravers and actress Tess Davy are visiting friends and touring Lord Dunford's stately home. Just as they're getting to be friends, Dunford is killed with a cricket ball. And even the old skeleton has gone missing. 2nd. [Ball Game]

RISENHOOVER, C. C. *Dead Even.* [Journalism]

ROBERTS, Les. *Not Enough Horses.* 1988 St. Martin/ St. Martin 1988. Robbie was young, he was gay, and he was dead. His friend Kevin wants Saxon to find out who killed Robbie. The trail leads to a TV studio's executive, injured when Robbie died. Which one was the intended victim? 2nd. [Television]

STEVENSON, Richard. *On The Other Hand, Death.* 1984 St. Martin/ Penguin 1985. The Millpond Company, shopping mall builders, hired PI Don Strachey to put an end to some vandalism. As Don's investigation gets underway, there's a kidnapping and several people are scrambling to raise a lot of money. 2nd. [Real Estate]

STEVENSON, Richard. *Ice Blues.* [Old Crime]

THOMPSON, Monroe. *The Blue Room.* [Suicide]

VARDEMAN, Robert E. *The Screaming Knife.* [Psychic]

WARD, Donald. *Death Takes The Stage.* 1988 St. Martin. Arnie wanted Jake Weissman to find out who had killed his lover, Bobby. After all, Jake had been Bobby's agent, once, a long time ago. Trouble comes from all sides as Jake and Arnie nose deeper and deeper. [Drugs]

WILLIAMSON, Chet. *McKain's Dilemma.* [Medical]

WILTZ, Chris. *A Diamond Before You Die.* 1987 Mysterious/ Mysterious 1988. Neal Rafferty was hired by Richard Cotton, candidate for New Orleans DA, to keep tabs on his wife. Neal discovers that female PI Lee Diamond is following *his* client. 2nd. [Holiday]

ZUBRO, Mark Richard. *A Simple Suburban Murder.* 1989 St. Martin. Tom Mason flipped on the lights in his high school classroom and stared at a body in the back row. Jim Evans, the math teacher, was dead. When Jim's son disappears, Tom and his lover Scott are asked to help find him. 1st. [Father]

ZUBRO, Mark Richard. *The Only Good Priest.* 1991 Scribner. Father Sebastian was found dead in the sacristy of the Chicago church just after evening mass. Someone had poisoned the altar wine. Friends of the priest convince high school teacher Tom Mason to look into the Father's death. 3rd. [Clergy]

GETTING AWAY WITH MURDER

As you close the covers of a mystery story, the last pages finished, there is a sense of satisfaction. All the loose ends have been tied neatly together, and justice prevails. Or does it? There are a growing number of murder mysteries in which someone is getting away with murder.

ASHFORD, Jeffrey. *A Question Of Principle.* 1987 St. Martin. Barrister Terence Elhan and struggling author Dennis Rickmore had little in common, except they were married to sisters. When a man dies in a hit-and-run accident, Dennis suspects Terence. And the lies begin.

BABSON, Marian. *Cover-Up Story.* [Television]

BARNARD, Robert. *Death Of A Perfect Mother.* [Mother]

BARNARD, Robert. *Political Suicide.* 1986 Scribner/ Dell 1987. MP James Partridge was found drowned in the Thames. Was it suicide or was he pushed? Superintendent Sutcliffe examines the political background and Partridge's love life. What he uncovers is the most frustrating case of his career. [Political]

BAXT, George. *A Queer Kind Of Death.* 1966 Simon & Schuster/ International Polygonics 1986. The cleaning woman found actor and model Ben Bently dead in the bathtub, with the radio still plugged in. NYPD Detective Pharoah Love, gay and black, investigates the murder that takes him to a never-ending list of suspects. 1st. [Black Detective]

BECKLUND, Jack. *Golden Fleece.* 1990 St. Martin. Harry Potter took off for a sail on Lake Superior. His wife reported him missing. Then logger Carl Hoffman was found murdered. Suddenly there's talk in the small town of Northport that there's gold on forestry land.

BRETT, Simon. *A Shock To The System.* 1985 Scribner/ Dell 1987. Graham Marshall killed a man one day. He discovered it was easy. Then he made a list of unpleasant people he could do without. He was going to get away with murder again, and again.

BRETT, Simon. *Dead Romantic.* 1986 Scribner/ Dell 1988. Madeleine Severen had been a virgin for thirty-seven years. Even though he was married, Bernard seemed the right person to succumb to. It was the perfect cottage: a fire in the hearth and death.

CAIRNS, Alison. *Strained Relations.* 1983 St. Martin/Critic's Choice 1986. It was the day after Melanie Quinn's party that they found Caroline's body; she'd been missing for several days. The tiny English village was shocked when another young woman died. Geoff Tavener quietly put the pieces together.

CARLSON, P. M. *Rehearsal For Murder.* [Theater]

CLARKE, Anna. *Desire To Kill.* 1982 Doubleday/ Charter 1988. When they could no longer live alone, a group of British elderly moved to Digby Hall, a country estate. Amy Langford saw it as the chance of a lifetime, the ideal place for her obsession to kill. But suddenly there were suspicions.

COHEN, Anthea. *Angel Without Mercy.* [Medical]

COHEN, Anthea. *Angel Of Vengeance.* 1982 Doubleday/ Tor 1988. Nurse Carmichael was now working at St. Matthew's Hospital, and her hay fever was menacing her. What she needed was an enemy. The father of a youngster was talking to the pediatrician about his badly battered child. Nurse's hay fever may soon improve. 2nd. [Medical]

CONSTANTINE, K. C. *Joey's Case.* 1988 Mysterious/ Mysterious 1991. Castelucci wants Police Chief Mario Balzic to do something about his son's murder. But it's out of Balzic's jurisdiction, and one of the witnesses refuses to testify. Mario gets slapped in the face with Joey's case. 8th.

CRIDER, Bill. *Too Late To Die.* 1986 Walker/ Ivy 1989. Jeanne Clinton was dead in her own living room. Texas sheriff Dan Rhodes hears stories about what she did while her husband worked nights. But when there are two other deaths, the tension in the town grows. 1st.

CRIDER, Bill. *Evil At The Root.* 1990 St. Martin. Mr. Babbit's stolen false teeth sent Sheriff Dan Rhodes to Sunny Dale Nursing Home. Dan's next visit was because Mr. Babbit was found dead with a plastic bag over his head. He scurries to solve the murder, and then another, before his wedding day. 5th. [Old Crime]

DEWHURST, Eileen. *A Private Prosecution.* 1987 Doubleday. Four young girls have died in Seaminster and then there's a fifth. Detective Maurice Kendrick is determined to find the killer. This last death is different, and Humphrey Barnes thinks Eleanor knows something.

DISNEY, Doris Miles. *Only Couples Need Apply.* 1973 Doubleday/ Zebra 1988. They had the routine down pat. Gretchen found a lonely widow and located the jewelry and money. Then Jay stepped in and used his gun efficiently. On to the next town. But something went wrong. Jay's dead, and Gretchen's charged with the crime.

GILBERT, Michael. *Overdrive.* 1968 Harper & Row/ Carroll & Graf 1988. Oliver Nugent was ruthless. He was going to get ahead. He never bothered about the means to his ambitious ends. Oliver never looked back, or cared about the troubles he caused others.

HALL, Adam. *Bishop In Check.* [Accident]

HILL, Reginald. *Deadheads.* [Botany]

HILTON, John Buxton. *Slickensides.* 1987 Scribner. On a visit to the High Peak district in 1911, Inspector Blunt is asked to investigate a break-in. The scene turns deadly when a body is found in the Slickensides mine. Now he has to find a killer. 6th. [Historical]

HORNIG, Doug. *Deep Dive.* 1988 Mysterious/ Mysterious 1989. Eric Vessey dove into the Charlotteville quarry and never came up. The air in his tank ran out. His sister suspects foul play and hires PI Loren Swift to investigate. 4th. [Medical]

JANCE, J. A. *Improbable Cause.* 1988 Avon/ PBO. Dentist Frederick Nielsen was dead in his own dentist's chair. Homicide Detective J. P. Beaumont is sifting through the list of suspects. He wants to question every member of the family. 5th.

JEFFERS, H. Paul. *Murder On The Mike.* [Television]

KIENZLE, William X. *Deadline For A Critic.* 1987 Andrews, McMeel & Parker/ Ballantine 1988. Critic Ridley Groendal was unloved by all. The power of his word closed plays, left books unread, and ruined concerts. One night Ridley read his mail and collapsed. Father Koestler, an old friend, wants to know more about Ridley's death. 9th.

LINSCOTT, Gillian. *Murder, I Presume.* [Victorian]

LIVINGSTON, Jack. *Hell-Bent For Election.* [Writer]

LIVINGSTON, Nancy. *Incident At Parga.* [On Vacation]

LUTZ, John. *Ride The Lightning.* 1987 St. Martin/ Tor 1990. Curtis Colt was due to die in the electric chair, the first in twenty-five years for Missouri. PI Nudger has been hired by Colt's girlfriend to reopen the case. She insists

Colt is innocent. Someone else is insisting Nudger get off the case. 3rd.

MATHIS, Edward. *From A High Place.* 1985 Scribner/ Ballantine 1987. In Butler Wells, Texas, for some R and R, PI Dan Roman has a visit from his old schoolteacher. She wants him to prove that her husband, fearful of heights, hadn't committed suicide by jumping off a cliff. 1st. [Revenge]

MATHIS, Edward. *Natural Prey.* [Missing Person]

MAXWELL, Thomas. *The Saberdene Variations.* [Revenge]

McCAFFERTY, Taylor. *Pet Peeves.* Pocket 1990/ PBO. Pigeon Fork, Kentucky, isn't the best place to make a living as a PI, but Haskell Blevins liked the town. Then Cordelia Turley, up from Nashville, has a case for him. Find out who killed Granny . . . and her cat and a parakeet. 1st.

McDERMID, Val. *Open And Shut.* [Gay]

McMULLEN, Mary. *The Bad-News Man.* 1986 Walker/ Jove 1987. May Lockett had run away from a miserable marriage and found seclusion in Provincetown. Now, after twenty-six years, *he* is crowding back into her life. She plans the only thing she can . . . his murder.

McMURRAY, Sarah, and Francesco P. Lualdi. *The Agreement.* 1986 Signet/ PBO. Three college classmates got together over lunch and discovered that none of them were particularly happy in their marriages. Putting their heads together, they worked out a very sensible plan that would make them wealthy widows.

MEEK, M. R. D. *A Worm Of Doubt.* 1988 Scribner/ Worldwide 1990. Frelis Lorimer consulted Lennox Kemp about divorcing her husband because he was having an affair. She quickly discovered that a lot of *her* money would be lost in a property settlement. Then the girlfriend died, and her husband went to jail. 4th. [Infidelity]

MEREDITH, D. R. *The Sheriff And The Panhandle Murders.* 1984 Walker/ Avon 1985. It was the first premeditated murder in Crawford County, Texas, and then there was another. Sheriff Charles Matthews, with his staff of two, pokes into hidden secrets, his own values, and friendship for his resolution. 1st.

NATSUKI, Shizuko. *The Third Lady.* [Oriental]

ORDE, A. J. *Death And The Dogwalker.* [Father]

ORMEROD, Roger. *A Death To Remember.* 1987 Scribner. Fifteen months after the brutal attack, Cliff Summers still had no memory of the past. As a former government inspector, he's doing his own investigation: reconstructing the hours just before the assault. [Fraud]

ORMEROD, Roger. *Death Of An Innocent.* [Mother]

PERRY, Anne. *Silence In Hanover Close.* [Victorian]

RANDISI, Robert J. *No Exit From Brooklyn.* [Art]

RAUCH, Constance. *A Deep Disturbance.* [Children]

ROOSEVELT, Elliott. *Murder At Hobcaw Barony.* [Famous People]

SMITH, Joan. *Why Aren't They Screaming?.* 1989 Scribner/ Fawcett 1990. Loretta Lawson, on her doctor's orders, has to take some time off from her teaching. With the loan of a cottage, she heads for the country and meets her hostess Clara Wolstonecraft. Loretta is soon caught up in Clara's causes and her murder. 2nd. [Old Crime]

SMITH, Julie. *New Orleans Mourning.* [Holiday]

SNOW, C. P. *A Coat Of Varnish.* 1979 Scribner/ Scribner 1988. The residents of quiet Belgravia Square were shocked when Lady Ashbrook was brutally murdered. And Superintendent Frank Briers stayed on the case long after the trail was cold.

TRENCH, Jason. *The Typescript.* 1988 Doubleday. Publisher William Dawnay received a manuscript in the mail, unsolicited. It was the story of his late wife, dead twenty-two years, and their life in the Middle East where he was a diplomat. Whoever sent him the MS wanted him to pay dearly. [Old Crime]

TRIPP, Miles. *The Frightened Wife.* [Infidelity]

TRUMAN, Margaret. *Murder On Embassy Row.* 1984 Arbor House/ Fawcett 1985. Geoffrey James, British ambassador to the U.S., saw out his guests, got comfortable in his study, and collapsed over the caviar. His Iranian valet was missing. Washington, D.C., Detective Sal Morizio follows the trail from London to Copenhagen and finds something more serious than smuggling. [Political]

TUROW, Scott. *Presumed Innocent.* 1987 Farrar, Strauss & Giroux/ Warner 1988. Carolyn Polhemus, from the County Prosecutor's Office, is dead, murdered in a terrible rape. Rusty Sabich is the chief investigator. When Rusty is accused of Carolyn's murder, he fights to clear himself. Is some of the evidence being hidden under a carpet of silence?

UNDERWOOD, Michael. *Hand Of Fate.* 1981 St. Martin/ Perennial 1987. Frank Wimble had committed the perfect murder. His wife was gone, never to be found. Then a hand wearing her ring surfaced, and the police had enough evidence to take Frank to trial. After he was acquitted, he received a letter. [Christmas]

WALKER, Walter. *Rules Of The Knife Fight.* 1986 Harper & Row/ Penguin 1987. Bobby O'Berry vanished on his wedding night. Months later, an unidentified body was found in San Francisco. PI Owen Carr not only tracks down the identity but also points a finger at attorney Leigh Rossville as the murderer. Chris Cage has to get his client off.

WHITE, Ned. *The Very Bad Thing.* [Computer Crime]

WILLEFORD, Charles. *New Hope For The Dead.* 1985 St. Martin/Ballantine 1987. Hoke Mosely, Miami PD, has a new partner—a woman—and a stack of old unsolved murder cases. But first, Hoke is going to follow through on the death of a junkie, no matter where it leads him. 2nd.

H . . . IS FOR

HISTORICAL

*M*ANY MURDER MYSTERIES *are set in the past. Some use historical events and real people. Others merely pick an interesting setting or period and make the most of it. For additional listings, please see "Medieval" and "Victorian," which are deserving of places of their own.*

ALEXANDER, Lawrence. *The Big Stick.* [Famous People]

ALEXANDER, Lawrence. *Speak Softly.* [Famous People]

CLARKE, Anna. *The Lady In Black.* [Writer]

DOHERTY, P. C. *The Fate Of Princes.* 1991 St. Martin. In 1483, Richard III staged a bloody coup shortly after his brother Edward IV died of a mysterious illness. Richard had himself crowned and his young nephews disappeared into the Tower of London. Did they die there? Or did they somehow escape? [Richard III]

EBERHART, Mignon G. *The Bayou Road.* 1979 Random House/ Warner 1987. During the Civil War, things were more than tense in New Orleans. Marcy Chastain was shocked when the man her family wanted her to marry was shot and killed. Then the handsome major, quartered in the house, was suspected. [Where There's A Will]

GRAYSON, Richard. *Death On The Cards.* 1988 St. Martin. The Sûreté has received a disturbing message. A number of men in Paris will be assassinated, including the president of the Republic. A playing card will announce the murder. Inspector Gautier gets to play every card in *his* deck. 7th. [Revenge]

HALL, Robert Lee. *Benjamin Franklin Takes The Case.* [Famous People]

HALL, Robert Lee. *Ben Franklin And A Case Of: Christmas Murder.* 1991 St. Martin. At a Christmas house party in London in 1757, wealthy Roderick Fairbrass collapsed and died while acting in a family play. A guest, Ben Franklin, is convinced it's a case of murder. Franklin is determined to uncover the truth. 2nd. [Christmas]

HAMBLEY, Barbara. *Those Who Hunt The Night.* [Vampire]

HELLER, Keith. *Man's Storm.* 1986 Scribner. The furious storm hit Winchester with a vengeance. While shopkeepers hurried to close up, a light burned in the ironmonger's shop. George Man, the parish watchman, will soon be investigating a murder. 2nd.

HILTON, John Buxton. *Slickensides.* [Getting Away With Murder]

JOHNSTON, Velda. *The Fateful Summer.* 1981 Dodd, Mead/ Warner 1987. It's 1910, and Emma is spending the summer with her friend Amanda on Long Island. When Amanda's foster father is found murdered, Michael, the man Amanda loves, is the first to be suspected.

MICHAELS, Barbara. *Wings Of The Falcon.* 1977 Dodd, Mead/ Berkley 1988. In 1880, when her father died, Francesca left England and journeyed to her mother's family in Italy. Her less-than-warm welcome is soon overshadowed by strange accidents, elusive secrets, and the appearance of the horseman known only as the Falcon.

PAUL, Raymond. *The Thomas Street Horror.* 1982 Viking/ Ballantine 1985. On April 10, 1836, in a New York City brothel, Helen Jewett was murdered with a hatchet. Criminal lawyer Lon Quinncannon is defending Richard Robinson for the crime. He leans heavily on one of the witnesses. 1st. [Prostitution]

PAUL, Raymond. *The Tragedy At Tiverton.* 1984 Viking/ Ballantine 1985. In 1832, Ephriam Avery was the first American minister to stand trial for murder. Lawyer Lon Quinncannon and his young assistant Christopher Randolph have the difficult task of defending him from the gallows. Except for outside interference, it would have been the perfect crime. 2nd. [Revenge]

ROBERTS, John Maddox. *SPQR.* Avon 1990/ PBO. Rome: 70 BC. Decius Caecilius Metellus serves on the Commission of Twenty-Six, investigating each morning the crimes of the city the previous night. A Thracian daggerman was found strangled in an alley. The first of a string of murders. 1st. [Political]

SHERBURNE, James. *Death's Pale Horse.* 1980 Houghton Mifflin/ Fawcett 1987. It's the 1880s in Saratoga Springs and the racing season is in full swing. Paddy Moretti has an eye on a beautiful young woman pushing a wheelchair. Between séances at the hotel and some high-level suspense at the racetrack, Paddy has both hands full. 1st. [Fraud]

SHERBURNE, James. *Death's Gray Angel.* 1981 Houghton Mifflin/ Fawcett 1987. The owner of the newspaper wants Paddy Moretti, sports columnist, to find out who conned his nephew and then get revenge. On the 1880s train to Kansas, Paddy finds the story of his life. 2nd. [Fraud]

SHERBURNE, James. *Death's Clenched Fist.* [Horse Racing]

SHERBURNE, James. *Death's White City.* [Horse Racing]

TEY, Josephine. *The Daughter Of Time.* [Richard III]

THOMAS, Donald. *Jekyll, Alias Hyde.* 1988 St. Martin. Scotland Yard Inspector Swaim has been turned loose on the Jekyll-Hyde mystery. Together with Sgt. Lumly, he follows a different path through London, and finds a different story.

TONE, Teona. *Full Cry.* 1985 Fawcett/ PBO. Nathaniel Howard was checking out the course the day before Race Weekend. They found him dead, his neck broken. Someone had wired the fence, spelling murder. Kyra Keaton, retired detective, feels she must investigate and steals a train. 2nd. [Drugs]

TOURNEY, Leonard. *The Bartholomew Fair Murders.* 1986 St. Martin/ Ballantine 1987. Queen Elizabeth I wants to attend the greatest fair in England. A puppeteer is murdered, and County Constable Matthew Stock is looking for the killer. But there's also a plot to kill the queen. 4th.

TOURNEY, Leonard. *Old Saxon Blood.* 1988 St. Martin/ Ballantine 1990. Queen Elizabeth I sends for Matthew Stock and his wife, Joan. They are to go to Derbyshire and look into the strange drowning of Sir John Challoner. The case becomes muddled when other deaths occur. 6th.

HOLIDAY FOR MURDER

Although Christmas is the most popular holiday on which to commit murder, we mustn't neglect the other days of celebration. They, too, can command the delight of the writer, as well as the reader, for an entertaining festival of mayhem.

ALDYNE, Nathan. *Slate.* [Gay]

ALEXANDER, Gary. *Kiet And The Golden Peacock.* [Art]

BLOCK, Lawrence. *When The Sacred Ginmill Closes.* [Fraud]

BOYLE, Thomas. *Post-Mortem Effects.* 1987 Viking/ Penguin 1988. It's Halloween, and Detective Frank De Sales' part of Brooklyn is going a litle crazy. A series of murders has him baffled and he's looking for some kind of connection. Then a young boy is kidnapped, and the chase is on. 2nd. [Psychological]

BURLEY, W. J. *Wycliffe And The Scapegoat.* 1978 Doubleday/ Avon 1987. Superintendent Charles Wycliffe took his wife to the coast for Halloween. As part of the festivities, a huge wheel is set ablaze and rolled into the sea. This year someone has tied onto the wheel the body of Jonathan Riddle. 8th. [Revenge]

DANIELS, Philip. *The Dracula Murders.* [Vampire]

DAVIS, Dorothy Salisbury. *Death Of An Old Sinner.* [Political]

DEAN, S. F. X. *Such Pretty Toys.* [Computer]

DEXTER, Colin. *The Secret Of Annexe 3.* 1987 St. Martin/ Bantam 1988. It was one of those New Year's Eve package deals for two at the Howorth Hotel. When the man in the Rastafarian costume is found dead in the hotel's annexe the next morning, Inspector Morse is called in. 7th. [Infidelity]

GREENBERG, Rosalind M., Martin Harry Greenberg, and Charles G. Waugh, eds. *Fourteen Vicious Valentines.* 1988 Avon/ PBO. February 14 is commemorated by this collection of fourteen tales of crime and horror.

HADDAM, Jane. *Precious Blood.* [Clergy]

HART, Carolyn G. *Deadly Valentine.* 1990 Doubleday/ Bantam 1991. Annie Laurence had no desire to attend Sydney Cahill's elaborate Valentine's Day bash. Especially since Sydney was chasing Max . . . and every other male on the island. To make matters worse, Max's mother has her eye on Sydney's husband. And now Sydney is dead. 6th. [Infidelity]

JEFFERS, H. Paul. *Rubout At The Onyx.* 1981 Ticknor & Fields/ Ballantine 1987. The Onyx Club was in full swing on New Year's Eve. But it wasn't noisy enough to drown out the shots when two hoods gunned down Joey Sedler. His widow is more than willing to pay PI Harry MacNeil to find out what is going on. 1st. [Jewels]

McCLINTICK, Malcolm. *Mary's Grave.* 1987 Doubleday/ Avon 1990. Investigating reports of a scream in the night, Detectives Kelso and Smith find, in a clearing outside St. Luke's Church, an old grave with a hand on top of it. Was the ghost of Mary Carter on the prowl this Halloween? 1st. [Witches]

McCRUMB, Sharyn. *Highland Laddie Gone.* [Imposter]

MICHAELS, Barbara. *Prince Of Darkness.* 1969 Meredith/ Berkley 1988. Dr. Kate More studied ancient folklore. When writer Peter Stewart came to town, she was suddenly caught up in the subject of her own work. It's Halloween and her life is threatened. [Imposter]

PULVER, Mary Monica. *Murder At The War.* 1987 St. Martin. At the Annual War for the Society for Creative Anachronism, Lord Thorston died in the deep woods, stabbed with an ice pick. One of his dying words was "mundane." It's up to Lord Stefan to marshal the evidence and find a murderer. 1st. [Blackmail]

RESNICOW, Herbert. *The Crossword Code.* [Crossword Puzzles]

RIGGS, John R. *The Last Laugh.* 1983 Dembner/ St. Martin 1988. It was April Fool's Day, and Si Buckles was dead. Garth Ryland, *Oglalla Reporter,* was doing a feature story on him. He finds in Si's diaries a lot of material for a column. Reports start coming in that Si has been seen around town, and two men are quickly dead. 1st. [Revenge]

SERAFIN, David. *The Body In Cadiz Bay.* [Intrigue]

SHANKMAN, Sarah aka Alice Storey. *Now Let's Talk Of Graves* [Journalism]

SMITH, Alison. *Someone Else's Grave.* 1984 St. Martin/ Critic's Choice 1986. For more than forty years, Miss Adams had gotten up early on Memorial Day and driven to Mount Morish Cemetery to decorate each grave. But this morning one of the graves is disturbed. For Police Chief Judd Springfield, this is just the first of several murders he will have to solve. [Revenge]

SMITH, Julie. *New Orleans Mourning.* 1990 St. Martin/ Ivy 1991. As the float came down St. Charles Street, carrying Rex, King of the Carnival, rookie cop Skip Langdon watched Dolly Parton on the second floor balcony pull a gun and fire off a shot. Now she'll have to tell Mrs. Chauncey St. Amant that her husband is dead. [Getting Away With Murder]

THAYER, Nancy. *Spirit Lost.* [Witches]

THOREAU, David. *The Good Book.* [Ball Games]

TURNBULL, Peter. *Two Way Cut.* [Arson]

WENDER, Theodora. *Murder Gets A Degree.* [Academic]

WILTZ, Chris. *A Diamond Before You Die.* [Gay]

HOLLYWOOD

In the land where more things happen on the streets and in the restaurants than on the screen, it's no wonder that the atmosphere is ripe for murder. Hollywood still reels over a variety of old crimes and unsolved murders, some stranger than anything that ever showed up at the movies. And even when the film crew goes on location, it's still "Hollywood."

BABSON, Marian. *Reel Murder.* 1987 St. Martin/ Bantam 1988. Silent film star Eve Sinclair and her friend Trixie Dolan went to London for a retrospective of Eve's films. Then someone started using scenes from the old movies as murder themes. The two aging women delight in playing detective. 1st. [Jealousy]

DE FELITTA, Frank. *Funeral March.* Bantam 1991/ PBO. William Hasbrouk died jogging on the beach, victim of a toy airplane loaded with explosives. After another death, Lt. Fred Santomassima, LAPD, discovers a pattern to the murders. But can he stop the next one? [Serial Killers]

FLIEGEL, Richard. *The Next To Die.* 1986 Bantam/ PBO. NYPD officer Shelly Lowenkopf had a little trouble. So his captain sent him off to Hollywood to be the police consultant on a film. He's plagued with difficulties and then finds the charred body of the film's director on the beach.

HAYES, Helen & Thomas Chastain. *Where The Truth Lies.* 1988 Morrow/ Knightsbridge 1990. It was Oscar night and TV viewers watched producer Arthur Strickland; he had a knife in his back and his Oscar at his side. Lt. John Staver is convinced the murderer is someone from Strickland's last film. Helen Hayes will help him find a killer. [Revenge]

HENDERSON, M. R. *The Killing Game.* 1989 St. Martin/ St. Martin 1990. It was going to be her big chance. Jeanne Donovan was hired as assistant director on a new film about a serial killer. Then someone starts following the script, body for body, and Jeanne's name is the next one on the list. [Serial Killers]

JACOBS, Nancy Baker. *Deadly Companion.* 1986 Dell/ PBO. Estelle Edwards, an old movie star, is bedridden. In desperation, she hires a live-in nurse to look after her. When things become aberrant, Estelle has to fight for her own life. [Medical]

KAISER, Ronn. *Made In Beverly Hills.* [Revenge]

KAMINSKY, Stuart. *The Fala Factor.* [Famous People]

McCONNER, Vincent. *The Man Who Knew Hammett.* 1988 Tor. Eighty-one-year-old PI Zeke Gahagan wanted one more good case before he died. Faye Manning gave him the chance. She wants him to find actor Lawrence Knight, who's disappeared. His remembrance of Hammett keeps him going. [Old Crime]

McGOWN, Jill. *Murder Movie.* 1990 St. Martin. Director Frank Derwent took his crew to Scotland to film *Three Clear Sundays,* a movie about a murder. Wanda, his wife, was the first to die. Next, his mistress Barbara. Then Detective Hugh Patterson is pulled off the case when he becomes involved with one of the suspects. [Infidelity]

PALMER, Stuart. *The Puzzle Of The Happy Hooligan.* 1941 Doubleday/ Bantam 1986. What a fluke. Schoolteacher Hildegarde Withers is in Hollywood as consultant on a movie. She lands right in the middle of the murder of Saul Stafford, half of a screenwriting team. 8th. [Old Crime]

RAY, Robert. *Bloody Murdock.* 1986 St. Martin/ Penguin 1987. Gayla Jean Kirkwood panted after the "good life," and no one expected her to die in a fiery crash. Her sister Meg arrives for the funeral, and Matt Murdock decides to help her find her sister's killer. 1st. [Pornography]

SANDERS, George. *Crime On My Hands.* 1944 Simon & Schuster/ International Polygonics 1990. Tired of playing detective, George Sanders agrees to star in the film *Seven Dreams,* a western. As Sanders rides into the big scene, shots ring out and there's a dead body not in the script. As the man holding the gun, he has to clear his own name. [Where There's A Will]

SERRIAN, Michael. *Fatal Exit.* Bantam 1991/ PBO. Director Neal Kane has trouble on the Mexico set of *Jungle Rot.* Film editor Matt Walker is doing everything he can to save the film. Wading through interference after interference, Matt has to track Kane down in his Mexican hideout. [Political]

STINSON, Jim. *Double Exposure.* 1985 Scribner/ Bantam 1988. Denise Tolman's little girl showed up in a porno film, and someone wants Denise to part with $50,000 for the original tape. What *Denise* wants is for Stoney Winston to get that tape. 1st. [Pornography]

STINSON, Jim. *Low Angles.* 1986 Scribner/ Bantam 1988. Stoney Winston was hired to ghost-direct a film. It was a low-budget biker movie having problems. It looks like someone wants to make sure the film never reaches the theaters. 2nd. [Revenge]

THOMPSON, Gene. *Murder Mystery.* 1980 Random House/ Ballantine 1989. Dade Cooley, San Francisco lawyer, told Rachael he'd come to Los Angeles for her stepmother's funeral. Then Rachael's father died, and Dade doesn't like the way things are shaping up. 1st. [Father]

THOMPSON, Gene. *Nobody Cared For Kate.* 1983 Random House/ Ballantine 1989. Kate Mulvaney was on a barge trip through France with her famous Hollywood relatives. Scared, she called her lawyer Dade Cooley. Before Dade reached France, Kate was dead and there was a murder to investigate. 2nd. [Where There's A Will]

UPTON, Robert. *Fade Out.* 1984 Viking/ Penguin 1986. The call came for PI Amos McGuffin from New York City. It was Ben Volper's father. Ben had just left a suicide note and walked into the Pacific. His father doesn't believe it, not his successful movie-producer son. Amos's job—find Ben Volper. 1st. [Suicide]

WESTBROOK, Robert. *Lady Left.* 1991 Crown. On vacation in Nicaragua, Beverly Hills police lieutenant Nicky Rachmanoff met Cory Heard, a radical Hollywood producer. When Cory vanishes, Nicky follows a path back to Beverly Hills and into the arms of Cory's activist wife. 3rd. [Political]

HORSES AND HORSE RACING

Dick Francis got the ball rolling with his mysteries about horse racing. Others have followed. There are now a number of murders committed around a racetrack, on both sides of the Atlantic, for big money, fixed races, and sometimes just for revenge.

ADAMSON, Lydia. *A Cat In The Manger.* [Cats]

ANDERSON, Virginia. *King Of The Roses.* 1983 St. Martin/ Bantam 1989. Jockey Chris England is about to ride the favorite in his sixth Kentucky Derby. He's just been offered a quarter million dollars not to win. Chris is up against a tough bunch, as well as murder.

ANDERSON, Virginia. *Blood Ties.* Bantam 1989/ PBO. Ted Whyse, exercise rider, drove back to Kentucky when he heard that his friend, jockey Alejo Aloso, was dead. The police called the trailer fire an accident, but

Ted's convinced it's murder. Now he's plunged into secrets from the past.

BIRKETT, John. *The Last Private Eye.* 1988 Avon/ PBO. Carl Walsh was missing. Kathleen Sullivan, TV reporter, wants Louisville PI Michael Rineheart to find him. Walsh had told Kathleen he had a story, something to do with the Derby. Three bodies later, Michael watches as justice is served. 1st.

BIRKETT, John. *The Queen's Mare.* Avon 1990/ PBO. PI Michael Rineheart was hired by the Grande Dame of the Bluegrass Country, Mrs. Hattie Beaumont, to deliver a million dollars to ransom a priceless mare and her foal. But something goes wrong. 2nd. [Revenge]

BURKEY, Dave. *Rain Lover.* 1985 Ballantine/ PBO. Ash Kramer came home just in time to hear about Rain Lover, a surefire horse. When Rain Lover collapses at the end of his first race and trainer Eddie Billman is murdered, Ash has to poke into it.

CHRISTOPHER, Paula. *The Dreaming Pool.* 1987 Dell/ PBO. Triple Crown winner Ganymede is missing. There's been no ransom note. Is the motive revenge? Psychic Eslin Hillary agrees to help Gage Roundtree and his brother find the horse, a search laced with danger. [Psychic]

FRANCIS, Dick. *Smokescreen.* [Africa]

FRANCIS, Dick. *The Danger.* 1984 Putnam/ Fawcett 1986. Andrew Douglas had a specialized job: finding people who were kidnapped. And someone is keeping him busy. Alessia Cenci, famous girl jockey, was the first to vanish. Then the daughter of a Derby-winning jockey and the senior steward of the Jockey Club are missing. [Kidnapping]

FRANCIS, Dick. *Break In.* 1986 Putnam/ Fawcett 1987. Kit Fielding's brother-in-law is in a lot of trouble and that hurts his twin sister, too. Two scandal sheets are printing stories about some horse trainers who are about to go under. Kit wants to know where they got their information. 1st. [Journalism]

FRANCIS, Dick. *Bolt.* 1987 Putnam/ Fawcett 1988. Someone is shooting horses with a "humane killer." Kit Fielding wants him stopped. As soon as Kit has one mystery solved, he finds another loose end that only a silent trip to the stables will resolve. 2nd. [Fraud]

FRANCIS, Dick. *Hot Money.* 1988 Putnam/ Fawcett 1989. Moira died in the greenhouse, her head stuffed in the potting soil. Then several attempts were made on the life of Malcolm Pembroke. He needs his jockey son, Ian, to find out what's going on. It's a large family to check out. [Father]

GELLER, Michael. *Dead Last.* 1986 Dell/ PBO. Kenneth Eagle, jockey, got the message clearly: lose all six races today or you won't get your daughter back. He did as he was told and was suspended. Then a trainer was shot to death. Ken wants to know who's behind it.

KENNEALY, Jerry. *Polo's Ponies.* 1988 St. Martin. Nick Polo was at Golden Gate Fields racetrack. On a trip to the men's room, he stumbles over the body of a small-time hood. Now he finds the body of a prospective employer, clearly marked with horse's hooves. 3rd.

MITCHELL, James. *Dead Ernest.* 1987 Holt. Ron Hoggert, London PI, was hired by the wealthy Imogen. She wants him to find two things for her: her horse and her fiancé, in that order. Ron gathers up his sidekick, Dave, and they go to work.

MORGAN, Kate. *A Slay At The Races.* Berkley 1990/ PBO. Librarian Dewey James knew just about everything that happened in Hamilton. It was a bit of a surprise to her that Leslie Downing was using a professional jockey for the annual charity race. Then Leslie's fiancé was found dead in the stall of a racehorse. 1st. [Real Estate]

MURRAY, William. *Tip On A Dead Crab.* 1984 Viking/ Penguin 1985. When Shifty Anderson wasn't performing his magic act, he hung around the racetrack, his real passion. Shifty met the beautiful Marina and found himself in the middle of a racing scam. 1st.

MURRAY, William. *The Hard Knocker's Luck.* [Art]

MURRAY, William. *When The Fat Man Sings.* [Revenge]

MURRAY, William. *The Getaway Blues.* 1990 Bantam/ Bantam 1991. Wealthy Lucius J. Bedlington has been planning his own death for months. He doesn't even go to the Winner's Circle when his horses come in first. Shifty Lou Anderson takes a part-time job driving Lucius around and stumbles into a sinister plot. 5th. [Fraud]

PALMER, Stuart. *The Puzzle Of The Red Stallion.* 1935 Doubleday/ Bantam 1987. Hildegarde Withers was walking her dog on the bridle path in Central Park when she came across the body of a young woman. The police saw it as a terrible accident, thrown from her horse. Hildegarde sees murder. 6th. [Revenge]

SHERBURNE, James. *Death's Clenched Fist.* 1982 Houghton Mifflin/ Fawcett 1987. It started out as an innocent prank: Paddy was going to smuggle a woman into McSorley's Bar. He ends up in the arms of a beautiful anarchist. When Marya is accused of murder, Paddy knows better. He'll be in deep trouble before this is straightened out. 3rd. [Historical]

SHERBURNE, James. *Death's White City.* 1988 Fawcett/PBO. Paddy Moretti is in Chicago to cover the American Derby. The beautiful woman he met on the train has disappeared, and there's something fishy about the race. Paddy has to juggle both mysteries at the same time. 4th. [Historical]

I . . . IS FOR

IMPOSTER

WHILE MOST OF US would find it fairly difficult or inconvenient to change our identity, in the mystery story people are, very frequently, not who they present themselves to be. The character may take on a false identity or may actually be impersonating someone else. Or one person may be mistaken for another. The mode chosen will fit the crime. Sometimes it can be funny. Sometimes it can be deadly.

ALLINGHAM, Margery. *The China Governess.* [Father]

BARNARD, Robert. *Death Of A Literary Widow.* [Writer]

BRAUN, Lilian Jackson. *The Cat Who Sniffed Glue.* [Cats]

CANNELL, Dorothy. *The Thin Woman.* [Cooks]

CARR, John Dickson. *Hag's Nook.* 1933 Harper & Row/ International Polygonics 1985. It seemed that the curse had returned. For Martin Starberth was dead; a fall from a balcony had broken his neck. It takes Dr. Gideon Fell to find out the truth. 1st.

CHASTAIN, Thomas. *The Case Of Too Many Murders.* [Lawyer]

CHRISTIE, Agatha. *The Body In The Library.* [Library]

CLARKE, Anna. *The Mystery Lady.* [Writer]

CORRINGTON, John William, and Joyce H. Corrington. *A Project Named Desire.* [Father]

D'ALTON, Martina. *Fatal Finish.* 1982 Walker/ Walker 1987. While Harry Liggett was running the New York City marathon, his friend Frank was trying to rescue a cat. Then Frank was dead, four floors below. Harry is convinced it's murder, but he'll have to run again to catch the killer.

DEXTER, Colin. *The Dead Of Jericho.* [Blackmail]

DISNEY, Doris Miles. *Do Not Fold, Spindle, Or Mutilate.* 1970 Doubleday/ Zebra 1987. At fifty-eight, Sophie was still playing the clown. She got her bridge club to fill in a computer dating card. The letters started to arrive. And then Sophie was dead.

DUNLAP, Susan. *Not Exactly A Brahmin.* [Fraud]

ELKINS, Aaron. *Old Bones.* 1987 Mysterious/ Mysterious 1988. Gideon Oliver was lecturing on forensics when a prominent Breton was accidently drowned at Mont-St.-Michel. Shortly after, parts of a skeleton are found under stone flooring at the Breton's home. Gideon investigates. 4th. [Anthropology]

ELKINS, Aaron. *Icy Clutches.* [Anthropology]

FISH, Robert. *Brazilian Sleigh Ride.* 1965 Simon & Schuster/ Foul Play 1988. Captain Jose Da Silva was meeting the plane to arrest a man suspected of embezzling bonds. His friend was meeting his old army buddy. They're both waiting for the same man. But Jimmy Martin wasn't on the plane. 5th. [Fraud]

GIROUX, E. X. *A Death For A Dancer.* [Blackmail]

GRAFTON, Sue. *"G" Is For Gumshoe.* [Mother]

HART, Roy. *Breach Of Promise.* [Suicide]

HEALY, Jeremiah. *The Staked Goat.* 1986 Harper & Row/Pocket 1987. An old army buddy called Boston PI John Cuddy about getting together. Instead, John had to identify him at the morgue—a body with a silent message. Cuddy takes matters into his own hands to find his friend's killer. 1st. [Old Crime]

HIGGINS, Joan. *A Little Death Music.* [Music]

JEFFRIES, Roderic. *Relatively Dangerous.* 1987 St. Martin. A car crashed in the mountains of Majorca and a man died. Inspector Alverez isn't convinced that bad driving caused the accident. As he plods through the case, he finds that few people are saddened by the death. 9th. [Fraud]

KAMINSKY, Stuart. *Red Chameleon.* [Russian]

LEE, Elsie. *Mansion Of Golden Windows.* 1988 Zebra/ PBO. Aunt Agnes all but insisted that Sable Lennox visit her ancestral home in Scotland. When Sable arrived, things felt strange, and bits and pieces didn't seem to fit the family history. She was finally convinced when someone tried to kill her.

LEMARCHAND, Elizabeth. *Who Goes Home?* [On Vacation]

MacLEOD, Charlotte. *The Withdrawing Room.* 1980 Doubleday/ Avon 1981. As a new widow, Sarah Kelling has turned her hand to making money, in a genteel manner, by renting rooms. The gentleman that has the withdrawing room ends up in front of a subway train at Haymarket Square. Max, now smitten with Sarah, is there to help. 2nd. [Where There's A Will]

MARON, Margaret. *Death In Blue Folders.* [Blackmail]

MARON, Margaret. *The Right Jack.* Bantam 1988/ PBO. At a cribbage tournament at a New York City hotel, two men finished the first game. One of them pegged the win on the cribbage board. The board exploded and both men died. Lt. Sigrid Harald, NYPD, has to find out which one of them was the intended victim. 4th. [Old Crime]

MATERA, Lia. *A Radical Departure.* 1988 Bantam/ PBO. At a law firm luncheon, Willa's boss and old friend sampled the garnish from his dessert and died a few hours later of hemlock poisoning. From that moment on, wherever Willa goes, death follows. She becomes suspect number one. 2nd. [Lawyer]

MATTHEWS, Patricia. *Mirrors.* 1988 Worldwide/ PBO. She'd arrived in Connecticut at the age of sixteen; she had no name and no past. Now, as Julie Malone, she was headed for Florida. They told her she was Suellen Devereaux. There was a series of accidents, and Julie was fighting to stay alive.

McCRUMB, Sharyn. *Highland Laddie Gone.* Ballantine 1991/ PBO. Elizabeth MacPherson was at the Western Virginia Scottish Festival with the clan mascot, a bobcat. The clans are still skirmishing, and a Campbell ends up dead. Elizabeth, together with a real Scot, uses her knowledge of culture to find the answer. 3rd. [Holiday]

McCRUMB, Sharyn. *Paying The Piper.* [Anthropology]

McGILL, E. J. *Immaculate In Black.* 1991 St. Martin. Wealthy, spoiled Shelly Egan liked to play games. After a call to 911 claiming someone was trying to break into her Tucson home, she was found dead: raped and strangled. Sherm Sherman is hired to defend Shelly's uncle of the crime. [Computers]

McIVER, N. J. *Come Back, Alice Smythereene!* [Writers]

MICHAELS, Barbara. *Prince Of Darkness.* [Holiday]

PENN, John. *A Deadly Sickness.* [Where There's A Will]

PENTECOST, Hugh. *Death By Fire.* [Arson]

PETERS, Elizabeth. *Die For Love.* [Writers]

PICKARD, Nancy. *Bum Steer.* [Where There's A Will]

PORTER, Anna. *Mortal Sins.* [Journalism]

PRATHER, Richard S. *The Kubla Khan Caper.* 1988 Tor/PBO. The Kubla Khan Hotel is about to open in Palm Desert, and one of the women in the beauty contest is missing. Monaco, the owner, hires Shell Scott to find her. Shell finds her dead, and a wealthy man is found shot. The case is taking too many turns. 24th. [Blackmail]

ROBERTS, Les. *An Infinite Number Of Monkeys.* [Mystery Writer]

TAYLOR, Andrew. *An Old School Tie.* 1986 Dodd, Mead/Penguin 1987. William Dougal saw the announcement of Hanbury's wedding in the *Times*. Seven weeks later, William read the bride's obituary. Hanbury asked William to look into Molly's death. Everyone is sure he's killed her. 3rd. [Old Crime]

THOMSON, June. *The Spoils Of Time.* 1989 Doubleday. They had all gathered at Howlett Hall where the elderly Edgar Aston lay dying of a massive stroke. Suddenly, in burst Rollo Saxby. He'd come to patch up an old feud with his childhood friend. In less than twelve hours, Inspector Rudd has two bodies and lots of questions. 12th. [Mother]

WENTWORTH, Patricia. *Dead Or Alive.* [Intrigue]

WILLIAMS, David. *Treasure In Roubles.* [Art]

WREN, M. K. *Curiosity Didn't Kill The Cat.* 1973 Doubleday/ Ballantine 1988. Someone is watching Conan Flagg's bookstore in the Oregon resort town, and he doesn't know why. A man dies on the beach, and Flagg discovers there's something fishy going on with his lending library. 1st. [Bookstore]

WRIGHT, Eric. *Death In The Old Country.* [On Vacation]

INCEST

Incest is such a nasty subject that most of us would rather shun it altogether. The victim is damaged and the community is shocked and broken when the truth emerges. Those who could have prevented it are shamed. But what of unknowing incest? What could be more deadly?

BARNES, Linda. *The Snake Tattoo.* 1989 St. Martin/Fawcett 1990. Jerry Toland was concerned about his friend and neighbor Valerie. She was missing from Emerson School and only Jerry seemed to care. He hires PI Carlotta Carlyle to find her. 2nd.

CORRIS, Peter. *The Dying Trade.* [Australian]

DUNDEE, Wayne D. *The Skintight Shroud.* [Pornography]

GEORGE, Elizabeth. *A Great Deliverance.* [Children]

GIROUX, E. X. *A Death For A Dilettante.* [Lawyer]

GRAFTON, Sue. *"E" Is For Evidence.* [Insurance]

GRAHAM, Caroline. *The Killings At Badger's Drift.* Avon 1989/ PBO. Miss Lucy Bellringer called in at the police station. She insists that Inspector Barnaby look into her friend's death. But more people will die in the village of Badger's Drift before Barnaby finds his answers. 1st. [Blackmail]

GREENAN, Russell H. *A Can Of Worms.* [Blackmail]

HOOPER, Kay. *Crime Of Passion.* Avon 1991/ PBO. Lane Montana finds things and people. A late-night message on her answering machine sends her to the Atlanta home of wealthy Jeffrey Townsend. She finds him stabbed on a peach couch in his living room. Soon Lane is seductively drawn into the investigation. 1st. [Father]

MANN, Jessica. *A Kind Of Healthy Grave.* [Art]

MATHIS, Edward. *Out Of the Shadows.* [Missing Person]

MOODY, Susan. *Penny Pinching.* [Black Detective]

PERRY, Anne. *Rutland Place.* [Victorian]

RENDELL, Ruth. *An Unkindness Of Ravens.* 1986 Pantheon/ Ballantine 1987. Rodney Williams was missing, and Inspector Wexford said he'd look into it. As he does, he discovers the family has a vast number of secrets. When Rodney's body is found, Wexford starts asking questions all over again. 13th. [Psychological]

REYNOLDS, William J. *Moving Targets.* [Father]

SIMPSON, Dorothy. *Last Seen Alive.* 1985 Scribner/ Bantam 1986. Alice Parnell died at the Black Swan—strangled. She'd just returned to the town where she'd grown up. Inspector Luke Thanet is forced to dig up past history to find out why she was murdered. 5th.

SIMS, L. V. *Death Is A Family Affair.* [Witches]

TAPPLY, William G. *Dead Winter.* [Lawyer]

WILCOX, Collin. *Night Games.* [Children]

WOOLRICH, Cornell. *Into The Night.* 1987 Mysterious/ Mysterious 1988. Madeline held the gun to her temple and pulled the trigger on an empty chamber. As she checks the gun, she fires it out the window, and the bullet hits a young woman, who dies in her arms. She vows to do whatever the woman wanted most to do.

YORKE, Margaret. *Evidence To Destroy.* [Revenge]

INDIANS

There is still some exotic quality about the Indians of North America and the Indian way of life. The religious practices are closer to nature, and life appears less complicated. But on closer examination we find a vast complexity of beliefs and intricate patterns of behavior. The mystery story draws on some of these nuances.

BURKE, James Lee. *Black Cherry Blues.* 1989 Little, Brown/ Avon 1990. Against his better judgment, Dave Robicheaux leaves his bayou country and heads for Montana. There's something going on with some oil leases and two Indians are missing. 4th. [Fraud]

HAGER, Jean. *Night Walker.* 1990 St. Martin. Graham Thornton, owner of the lodge in Buckskin, was found dead in the car of one of his employees on a very snowy night. Chief Mitch Bushyhead has almost more suspects than he can deal with. 2nd. [Mother]

HILLERMAN, Tony. *The Blessing Way.* 1970 Harper & Row/ Avon 1978. Ellen Leon wandered onto the Navajo Reservation looking for her missing boyfriend. Soon Lt. Joe Leaphorn, from Law and Order, was involved, and so was murder and witchcraft. 1st. [Anthropology]

INDIANS

HILLERMAN, Tony. *People Of Darkness.* 1980 Harper & Row/ Avon 1982. Why would anyone want to kill an old Indian who was already dying of cancer? Then a box of old rocks is stolen, and the owner will pay dearly for its return. Sgt. Jim Chee follows a cold trail and finds a false identity. 1st. [Anthropology]

HILLERMAN, Tony. *The Dark Wind.* 1982 Harper & Row/Avon 1983. A small plane crashed in a deserted part of the Navajo Reservation. Soon several men were dead, and Sgt. Jim Chee of the Tribal Police was awash in witchcraft and drugs. 2nd. [Anthropology]

HILLERMAN, Tony. *The Ghostway.* [Witness Protection Program]

HILLERMAN, Tony. *Skinwalker.* 1986 Harper & Row/ Harper & Row 1987. Three men have died on the Navajo Reservation and there's more than a hint of witchcraft. Joe Leaphorn and Jim Chee of the Tribal Police are working from different parts of the reservation to solve the case. 8th. [Anthropology]

HILLERMAN, Tony. *A Thief Of Time.* 1988 Harper & Row/ Harper & Row 1990. Archaeologist Dr. Eleanor Freedman-Bernal was angry when she got to Many Ruins Canyon and found burial sites recently disturbed. Tribal Police Joe Leaphorn and Jim Chee get the report that she's now missing. 9th. [Anthropology]

HILLERMAN, Tony. *Talking God.* 1989 Harper & Row/ Harper Collins 1991. Smithsonian conservator Highhawk was arrested by Jim Chee for grave robbing while Joe Leaphorn was trying to identify the body of a man found near the railroad tracks. So far, all leads take both Chee and Leaphorn to Washington, DC, and the Smithsonian. 10th. [Anthropology]

HOYT, Richard. *Fish Story.* 1985 Viking/ Tor 1987. Melinda Prettybird, a young Indian woman, is convinced that her ex-husband is responsible for the beating of her boyfriend. She wants PI John Denson to find out. And what does it have to do with the lawsuit concerning fishing rights?

McBRIARTY, Douglas. *Whitewater VI.* [Smuggling]

McBRIARTY, Douglas. *Carolina Gold.* 1990 St. Martin. Terry and Stacey arrived in the small Carolina mountain town to open "Carolina Gold," a jewelry shop. They had located a vein of gold for use in the shop. With Terry missing, Sheriff McPhee and his Cherokee deputy Billy Birdsong are looking for a gold-hungry killer. 3rd. [Missing Person]

McCORMICK, Claire. *Murder In Cowboy Bronze.* 1986 Walker. John Waltz took his spring vacation in Ember Hills, Arizona. After all, his novelist mother wants him to meet her fiancé, Navajo jewelry designer Jefferson Horse. In just a few days, sculptor Cal Morefield is found shot and then beaten with one of his own bronzes. 3rd. [Art]

McCRUMB, Sharyn. *Lovely In Her Bones.* 1985 Avon/ PBO. Elizabeth MacPherson was taking a summer course in Folk Medicine in Appalachia. Her assignment was to find three woodland herbs. Instead, she found a skull. Hired by the Cullowhee Tribe for a real dig, she turns up a whole body. 2nd. [Anthropology]

MOORE, Barbara. *The Wolf Whispered Death.* 1986 St. Martin/ Dell 1988. An old man died, just off the Navajo Reservation, killed by a wolf. The Benally family is suspected of witchcraft. Unconvinced, Sam Benally asked his friend Gordon Christy to help track down the murderer and put superstitions to rest. 2nd. [Dogs]

SATTERTHWAIT, Walter. *At Ease With The Dead.* 1990 St. Martin/ Worldwide 1991. On a fishing trip, Joshua

Croft saves an old Indian from bullying red-necks. A short time later, the Indian, Daniel Begay, enters Croft's office. He wants him to locate a skeleton taken from the Navajo Reservation in 1925. It must be returned to its resting place. 2nd. [Old Crime]

STERN, Richard Martin. *Tangled Murders.* 1989 Pocket/ PBO. Charlie Harrington, a young computer genius, was found dead of a shotgun blast in a ditch. Then the Cathcart house was broken into and trashed, and Mr. Cathcart ended up in the hospital. The man who was supposed to be house-sitting is missing. Lt. Johnny Ortiz is perplexed. 4th. [Computer]

STERN, Richard Martin. *You Don't Need An Enemy.* Pocket 1989/ PBO. They found wealthy Miss Lucy Carruthers dead on the polished tile floor in her Santo Cristo home. Beside the dried blood were dusty footprints. Detective Johnny Ortiz investigates the town's darker side while trying to keep Cassie from being killed. 2nd. [Smuggling]

STERN, Richard Martin. *Interloper.* Pocket 1990/ PBO. FBI agent Walter Higgins showed up at the police station to ask Johnny Ortiz about Leon Bascomb, a newcomer to Santo Cristo. A few days later, Higgins was found dead by hikers. Now Johnny has to get involved. 7th. [Drugs]

YARBRO, C. Q. *Bad Medicine.* 1976 Putnam/ Jove 1990. Charlie Moon, Ojibwa Indian, is partner in a San Francisco law firm. His friend Dr. Miranda Trobridge retains him. She's being sued for malpractice in the death of a young boy. Charlie suspects something sinister behind the boy's death. 1st. [Medical]

INFIDELITY

Since infidelity has been with us almost forever and has played an important part in history, theater, and literature, it would be expected to be a theme in the murder mystery. The trials, the torment, and the frictions add up to murder.

ADAMS, Harold. *When Rich Men Die.* 1987 Doubleday/Avon 1988. Wealthy Oren Fletcher vanished in Mexico. His young wife, Daphne, hired unemployed investigative reporter Kyle Champion to find him, dead or alive. Kyle discovered that several of Fletcher's friends prefer "dead." 1st.

ANDERSON, James. *Additional Evidence.* 1988 Doubleday. Linda Matthews was strangled in her apartment at the wealthy Fermouth seaside resort. Stephen Grant, a literary agent, is arrested. He was Linda's lover. Grant's wife, Alison, and Linda's brother Roger, of Scotland Yard, are determined to clear his name. [Revenge]

BABSON, Marian. *In The Teeth Of Adversity.* [Medical]

BOROWITZ, Albert. *This Club Frowns On Murder.* 1990 St. Martin. After a fire at their home, Paul and Alice Prye are staying at the Alumni Club in New York City. Some of the members start receiving condolence letters when their spouses are very much alive. But when a member accidently falls from a balcony, Paul is invited to investigate. 2nd. [Revenge]

CAUDWELL, Sarah. *The Sirens Sang Of Murder.* [Lawyer]

COHEN, Charles. *Silver Linings.* [Christmas]

COKER, Carolyn. *The Balmoral Nude.* [Art]

CORMANY, Michael. *Lost Daughter.* 1988 Lyle Stuart. Terrance Dawson hired Chicago PI Dan Kruger to find his missing teenage daughter, Asia. But Asia doesn't want to stay found, especially when there are a couple of bodies around. [Missing Person]

CRIDER, Bill. *Death On The Move.* 1989 Walker/ Ivy 1990. Clyde Ballinger, from the local funeral home, wants Sheriff Dan Rhodes to find out who's stealing the jewelry from the bodies he's prepared for burial. Then a rash of house break-ins leads to a body wrapped like a mummy. 4th. [Jewels]

DEAN, S. F. X. *It Can't Be My Grave.* 1983 Walker/ Tor 1987. While in England to publicize his book, Professor Neil Kelly is asked to authenticate an anonymous sixteenth-century play. Gordon Fairly, the owner of the MS, is killed soon after. Neil has to look beyond the old MS to find the murderer. 4th. [Manuscript]

DEXTER, Colin. *Last Bus To Woodstock.* 1975 St. Martin/ Bantam 1989. Sylvia Kaye was found murdered in the parking lot outside of the *Black Prince* pub. Her ride with a stranger was a fatal one. But two girls, waiting at the bus stop, were seen getting into that car. Inspector Morse has to find the missing girl and the murderer. 1st. [Jealousy]

DEXTER, Colin. *The Secret Of Annexe 3.* [Holiday]

DISNEY, Doris Miles. *Three's A Crowd.* 1971 Doubleday/ Zebra 1987. Julie ran home to Virginia and her older sister Alix. Because of her drinking and being married three times, Julie was denied control of her money. Now Alix, in charge of the trust, is dead and Julie's out cold, a gun on the floor beside her chair.

DOBYNS, Stephen. *Saratoga Snapper.* 1986 Viking/ Penguin 1987. Saratoga PI Charlie Bradshaw is moonlighting as night manager at the Bently Hotel. His partner Victor is taking pictures of the tourists. Then Victor's camera is stolen and someone tries to run him down. 4th.

ECCLES, Marjorie. *Requiem For A Dove.* 1990 Doubleday. Elderly Marion Dove was found floating in the canal near the lock keepers' house where she lived. As Inspector Gil Mayo investigates, he discovers Marion had more than her own share of secrets. 3rd. [Mother]

FRIEDMAN, Mickey. *A Temporary Ghost.* [Writer]

GAULT, William Campbell. *Come Die With Me.* 1959 Random House/ Charter 1987. Gloria Malone thinks her jockey husband might be playing around, and she wants Brock Callahan to find out for sure. When Tip is found dead at the lake house, the case becomes something entirely different for Brock. 4th.

HART, Carolyn G. *Deadly Valentine.* [Holiday For Murder]

HENSLEY, Joe L. *Robak's Cross.* [Lawyer]

HOLT, Hazel. *Mrs. Malory Investigates.* [Real Estate]

JONES, Cleo. *The Case Of The Fragmented Woman.* [Television]

KELLERMAN, Faye. *Milk And Honey.* 1990 Morrow/ Fawcett 1991. Peter Decker was returning home late one night when he discovered a small girl in a strange yard. The only clue to her identity is a cluster of bee stings. As Peter investigates he discovers a family slaughtered. 3rd. [Real Estate]

KENYON, Michael. *A Free-Range Wife.* 1983 Doubleday/ Avon 1988. Although on holiday in France, Inspector Peckover was asked to call in on Mrs. Mercy McClusky, to help interpret. It seems that a former lover had turned up dead. Soon there was a rash of murders and they all had one thing in common: Mercy. 2nd. [On Vacation]

KRICH, Rochelle Majer. *Where's Mommy Now?* [Medical]

McCLINTICK, Malcolm. *The Key.* [Revenge]

McCLINTICK, Malcolm. *Death Of An Old Flame.* 1988 Doubleday/ Avon 1989. George Kelso, Clairmont PD, ran into an old flame, Clara Ott. A few days later Clara found her husband shot twice. Kelso winds up with the case and finds the world full of liars. 3rd. [Christmas]

McGOWN, Jill. *Murder Movie.* [Hollywood]

McINERNY, Ralph. *Basket Case.* 1987 St. Martin/ St. Martin 1988. After a messy divorce, Connie Rush left her baby at St. Hilary's with a note to Father Dowling to take care of him. Within days, the baby's father is murdered and a whole family is in absolute distress. 11th. [Clergy]

McINERNY, Ralph. *Cause And Effect.* [Medical]

McMULLEN, Mary. *Funny, Jonas, You Don't Look Dead.* [Blackmail]

MEEK, M. R. D. *A Worm Of Doubt.* [Getting Away With Murder]

MEREDITH, D. R. *The Sheriff And The Panhandle Murders.* 1984 Walker/ Avon 1985. The young boy died in a car wreck, and a young girl was found murdered in a Texas barbecue pit. Sheriff Charles Matthews has his hands full in this quiet town. He's asking questions of his friends. 1st.

MITCHELL, Kay. *A Lively Form Of Death.* 1991 St. Martin. Betty Hartley, the biggest gossip in Little Henge, was found poisoned in her own kitchen. But Chief Inspector Morrissey suspects the poison was really meant for her employer Marion Walsh, known to be involved with several men in the community. 1st. [Clergy]

MURRAY, Stephen. *A Cool Killing.* 1988 St. Martin. Dr. Geoffrey was found dead in the hospital mortuary drawer. As Inspector Alec Stainton takes on the inquiry, the first murder case he's done on his own, he learns a lot about the man that few mourn. 1st.

NATSUKI, Shizuko. *The Obituary Arrives At Two O'Clock.* [Oriental]

O'DONNELL, Lillian. *Cop Without A Shield.* [Smuggling]

OLIPHANT, B. J. *The Unexpected Corpse.* [Antiques]

PENTECOST, Hugh. *Kill And Kill Again.* 1987 Dodd, Mead. Martha Best's frozen body was found in the trunk of her car; she'd been strangled. Martha's brother turned to Julian Quist for help. Before it's over, Julian has to rescue his kidnapped girlfriend. 16th.

PENTECOST, Hugh. *Murder In Luxury.* 1981 Dodd, Mead/Worldwide 1991. After finding a dead man in her living room, Valerie Summers has taken refuge at the Hotel Beaumont. In less than twenty-four hours, Valerie is involved in a second murder. While the police investigate, Pierre Chambrun starts his own inquiry. 15th. [Revenge]

RESNICOW, Herbert. *The Gold Gamble.* [Theater]

RICE, Craig. *Having A Wonderful Crime.* [Lawyer]

ROBINSON, Peter. *A Dedicated Man.* 1991 Scribner. History professor Hanry Steadman's body was found buried under a tumbled stone wall in a field in Helmthorpe. Detective Chief Inspector Alan Banks has to go back to a glorious summer ten years ago to find out what led up to this murder. 2nd. [Where There's A Will]

ROOSEVELT, Elliott. *Murder In The Blue Room.* [Famous People]

ROSS, Jonathan. *Fate Accomplished.* 1987 St. Martin. The car was demolished by the night train, but the man inside the auto had been dead for several hours. Detective Superintendent George Rogers follows the clues of false papers and a love nest to identify the body. 5th.

ROSS, Jonathan. *Sudden Departures.* 1988 St. Martin. Superintendent George Rogers got a tip that a murder was about to be committed. Then Andrew Lattimer was killed in a car explosion. Audrey Lattimer is missing, and so is a lot of money. 6th.

SHAH, Diane K. *As Crime Goes By.* [Journalism]

SIMON, Roger L. *Wild Turkey.* 1975 Simon & Schuster/ Warner 1986. TV's anchorwoman Deborah Frank was dead at the Beverly Wilshire, and author Jock Hecht had the attention of the police. PI Moses Wine was trying to clear him. Hecht died a day later, a confession in his typewriter. His wife, Nancy, said it was a fake. 2nd.

SIMPSON, Dorothy. *Element Of Doubt.* 1988 Scribner/ Bantam 1989. Nerine Tarrant died of a nasty fall on the terrace. She wasn't a particularly nice woman, distant to her son and unfaithful to her husband, many times over. Still, it's up to Inspector Luke Thanet to clear up the matter. 7th. [Father]

SMITH, J. C. S. *Jacoby's First Case.* 1980 Atheneum/ Signet 1985. Mostly-retired transit cop Jacoby hung around the racetrack. His friend Peter Hecht is worried about a woman friend. The young lady was found dead, and her death is tied to a series of killings. [Serial Killers]

THOMSON, June. *No Flowers, By Request.* [Father]

TOURNEY, Leonard. *The Player's Boy Is Dead.* [Historical]

TRIPP, Miles. *The Frightened Wife.* 1988 St. Martin. Jessica Lee had a premonition. She came to PI John Samson with the forecast of her own death. She paid him in advance to investigate if she happened to die. Samson didn't wait; he started looking into her life at once. 8th. [Getting Away With Murder]

WALKER, Walter. *The Two Dude Defense.* 1985 Harper & Row/ Penguin 1986. San Francisco PI Hector Gronig took a job he didn't want, just for the money. He was to take pictures of a woman and a man in a motel room. Things started to go wrong, fast. He didn't get paid, the motel burned, and Hector's about to be arrested for murder.

WALKER, Walter. *The Immediate Prospect Of Being Hanged.* 1989 Viking/ Onyx 1990. Rebecca Chesley Carpenter was found strangled with a scarf in her own Mercedes at the end of a lover's lane. The county DA assigns Patterson Starbuck to the investigation. But Starbuck has secrets of his own, and they all lead to the town of Woodedge.

WEEKS, Delores. *The Cape Murders.* 1987 Dodd, Mead. Lawyer Owen Wentworth was found dead in his Cape San Juan summer house. Surgeon Scott Eason was called from his cabin to help. And there in Owen's wallet was a picture of Scott's dead wife, Toni. He's in for more surprises. [Drugs]

WILLIAMS, David. *Divided Treasure.* [Fraud]

WINGFIELD, Rodney. *A Touch Of Frost.* 1987 Paperjacks/ PBO. Inspector Jack Frost, plodding along, working at tangents, irritates his superiors. God, they'd like to get rid of him! A cop, one of their own, is dead. If they can just keep Frost out of the case—but he bumbles in. 2nd.

WITTEN, Barbara Yager. *The Isle Of Fire Murder.* 1987 Walker. Lily Lambert, recent widow, went to her summer house on Fire Island. There was a lot of gossip about Scotty Banks, the tennis coach. Scotty's body was found on the beach, and Homicide Detective Harry Ball can't keep Lily from nosing around. [Revenge]

WOLZIEN, Valerie. *The Fortieth Birthday Body.* 1989 St. Martin/ Fawcett 1991. Susan was going to have her fortieth birthday. She knew about the surprise party her husband had planned. But she was as surprised as the rest of the guests when the body of a femme fatale was found in her birthday car. 2nd.

WOODS, Sara. *Most Deadly Hate.* [Lawyer]

WREN, M. K. *Seasons Of Death.* [Old Crime]

WRIGHT, Eric. *A Sensitive Case.* [Canadian]

YORKE, Margaret. *The Small Hours Of The Morning.* 1975 Walker/ Penguin 1988. Lorna was addicted to spying on Cecil Titmus and his wife. Their life was a storybook, with happy loving children and the good wishes of the community. Then Lorna discovered June's secret.

ZOLLINGER, Norman. *Lautrec.* [Lawyer]

INSURANCE

Thousands of crimes are committed yearly for the insurance money, and millions of dollars are paid out to unworthy claimants. It soothes our sense of justice that in the mystery story the culprit doesn't come off clean.

BANKS, Joan. *Death Claims.* [Accident]

BARNES, Linda. *Dead Heat.* 1984 St. Martin/ Fawcett 1985. When Senator Donagher started to receive threatening letters, his bodyguard hired his old friend Michael Spraggue to help out. Pete died, and Michael struggled to solve the mystery. 3rd. [Political]

BOND, Michael. *Monsieur Pamplemousse.* [Cooks]

BRAUN, Lilian Jackson. *The Cat Who Ate Danish Modern.* [Cats]

CANNELL, Dorothy. *The Widow's Club.* [Revenge]

GRAFTON, Sue. *"E" Is For Evidence.* 1988 Holt/ Bantam 1989. Just before Christmas, PI Kinsey Millhone discovered $5,000 had been deposited in her checking account. Still, she doesn't believe in Santa. Working on a warehouse fire, she discovers she's being accused of being on the take. 5th. [Incest]

HAMMOND, Gerald. *The Worried Widow.* [Suicide]

HANSEN, Joseph. *Trouble Maker.* 1975 Harper & Row/Owl 1984. Richard Wendell was shot in his den, and a naked man stood over his body wiping off the gun. As Dave Brandstetter investigated, one of his first stops was the Hang Ten, a gay bar co-owned by the dead man. 3rd. [Gay]

HART, Jeanne. *Threnody For Two.* 1991 St. Martin. Eugenia was a bag lady who sneaked into an empty hospital bed to sleep. Now she was stabbed to death. Across town, Ann Koppleman crawled into bed one night and missed her lunch date with her brother the next day. Why would someone purchase two identical knives to murder two unrelated women? 3rd.

HENSLEY, Joe L. *Robak's Fire.* [Lawyer]

HILL, Reginald. *An April Shroud.* 1986 Foul Play/ Signet 1987. Superintendent Dalziel is on holiday in Lincolnshire. He's rescued from flood waters and taken to Lake House, an old mansion being restored as a posh medieval restaurant. Quickly, he becomes mired in murder and romance. 5th. [On Vacation]

LUTZ, John. *Diamond Eyes.* [Jewels]

LYONS, Arthur. *At The Hands Of Another.* [Suicide]

MILNE, John. *Dead Birds.* 1987 Viking/ Penguin 1988. George Duncan wanted London PI Jimmy Jenner to keep an eye on his wife—his life has been threatened. When the wife was found dead, Jenner was suspicious. It wasn't till much, much later, and in another country, that Jenner found his answers. 1st.

MOYES, Patricia. *Down Among The Dead Men.* [On Vacation]

RAY, Robert J. *Dial "M" For Murdock.* 1988 St. Martin/ Dell 1990. From coast to coast, rich men, saddled with rich debts, jump into the perfect scam: fake their own deaths and start their lives over with the insurance money. Murdock gets called in. He works closely with the wife of one of the "dead" men. 3rd. [Fraud]

RESNICOW, Herbert. *The Gold Solution.* [Locked Room]

RINEHART, Mary Roberts. *Miss Pinkerton.* 1932 Holt/ Zebra 1986. Miss Juliet was quite shaken when her nephew committed suicide. Hilda Adams, nurse, was determined to keep a close eye on her. But the household was hardly ever still, and Miss Juliet vanished. 1st. [Suicide]

TAPPLY, William G. *The Spotted Cats.* [Antiques]

WEBSTER, Noah. *Witchline.* 1988 Doubleday. A woman in Spain had written a furious letter about her washing machine not working. To marine investigator Andrew Laird, it was a mystery: that particular shipment was supposed to be at the bottom of the Bay of Biscay. 10th. [Drugs]

WRIGHT, Eric. *A Question Of Murder.* [Canadian]

WUAMETT, Victor. *Deeds Of Trust.* [Real Estate]

INTRIGUE

As long as we have international conflicts, we'll have spy stories and mysteries with intrigue. But some of these tales involve various branches of our own government, on our own soil, and leave the average citizen aghast.

ARNOLD, Margot. *Sinister Purposes.* 1988 Fawcett/ PBO. Just out of the hospital and recuperating from the accident that killed her husband and unborn child, Elizabeth Marchant was approached by a man with a mission. Michael wanted her to help rescue her old roommate, Lelia. Feeling she hasn't much to live for, she agrees.

BABSON, Marian. *Fatal Fortune.* 1991 St. Martin. Grandfather Buck Bradstone is dying and the family has gathered. His granddaughter Hope gets an urgent call from her sister-in-law. Inga wants Hope to fly to Brussels, collect her son, and bring him to Massachusetts where he'll be safe.

BANDY, Franklin. *Athena.* 1987 Tor/ Tor 1989. Athena was acquitted of the murder of her husband. Only later does the news break that seven of the jurors had been bribed. Athena knows *why,* but she doesn't know *who.* She just knows that she has earthshaking papers in her possession.

BASS, Milton. *The Moving Finger.* 1986 Signet/ PBO. Benny Freedman has just buried his wife of only a few months. He's back at the San Diego PD, assigned to work on the Dienben case, a used car dealer found strangled. As he investigates, he keeps finding out new things about his late wife. 1st.

BAXT, George. *The Alfred Hitchcock Murder Case.* [Famous People]

BAYER, William. *Pattern Crimes.* [Serial Killer]

BECK, K. K. *Young Mrs. Cavendish And The Kaiser's Men.* [Journalism]

BECK, K. K. *Without A Trace.* Jove 1988/ PBO. Fellow spy Billie St. Clair showed up after thirty-five years in retirement. He wants Sunny Sinclair for one more mission. He needs help to locate Sunny's wartime lover Alex Markoff, rumored to be dead. [Missing Person]

BEECHCROFT, William. *The Rebuilt Man.* 1987 Dodd, Mead/ Berkley 1988. When Don Franklin regained consciousness, he was in a strange room and a woman was watching him. She claimed to be his wife. Recuperating in Hawaii, there were more questions than answers.

BOUCHER, Anthony. *The Case Of The Baker Street Irregulars.* [Sherlock Holmes]

BRANDON, Ruth. *Out Of Body, Out Of Mind* [Psychological]

BRINGLE, Mary. *The Man In The Moss-Colored Trousers.* 1986 Doubleday. The body was found on the racecourse in Balgriffin by a group of children. The corpse was dressed in moss-colored trousers. As rumors run rampant in the village, the children decide to take matters into their own hands. [Children]

BUCKLEY, William F., Jr. *Mongoose, R.I.P.* 1987 Random House/ Dell 1989. The CIA's Blackford Oakes is point man in Operation Mongoose. It's 1963 and at Miami headquarters the plans for ending the Caribbean menace are unfolding. Then Oakes is faced with a dreadful decision: the life of one man or millions. 8th. [Famous People]

BYRD, Max. *Target Of Opportunity.* 1988 Bantam. Gilman and his brother-in-law stopped at the 7-Eleven to pick up some doughnuts. Minutes later, Kevin was dead, shot by a masked gunman. The killers' trail took Gilman to Boston and back to World War II. [Old Crime]

CHARLES, Hampton. *Miss Seeton, By Appointment.* [Jewels]

CHESBRO, George C. *City Of Whispering Stone.* 1978 Simon & Schuster/ Dell 1988. Mongo, the dwarf, is back in the circus. He's looking for one of their favorite stars. He ends up in the center of a Middle Eastern intrigue and the end of a broken love. 2nd.

CHESBRO, George C. *The Beasts Of Valhalla.* 1985 Atheneum/ Dell 1987. Mongo is back in his Nebraska hometown, investigating the grisly death of a teenager. Then he stumbles onto something strange—the Valhalla Project. 4th.

CHESBRO, George C. *Two Songs The Archangel Sings.* 1986 Atheneum/ Dell 1988. Mongo's friend Veil Kendry is missing. Mongo starts with three clues: a bullet hole, a cryptic oil painting, and $10,000. He ends up in Washington, D.C., and a secret CIA mission called Archangel. 5th.

CLIFT, A. Denis. *A Death In Geneva.* 1988 Ivy/ PBO. On a street in Geneva, Constance Burdette was gunned down. Not only was she the newly-appointed U.S. ambassador to the U.N. in Europe, but she'd also been the president's lover. U.S. intelligence agent Sweetman is going to be in on the last act.

CUNNINGHAM, E. V. *The Wabash Factor.* [Political]

DAVIS, Dorothy Salisbury. *The Pale Betrayer.* 1965 Scribner/ Avon 1987. Professor Eric Mather has just one job to do: trick physicist Peter Bradley into carrying some secret documents from Greece back to New York City. But there's one complication. Mather's in love with Peter's wife.

DAVIS, Dorothy Salisbury. *The Habit Of Fear.* [Missing Person]

DeANDREA, William. *Snark.* 1986 Mysterious/ Mysterious 1987. Clifford Driscoll flew to England to help look for the missing chief of British intelligence, Lewis Alfot. He was greeted at Heathrow with a hail of bullets. Now he has someone else to hunt for. 2nd.

DeANDREA, William. *Azreal.* 1987 Mysterious/ Mysterious 1988. Petra Hudson controlled one of the most powerful newspaper syndicates in the world. On command, she was supposed to put a Cronus operation into effect. Instead, she disobeys. Trotter has to come out of hiding. 3rd.

DEFORD, Frank. *The Spy In Deuce Court.* [Ball Games]

DELMAN, David. *Murder In The Family.* 1985 Doubleday. Nassau County Homicide Detective Jacob Horowitz was on his way to Lisbon to find the person who killed his son. On the plane he meets former football star Ray Stickney. Their paths continue to cross on Jacob's tortuous pursuit of justice. 6th.

DELMAN, David. *The Last Gambit.* 1991 St. Martin. Jacob Horowitz is at his first chess tournament, the Capa Open, in Philadelphia. His reporter cousin Buddy is in a snit. Chessmaster Demitri Kaganovich, who jilted Buddy, is also part of the game. When Demitri is shot, Buddy tops the list of suspects. 10th. [Journalism]

DENHAM, Bertie. *Foxhunt.* 1988 St. Martin. Derek was following along behind a silver BMW when it disappeared under the Thames. He knew there were only twelve tunnels under the river, so where did the car go? Derek is searching for another tunnel. 2nd. [Blackmail]

DEWHURST, Eileen. *Playing Safe.* 1987 Doubleday. Bored with her comfortable life, retired actress and wife of a member of British intelligence, Helen Johnston looked for something to do. She hired out to play a relative for someone and ended up in an international espionage operation.

DEWHURST, Eileen. *The Sleeper.* 1988 Doubleday. Olga Trent's memories of Russia have faded. She's married to Henry, and living in England with two children. Then one afternoon she gets a phone call and her life becomes a nightmare.

DOWLING, Gregory. *See Naples And Kill.* 1988 St. Martin. January Esposito couldn't understand why his brother's visit ended up with Gigi heading out the kitchen window or the two Italians coming in his door. They took Jan for a ride, all the way to Naples.

DUFFY, Margaret. *A Murder Of Crows.* 1988 St. Martin/ Fawcett 1989. Shortly after her husband was gunned down by thugs, romance writer Ingrid Langley was confronted by Patrick, her first husband. He wants Ingrid's help in solving her second husband's murder. She'll have to pose as Patrick's wife. 1st. [Writer]

DUFFY, Margaret. *Death Of A Raven.* 1988 St. Martin/ Fawcett 1990. Patrick Gillard and his romance-writer wife Ingrid Langley are on an MI5 assignment in

Canada. There's a problem with the Devonport Admiralty Research Executive personnel gathering. One engineer is dead, and threats have been made against DARE. 2nd. [Writer]

DUFFY, Margaret. *Who Killed Cock Robin?* 1990 St. Martin. Terry Meadows, code name "Robin," had died when his beloved sports car blew up. As Patrick Gillard and his wife Ingrid investigate the murder of an MI5 official, Ingrid is kidnapped and discovers that Terry might just be still alive. 4th. [Kidnapping]

ESTLEMAN, Loren D. *Silent Thunder.* [Smuggling]

FISH, Robert L. *Always Kill A Stranger.* 1967 Putnam/ Foul Play 1988. Capt. Jose Da Silva, liaison between Interpol and the Brazilian police, received an anonymous letter. The life of Argentinian Juan Dorcas, arriving for the OAS meeting, was on the line. Da Silva was in a race against death. 6th. [Where There's A Will]

FOOTMAN, Robert. *Always A Spy.* 1986 Dodd, Mead/ Berkley 1988. The agency had blackmailed Harry Ryder back into the service. His job was to rescue an agent from behind the Iron Curtain. The man is Harry's old partner, thought to have been killed years ago. To rescue him, Harry puts his life in the hands of his new partner. 2nd.

GARDNER, John. *No Deals, Mr. Bond.* 1987 Putnam/ Charter 1988. M wants Bond to find and rescue the remnants of "Cream Cake," a failed sex-entrapment operation they had going in East Germany. Two young women have already been killed and their tongues cut out. 18th.

GARVE, Andrew. *Two If By Sea.* 1949 Harper & Row/ Perennial 1986. While on duty in Moscow in 1943, Jack Denny and Philip Sutterland both married Russian women. Returning to England, they find their wives cannot leave Russia. There's bound to be a way to rescue them.

GERSON, Jack. *Deathwatch.* 1991 St. Martin. Ex-Berlin police chief, Ernst Lohmann, fled Germany for London as Hitler rose to power. As England declares war on Germany, Lohmann is taken into custody as an enemy alien. Suddenly he's summoned before Winston Churchill; he's to be sent to Washington, DC, on a secret mission and on a matter of multiple murder. 3rd. [Serial Killers]

GILMAN, Dorothy. *Uncertain Voyage.* 1967 Doubleday/ Fawcett 1988. By way of putting aside a bad marriage, Melissa Aubrey sailed to Europe, on her own for the first time. A desperate stranger asks her to deliver a book to a secret address. As soon as she agrees, her life is threatened.

GILMAN, Dorothy. *The Elusive Mrs. Pollifax.* 1971 Doubleday/ Fawcett 1974. On a courier mission for Carstairs of the CIA, Mrs. Pollifax was bringing passports into Bulgaria. She teams up with the local underground to break into prison to free some captured men. 3rd.

GILMAN, Dorothy. *Mrs. Pollifax And The Golden Triangle.* 1988 Doubleday/ Fawcett 1989. Mrs. Pollifax and her husband, Cyrus Reed, are on vacation in Thailand. The department wants just one little favor: pick up a letter. That's all. But the man who's to deliver the letter is dead, and Cyrus gets kidnapped. 8th. [On Vacation]

GOLIN, James. *The Philomel Foundation.* [Music]

HAMMOND, Gerald, w/a Arthur Douglas. *A Worm Turns.* 1988 St. Martin. Jonathan Craythorne's Aunt Joy was attacked and robbed. He's just discovered that she's not the innocent he'd thought. Aunt Joy has carried on her late husband's business as a fence. She manages to get Jonathan to retrieve her stolen goods. 2nd.

HARRISON, Harry. *Queen Victoria's Revenge.* 1974 Doubleday/ Tor 1987. FBI Special Agent Tony Hawkins was delivering $2 million in ransom money to a hijacked DC-10. Before long he and the money have parted, and he's being chased across Scotland. 2nd.

HESS, Joan, w/a Joan Hadley. *The Night-Blooming Cereus.* 1986 St. Martin/ Ballantine 1989. Theo Bloomer, retired florist, got an emergency call from his sister. She wants him to go rescue his niece, Dorrie, from a kibbutz in Israel. But Dorrie has ideas of her own, and Theo needs a large shoehorn. 1st. [Anthropology]

KAMINSKY, Stuart M. *Smart Moves.* [Famous People]

KAMINSKY, Stuart M. *Death Of a Dissident.* [Russian]

KAYE, M. M. *Death In Zanzibar.* [Africa]

KUNETKA, James. *Shadow Man.* [Anthropology]

LEE, Elsie. *The Drifting Sands.* 1986 Zebra/ PBO. Fran Kennett was joining her husband John in Qeman. On the flight out, she met Ross Elvig, on assignment for *Life.* John was behaving strangely, and Ross ended up dead in the garden. Fran was willing to fight to hang onto her husband, even if it meant solving a murder.

LEE, Elsie. *Season Of Evil.* 1987 Zebra/ PBO. When Bianca Trael went to stay at her brother's house in Chevy Chase, she was in shock. Out of the blue, Ludo had divorced her. Instead of quiet, she walked into calamity and danger, with strange things going on next door.

MacLEOD, Charlotte. *The Silver Ghost.* 1988 Mysterious/ Mysterious 1989. Bill and Abigail Billingsgate were holding their annual Renaissance Ball. A vintage Rolls vanishes, and Sarah and Max are sleuthing. Then the gatekeeper is killed and another Rolls disappears. 8th.

MARTIN, Nancy. *Black Bridge To China.* 1988 Pocket/PBO. Paul Keller gets a midnight call from his father: "I'm in Kathmandu and I need that map." When he reaches Nepal, Paul teams up with Jane Parish. She's looking for her husband's downed plane. But no plans are entirely smooth.

MELVILLE, James. *The Wages Of Zen.* [Oriental]

MORROW, J. T. *Prophet.* 1988 Paperjacks/ PBO. Lynn McCall, PI and ex-lover, asks Jason Prophet for some help on a case involving computer research. When Lynn disappears, Prophet discovers that the Soviets were involved.

MYERS, M. Ruth. *A Touch Of Magic.* 1988 Dell/ PBO. Channing Stuart, fourth generation of magicians, chose instead to become a geologist. Yussuf, a friend of her grandfather's, hands her a tape just minutes before he is killed. Now the State Department is knocking at her door.

NABB, Magdalen, and Paolo Vagheggi. *The Prosecutor.* 1988 St. Martin. Lapo Mardi, the prosecutor, had never abandoned his search for the mastermind of the Red Brigades' kidnapping and murder of Italian statesman Carlo Rota. A breakthrough in the case seems imminent.

O'HAGAN, Joan. *Against The Grain.* [Botany]

PARKER, T. Jefferson. *Little Saigon.* 1988 St. Martin/ St. Martin 1989. It's called Little Saigon, home to a hundred thousand refugees in Orange County. Chuck Frye's brother Bennett is right in the middle of a mess.

As Chuck noses around, the evidence points to a transpacific espionage network.

PENTECOST, Hugh. *The Fourteenth Dilemna.* 1976 Dodd, Mead/Worldwide 1990. The Watson family had won a week at New York's Hotel Beaumont. But their young daughter was found murdered. What had the innocent deaf-mute child seen that caused someone to kill her? Pierre Chambrun is pushed almost beyond his limits. 12th. [Children]

PENTECOST, Hugh. *Nightmare Time.* 1986 Dodd, Mead/Worldwide 1988. Major Willis and his wife left their room at the Beaumont Hotel to go downstairs to listen to jazz. At 1 a.m., their son Guy demands to see Pierre Chambrun, the hotel manager. His parents are missing, and Pierre has to find them. 20th.

PUMPHREY, Janet Kay. *A House Full Of Love.* Vantage 1990/ PBO. Lynn Swanson ran into her husband in the mall parking lot; she'd run away from the Senator five years ago. Against her will, she returns to his old family home. But something's wrong and his sister Melody seems to have aged terribly. [Old Crime]

SCHUTZ, Benjamin M. *A Tax In Blood.* 1987 Tor/ Bantam 1989. The law firm hired Washington, D.C., PI Leo Haggerty to check out the death of a client's husband. Divorce proceedings had started, and now the man was dead—suicide, the police said. If that was correct, the insurance company wouldn't pay. Leo finds something else. 3rd. [Suicide]

SERAFIN, David. *The Body In Cadiz Bay.* 1985 St. Martin. Superintendent Luis Bernal and his wife were spending *Semana Santa* in Cadiz when the local police drew him into an investigation. The body of a frogman was found in the bay, and he didn't drown. 4th. [Holiday]

SERAFIN, David. *Port Of Light.* 1987 St. Martin. Superintendent Luis Bernal is in the Canary Islands to insure that the visit of the president of the Council of Ministers doesn't run into trouble. Then Consuelo, his mistress, is kidnapped. 5th. [Political]

SPILLANE, Mickey. *The Killing Man.* [Revenge]

STUART, Anne. *Darkness Before Dawn.* 1987 Dell/ PBO. Mack had been dead for two years when Maggie Bennett found herself teamed up with a former lover for a job she didn't really want. But she and Randall have to get behind the Iron Curtain, and out again. 2nd.

STUART, Anne. *At The Edge Of The Sun.* 1987 Dell/ PBO. Timothy Flynn picked out rich women and took what he could get. This time, he lifted cash and jewels from Maggie's mother, and Sybil is in the hospital in a coma. Maggie vows to get Flynn. She has lots of help. 3rd.

SWIGART, Rob. *Toxin.* 1989 St. Martin. Out jogging, Victor Linz, Kauai land developer, was shot to death. Detective Cobb Takamura and microbiologist Chazz Koenig have just gotten the case when a second crisis occurs. A satellite carrying deadly toxin has gone out of control and landed on the island. 2nd. [Revenge]

TAPPLY, William G. *The Marine Corpse.* [Social Issues]

THOREAU, David. *The Book Of Numbers.* Pocket 1990/ PBO. Sports bookmaker Jimmy Lujack did a favor for a friend. He picked up Ginger Lowe as she was discharged from the Betty Ford Clinic. A week later Ginger was found dead, decapitated. To Lujack it looked like a satanic ritual. 2nd. [Witches]

TRUMAN, Margaret. *Murder At The FBI.* [Manuscript]

TRUMAN, Margaret. *Murder In The CIA.* 1987 Random House/ Fawcett 1988. Barrie Mayer was a literary agent for authors behind the Iron Curtain. When she died at Heathrow Airport, her friend, Colette Cahil, wanted to know why. Using her own State Department skills, she asks a lot of questions and puts her own life in jeopardy.

TRUMAN, Margaret. *Murder In the Kennedy Center.* [Political]

TUCKER, Bartholomew. *The Man Who Looked Like Howard Cosell.* [Famous People]

TYLER, Alison. *Chase The Wind.* 1987 Dell/ PBO. Jenny Heath, on a buying trip in Rome, outbid a man for an antique silver pillbox. It didn't take long for her to discover that a lot of people were ready to chase her across Italy to get it back. 1st. [Antiques]

TYLER, Alison. *Chase The Storm.* 1987 Dell/ PBO. Since her last adventure, Jenny Heath has only a few questions about doing a favor for the CIA. She starts out to pick up a package from the Louvre. But that turns into finding a body instead. She's on the run again. 2nd.

VALENTINE, Paul W. *Crime Scene At "O" Street.* [Black Detective]

WAKEFIELD, Hannah. *A Woman's Own Mystery.* 1990 St. Martin. Dee Street's client Gillian Shiroz is threatening not to show up at the custody hearing for her young daughter. Her main witness has vanished. Dee gets a postponement and rushes to the woman's house, only to find her dead. 2nd. [Lawyer]

WENTWORTH, Patricia. *Dead Or Alive.* 1936 Lippencott/ Warner 1990. The day Meg O'Hara asked Robin for a divorce, he disappeared. The Colonel said he was on a dangerous assignment. Then a body was found in the Thames with Robin's wallet. But why is Meg receiving messages that say "I AM ALIVE"?

WESTLAKE, Donald E. *Kahawa.* [Africa]

WILSON, Gahan. *Everybody's Favorite Duck.* 1988 Mysterious/ Mysterious 1989. Some of the greatest villains of popular fiction are planning to menace modern America. Their first target is Waldo World, the home of everyone's favorite duck. John Weston and Bone have to work fast to stop them.

WINDNER, Robert. *No Admission.* [Computer]

WOODS, Sara. *The Third Encounter.* 1963 Harper & Row/Avon 1986. Kindly Dr. Martin of Streatham was strangled just after he'd placed a call to Antony Maitland. Antony knows the man charged with the crime is innocent. He has to return to his own World War II experiences for this case. 4th. [Lawyer]

J . . . IS FOR

JEALOUSY

*J*EALOUSY IS ONE OF THOSE EMOTIONS *which is difficult to explain. It can arise suddenly out of nowhere with devastating impact. And terrible crimes have been committed in the name of jealousy.*

ADAMS, Harold. *The Fourth Widow.* 1986 Mysterious/ Mysterious 1987. Carl Wilcox had recently returned to Corden, South Dakota, when Flory Fancett was found beaten to death out behind the hotel. As a prime suspect, Carl is forced to do his own investigating, especially when the bodies become numerous. 5th.

BABSON, Marian. *Reel Murder.* [Hollywood]

BABSON, Marian. *Untimely Guest.* [Accident]

BAXT, George. *The Affair At Royalties.* [Mystery Writer]

BOHJALION, Christopher A. *A Killing In The Real World.* 1988 St. Martin. Lisa Stone and her roommate Melanie from Crosby College bemoan the murder of Penny, another roommate. Penny was found in the apartment of a porno photographer and petty pusher. Then Melanie is stabbed to death before Lisa's eyes. Is Lisa next?

BRAND, Christianna. *Tour De Force.* [On Vacation]

CARR, John Dickson. *Dark Of The Moon.* 1967 Harper &

Row/ Carroll & Graf 1987. It was a strange house party at Maynard Hall, and Henry Maynard was being cryptic. Someone stole a scarecrow, and then Henry was found dead on the terrace. Dr. Gideon Fell is about to solve his last case. 23rd.

CLARK, Mary Higgins. *Weep No More My Lady.* 1987 Simon & Schuster/ Dell 1988. Elizabeth Lange has just returned to New York City to be the star witness at her sister's murder trial. In response to a letter from Sammy, she flew to Cypress Point Spa. There she's confronted by Ted Winters, the man she's to testify against. Sammy dies, another guest is attacked, and Elizabeth is willing to swap her life for the truth.

DeANDREA, William. *Killed With A Passion.* [Television]

DEXTER, Colin. *Last Bus To Woodstock.* [Infidelity]

FERRARS, E. X. *Trial By Fury.* [Mother]

FRASER, Antonia. *Cool Repentance.* [Theater]

FRIEDMAN, Kinky. *Greenwich Killing Time.* 1986 Birch Tree/Berkley 1987. Kinky found a man lying on the floor of his apartment holding eleven pink roses. Kinky's reporter friend, McGovern, is being held for the murder. Kinky wades through strange people who live in Greenwich Village to help his friend. 1st.

FULTON, Eileen. *Lights, Camera, Death.* [Television]

GAULT, William Campbell. *Day Of The Ram.* 1956 Random House/ Charter 1988. Johnny Quirk had received a rather nasty note, and he wanted Brock Callahan to protect him. Then as Johnny visits his mother's grave, he's shot to death. Brock questions Johnny's friends and even an old school teacher in Phoenix. 2nd.

GILLIGAN, Roy. *Chinese Restaurants Never Serve Breakfast.* 1986 Perseverance/ PBO. PI Pat Riordan just moved to Carmel. He's checking on the wife of his rich friend. But almost before he can get started, he's hauled out of bed to investigate the death of an artist friend, Sheila Lord. There's double trouble.

GREELEY, Andrew M. *Happy Are The Clean Of Heart.* [Clergy]

HESS, Joan. *Malice In Maggody.* 1987 St. Martin/ Onyx 1991. Arly Hanks has just been made the first woman sheriff of Maggody, Arkansas, population 852, and she has problems. The man from the EPA, in town to see about the dumping of garbage in Boone Creek, has disappeared. There's an escaped prisoner, and Jaylee was shot to death with a crossbow. 1st. [Kidnapping]

HILARY, Richard. *Pillow Of The Community.* [Black Detective]

HUXLEY, Elspeth. *The African Poison Murders.* [Africa]

JERINA, Carol. *The Tall Dark Alibi.* 1988 Charter/ PBO. Jillian Fletcher has a new job with Dallas PI Jackson Fury. When she reads that Sterling Wyatt has been arrested for murder, she knows better. At the time of the killing, she'd been with him. Jillian and Fury argue their way to the real killer. 1st.

JOHNSTON, Velda. *Voice In The Night.* 1984 Dodd, Mead/Warner 1987. After her husband, Neil, died in a drowning accident, Carla left behind the memories of her unhappy marriage. In New York City she started a new life and a new love. Then in the middle of the night, the phone calls start.

LLEWELLYN, Sam. *Dead Reckoning.* [At Sea]

McBAIN, Ed. *Poison.* 1987 Arbor House/ Avon 1988. He had just managed to get to the telephone when he died. The redial on the phone reached Marilyn Hollis. Then someone else she dated died. Detective Steve Carella of the 87th Precinct has to make the right connections to save Marilyn's sanity. 39th.

McGIVERN, William P. *Shield For Murder.* 1951 Dodd, Mead/ Berkley 1988. Mark Brewster, reporter, was at the police station when the call came in: Barny Nolan, Philadelphia PD, had shot a man. Then it develops that Mark and Barny are both stuck on the same woman, Linda. This will be a deadly triangle.

MELVILLE, James. *The Reluctant Ronin.* [Oriental]

MOFFAT, Gwen. *Rage.* [Writer]

MORGAN, D. Miller. *Money Leads To Murder.* [Blackmail]

ORMEROD, Roger. *The Second Jeopardy.* 1988 Doubleday. Although Harry went to jail for a jewel theft, he was found innocent of the murder of Angela. Harry's out now, and a woman named Virginia has contacted him. She knows he didn't commit the murder and she'll help him prove it. [Jewels]

PAGE, Emma. *Final Moments.* 1987 Doubleday/ Worldwide 1988. When Venetia Franklin didn't pick up the children at school, her ex-husband went looking for her. And there she was, crammed into the back of her car, dead. Inspector Kelsey finds a lot of suspects and the missing pieces that spell murder. 5th.

PENN, John. *Mortal Term.* [Academic]

PERRY, Anne. *Paragon Walk.* [Victorian]

RICH, Virginia. *The Cooking School Murders.* [Cooks]

RICH, Virginia. *The Nantucket Diet Murders.* [Cooks]

RISENHOOVER, C. C. *Blood Bath.* [Journalism]

ROBERTS, Les. *An Infinite Numbers Of Monkeys.* [Mystery Writer]

SMITH, Joan. *Don't Leave Me This Way.* [Accident]

SUCHER, Dorothy. *Dead Men Don't Give Seminars.* 1988 St. Martin. PI Vic Newman joins his boss on Lake Champlain for the weekend. Sabina's husband is at the Physics Institute. At the opening ceremonies, a Nobel laureate drops dead. Sabina knows who the murderer is but has no evidence. 1st.

TRAVIS, Elizabeth. *Under The Influence.* 1989 St. Martin. Underneath the country serenity of Riverside, Connecticut, Ben and Carrie Porter discover murder. Carrie found the body of local artist Greg Dillon in the office of their small publishing company. Then Greg's studio burns down. There are some paintings someone wants kept a secret. 1st. [Art]

UPTON, Robert. *Dead On The Stick.* [Ball Games]

JEWELS AND JEWELRY

Jewels: they glitter, they sparkle, and they're tempting. Jewels are stolen, copied, faked, and smuggled. Jewels form a solid foundation for a good murder mystery.

ALBERT, Marvin. *Bimbo Heaven.* Fawcett 1990/ PBO. PI Pete Sawyer looked up to see a bikini-clad young woman on his patio. She wanted Pete to deliver a letter for her. Instead, the addressee was missing and a couple of thugs were working over his wife. 7th. [Father]

BABSON, Marian. *Bejeweled Death.* 1981 Walker/ Warner 1991. As Stacey dozed on her flight to London, a little girl got into her hatbox, playing with the fortune in jewels. Aunt Eustace had donated them to a museum instead of leaving them to Stacey. In London, the jewels are missing. Stacey has the wrong hatbox.

BIGGERS, Earl Derr. *The Chinese Parrot.* [Oriental]

BLOCK, Lawrence. *The Burglar In The Closet.* [Bookstore]

CHARLES, Hampton. *Miss Seeton, By Appointment.* Berkley 1990/ PBO. Miss Seeton is invited to Buckingham Palace to keep her eye on a royal retainer who just might be working for the Russians. At the same time, she gets word that there is about to be a well-planned jewel robbery in Kent. 6th. [Intrigue]

CRIDER, Bill. *Death On The Move.* [Infidelity]

DOBSON, Margaret. *Touchstone.* 1987 Dell/ PBO. Phillip Decker came to Tulsa to tell Jane Bailey about her brother's death. After the funeral, a cryptic message arrived for Jane, together with a pair of combs. Jane's determination to find out more about her brother's death takes her away from her bookstore and to Aruba. [Bookstore]

FRASER, Anthea. *The Nine Bright Shiners.* 1988 Doubleday. Jan Cloverdale's husband left. She accepted her half-brother's invitation to return to England for Christmas, even though he and his wife were leaving after the holidays for Peru. At Rylands Jan is soon caught up in a hunt for lost treasures and murder. [Old Crime]

GARDNER, Erle Stanley. *The Case Of The Terrified Typist.* [Lawyer]

GORES, Joe. *Come Morning.* 1986 Mysterious/ Mysterious 1987. Only minutes after Runyon walked out of the gate, having served seven years at San Quentin, two

JEWELS AND JEWELRY

people were after him. They were looking for two million in diamonds.

HUXLEY, Elspeth. *Murder On Safari.* [Africa]

JACKSON, Marion J. A. *The Punjat's Ruby.* Pinnacle 1990/PBO. One of the highlights of her trip was to have dinner with the Prince of Wales when he's to be presented the Punjat's Ruby. But when the jewel was stolen, Miss Abigail Danforth vowed to put her skills to work as the first female consulting detective. 1st. [Victorian]

JEFFERS, H. Paul. *Rubout At The Onyx.* [Holiday]

KAYE, M. M. *Death In Berlin.* 1985 St. Martin/ St. Martin 1986. Miranda Brand had a month's holiday visiting Germany. Then a story about a lost fortune in diamonds turns the trip into suspicions and murder. [On Vacation]

KERR, Philip. *March Violets.* [Political]

KRAFT, Gabrielle. *Bloody Mary.* Pocket 1990/ PBO. Jerry Zalman's young nephew showed up at his office with a real problem; his 13-year-old girlfriend has stolen a Picasso medallion and wants to return it. Jerry is quickly knee-deep in murder. 4th.

LUTZ, John. *Diamond Eyes.* 1990 St. Martin. Vanita White gave PI Arlo Nudger a $1,000 retainer. She was scared and needed help. Now she's a corpse, and a million dollars worth of diamonds are missing. Arlo is out to find them and stay alive. 6th. [Insurance]

MacLEOD, Charlotte, w/a Alisa Craig. *The Grub-And-Stakers Quilt A Bee.* [Canadian]

MANN, Jessica. *Grave Goods.* 1985 Doubleday. The Crown Jewels of Charlemagne, along with other treasures, are on their way from East Germany for exhibit in London. Margo Ellice was working on a manuscript that proved the jewels were fake. Now Margo's dead and Tamara, archaeologist and British agent, must find the real jewels to solve Margo's murder. 1st.

MATHESON, Don. *Stray Cat.* 1987 Summit/ Pocket 1988. She was sound asleep in her Ferrari, parked on the dock at Boston Harbor. To Charlie Gamble, living on a boat, she was like a stray cat that wandered in to be fed. A glint from a pair of binoculars convinced Charlie that someone was watching her. 1st.

MICHAELS, Barbara. *Into The Darkness.* 1990 Simon & Schuster/Berkley 1991. At the death of her grandfather, Meg Venturi returns to Seldon, Massachusetts. She's shocked to learn that Daniel Mignot has left her his antique jewelry business . . . and a partner, jewelry designer Riley. But that's just the beginning of a long list of surprises. [Old Crime]

MINAHAN, John. *The Great Hotel Robbery.* 1982 Norton/ Signet 1985. It was quite a heist. Three men in tuxedos arrived at the posh hotel in a limo and walked out with three and a half million in cash and jewels. NYPD Detective John Rawlings tracks the thieves across town and up to the thirty-eighth floor. 1st.

NABB, Magdalen. *Death In Autumn.* 1985 Scribner/ Penguin 1986. They found the woman's body in the Arno River clad only in her fur coat and her jewelry. As Marshal Guarnaccia traces the woman's identity, he discovers an intricate crime network. 4th.

NEGGERS, Carla, w/a Anne Harrell. *Minstrel's Fire.* 1989 Berkley/ PBO. Pianist Juliana Fall inherited the Minstrel's Rough, the largest uncut diamond in the world. It carried with it heartache and danger. Things will never be the same for Juliana as she races to escape death. [Journalism]

NEGGERS, Carla, w/a Anne Harrell. *Betrayals.* Berkley 1990/ PBO. Rebecca Blackburn has had the Jupiter Stones in her possession for years, without having any idea what they are or who they belong to. Now, caught up in the middle between two warring Boston families, she discovers that someone wants them back. [Old Crime]

O'CALLAGHAN, Maxine. *Hit & Run.* 1989 St. Martin/ St. Martin 1991. One rainy night, Mike Morales was driving too fast. He grazed PI Delilah West and ran down old Joe Collins. Mike's mother hires Delilah to prove her son innocent. As Delilah investigates, she remembers something strange about the "accident." 2nd. [Blackmail]

ORMEROD, Roger. *The Second Jeopardy.* [Jealousy]

PAUL, Barbara. *But He Was Already Dead When I Got There.* 1986 Scribner/ Bantam 1988. Uncle Vincent had called them all together. He'd decided not to extend the loan for Ellandy Jewels. Later that night, Vincent died in the library. The suspects all declare that he was already dead when they got there.

ROBERTS, Nora. *Hot Ice.* 1987 Bantam/ PBO. Doug Lord, thief by profession, had some papers about a treasure buried two hundred years ago in Africa. Fleeing from certain death, he hitched a ride with bored Whitney MacAllister. Together they head for Madagascar and the jewels of Marie Antoinette. [Africa]

ROBERTS, Nora. *Sweet Revenge.* 1989 Bantam/ PBO. By day Adrianne was the beautiful princess, part of the glittering jet set. By night she's heralded as the Shadow, an extraordinary jewel thief. She's getting ready for her last heist, her sweet revenge. [Revenge]

ROOSEVELT, Elliott. *Murder And The First Lady.* [Famous People]

SATTERTHWAIT, Walter. *Wall Of Glass.* 1987 St. Martin/ Worldwide 1989. Santa Fe PI Joshua Croft was approached about a piece of jewelry on which the insurance company had already paid the claim. The next day, the man making the offer was found dead in the mountains. With the promise of a finder's fee, Josh takes off, only to stumble over more bodies. 1st.

TAYLOR, Andrew. *Caroline Minuscule.* [Manuscript]

WATSON, Peter. *Landscape Of Lies.* [Art]

WENTWORTH, Patricia. *Outrageous Fortune.* [Missing Person]

WENTWORTH, Patricia. *Run!* 1939 Lippincott/ Warner 1990. James Elliot, lost in the fog, stopped at a country house. He ran into a very strange young woman with an even stranger story. She said she was trying to find her late Aunt Clementa's diamonds.

WENTWORTH, Patricia. *The Brading Collection.* 1950 Lippincott/ Perennial 1990. Lewis Brading consulted Miss Silver on the security of his famous collection of jewelry, then absolutely disregarded her advice. A few weeks later, he was found murdered among the jewels. Chief Constable March asks Miss Silver to investigate. 17th. [Where There's A Will]

WESTLAKE, Donald. *Hot Rock.* 1970 Simon & Schuster/ Mysterious 1987. In a failed plot to steal the famous Balabomo Emerald, one of Dortmunder's convict friends was picked up by the cops. Dortmunder springs him from jail only to discover that the emerald has been stashed in a holding cell. Now they have to break *into* jail. 1st.

WHITE, Teri. *Tight-Rope.* 1986 Mysterious/ Mysterious 1987. She's wandered into the LAPD and now she's dead. She died execution style, killed with the same gun that had taken out Hua in Little Saigon. Los Angeles Detectives Blue Maguire and Spaceman Kowalski are all over the city following leads.

ZIMMELMAN, Lue. *Honolulu Red.* 1990 St. Martin/ St. Martin 1990. LAPD detective Rachael Starr just saw her ex-partner gunned down in an illegal search. She arranges two weeks off to follow up, on her own, on the jewelry ring. What better companion than art professor Nicholas Snow? Especially since he's a jewel thief. 1st. [Drugs]

JOURNALISM

Journalists should make great detectives. They've been trained to ask questions, poke their noses into places most of us hope forever to avoid, and bluff their way into grabbing just the right information. But none of that will protect them from the danger of being a victim.

BAYER, William. *Blind Side.* 1989 Villard/ Signet 1990. Burned-out news photographer Geoffrey Barnett met Kimberly Yates on the street and he fell in love. When she disappeared and her roommate was murdered, Geof felt compelled to find her. The final showdown took him all the way to Santa Fe. [Blackmail]

BEATON, M. C. *Death Of A Gossip.* 1985 St. Martin/ Ivy 1988. Eight people gather in a Scottish hamlet for lessons in fly casting. Lady Jane collects and broadcasts damaging gossip. One of the group is determined to stop her. She's found strangled at the bottom of a quiet pool. Constable Hamish Macbeth has to find the killer. 1st.

BECK, K. K. *Young Mrs. Cavendish And The Kaiser's Men.* 1987 Walker/ Ivy 1989. 1916: Maude Teasdale Cavendish, society columnist for the *San Francisco Globe,* was attending a dinner party when she looked up to see another young woman wearing her identical dress. That was shortly before Maude was kidnapped. [Intrigue]

BECK, K. K. *Murder In A Mummy Case.* 1986 Walker/ Ivy 1987. It's the 1920s and Iris Cooper, Stanford student, is spending Easter with her classmate Clarence. He wants her to see his mummy. But the body in the mummy case isn't very old. Iris's friend, reporter Jack Clancy, shows up on the doorstep almost before the police. 2nd. [Blackmail]

BELSKY, Dick. *One For The Money.* 1986 Academy/ PBO. Sharp-tongued Lucy Shannon, reporter for the *Blade,* is covering the murder of a young woman on the Upper East Side. As she follows the story, she stumbles on body after body until her own life is threatened.

BLACK, Lionel. *Death Has Green Fingers.* [Botany]

BRAUN, Lilian Jackson. *The Cat Who Could Read Backwards.* [Cats]

BRAUN, Lilian Jackson. *The Cat Who Knew Shakespeare.* [Cats]

BREAN, Herbert. *Wilders Walk Away.* [Where There's A Will]

BROWN, Frederic. *The Screaming Mimi.* 1949 Dutton/ Carroll & Graf 1989. Reporter Bill Sweeney is on the last skids. When Chicago's Ripper gets his fourth victim, he pulls himself together to go after a killer and a big story. And somewhere there's a statuette of a slim nude girl . . . screaming. [Serial Killers]

CASE, Peg, and John Migliore. *Death Blade.* 1988 Paperjacks/ PBO. Reporter Molly Magee promised Cornelia she'd herd a bunch of third-graders through the

Alsbury Historical Museum. And there in the rocking chair was Cornelia, run through with a rapier. [Old Crime]

CHASE, Elaine Raco. *Dangerous Places.* [Blackmail]

CHASE, Elaine Raco. *Dark Corners.* 1988 Bantam/ PBO. Journalist Nikki Holden is on assignment to check out UFO sightings. Meanwhile, Roman Cantrell, security specialist, has to find out how a shipment of precious metals was stolen. What neither knows is how their investigations will tangle with genius and murder. 2nd. [Revenge]

CORRINGTON, John William, and Joyce H. Corrington. *So Small A Carnival.* 1986 Viking/ Fawcett 1987. Police reporter Wes Colvin arrived at a New Orleans bar just moments after everyone was gunned down. One of the corpses was Aguste Lemoyne from a fancy Uptown family. As Wes digs into the story, he finds a trail back to Huey Long. 1st. [Old Crime]

D'AMATO, Barbara. *Hardball.* 1989 Scribner/ Worldwide 1991. Freelance journalist Cat Marsala is at a sherry reception at the University of Chicago. As she sits next to Louise Sugarman, Louise is blown to bits, and Cat ends up in the hospital. Quiet, mild-mannered Louise was out to legalize drugs and someone wanted her stopped. 1st. [Drugs]

DeBROSSE, Jim. *The Serpentine Wall.* [Arson]

DELMAN, David. *The Last Gambit.* [Intrigue]

DOWNEY, Timothy. *A Splendid Executioner.* 1987 Dutton/ Ivy 1988. Columnist Pete Killharney had an established hit list of the greedy, corrupt, and evil. All of a sudden, someone was taking him seriously and was eliminating people from the list. Pete, and fellow reporter Sheila McGrath, can't seem to put the pieces together. Now the killer is stalking Pete. [Serial Killer]

ESTLEMAN, Loren D. *Every Brilliant Eye.* 1986 Houghton Mifflin/ Fawcett 1987. Detroit PI Amos Walker has been hired to find his old friend Barry Stackpole. His newspaper wants him, and so does his editor. It looks like Barry doesn't want to be found. Amos would call it quits, but too many people are dying. 6th.

FELD, Bernard. *Blood Relatives.* [Mother]

FLYNN, Don. *Murder On The Hudson.* 1985 Walker/Walker 1986. For Howard Ritter, it was a simple messenger job: drop the package off the Hudson River Cruise Boat. Not one of the 1,424 passengers saw who shot him. Reporter Ed Fitzgerald has the story and he won't let go. 2nd. [Kidnapping]

FLYNN, Don. *Murder In A-Flat.* [Music]

FRANCIS, Dick. *Break In.* [Horses]

FRIEDMAN, Mickey. *Paper Phoenix.* [Revenge]

FRIEDMAN, Mickey. *Magic Mirror.* [Art]

GOLDSBOROUGH, Robert. *Death On Deadline.* 1987 Bantam/ Bantam 1988. British scandal-sheet owner Ian MacLaren was out to possess the *Gazette.* When Nero Wolfe heard that owner Harriet Haverhill had committed suicide, he's bound to call it murder. He'll solve this one even if he goes without a fee. 2nd. [Suicide]

GORDON, Alison. *The Dead Pull Hitter.* [Ball Games]

GRANGER, Bill, w/a Joe Gash. *Newspaper Murders.* 1985 Holt/ Warner 1987. He was an old, boozing reporter: Francis X. Sweeney was found at four in the morning in a Chicago alley, his head bashed in. Sergeant Terry

Flynn and Detective Karen Kovak check with all his co-workers and the stories he worked on, looking for a clue. 3rd.

GRANT-ADAMSON, Lesley. *The Face Of Death.* 1986 Scribner/Fawcett 1987. She'd been in an auto accident and remembered nothing. Peter Dutton claimed she was his wife, Carol. But it didn't feel right to her. Holly, assistant to columnist Rain Morgan, lived next door to the Duttons. She's about to involve Rain. 2nd.

GRANT-ADAMSON, Lesley. *Wild Justice.* 1988 St. Martin/ Perennial 1990. Hal MacQuillan, new owner of London's *Daily Post,* was found dead at his desk, a knife in his back. The list of enemies was long and reached into the past. Columnist Rain Morgan uses her fine-honed skills to find the murderer. 4th. [Revenge]

GRISSOM, Ken. *Drop-Off.* [Drugs]

HIAASEN, Carl. *Tourist Season.* [Social Issues]

HILL, Reginald. *Underworld.* [Old Crime]

JERINA, Carol. *Flirting With Danger.* Pocket 1990/ PBO. Rival reporters Catherine Harrison and Tom Devlin overhear a serious argument at a Maryland fox hunt. When the woman disappears, Catherine tracks her down in Georgetown and helps smuggle her out of the city. Tom Devlin is in close pursuit. [Political]

JOHNSTON, Jane. *Paint Her Face Dead.* 1987 St. Martin/ Worldwide 1988. Reporter Louisa Evans signed up for SUM, a marathon similar to est, to get a story. The green-haired woman sitting next to her collapsed and died. This will be a bigger story—or Louisa's death sentence. 2nd. [Where There's A Will]

KALLEN, Lucille. *C. B. Greenfield: The Piano Bird.* [Real Estate]

KALLEN, Lucille. *C. B. Greenfield: A Little Madness.* 1986 Random House/ Ballantine 1987. Maggie Rome joined an antinuclear group picketing the air force base. As the pro and anti groups clash, one of the leaders is found dead in a stream behind the base. Maggie and her boss solve the crime. 5th. [Social Issues]

KIKER, Douglas. *Murder On Clam Pond.* 1986 Random House/ Ballantine 1988. Mac McFarland, ex-reporter and husband, with his toothless poodle, find refuge on Clam Pond. The dog sniffs out the snow-covered body of the lady next door. Jane Drexel had been rich and had a secret. Mac had a story. 1st.

KIKER, Douglas. *Death At The Cut.* [Political]

KOHLER, Vincent. *Rainy North Woods.* 1990 St. Martin/ Pocket 1990. It started out as a simple story for reporter Eldon Larkin of the *South Coast Sun.* A Vietnamese refugee had been trampled to death by a circus elephant. But something strange is going on in the rainy woods of Port Jerome, Oregon. [Drugs]

LAMB, Margaret. *Chains Of Gold.* [Old Crime]

LEWIS, Roy Harley. *Miracles Take A Little Longer.* 1986 St. Martin. Enjoying his life as a bookstore owner, Matthew Coll was disturbed by a visit from an old newspaper colleague. Bill had become a faith healer, and the first person he cured had been murdered. Bill doesn't know if he's the killer or not. 4th. [Bookstore]

LOGUE, John. *Follow The Leader.* [Ball Games]

LOGUE, John. *Replay: Murder.* [Ball Games]

McDONALD, Gregory. *Fletch Won.* 1985 Warner/ Warner 1986. Noted attorney Donald Habeck was found in the *News-Tribune* parking lot. He was sitting in his car with a bullet in his temple. Fletch wants the story. Soon he's up to his knees in dirty tricks. 9th. [Prostitution]

McMULLEN, Mary. *A Dangerous Funeral.* [Where There's A Will]

NAHA, Ed. *On The Edge.* [Serial Killer]

NEGGERS, Carla, w/a Anne Harrell. *Minstrel's Fire.* [Jewels]

O'BRIEN, Meg. *The Daphne Decisions.* Bantam 1990/ PBO. Reporter Jessica James woke up in a hospital room. The Judge and a doctor kept calling her Mrs. Malcross. Jessica knew she wasn't the Judge's daughter-in-law. She also smelled a great story. 1st. [Real Estate]

O'BRIEN, Meg. *Salmon In The Soup.* Bantam 1990/ PBO. Marcus Andrelli's lawyer, beautiful Barbara Sloan, was shot to death on Marcus's boat. The police have tagged him as prime suspect. It's up to reporter Jesse James to get the truth that sets Marcus free. 2nd. [Drugs]

PETERSON, Keith. *The Trap Door.* 1988 Bantam/ PBO. John Wells has an editor who doesn't care much for him. He took Wells off the big trial that was about to start and sent him to Grant County to cover a rash of teen suicides. Under the surface, Wells found that things were not country quiet. 1st. [Father]

PETERSON, Keith. *There Fell A Shadow.* 1988 Bantam/ PBO. Crime reporter John Wells stopped off at the Press Club for a drink and was introduced to Timothy Colt. Colt was knifed as John watched, helpless—the only witness. John has to find the answers, quickly, before he's next. 2nd. [Old Crime]

POLLACK, Richard. *The Episode.* 1986 NAL/ Signet 1987. Journalist Daniel Cooper has a problem. The .45 that killed the real estate owner, Billy Roarke, was found in Daniel's apartment. He had to recapture the twenty-four hours that he lost to his first epileptic seizure in twenty years. [Real Estate]

PORTER, Anna. *Mortal Sin.* 1988 NAL/ Onyx 1989. Free-lance journalist Judith Hayes finally got her interview. But on the night of Paul Zimmerman's belated birthday party, he collapsed and died. Judith thinks there's a connection between Paul's death and that of a shoeless corpse. She's out to prove it. 2nd. [Imposter]

RISENHOOVER, C. C. *Dead Even.* 1986 McLennon/ Paperjacks 1988. His editor wants Matt McCall, *San Antonio Tribune,* to cover the murder of an attorney's wife. It's looking like a setup when Matt finds out that a year earlier another lawyer's wife died mysteriously. But the killings aren't over yet. 1st. [Gay]

RISENHOOVER, C. C. *Blood Bath.* 1987 McLennon/ Paperjacks 1988. Reporter Matt McCall is on assignment, looking into the brutal murder of a young woman. When another woman dies, it looks like a serial killer. 2nd.

RISENHOOVER, C. C. *Matt McCall.* 1988 Paperjacks/ PBO. Matt McCall, working as an investigative reporter, is disgusted. On a technicality, a man had just beaten charges of murdering a child. Matt's out to see that his wife and children stay safe. 3rd. [Children]

SHAH, Diane K. *As Crime Goes By.* Bantam 1990/ PBO. Hollywood 1947: Paris Chandler, young widow, took a job doing the leg work for gossip columnist Ette Rice. One morning a woman walked into Paris's office asking her to print her affair in the gossip column. Days later, the lady was dead on the beach. 1st. [Infidelity]

SHANKMAN, Sarah aka Alice Storey. *Now Let's Talk Of Graves.* 1990 Pocket. Journalist Sam Adams is in New Orleans for Mardi Gras, visiting her college friend Kitty Lee. On the way home from the last ball, Kitty's brother is run down and killed by a vintage Buick with a masked driver. And Sam sees it happen. 3rd. [Holiday]

SMITH, Kay Nolte. *Catching Fire.* [Theater]

SQUIRE, Elizabeth Daniels. *Kill The Messenger.* 1989 St. Martin/ St. Martin 1991. Owner and publisher of *The Defender,* Isaiah Justice, died of cyanide poisoning and made his own front page. His son Howard and reporter Leeroy Hicks start their own investigation and fight to prevent the paper from being sold. [Blackmail]

STANSBERRY, Dominic. *The Spoiler.* [Ball Games]

STEVENS, Christian D. *Printer's Devil.* 1987 St. Martin. Reporter Steve Hadleyman received an urgent plea from Birdie Johnson, publisher of a small Montana newspaper. He arrived to find Birdie stabbed to death. When he's knocked over the head, the body disappears. Steve discovers that the paper is in trouble. [Fraud]

STOREY, Alice. *First Kill All The Lawyers.* 1988 Pocket/ PBO. Reporter Samantha Adams returned to her home in Atlanta and was looking for a story. She thought she'd found one in the corruption of small-town law. Then attorney Forrest Ridley died—an accident. Samantha sharpened her pencil and went to work. 1st. [Real Estate]

TAYLOR, Matt & Bonnie. *Neon Flamingo.* 1987 Dodd, Mead/ St. Martin 1990. Haskins Delano, a thirty-year cop, retired for eighteen months, was knifed to death in his own home. The house is ransacked, and the police think his murder has to do with Delano's past history. Journalist Palmer Kingston of the Marlinsport *Tribune* has to go back in time for the answers. 1st. [Old Crime]

TRUMAN, Margaret. *Murder In Georgetown*. 1986 Arbor House/ Fawcett 1987. Joe Potamos, *Post* reporter, was covering the death of Valerie, the senator's daughter. Tony, a friend of Valerie, has her diary and everyone wants it, especially after Tony's also found dead. Joe wants to find the killer. [Political]

WARMBOLD, June. *June Mail*. 1986 Permanent/ Jove 1986. Free-lance journalist Sarah Colloway was onto a top-notch story, a vaccine for AIDS. The research was being done by an ex-lover. He's missing, and she's the only one trying to find him. 1st.

WEISS, Mike. *No Go On Jackson Street*. 1987 Scribner/ Fawcett 1989. He's been bumped from the *San Francisco Courier* for probing too deeply. So Ben Henry drives a taxi. He answered a call for 3670 Jackson Street, and it was a "no-go." Next day, he learns that a columnist was murdered at that address, and his friend Vollo is in trouble. 1st. [Revenge]

WESTLAKE, Donald. *Trust Me On This*. 1988 Mysterious/ Mysterious 1989. On the way to her new job, Sara Joslyn spotted a dead man in a blue Buick. When no one seems interested in the story, she digs at it anyway. Then the body disappears, and her notes are stolen. Her editor, Jack, finally decides to help. [Old Crime]

WOODS, Sheryl. *Reckless*. [Cooks]

WOODS, Sheryl. *Body & Soul*. Popular 1989/ PBO. Amanda Roberts is doing a story on health clubs for *Inside Atlanta*. She's on the scene when a woman is found dead in the steam room. Suddenly her boss at the magazine wants her to drop the story. But, with Joe Danelli, she digs even deeper. 2nd. [Drugs]

WOODS, Sheryl. *Stolen Moments.* Popular 1990/ PBO. Amanda Roberts, on assignment for *Inside Atlanta,* is writing up historic homes in the city. But valuable antiques are disappearing from these same stately mansions. To complicate matters, her ex-husband Mack is on the scene and Joe Danelli doesn't like it. 3rd. [Antiques]

ZELMAN, Anita. *The Right Moves.* 1988 St. Martin. Linda was on her way to a Caribbean island for a chess tournament, the first woman to represent the U.S. When she had a series of accidents, it became obvious that someone didn't want her to be world champion. Journalists Debs and Calvin are going to write the story. [Political]

K . . . IS FOR

KIDNAPPING

*K*IDNAPPING IS A CRIME *we are all beginning to fear. In times past, it was only the very rich or the very powerful who were the victims of this crime. That's no longer the case. Even the ordinary person has cause for concern.*

ALBERT, Marvin. *Long Teeth.* [Blackmail]

BABSON, Marian. *Unfair Exchange.* 1986 Walker. Zita Falbridge agreed, with a faint heart, to look after her husband's ex-wife's nine-year-old daughter Fanny. Fanny's mother was going on a Mediterranean cruise. Fanny arrived from America, was kidnapped, and Caroline was really on a boat in the Thames. [On Vacation]

BUNN, Thomas. *Worse Than Death.* 1989 Holt. Nora Toland had wanted a baby for a long time and was thrilled when Mai came along. When Mr. Agnew said he still needed $13,000, the baby disappeared. Unable to go to the police, Nora turns to PI Jack Bodine. 2nd. [Children]

CHARLES, Hampton. *Advantage Miss Seeton.* [Ball Games]

COLLINS, Max Allan. *Spree.* 1987 Tor/ Tor 1988. Nolan is a thief who's decided to go straight. He runs a restaurant in the Brady Eighty Mall and has found himself a beautiful companion. The Comforts arrive. They kidnap Sherry and start making demands.

CRAIS, Robert. *Stalking The Angel.* [Manuscript]

DUFFY, Margaret. *Who Killed Cock Robin?* [Intrigue]

FLYNN, Don. *Murder On The Hudson.* [Journalism]

FRANCIS, Dick. *The Danger.* [Horses]

GREENLEAF, Stephen. *Toll Call.* 1987 Villard/ Ballantine 1988. Tanner's secretary Peggy is receiving strange phone calls. Despite her phone number changes, the calls continue. In the process of tracing down the caller, Tanner meets Peggy's neighbor, a woman in fear of her daughter's being kidnapped. 5th.

HEBDEN, Mark. *Pel And The Party Spirit.* [Old Crime]

HESS, Joan. *Malice In Maggody.* [Jealousy]

KENYON, Michael. *Peckover Holds The Baby.* [Drugs]

LaPIERRE, Janet. *The Cruel Mother.* 1990 Scribner. Meg Hallaran and her police-chief boyfriend Vince Gutierrez are on vacation. Along for the ride is Cass, his niece. Vince has to fly home, and Meg and Cass are in an accident where a young child is injured. Soon after, they're kidnapped. 3rd. [Mother]

LORNE, David. *Sight Unseen.* Signet 1990/ PBO. Janey Granville was kidnapped when her class took a field trip to the local museum. Her Uncle Spike Halleck, one of Hollywood's greatest sound-effects men, has to save the little girl he adores. But Spike is blind.

LUTZ, John. *The Right To Sing The Blues.* 1986 St. Martin/Tor 1988. PI Nudger flew to New Orleans to help out night club owner Fat Jack McGee. He wants Nudger to check out jazz piano player Willie Hollister and his romance with Ineida, which is about to go sour. 3rd.

MARTIN, Lee. *A Conspiracy Of Strangers.* 1986 St. Martin. Deb Ralston, Ft. Worth PD, was jogging near her home when she discovered the body of a young woman in a culvert—another in a long list getting longer. All the women were pregnant when they disappeared. Deb is about to open up a nasty case. 2nd.

McSHANE, Mark. *Séance On A Wet Afternoon.* [Psychic]

NABB, Magdalen. *Death In Springtime.* 1984 Scribner/Penguin 1985. Two young women were kidnapped from the Piazza San Felice in Florence in broad daylight. Marshal Guarnacci was joined by Capt. Maestrangelo in a hunt through the Tuscan hills in a fight against time. 3rd.

O'HARA, Kenneth. *Death Of A Moffy.* 1987 Doubleday. Trouble found the English country hotel. Helmer, the owner, may not be on the up-and-up. His daughter was kidnapped, and assistant Caroline Skene hired a security agent. She got more than she bargained for. [Revenge]

PETERS, Elizabeth. *The Copenhagen Connection.* [Anthropology]

PHILBIN, Tom. *Cop Killer.* [Gay]

PHILBRICK, W. R. *Ice For The Eskimo.* 1986 Beaufort/Signet 1988. Two children have been kidnapped. The ransom? Their father, lawyer Finian A. Fitzgerald, is to drop his latest case. Mystery writer Jack Hawkins is helping to find the children. Then the whole case blows up. 2nd. [Blackmail]

RITCHIE, Simon. *The Hollow Woman.* [Canadian]

SHERWOOD, John. *The Sunflower Plot.* [Botany]

SMITH, Janet L. *Sea Of Troubles.* [Revenge]

SMITH, Julie. *True-Life Adventure.* 1985 Mysterious/ Mysterious 1986. Paul McDonald had quit his job on the newspaper to write mysteries. But to earn a living, he ghost-wrote reports for PI Jack Birnbaum. When Jack keels over on his living room floor from too much saccharin in his coffee, Paul takes over the cases. 1st. [Mystery Writer]

TAYLOR, Andrew. *Waiting For The End Of The World.* [Smuggling]

WESTLAKE, Donald. *Good Behavior.* 1986 Mysterious/ Mysterious 1987. The heist had gone bad, and Dortmunder was hanging from the rafters in the chapel of the convent. He was about to do the good sisters a favor: kidnap back Sister Mary Grace who was being held for deprogramming in her father's very secure penthouse. 6th. [Clergy]

WHITNEY, Phyllis A. *Feathers On The Moon.* 1988 Doubleday/ Fawcett 1989. It had been seven years since Jenny Blake's three-year-old daughter had been kidnapped. Suddenly she received a letter from a wealthy woman in Victoria, Canada. Mrs. Arles wants to have Jenny prove that the child in her home cannot be Jenny's daughter. Mrs. Arles wants Alice to be her great-granddaughter. [Children]

L . . . IS FOR

LAWYERS

ERLE STANLEY GARDNER made the name of attorney Perry Mason almost a household word. Gardner had hardly finished law school when he decided that his practice of the law would be between the covers of the mystery novel. Since lawyers are avid mystery readers, it's no surprise to find them also writing some.

BERRY, Carole. *The Letter Of The Law.* [Old Crime]

BORGENICHT, Miriam. *Undue Influence.* 1989 St. Martin/ Worldwide 1990. Attorney Lydia Ness has a case she doesn't want. Kindly Jerry Eldstrom is accused of raping and murdering a young girl. As the trial gets underway, the dead girl's family starts to put pressure on Lydia. And now her daughter is missing. [Mother]

BOWMAN, Robert J. *The House Of Blue Lights.* [Real Estate]

CAUDWELL, Sarah. *Thus Was Adonis Murdered.* [Art]

CAUDWELL, Sarah. *The Shortest Way To Hades.* [Accident]

CAUDWELL, Sarah. *The Sirens Sang Of Murder.* 1989 Delacorte/ Dell 1990. Michael Cantrip volunteered his legal services for the Daffodil Settlement. After all, who could resist a trip to Monaco and the Cayman Islands? But some of the advisors for the wealthy trust are killed off. Hilary Tamar has to rescue poor Cantrip. 3rd. [Infidelity]

CHASTAIN, Thomas. *The Case Of Too Many Murders.* 1989 Morrow/ Avon 1990. Just as they left the restaurant, notorious Los Angeles businessman Gil Adrian turned and shot his dinner companion, in front of a room full of witnesses. Minutes later, Gil was murdered in his own den. Perry Mason was hired to clear Gil's estranged wife of the crime. 1st. [Imposter]

DOWNING, Warwick. *A Clear Case Of Murder.* Pocket 1990/ PBO. Ex-rodeo star Johnny Blue ran down public defender Ami O'Rourke as she left the courthouse and jaywalked across the street in Sopris County, Colorado. Special prosecutor David Reddman has been sent down from Denver to try the case. He's looking for Murder One. [Accident]

GARDNER, Erle Stanley. *The Case Of The Crooked Candle.* 1944 Morrow/ Ballantine 1987. A series of incidents leads Perry Mason to dig deep into Roger Burbank's business dealings. His client is accused of the murder of Fred Milfield on Burbank's yacht. Milfield is a partner in a company that has suspicious commercial dealings. 24th. [Fraud]

GARDNER, Erle Stanley. *The Case Of The Terrified Typist.* 1956 Morrow/ Ballantine 1987. Perry called for a temporary typist to help with some briefs. When a young woman showed up at the office, Gertie put her to work. Later, the South African Gem Company was robbed and the typist was gone. Perry has to defend a murderer where there's no body. 50th. [Jewels]

GIROUX, E. X. *A Death For Adonis.* [Revenge]

GIROUX, E. X. *A Death For A Darling.* [Imposter]

GIROUX, E. X. *A Death For A Dancer.* [Blackmail]

GIROUX, E. X. *A Death For A Doctor.* [Revenge]

GIROUX, E. X. *A Death For A Dilettante.* 1987 St. Martin/ Ballantine 1988. Barrister Robert Forsythe and his secretary, Miss Sanderson, are posing as guests at the home of Winslow Maxwell Penndragon. Several attempts have been made on his life and he wants them stopped. They aren't able to prevent Winslow's death. 5th. [Incest]

GIROUX, E. X. *A Death For A Dietitian.* [Mystery Games]

GREENLEAF, Stephen. *Impact.* 1989 Morrow/ Bantam 1990. SurfAir 617 crashed on approach to San Francisco airport. Jack Donahue survived, but just barely. Aviation lawyer Alec Hawthorne joined Keith Tollison to fight the airlines. Despite Keith's affair with Laura, Jack's wife, it almost seems as though Laura is on trial. [Accident]

HENSLEY, Joe L. *Robak's Cross.* 1985 Doubleday. Ed Sage was found near the body of his wife, a gun in his hand. He doesn't remember shooting Beth, but seems perfectly willing to take the blame. Don Robak is trying to defend him when he finds Beth's diary. 6th. [Infidelity]

HENSLEY, Joe L. *Robak's Fire.* 1986 Doubleday/ Paperjacks 1988. Avery Benjamin died when his house burned. But the insurance company thinks his two sons and second wife, Hilda, are pulling a gigantic scam. Don Robak was asked to come to Drewville to sort things out. The Benjamins aren't very friendly. 7th. [Insurance]

HUEBNER, Frederick D. *The Black Rose.* [Social Issues]·

HUEBNER, Frederick D. *Judgment By Fire.* [Arson]

ISRAEL, Peter. *If I Should Die Before I Die.* [Serial Killer]

KAHN, Michael A. *The Canaan Legacy.* [Where There's A Will]

KRAFT, Gabrielle. *Bullshot.* [Fraud]

LACHMAN, Charles. *In The Name Of The Law.* 1988 St. Martin. As he practices law in New York City, Jimmy Janos operates scams, mixes with mobsters, and flouts the legal profession. Things come to a head when he defends the Sick Assassins, a youth gang. Now he's up for disbarment.

LEVINE, Paul. *To Speak For The Dead.* 1990 Bantam. Jake Lassiter takes on a malpractice case. Dr. Roger Salisbury has been charged in the death of wealthy Philip Corrigan. Corrigan's daughter is convinced her father was murdered, and his second wife makes a play for Jake. 1st. [Medical]

LEWIS, Roy. *The Salamander Chill.* 1989 St. Martin. Eric Ward, solicitor, is being kept busy. There's the threat of a hostile takeover at Martin & Channing. Then his wife's advisor to her Marcomb Estates is charged with the murder of his fiancée. Eric will represent him. 7th. [Fraud]

MATERA, Lia. *Where Lawyers Fear To Tread.* 1987 Bantam/PBO. Willa Jansson, law student, is an editor for the Law Review. The editor-in-chief is found dead at her desk, her head bashed in. When two more editors turn up dead, it seems to be open season on the Law Review. 1st. [Academic]

MATERA Lia. *A Radical Departure.* [Imposter]

MATERA, Lia. *The Smart Money.* [Where There's A Will]

MATERA, Lia. *Hidden Agenda.* 1988 Bantam/ PBO. Bob Hopper is a top honcho in the Republican Party. So why is he promoting left-leaning Willa Jansson to a top-notch law firm? At a retreat in the Sierras, a law partner dies of hemlock poison. Willa seems a likely suspect. 3rd. [Revenge]

McBAIN, Ed. *Jack and The Beanstalk.* 1984 Holt/ Pinnacle 1988. Young Jack McKinney was dead, stabbed fourteen times, and $36,000 was missing. He had Matthew Hope's card in his pocket. Matt remembered him: the kid had bought a snap-bean farm. Soon there's another body and a bushel of suspects with a couple of leads. 4th. [Drugs]

McBAIN, Ed. *Cinderella.* [Drugs]

McBAIN, Ed. *Puss In Boots.* [Pornography]

McBAIN, Ed. *The House That Jack Built.* 1988 Holt/ Mysterious 1989. Frank Parrish flew to Florida for his brother's fortieth birthday. Appalled at Jonathan's gay life-style, they have a terrible fight. In the morning, Jonathan is dead on the kitchen floor and Frank's charged with his murder. Attorney Matthew Hope is convinced that Frank is innocent. 8th. [Blackmail]

McINERNY, Frank. *Body And Soil.* [Psychological]

MEEK, M. R. D. *The Split Second.* 1987 Scribner/ Worldwide 1989. After her mother died, Fiona had taken off and married. Now Aunt Grace was concerned. She hadn't heard from Fiona at Christmas. She wants Lennox Kemp to find her. Kemp traces her to Scotland. He arrives to find she's drowned. But that's not the worst. 2nd. [Psychological]

MEEK, M. R. D. *In Remembrance Of Rose.* [Manuscript]

MEEK, M. R. D. *This Blessed Plot.* 1991 Scribner. Poor, ill-kempt Julie Sorrento arrives at lawyer Lennox Kemp's office with her two dirty children. Her husband is missing and she wants him found. At the same time, the Courtenay twins have inherited a vast fortune. Lennox gets edgy when he discovers a connection between the two families. 7th. [Where There's A Will]

LAWYERS

MEREDITH, D. R. *Murder By Impulse.* [Revenge]

MITTERMEYER, Helen. *Brief Encounter.* [Smuggling]

PIESMAN, Marissa. *Unorthodox Practices.* [Real Estate]

RESNICOW, Herbert. *The Hot Place.* 1990 St. Martin. Lawyer Barney Brodsky was found strangled in the steam room in the Oakland Country Club. Warren Baer just happened to be the one who found him. Ed, Warren's father, jumps into the investigation. Barney had a lot of enemies. 2nd. [Fraud]

RICE, Craig. *Having A Wonderful Crime.* 1943 Simon & Schuster/ Bantam 1986. Dennis Morrison, in a smart move, married heiress Bertha Lutis. In the morning, his bride is dead. When the police want him to identify the body, he discovers someone else's head on Bertha's torso. Lawyer J. J. Malone is nearby. 7th. [Infidelity]

RICE, Craig. *My Kingdom For A Hearse.* 1957 Simon & Schuster/ Bantam 1986. The advertising model for Delora Deanne Cosmetics is a composite, made from parts of many women. Hazel Swackhammer is the brains of the business, and she's just received a package containing Delora's hands. She calls for J. J. Malone. 11th. [Blackmail]

SMITH, Julie. *Death Turns A Trick.* [Prostitution]

TAPPLY, William G. *Death At Charity's Point.* [Suicide]

TAPPLY, William G. *The Dutch Blue Error.* [Father]

TAPPLY, William G. *Follow The Sharks.* [Ball Games]

TAPPLY, William G. *The Marine Corpse.* [Social Issues]

TAPPLY, William G. *The Vulgar Boatman.* [Drugs]

TAPPLY, William G. *A Void Of Hearts.* 1988 Scribner/ Ballantine 1990. Les Katz was hired by Brenda Hayden to follow her husband to find out what he was up to. Les took pictures, then he was run over. His friend Brady Coyne is helping his widow to sort things out. It's double trouble all the way. 7th. [Economics]

TAPPLY, William G. *Dead Winter.* 1989 Delacorte/ Dell 1990. Desmond Winter, retired minister, called Brady Coyne in the middle of the night. His daughter-in-law Maggie has just been found murdered and his son is being held at the police station. As Brady digs into the case, another murder surfaces. 8th. [Incest]

TAPPLY, William G. *Client Privilege.* [Father]

THOMPSON, Gene. *A Cup Of Death.* [Art]

TRUMAN, Margaret. *Murder In The Supreme Court.* 1982 Arbor House/ Fawcett 1985. Up and coming Clarence Sutherland was shot to death while he sat in the chief justice's chair at the Supreme Court. Detective Martin Teller and Susanna Pinscher, from Justice, after several setbacks, finally find a solid lead. [Blackmail]

VAN GIESON, Judith. *North Of The Border.* [Real Estate]

VAN GIESON, Judith. *Raptor.* [Bird Watching]

VAN GIESON, Judith. *The Other Side Of Death.* 1991 Harper Collins. In Santa Fe for a party, Neil Hamel drove her friend Lonnie home. Within minutes, Lonnie took off. In the morning her body was found in an Indian cave where she liked to meditate. The police call it suicide, a drug overdose; Neil calls it murder. 3rd. [Psychic]

WAKEFIELD, Hannah. *A Woman's Own Mystery.* [Intrigue]

WHEAT, Carolyn. *Dead Man's Thoughts.* [Corruption]

WHEAT, Carolyn. *Where Nobody Dies.* [Blackmail]

WILLIAMS, Philip Carlton. *Mission Bay Murder.* [Fraud]

WOLFE, Susan. *The Last Billable Hour.* 1989 St. Martin/ Ballantine 1990. Leo Slyde sat in his chair at Tweedmore and Slyde law offices. He'd been stabbed with a message spindle from his own desk. Howard Rickover, young attorney, is the inside man for Inspector Sarah Nelson. 1st. [Fraud]

WOODS, Sara. *Malice Domestic.* [Old Crime]

WOODS, Sara. *Bloody Instructions.* [Where There's A Will]

WOODS, Sara. *The Third Encounter.* [Intrigue]

WOODS, Sara. *Most Deadly Hate.* 1986 St. Martin/ Avon 1987. When Phillipa Osmond was strangled, the best suspect was her ex-husband. Phillipa had walked out on him and her child. Then she wanted custody of her daughter at any cost. Antony Maitland has to prove him innocent. 49th. [Infidelity]

ZOLLINGER, Norman. *Lautrec.* 1990 Dutton. Attorney Jack Lautrec took the tough cases. This time, young Luis Esquibel was found filling in a grave, the grave of a beautiful young woman. Together with his daughter and law partner Martine, they have to break the air-tight case against him. 1st. [Infidelity]

LIBRARIES

Musty stacks, signs that caution the visitor to behave in a quiet manner, and hushed footsteps approaching from behind all conjure up a setting conducive to foul play and murder. The stalker seems to be all but anonymous in the dim lighting. Not neglected is the private library in the Stately Home.

BLACKSTOCK, Charity. *Dewey Death.* 1958 London House/ Ballantine 1985. Mrs. Warren, the library gossip, was the first to die. As the police roam the stacks and offices, Barbara Smith falls in love. But there will soon be another murder. [Drugs]

CHRISTIE, Agatha. *The Body In The Library.* 1942 Dodd, Mead/ Pocket 1985. When the body of a young woman is found on the hearth rug in Colonel Bantry's library, his wife Dolly summons Jane Marple to clear up the mystery. But first they must visit the nearby resort of Danemouth. 2nd. [Imposter]

CURRAN, Terrie. *All Booked Up.* [Manuscripts]

DEAN, S. F. X. *By Frequent Anguish.* [Academic]

GOODRUM, Charles A. *Dewey Decimated.* 1977 Crown/ Perennial 1988. At the spring concert at Werner-Bok Library, Murchison DeVeer died. Earlier that day, a letter had declared the Gutenberg Bible a fake. Dr. George and his cohorts, Crighton and Carson, are not about to let the crime go unsolved. 1st. [Manuscripts]

GOODRUM, Charles. *The Best Cellar.* 1987 St. Martin/ Perennial 1988. In a wild gesture, Crighton Jones invited Durance, a student doing research on Thomas Jefferson at the Library of Congress, to stay with her. Then Durance disappears, and simple research leads to murder. 3rd. [Manuscripts]

HARRIS, Charlaine. *Real Murder.* 1990 Walker. Librarian Aurora Teagarden belonged to Real Murders, a small group devoted to the study of famous murder cases. But when Mamie Wright is found dead in the VFW kitchen, Aurora recognizes it as a reenactment of her Murder of the Month. 1st. [Mystery Games]

HARRISS, Will. *The Bay Psalm Book Murder.* 1983 Walker/ Pinnacle 1985. Librarian Link Schofield was mugged and killed for fourteen dollars, with a rare manuscript left in his hand. His friend English professor Cliff Dunbar starts an investigation. Aided by proofreader Mona Moore, he discovers the MS is a forgery. [Manuscript]

LATHEN, Emma, w/a R. B. Dominic. *Murder, Sunny Side Up* [Political]

McALEER, John. *Coign Of Vantage.* [Manuscripts]

LOCKED ROOM

Although he'd never been to Paris, and there is no Rue Morgue in the city, Edgar Allan Poe delighted us with the most famous impossible crime—the ultimate puzzle—the locked room murder. The tradition has continued to keep us on our toes. The master of the locked room drama, John Dickson Carr, even included an essay on the subject in his mystery, The Three Coffins.

BOUCHER, Anthony. *Nine Times Nine.* [Clergy]

BOWEN, Michael. *Washington Deceased.* 1990 St. Martin. Wendy Gardner made arrangements to meet Richard Michaelson, late of the State Department. Her father, Senator Gardner, in prison for misdeeds, feels that his life is in danger. And when there is a murder in a locked room in the prison, the Senator stands accused. [Political]

CARR, John Dickson. *The Dead Man's Knock.* 1958 Harper & Row/ Zebra 1987. Mark received an early morning phone call and rushed out of the house straight into a death scene. Rose Lestrange was stabbed in a locked room. Dr. Gideon Fell knew it was murder. 18th.

CHRISTIE, Agatha. *A Holiday For Murder.* [Christmas]

GODFREY, Ellen. *Murder Behind Locked Doors.* [Canadian]

GRAY, Malcolm. *Stab In The Back.* [Mystery Writer]

GREENBERG, Martin, and Bill Pronzini, eds. *Locked Room Puzzles.* 1986 Academy Chicago/ PBO. Four novellas featuring locked room mysteries.

GREENE, Douglas G., and Robert C. S. Adey, eds. *Death Locked In.* 1987 International Polygonics/ PBO. Five hundred pages of locked room mysteries from the pens of some of the best writers.

MILNE, A. A. *The Red House Mystery.* 1922 Dutton/ Dell 1984. Robert Ablett returned from Australia to stay with his wealthy brother Mark at the Red House. Robert died in a locked room, and Mark is missing. Antony Gillingham and Bill Beverley are asking a lot of questions. [Revenge]

MURPHY, Warren. *Leonardo's Law.* 1978 Carlyle/ Paperjacks 1988. Mystery writer Barry Dawson was found with his skull crushed. The room had been locked from the inside, and the corpse was holding the key. Professor David Leonardo is called in. He quickly discovers the murderer, but the puzzle of the locked room becomes an obsession. [Mystery Writer]

RESNICOW, Herbert. *The Gold Solution.* 1983 St. Martin/ Avon 1984. Alexander Gold is recuperating from a heart attack, and Norma is trying to keep him occupied with puzzles. He's persuaded to figure out the murder of architect Roger Allen Talbot, a locked room murder. 1st. [Insurance]

RESNICOW, Herbert. *The Dead Room.* 1986 Dodd, Mead/ Worldwide 1989. Walter Kassel had just invented a new speaker system. Now he was dead in an anechoic chamber where he was testing the sound system. Not only does Ed Baer have to find out who killed him, but also how it was done. 1st. [Fraud]

RHODE, John, and Carter Dickson. *Fatal Descent.* 1939 Dodd, Mead/ Dover 1987. Police surgeon Dr. Horatio Glass and Inspector David Hornbeam have a baffling case to solve. Publishing magnate Sir Ernest Tallent rode down in the elevator alone, made no stops, and was dead when the doors opened. No weapon was found. [Revenge]

SIMS, L. V. *To Sleep, Perchance To Kill.* [Revenge]

WILLIAMS, David. *Murder In Advent.* 1985 St. Martin/ Avon 1987. The church elders were divided on whether to sell the 1225 version of Magna Carta for money to repair the church. Mark Treasure was to be the deciding vote. When he arrived, he found a fire had destroyed the document, and someone was dead. 9th. [Manuscript]

M . . . IS FOR

MANUSCRIPTS

MANUSCRIPTS AND RARE BOOKS figure prominently on the pages of the mystery story. Rare books disappear, old manuscripts surface, and priceless collections go on the auction block—all to the delight of the reader and to the detriment of the victim.

BABSON, Marian. *Encore Murder.* [Television]

BARNARD, Robert. *The Case Of The Missing Brontë.* 1983 Scribner/ Dell 1986. Superintendent Perry Trethowan and Jan are motoring through the Yorkshire villages. In a pub, they strike up a conversation with Miss Edith Wing. She claims to have either an unpublished Brontë or a clever forgery. Then Miss Wing is brutally attacked. 3rd. [On Vacation]

BEATON, M. C. *Death Of A Hussy.* 1990 St. Martin/ Ivy 1991. Maggie Baird brought her niece Alison Kerr with her to the new house in the Highlands. Overweight and tweedy Maggie flirted with Constable Hamish Macbeth. Then she shed pounds, had a makeover and invited former lovers for a visit and a proposal. 5th. [Revenge]

BLOCK, Lawrence. *The Burglar Who Liked To Quote Kipling.* [Bookstore]

COLLINS, Max Allan. *Kill Your Darlings.* [Mystery Writer]

CRAIS, Robert. *Stalking The Angel.* 1989 Bantam. PI Elvis Cole was hired to find a rare eighteenth century Samurai manuscript, stolen from Bradley Warren's Los Angeles home. While Warren's wife makes a play for Elvis, his daughter Mimi is kidnapped. 2nd. [Kidnapping]

CURRAN, Terrie. *All Booked Up.* 1987 Dodd, Mead/ Worldwide 1989. Five weeks ago, Basil Killingsly was holding the rare book in his own two hands. Today, it was missing from the Smedley Library in Boston. Well, Basil is raising a fuss. Within days, two members of the staff are dead and more books are missing. [Library]

DEAN, S. F. X. *It Can't Be My Grave.* [Infidelity]

FISKE, Dorsey. *Bound To Murder.* 1987 St. Martin. Thieves are at work at the Cambridge University Library. At first, just color plates, then a whole medieval text vanishes. When the thief is murdered, the staff is relieved. For Inspector Bunce and Fen Church, it's just the beginning of the chase. 2nd. [Academic]

GOLLIN, James. *Eliza's Galiardo.* [Music]

GOODRUM, Charles A. *Dewey Decimated.* [Library]

GOODRUM, Charles A. *The Best Cellar.* [Library]

HARRISS, Will. *The Bay Psalm Book Murder.* [Library]

HAUSER, Thomas. *The Beethoven Conspiracy.* [Music]

HEALD, Tim. *Brought To Book.* [Smuggling]

HEBDEN, Mark. *Pel Among The Pueblos.* 1987 Walker. Pel is hunting a murderer in Mexico. But the killer escapes and heads back for France. Pel sets a trap to buy the lost letters and diary of Maximilian on a dark deserted road, and gets his man. 9th.

HENDRICKS, Michael. *Friends In High Places.* 1991 Scribner. Rita Noonan, PI, returned to her apartment and found ex-cop Wilsey Weiss shot to death on her floor. Wilsey had been an undercover cop who had taken too many wrong turns. Now his girlfriend says he was writing a book, an expose. Rita wants the manuscript. 2nd. [Blackmail]

KELLEY, Patrick A. *Sleightly Murder.* [Psychic]

LEWIS, Roy. *A Trout In The Milk.* [Real Estate]

LEWIS, Roy. *The Devil Is Dead.* [Witches]

LORENS, M. K. *Sweet Narcissus.* Bantam 1990/ PBO. Thirty years ago, Winston Marlowe Sherman attended a party in honor of Dylan Thomas. That night the folio of Webster's *Duchess of Malfi* was stolen and a man died. Now the manuscript has surfaced and there's going to be another murder. 1st. [Theater]

LOVELL, Marc. *The Spy Who Fell Off The Back Of The Bus.* 1988 Doubleday. Disguised as a wealthy Canadian, spy Appleton Porter is on a mission in Cannes. He's at a book convention to buy a manuscript that's supposed to be an attack on Sherlock Holmes by Arthur Conan Doyle. It's a matter of national security. 12th.

McALEER, John. *Coign Of Vantage.* 1988 Foul Play. The Smedley Barlow papers, missing for years, have turned up at the Boston Athenaeum, the foremost of gentlemen's libraries. In short order, several members of the Cart-tail Club, a literary society, die. Austin Layman is called in to investigate. 1st. [Library]

McGIVERN, William P. *Very Cold For May.* 1950 Dodd, Mead/ Penguin 1987. Hostess May Laval decided to have her diaries published. Jake Harrison was hired to protect Dan Riordan's honor. When May was murdered, Jake had to look at Dan's past. He didn't like what he found.

MEEK, M. R. D. *In Remembrance Of Rose.* 1987 Scribner/ Worldwide 1989. Rose Amaury had just finished signing her will. She turned to Lennox Kemp, her solicitor, and told him that someone was trying to kill her. Sure enough, one week later she was dead. And what's happened to the manuscript she wanted typed? 3rd. [Lawyer]

MONTGOMERY, Yvonne. *Scavengers.* 1987 Arbor House/ Avon 1990. When Elliot Fulton, Denver broker, died, there was a scavenger hunt for a missing Mark Twain manuscript. Fenny Aletter teams up with Detective Barelli to get herself off the hook for murder. 1st. [Revenge]

O'DONNELL, Lillian. *Falling Star.* [Theater]

RANDISI, Robert J. *The Steinway Collection.* 1988 Paperjacks/ PBO. Aaron Steinway called on PI Miles Jacoby. His prize collection of pulp detective magazines had been stolen, and he wanted Miles to find it. Then Steinway was killed, and someone wanted Miles off the case. 2nd.

RICHARDSON, Robert. *The Latimer Mercy.* 1985 St. Martin/ Signet 1987. Agustus Maltravers's mystery plays were to be performed at the Arts Festival in Vercaster. Diana Parker was the featured actress. As they arrived, a rare Bible, the Latimer Mercy, was stolen. Then Diana disappeared. 1st.

ROBINSON, Robert. *Landscape With Dead Dons.* [Academic]

ROOSEVELT, Elliott. *Murder At The Palace.* [Famous People]

SKOM, Edith. *The Mark Twain Murders.* 1989 Council Oak/Dell 1990. Professor Beth Austin, at Midwestern University, is shocked when Marylou Peacock is found murdered in the library, just as the semester is ending. Almost as disturbing is the loss of rare books from the open stacks. [Academic]

SMITH, Joan. *A Masculine Ending.* [Revenge]

SMITH, Julie. *Huckleberry Fiend.* 1987 Mysterious/ Mysterious 1988. Paul McDonald's friend Booker Kessler burgled an apartment and found a handwritten manuscript for Huckleberry Finn. Now the woman who had it is dead and Booker wants Paul to find out if it's real. Paul has to follow a paper trail. 2nd.

SWAIM, Don. *The H. L. Mencken Murder Case.* [Famous People]

TAYLOR, Andrew. *Caroline Minuscule.* 1983 Dodd, Mead/ Penguin 1984. Professor Sumpter, an authority on medieval scripts, was found strangled in his office. One of his graduate students, William Dougal, is also interested in the Caroline Minuscule. The manuscript is supposed to hold a secret to a treasure. 1st. [Jewels]

TRUMAN, Margaret. *Murder At The FBI.* 1985 Arbor House/ Fawcett 1986. The tour group going through the FBI building stopped at the firing range. The body of George Pritchard, special agent, is hanging behind the target, very dead. Half-Indian Christine Saksis and loner Ross Lizenby head up the investigative team. [Intrigue]

WARGA, Wayne. *Hardcover.* 1985 Arbor House/ Penguin 1987. Jeffrey Dean, rare book dealer, was poking around at the Los Angeles Antiquarian Book Fair. He spotted two first editions of Steinbeck, books he'd once owned. Only now they are both inscribed. His discovery causes someone to want him dead. 1st. [Bookstore]

WILLIAMS, David. *Murder In Advent.* [Locked Room]

WILTZ, Chris. *The Killing Circle.* [Father]

MEDICAL

Medical professionals are seen as possessing curative powers and promoting vigorous health. But the trappings of medicine are often used for sinister purposes by someone who has access to the supplies. The temptation can be great to slip a little something extra into the warm milk at bedtime.

BABSON, Marian. *In The Teeth Of Adversity.* 1990 St. Martin. Endicott Zayle, London dentist, used a new anesthetic on his patient Morgana Fane, a fashion model. When she died in the chair, he rushed to Doug Perkins for help. When Zayle and Perkins returned to the office, Morgana was gone, but Zayle's partner was dead. 4th. [Infidelity]

BURNS, Rex. *Parts Unknown.* [Missing Persons]

CANDY, Edward. *Which Doctor.* 1954 Doubleday/ Ballantine 1985. The body of Dr. Sandeman was found on the grounds at the Children's Hospital. And a nine-year-old boy is missing. While Inspector Burnivel investigates the crime, visiting professor Fabian Honeychurch plays detective. 1st. [Fraud]

CARLSON, P. M. *Murder Is Pathological.* [Academic]

COHEN, Anthea. *Angel Without Mercy.* 1984 Doubleday/ Tor 1987. Nurse Marion Hughes was night supervisor at St. Jude's, and she delighted in collecting information about her staff. But then one day, Nurse Hughes went much too far. Someone decided to do her in. 1st. [Getting Away With Murder]

COHEN, Anthea. *Angel Of Vengeance.* [Getting Away With Murder]

COHEN, Anthea. *Guardian Angel.* 1985 Doubleday. Nurse Carmichael's life is being disturbed by the porter at the hospital. Sampson is trying to get the nurses to join a union. Then there are the two punk visitors who are disturbing the ward. Worst of all, her cottage is broken into and her cats are missing. She has to take drastic action. 4th [Revenge]

CUTTER, Leela. *Death Of The Party.* 1985 St. Martin. The servants rolled in the diorama for the Romance Writer's Museum. But there was an extra figure: Lettie's nephew Freddie was very dead. Lettie and her niece Julia are joined by Max for a roam in the south of France to unravel a dangerous scheme. 3rd. [Mystery Writer]

DAVIDSON, Diane Mott. *Catering To Nobody.* [Cooks]

DAWSON, David Laing. *Last Rights.* [Canadian]

DILLON, Eilís. *Death At Crane's Court.* 1963 Walker/Perennial 1988. George Arrow, hearing that he had a heart condition that would soon make him an invalid, retired to the Irish coast and took up residence at a hotel-spa. When Mr. Burder, the owner, is found stabbed before his evening fire, George is a major suspect. 1st. [Where There's A Will]

DONALDSON, D. J. *Blood On The Bayou.* 1991 St. Martin. The French Quarter has a plague. A stripper, a homeless man and now a tourist have been found mutilated on the streets. Medical Examiner Andy Broussard has to bring modern techniques to bear on an ancient curse. 2nd. [Pathologist]

FARRELL, Maud. *Skid.* 1989 Dutton. New York City PI Victor Childes was murdered. A case the police quickly closed. Six months later his daughter Violet has decided that by fair means or foul, she's going to take over his practice and track down his killer. 1st. [Gay]

FRANKEL, Valerie. *A Deadline For Murder.* [Where There's A Will]

GREENLEAF, Stephen. *Death Bed.* [Missing Person]

HORNIG, Doug. *Deep Dive.* [Getting Away With Murder]

JACOBS, Nancy Baker. *Deadly Companion.* [Hollywood]

JOSHUA, Benjamin, MD. *A Drop Of Murder.* Avon 1990/ PBO. Several patients have died suddenly at Manhattan's Memorial Hospital. The autopsies show nothing definitive, but the police sense murder. Dr. Chuck Barone may be the only one who can stop a murderer that stalks the hospital corridors. [Psychological]

KIENZLE, William X. *Sudden Death.* 1985 Andrews, McMeel & Parker/ Ballantine 1986. Superstar for the Pontiac Cougars, "Hun" Hunsinger, stepped into his shower and soaped up his head. It was the last thing he ever did. The police know how he was murdered; Father Koesler finds out the who and why. 7th. [Mother]

KIENZLE, William X. *Deathbed.* 1986 Andrews, McMeel & Parker/ Ballantine 1987. Father Koesler is on assignment at St. Vincent's Hospital filling in for the chaplain. He begins to discover that someone is out to make a few of the patients a little bit sicker. He has to find the perpetrator before someone dies. 8th. [Clergy]

KITTREDGE, Mary. *Fatal Diagnosis.* 1990 St. Martin. Bill and Jane Claymore are taking the case to court. They insist their daughter was switched at birth with a terminally ill baby. In the hospital tissue lab, a technician and a volunteer have just been shot and the samples stolen. Edwina Crusoe is supposed to quiet the scandal. 1st. [Children]

KITTREDGE, Mary. *Rigor Mortis.* 1991 St. Martin. Millie Clemens insists the nurse fiddled with her husband's IV just before he died. Soon another patient is dead. Edwina Crusoe sets out to clear the nurse about to be charged with the crimes. 2nd. [Real Estate]

KRICH, Rochelle Majer. *Where's Mommy Now?.* Pinnacle 1990/ PBO. Kate Bauers loved her children and physician husband. She also loved her gift shop. As work demanded more time, she hired Janine, an *au pair.* Suddenly Kate was tired all the time, couldn't concentrate, and her perfect world was falling apart. [Infidelity]

LEVINE, Paul. *To Speak For The Dead.* [Lawyer]

LINDSEY, David L. *A Cold Mind.* [Serial Killer]

MANN, Jessica. *Faith, Hope & Homicide.* [Anthropology]

McINERNY, Ralph. *Cause And Effect.* 1987 Atheneum/ Worldwide 1990. Attorney Andrew Broom has just received a fatal diagnosis—leukemia. As he works to defend his client in a murder trial, his own life becomes more bizarre. 1st. [Infidelity]

MELVILLE, Jennie. *Windsor Red.* 1988 St. Martin/ Worldwide 1990. Studying the female criminal and the possible existence of feminist crime, police woman Charmian Daniels took rooms in Windsor to be near the university. Suddenly there are unidentified limbs in rubbish sacks, and a child is kidnapped. 1st. [Revenge]

O'DONNELL, Lillian. *Casual Affairs.* 1985 Putman/ Fawcett 1987. For her first case as lieutenant, Norah

Mulcahaney is confronted with the puzzle of a wealthy socialite in a coma from alcohol and drugs . . . again. The sister said it was attempted murder. One death leads to another, and Norah sets up a trap to smoke out the murderer. 10th. [Revenge]

PARETSKY, Sara. *Bitter Medicine.* 1987 Morrow/ Ballantine 1988. A friend of V. I. Warshawski's, Consuela, dies in the emergency room at a local hospital. Then the doctor is murdered in his apartment. Consuela's death starts to smell like malpractice, with a little cover-up thrown in. 4th.

SINGER, Shelley. *Spit In The Ocean.* 1987 St. Martin/ Worldwide 1989. Rosie convinces Jake Samson to investigate the plight of a friend. Someone has taken the assets of the North Coast Sperm Bank and dumped them into the Pacific. Soon they're looking for a murderer as well as a thief. 4th.

VAN DE WETERING, Janwillem. *The Rattle-Rat.* 1985 Pantheon/ Ballantine 1986. The burned body was floating in a blackened rowboat. Grijpstra and de Gier are sent to Friesland to find out who the victim is and who did it. Neither is pleased about their findings. 10th. [Drugs]

WEINMAN, Irving. *Virgil's Ghost.* [Corruption]

WILLIAMSON, Chet. *McKain's Dilemma.* 1988 Tor. Carlton Runnels had made his own adjustments. He'd made a marriage of convenience and made a lot of money. Now his lover Christopher is missing, and PI McKain is supposed to find him. When Chris turns up dead, McKain is suspicious. [Gay]

WOODS, Sara. *They Stay For Death.* 1980 St. Martin/ Avon 1988. Aunt Vera wants Antony Maitland to travel down to Chedcombe for a few days. During the past six months three patients have died at the Restawhile

Nursing Home. As Antony arrives, there's another death and Dr. Swinburne is arrested for murder. 31st. [Where There's A Will]

YARBRO, C. Q. *Bad Medicine.* [Indian]

YORK, Rebecca. *Life Line.* Harlequin 1990/ PBO. Psychologist Abby Franklin got a frantic call from a former patient. Unable to locate Sharon, Abby called her brother Derrick only to learn that Sharon was hospitalized. A short time later, Sharon is dead and her brother Steve accuses Abby of causing her death. 1st. [Psychological]

MEDIEVAL

The Middle Ages conjure up an image of drafty castles and silent monasteries. Travel was difficult and times were not easy. There were a multitude of wars, and the aftermath of the conflicts found families destitute. Life was undervalued and murder abounded. But isn't it a wonderful setting for mystery?

DOHERTY, P. C. *The Death Of A King.* 1986 St. Martin/ Bantam 1987. In 1344 Edward III commissioned a royal clerk, Edmund Beche, to carry out a secret investigation into the murder of Edward II at Berkeley Castle. As he travels the Continent, Beche discovers that others are following him.

DOHERTY, P. C. *Satan In St. Mary's.* 1987 St. Martin/ St. Martin 1989. King Edward I commissions Hugh Corbett, a clerk, to investigate the apparent suicide of a man in the London church of St. Mary. Hugh discovers murder and a coven of witches, together with a plot to remove the king, and a little love. 1st.

DOHERTY, P. C. *The Whyte Harte.* 1988 St. Martin. In 1399 Bishop Beaumont sends mercenary and ex-scholar Matthew Jankyn on a mission. He is to spy on Whyte Harte, a secret society. Was Richard II dead or in exile? Jankyn's reward would be his own freedom.

PETERS, Ellis. *A Morbid Taste For Bones.* 1977 Morrow/ Fawcett 1988. Brother Cadfael is sent out to his Welsh village to help the prior obtain the bones of St. Winifred. The man who most opposes the removal of the relics is murdered, and Brother Cadfael has his first case. 1st.

PETERS, Ellis. *One Corpse Too Many.* 1979 Morrow/Fawcett 1988. After the struggle between King Stephen and his cousin, Empress Maud, Brother Cadfael is called to perform funeral services for the ninety-four defenders who were hanged. He discovers an extra corpse, not hanged but killed with a knife. 2nd.

PETERS, Ellis. *Monk's Hood.* 1980 Morrow/ Fawcett 1988. When Gervase Bonel was taken ill, Brother Cadfael hastened to his side. He recognized Bonel's wife as the woman he had loved before he took his vows. Master Bonel had been poisoned by monk's hood oil from Brother Cadfael's own supply. 3rd.

PETERS, Ellis. *St. Peter's Fair.* 1981 Morrow/ Fawcett 1986. St. Peter's Fair was the grandest; merchants attended from miles around. Thomas of Bristol was murdered on the eve of the fair. As Brother Cadfael offers to assist his niece to find the killer, Thomas's booth is ransacked and two more men are dead. 4th.

PETERS, Ellis. *The Leper Of St. Giles.* 1981 Morrow/ Fawcett 1988. Huon de Domville died on the eve of his wedding to lovely Iveta. Iveta's only concern at the death of her betrothed is that her true love, Joscelin, a noble squire, is suspected and forced to hide in a leper sanctuary. Brother Cadfael doesn't believe in his guilt. 5th.

PETERS, Ellis. *The Virgin In The Ice.* 1982 Morrow/ Fawcett 1985. In 1139 Brother Cadfael journeys to Ludlow to minister to a wounded traveler. The local sheriff asks him to keep an eye out for two orphans and their chaperone. Then Cadfael discovers the body of a young girl frozen in the ice of a shallow brook. 6th.

PETERS, Ellis. *The Sanctuary Sparrow.* 1983 Morrow/ Fawcett 1988. A poor minstrel is offered sanctuary at the Abbey of St. Peter and St. Paul. He'd arrived just steps ahead of an angry mob, convinced that he was guilty of robbing a strong box at the goldsmith's house. Brother Cadfael is determined to clear Liliwin. 7th.

PETERS, Ellis. *The Devil's Novice.* 1983 Morrow/ Fawcett 1987. A novice from a good family shatters the quiet of the monastery, screaming in the night. Shunned by the other brothers, Aspley is noticed by Brother Cadfael. Then a young priest is found murdered and Aspley is implicated. Another mystery for Cadfael. 8th.

PETERS, Ellis. *Dead Man's Ransom.* 1984 Morrow/ Fawcett 1986. The war between King Stephen and Empress Maud still rages. Each side has a prisoner: the sheriff of Shropshire and Eli ap Cynan. Just as they are about to be exchanged, the sheriff is murdered and Eli has fallen in love. Brother Cadfael has to intervene. 9th.

PETERS, Ellis. *The Pilgrim Of Hate.* 1984 Morrow/ Fawcett 1987. The pilgrims flock to the abbey during the feast of St. Winifred. Ciaran has vowed to walk barefoot across England to Wales, and Matthew follows. Brother Cadfael has concern about their relationship, especially when news reaches him of the murder of a knight in Winchester. 10th.

PETERS, Ellis. *An Excellent Mystery.* 1985 Morrow/ Fawcett 1988. After Winchester was destroyed, brothers Humilis and Fidelis sought refuge at the abbey. Wounded in the Crusades, Humilis had released his betrothed Julian. Now a fellow crusader comes to request her hand. But Julian, together with the church plate and jewelry, has disappeared. 11th.

PETERS, Ellis. *The Raven In The Foregate.* [Christmas]

PETERS, Ellis. *The Rose Rent.* 1986 Morrow/ Fawcett 1988. For the past three years, Brother Eluric has delivered the rent for the house to Judith Perle: one rose from the bush beside the house. Now Eluric has been murdered and Judith has disappeared. Besides, the rose bush has been destroyed. Brother Cadfael is puzzled. 13th.

PETERS, Ellis. *The Hermit Of Eyton Forest.* 1988 Mysterious/ Mysterious 1989. It's 1142 and England is still caught up in a cruel war when the hermit Cuthred arrives at the Abbey of St. Peter and St. Paul. Richard, Lord Eaton's heir, has disappeared, and a body is found in Eyton Forest. Cuthred is suspected, but Brother Cadfael thinks otherwise. 14th.

PETERS, Ellis. *The Confession Of Brother Haluin.* 1988 Mysterious/ Mysterious 1989. Winter forced repairs to the guest-hall roof at the abbey. Brother Haluin falls to the frozen ground. Convinced he's dying, he confesses to Brother Cadfael and the abbot. It's a wicked story, hard to forgive. But Haluin recovers and vows a journey of expiation. 15th. [Father]

PETERS, Ellis. *The Potter's Field.* 1990 Mysterious. They were plowing the land that had once belonged to Brother Ruald before he left his wife and joined the Abbey. The body of a woman is discovered and she may be the woman Ruald left behind. Brother Cadfael makes inquiries. 17th. [Old Crime]

MISSING PERSONS

As our world grows ever larger, it becomes easier for anyone to turn into a missing person. Sometimes it is by choice, sometimes by the instigation of another. Finding missing persons must be the major source of income for private investigators. The topic certainly consumes vast amounts of words and paper in the murder mystery.

ALBERT, Marvin. *Stone Angel.* 1986 Fawcett/ PBO. Half-American, half-French, Pete Sawyer has gone into the detective business on the Riviera. Hired by the Byrnes to find their missing daughter, his chase leads him into Champagne country and a link to terrorists. 1st.

BARNES, Linda. *A Trouble Of Fools.* 1987 St. Martin/ Fawcett 1988. Things were pretty quiet, and PI Carlotta Carlyle needed the money, so she agreed to look for Margaret's missing brother. As she checks out his hangouts, Margaret is beaten up. She whispers to Carlotta about a secret cache of money. Where did it come from? 1st.

BAXT, George. *A Parade Of Cockeyed Creatures.* 1967 Random House/ International Polygonics 1986. Tippy Blarney is missing. It's been five days, and his parents are just getting around to reporting it to NYPD's Max van Larsen. Schoolteacher Sylvia Plotkin joins in the search. 1st. [Drugs]

BAXT, George. *"I!" Said The Demon.* 1969 Random House/ International Polygonics 1987. Max is doing a story for *True Mystery Magazine* on the missing Judge Matthew Kramer and a lot of money. But when a Hollywood director shows up in New York City and bodies start to fall, Max and Sylvia Plotkin nose into hidden secrets. 2nd.

BECK, K. K. *Without A Trace.* [Intrigue]

BECKLUND, Jack. *Golden Fleece* [Getting Away With Murder]

BLOCK, Lawrence. *Out On The Cutting Edge.* 1989 Morrow/ Avon 1990. Matt Scudder takes on a case of a missing young woman who came to New York City to get into the theater. Then his new friend Eddie is found dead in his rent-controlled apartment. 7th. [Real Estate]

BOWERS, Elizabeth. *Ladies' Night.* Seal 1988/ PBO. Fifteen-year-old runaway girls are a dime a dozen. At least that's what the police told Stan Kubicek. So he turned to PI Meg Lacey to find his daughter Lillian. A year later her body was found on the beach. 1st. [Pornography]

BURNS, Rex. *Parts Unknown.* 1990 Viking. Devlin Kirk isn't too happy about his associate Bunchcroft taking on a missing persons case from a family friend. Before long the trail leads to a medical clinic and a couple of suspicious doctors. 2nd. [Medical]

CLINE, Edward. *First Prize.* 1988 Mysterious/ Mysterious 1989. PI Chess Hanrahan took the case for the well-known Eunice Davies-Granville Foundation. Gregory Compton has won this year's Granville Prize and he's missing. Chess thought Compton wanted to stay missing—until his body was discovered. [Writer]

CORMANY, Michael. *Lost Daughter.* [Infidelity]

CORRIS, Peter. *White Meat.* [Australian]

CORRIS, Peter. *The Marvelous Boy.* [Australian]

CORRIS, Peter. *The Empty Beach.* [Australian]

CORRIS, Peter. *Make Me Rich.* [Australian]

CROSS, Amanda. *No Word From Winifred.* 1986 Dutton/ Ballantine 1987. At a party, Kate's niece draws her into the hunt for Winifred. It seems Winifred disappeared just after she agreed to help with the biography of her "aunt," novelist Charlotte Stanton. 8th.

DAVIS, Dorothy Salisbury. *The Habit Of Fear.* 1987 Scribner/Worldwide 1989. Things have not gone well for Julie Hayes. Her husband wants a divorce and she's been badly assaulted. She goes to Ireland, hoping to locate the father she's never known. This is not an easy trip. 4th. [Father]

DOBSON, Margaret. *Soothsayer.* [Bookstore]

DOLD, Gaylord. *Hot Summer, Cold Murder.* 1987 Avon/ PBO. Carl Plummer hired PI Mitch Roberts to find his son Frankie, who's been missing for three days. The pay was too good to turn down. But Plummer neglected to mention that Frankie had stolen something and made someone very mad. 1st. [Drugs]

DUNLAP, Susan. *The Bohemian Connection.* 1985 St. Martin. At the start of Bohemian Week at Russian River, Michelle Davidson was missing. She'd been harassing everyone about the cesspool problem. Then Vejay Haskell, meter reader and amateur sleuth, stumbles over the first body. 2nd. [Drugs]

ELLROY, James. *Because Of The Night.* 1984 Mysterious/ Avon 1987. Sgt. Lloyd Hopkins had two messy cases. In one, there were three bodies in a Hollywood liquor store. The other involved a missing undercover cop. Hopkins is about to travel to the very edge of madness. 2nd. [Psychological]

ENGLEMAN, Paul. *Catch A Fallen Angel.* 1986 Mysterious/ Mysterious 1987. New York City PI Mark Renzler takes a Chicago job. He's hired to find Sherri West, soon to be the Angel-of-the-Month centerfold for *Paradise* magazine. The case becomes a lot more complicated before it's over. 2nd.

ESTLEMAN, Loren D. *Angel Eyes.* 1981 Houghton Mifflin/ Fawcett 1987. Ann Maringer hired Amos Walker to find her; she's about to disappear and it won't be voluntary. Then she does vanish, leaving a man's body in her apartment. Amos gets to work; he's already been paid for three days. 2nd. [Fraud]

ESTLEMAN, Loren D. *Sugartown.* 1984 Houghton Mifflin/ Fawcett 1986. Martha Evancek hires PI Amos Walker to find her grandson who's been missing for nineteen years. Then an editor wants Amos to help her. A Russian novelist is being pressured not to publish. The trail crosses itself. 5th. [Old Crime]

ESTLEMAN, Loren D. *Lady Yesterday.* 1987 Houghton Mifflin/ Ballantine 1988. When PI Amos Walker ran into Iris, she needed help. She was trying to find the man she'd just found out was her father. Suddenly someone is after Iris, and Amos has to do a lot of legwork to keep them both alive. 7th. [Father]

FLETCHER, Lucille. *Mirror Image.* 1988 Morrow/ Avon 1990. Aging actress Francesca Chodoff is dying. She receives a letter from France indicating that Marya, the four-year-old kidnapped from Central Park two decades ago, might still be alive. Her daughter Robin reluctantly agrees to search her out. [Theater]

GASH, Jonathan. *Pearlhanger.* [Antiques]

GREENLEAF, Stephen. *Death Bed.* 1980 Dial/ Ballantine 1982. Maximilian Kottle, wealthy old man, is dying from cancer. He wants PI John Marshall Tanner to find his son Karl . . . and he has only two months to do it. 2nd. [Medical]

GRETH, Roma. . . . *Now You Don't.* Pageant 1988/ PBO. Businesswoman Hana Shaner had a problem. Grace Urich, an employee, was missing. As Hana sets out to find her, she runs into a teenager who looks just like Grace. Now she can hardly believe that Grace is dead. [Social Issues]

HOLLAND, Isabelle. *Bump In The Night.* 1988 Doubleday/ Fawcett 1990. Martha Tierney wakes up in a nightmare. She's hung over and Jonathan, her eight-year-old son, is gone. As she dives into the mystery to find her child, she struggles with her awful desire to drink. [Children]

HOWATCH, Susan. *Call In The Night.* 1967 Stein & Day/Fawcett 1986. Claire Sullivan received a frantic call from her sister Gina from London. Catching the earliest flight, Claire hurried to respond, only to find Gina missing. She bumps into one body, then another, before she locates her sister. [Fraud]

LATIMER, Jonathan. *The Lady In The Morgue.* 1936 Doubleday/ International Polygonics 1988. They'd found her body in the cemetery and now she was the prettiest corpse in the Cook County Morgue. PI William Crane is hustling to find out who she is. Suddenly the body vanishes, and now he has to find out who took her. 3rd.

LUPICA, Mike. *Dead Air.* [Television]

LYONS, Arthur. *Fade Fast.* 1987 Mysterious/ Mysterious 1988. Jacob Asch was hired to prove that Walter Cairns was the missing husband of Lori Norris. Cairns, now a movie director shooting a film in Palm Springs, has a whole cast of enemies, and is soon found dead. 9th. [Blackmail]

LYSAGHT, Brian. *Sweet Death.* 1984 St. Martin/ Tor 1986. Anna Bradley got no satisfaction from the Los Angeles

PD. So she turned to lawyer Benjamin O'Malley. Her husband was missing and so was his secretary. But she knew they hadn't run off together. 2nd. [Psychological]

MATHIS, Edward. *Natural Prey.* 1987 Scribner/ Ballantine 1988. PI Dan Roman was hired to locate Ralph Kincade. The day after Kincade returned to his Texas home, he was found dead—four bullets in his head. It was not the loving reception Dan had anticipated. 3rd. [Getting Away With Murder]

MATHIS, Edward. *Out Of The Shadows.* 1990 Scribner. Philip Arganian hired PI Dan Roman to find his step-sister who disappeared when she was sixteen. His step-mother is old and ill; she wants to see her daughter before she dies. Besides, there's a lot of money involved. 6th. [Incest]

McBRIARTY, Douglas. *Carolina Gold.* [Indians]

McCALL, Wendell. *Aim For The Heart.* [Real Estate]

McDONALD, Gregory. *Fletch, Too.* [Father]

McSHEA, Susanna Hofmann. *Hometown Heroes.* [Old Crime]

NABB, Magdalen. *The Marshal And The Murderer.* 1987 Scribner/ Penguin 1988. A young Swiss teacher came to Florence to learn Italian and stayed on to study pottery. No one has seen her since last Friday. When her body is found under a heap of shards, Guarnaccia must intrude into the quiet village. 5th. [Old Crime]

NEEL, Janet. *Death Of A Partner.* 1991 St. Martin. Lobbyist Angela Morgan, engaged to the Financial Secretary to the Treasury, failed to meet her fiancé for lunch. When he reported her missing, Chief Inspector John McLeish gets his team into action. 2nd. [Economics]

PAGE, Emma. *Scent Of Death.* 1986 Doubleday/ Worldwide 1988. Helen Mowbray was missing and her sister Joanne wanted to find her. There was a little money involved. When both women are discovered dead, Inspector Kelsey and Detective Lambert have to solve Helen's murder first. 4th.

PALMER, Stuart. *The Puzzle Of The Silver Persian.* [Revenge]

PAYNE, Laurence. *Vienna Blood.* [Revenge]

PAYNE, Laurence. *Dead For A Ducat.* 1986 Doubleday. Ex-Inspector Sam Birkett needs a favor. He wants PI Mark Savage to find his son-in-law. Unfortunately, Anthony's wanted for the murder of his best friend. 4th. [Smuggling]

PHILBRICK, W. R. *Walk On The Water.* [Mystery Writer]

PRATHER, Richard S. *Shellshock.* 1987 Tor/ Tor 1988. A man with a shady past has been shot. His lawyer wants Shell Scott to find the man's daughter. He's enjoined from using the daughter's last name, her picture is twenty years old, and her birthmark is not easily accessible. 31st.

RADLEY, Sheila. *Fate Worse Than Death.* 1986 Scribner/ Bantam 1987. In the hamlet of Fodderstone Green, Sandra Websdell disappears just before her wedding day. Nemesis to Inspector Quantrill, Martin Tate clouds the issue when his rich Aunt Con dies and Martin is the suspect. Then another woman vanishes. 6th. [Accident]

ROBERTS, Les. *Pepper Pike.* 1988 St. Martin/ St. Martin 1990. Cleveland PI Milan Jacovich was hired as a bodyguard for Richard Amber. When he arrived at Amber's home, Amber wasn't there. His wife called the next day to report him missing. Four days later, Amber's body is found in the river. 1st. [Advertising]

ROBINETT, Stephen. *Final Option.* [Economics]

ROSS, Jonathan. *Daphne Dead And Done For.* 1991 St. Martin. The editor of the *Daily Echo* called Superintendent George Rogers about a strange item in the personal column. Mrs. Daphne Gosse was missing and might be the victim of foul play. Her husband says nonsense, a cruel joke. Then Mr. Gosse is found dead. 6th. [Fraud]

SCHOPEN, Bernard. *The Big Silence.* 1988 Mysterious/ Mysterious 1989. Reno PI Jack Ross is hired by a young hooker dressed in black. Forty years ago, after having killed a man, her grandfather vanished into the Nevada desert. She wants him found. 1st.

SERAFIN, David. *The Angel Of Torremolinos.* 1988 St. Martin. Superintendent Luis Bernal has been sent to Torremolinos to take care of a Basque bomb threat. As soon as he arrives, he's caught up in cases of missing young people. Setting a trap, one of his own men vanishes. 5th. [Psychological]

SIMPSON, Dorothy. *Close Her Eyes.* 1984 Scribner/ Bantam 1985. Charity Pritchard, age fifteen, had been missing for three days. As they search the footpath, Inspector Luke Thanet almost falls over her body. Further search leads to questions about Charity's innocence. 4th. [Father]

SPENCER, Ross. *Monastery Nightmare.* [Mystery Writer]

STEWART, Gary. *The Tenth Virgin.* 1983 St. Martin/Critic's Choice 1988. Gabe Utely flew into Salt Lake City to do a favor for an old flame. Linda wanted him to find her sixteen-year-old daughter. She's been missing for a week. Gabe's caught up in Mormon infighting and a lot of hypocrisy. [Clergy]

VALIN, Jonathan. *Second Chance.* 1991 Delacorte. Psychiatrist Philip Pearson hired Harry Stoner to find his daughter. Kirsten had planned to fly to Cincinnati for Christmas, but no one knew where she was. Kirsten had been working on an autobiographical novel. 9th. [Old Crime]

WENTWORTH, Patricia. *Outrageous Fortune.* 1933 Lippincott/ Warner 1990. Caroline Leigh knew her cousin Jim Randal was on the coast steamer when it sank in the storm. A radio broadcast sent her to the hospital, only to discover that "Jimmy Riddel" had been taken away by his wife. But what about the shooting of Van Berg and the missing emeralds? [Jewels]

WINGATE, Anne, aka Lee Martin. *Death By Deception.* 1988 Walker/ Harper Collins 1991. Fourth-generation Japanese-American Mark Shigata has a woman's body in the backyard, a woman he doesn't know. His more pressing problem is his missing twelve-year-old stepdaughter. He gets some help from local policeman Al Quinn. 1st.

WINSLOW, Don. *A Cool Breeze On The Underground.* 1991 St. Martin. Rhode Island Senator John Chase has a missing daughter and he wants her found in time for the Democratic Convention. Graduate student Neal Carey is sent off to London to find her and bring her back. But Allie Chase is in more trouble than Neal knows. 1st. [Political]

YORKE, Margaret. *No Medals For The Major.* 1987 Penguin/ PBO. In retirement, Major Frederick Johnson is trying to start a new life, making up for what he's missed. He's just settling in when he finds the body of a missing girl in the trunk of his car. [Children]

MOTHERS

The relationship between a mother and her child can be very intense, especially in terms of the extreme emotions of love and hate. While mothers seem to be genetically programmed to go to the limits for a child, something else may be motivating the offspring. One of the most charged themes is the search for the lost mother.

BALLARD, Mignon F. *Raven Rock.* 1986 Dodd, Mead. Henri Meredith finds out, as her mother is dying, that she was adopted. In Raven Rock, she's trying to find out what happened to her real mother. The closer she comes to the answer, the harder someone is trying to stop her. [Psychological]

BANKS, Carolyn. *Patchwork.* 1986 Crown/ Avon 1987. Rachael had to send her son away, when he was still a child, to a place where he could get "special" care. Now she's afraid that he's coming home and that he wants to kill her. [Psychological]

BARNARD, Robert. *Death Of A Perfect Mother.* 1981 Scribner/ Dell 1985. Brian and Gordon Hodsden would sprawl on their bed and plan the murder of their mother Lill, that tyrranical and oppressive woman. All of a sudden Lill was dead, and Inspector McHale discovers that a lot of other people wanted her dead, too. [Getting Away With Murder]

BORGENICHT, Miriam. *Undue Influence.* [Lawyer]

CAMPBELL, Robert. *The Gift Horse's Mouth.* [Political]

CHEHAK, Susan Taylor. *The Story Of Annie D.* 1989 Houghton Mifflin/ Ballantine 1990. Widowed, Annie D. lives out her days in Wizen River, Nebraska. The peaceful town has suddenly become a dangerous place. Several women have been raped and killed. Annie D. wonders about the neighbors. [Psychological]

CHRISTMAS, Joyce. *Suddenly In Her Sorbet.* [Where There's A Will]

CLARKE, Anna. *The Poisoned Web.* 1979 St. Martin/ Charter 1990. Brenda and Laurie had a tiny apartment in the house of an Oxford professor's widow. When Mrs. Merriman asked Brenda to fetch her notebook, Brenda read the first page: "I'm sure my daughter Romala is planning to murder me." [Where There's A Will]

DAWSON, Janet. *Kindred Crimes.* [Old Crime]

ECCLES, Marjorie. *Requiem For A Dove.* [Infidelity]

EVERSON, David. *Suicide Squeeze.* [Ball Games]

FELD, Bernard. *Blood Relations.* 1987 Little, Brown/ Avon 1988. Nick Phillips got a job as reporter on the *Birmingham Examiner* and ran into Cassie Fairchild . . . again. Nick is working on a murder case, and somehow Cassie's brother is involved. It turns out to be a family affair. [Journalism]

FERRARS, E. X. *Trial By Fury.* 1989 Doubleday. Constance Lawley, widow, worked part-time for the Bracklington Helpers. She went off to help out Colonel and Mrs. Barrows and their orphaned grandson. Out of the blue, Margo, the boy's mother, arrives. Resentment explodes. [Jealousy]

FINK, John. *The Leaf Boats.* [Old Crime]

GORMAN, Edward. *Several Deaths Later.* [At Sea]

GRAFTON, Sue. *"G" Is For Gumshoe.* 1990 Holt/ Fawcett 1991. The ailing Irene Gersh wants Kinsey to locate her mother, Agnes Grey, who's living at the Slabs in Mohave. Agnes doesn't seem to want to stay found, and between times, Kinsey is ducking a hit-man who has a contract on her life. 7th. [Imposter]

GUTHRIE, Al. *Private Murder.* [Revenge]

HAGER, Jean. *Night Walker.* [Indians]

HAYMON, S. T. *Death Of A God.* 1987 St. Martin/ Bantam 1990. Inspector Ben Jurnet was coaxed into attending a performance of the Second Coming, a rock group. He gets caught up by the lead singer Loy Tanner. But by the next morning Loy Tanner is hanging from a cross in Angleby Market Place. 4th. [Music]

JANCE, J. A. *Minor In Possession.* Avon 1990/ PBO. J. P. Beaumont is at Ironweed Ranch, Arizona, in an alcohol rehab program. His roommate is a teenage drug dealer, Joey Rothman. But when Joey is murdered with Beau's .38, he's forced to look into Joey's death. 8th. [Drugs]

KIENZLE, William X. *Sudden Death.* [Medical]

LaPIERRE, Janet. *The Cruel Mother.* [Kidnapping]

LYONS, Nan, and Ivan Lyons. *The President Is Coming To Lunch.* [Cooks]

MARTIN, James E. *The Mercy Trap.* 1989 Putnam/ Avon 1990. PI Gil Disbro was hired to find a missing woman, the mother of Howard Eberly's adopted daughter. Heather needs a kidney transplant, she's failing rapidly. This time, the skeletons Gil finds are for real. [Old Crime]

McBAIN, Ed. *Snow White and Rose Red.* 1985 Holt/ Mysterious 1986. Sarah Whittaker was incarcerated at Knott's Retreat, certified crazy. She hired attorney Matthew Hope. She wants her freedom and the fortune her mother controls. As Matt takes the case, his reality becomes blurred. 5th. [Psychological]

McGOWN, Jill. *Murder At The Old Vicarage.* [Christmas]

NORDAN, Robert. *All Dressed Up To Die.* [Clergy]

O'DONNELL, Lillian. *Lady Killer.* 1984 Putnam/ Ballantine 1985. Norah Mulcahaney has been a widow for eight months. Work helps to fill the emptiness, so that when a young woman is killed in Central Park, she gives the case everything she has. Norah was not prepared for how the case would end. 9th. [Serial Killer]

ORMEROD, Roger. *Death Of An Innocent.* 1990 St. Martin. Amelia was invited by her school friend Olivia Dean to come and stay at Mansfield Park. And to bring her husband, ex-inspector Richard Patton. There had been a break-in at Olivia's house, but nothing seemed to be missing. Then a young woman was discovered, drowned in the river. 4th. [Getting Away With Murder]

PARKER, Robert B. *Crimson Joy.* 1988 Delacorte/ Dell 1989. Someone is murdering women in Boston; his calling card is a long-stemmed red rose. When Spenser joins the chase, he discovers that the killer may be a client of Susan's. Will she be next? 15th. [Psychological]

PETERS, Elizabeth. *The Love Talker.* [Psychological]

PHILBIN, Tom. *Precinct: Siberia.* [Revenge]

PICKARD, Nancy. *I. O. U.* 1991 Pocket. Jenny Cain's mother has died, after years in a coma at the Hampshire Psychiatric Hospital. At the funeral, someone pushed Jenny, hissing "Forgive me. It was an accident." Suddenly Jenny has a lot of questions, and most of them are about her mother. 7th. [Old Crime]

ROBERTS, Nora. *Public Secrets.* [Music]

THOMSON, June. *The Spoils Of Time.* [Imposter]

TRAVIS, Elizabeth. *Finders, Keepers.* 1990 St. Martin. Carrie and Ben Potter, publishers, are on the Riviera. Charles Melton has just died and they want to publish his last book. There's just one hitch: at least five people have parts of the novel and the one person who manages to collect all the parts gets the copyright. 2nd.

WHITNEY, Phyllis A. *Silversword.* [Old Crime]

YAFFE, James. *A Nice Murder For Mom.* [Academic]

YAFFE, James. *Mom Meets Her Maker.* 1990 St. Martin/ Worldwide 1991. Mr. and Mrs. Meyer were enjoying their retirement in Mesa Grande, Colorado. Until just before Christmas when Reverend Chuck Candy decorated his house and played carols at high volume till late at night. Meyer's son Roger, home from college, has just been accused of shooting the reverend. It's up to Dave and Mom to save him. 2nd. [Real Estate]

ZILINSKY, Ursula. *A Happy English Child.* [Theater]

MUSIC

Making music is one of the gentlest of occupations. Making murder seems a violation. Yet our new breed of musicians can be a magnet for violent means to personal ends.

CLARK, Dick. *Murder On Tour.* 1989 Mysterious/ Mysterious 1990. Reporter Del Barnes, from a music magazine, is following the tour of the newest rock band ROOTS. The producer died from a drug overdose, but a note hints that it was murder. Then in Madison, a huge amplifier fell and killed the guitar player. Del's curiosity may be unhealthy. [Revenge]

CODY, Liza. *Under Contract.* 1987 Scribner/ Bantam 1990. Rock star Shona Una has been receiving threatening letters. Before her startling career rise is ruined, PI Anna Lee is hired to stop the threats and find the sender. Dressing for the part in a black leather outfit, Anna joins the entourage. 5th.

FLYNN, Don. *Murder In A-Flat.* 1988 Walker. At the Algonquin, Erik Halvorsen was buying drinks and bragging about a priceless Stradivarius violin. Then Erik dies in his Greenwich Village flat, six bullets in his chest. Fitz Fitzgerald of the *Daily Press* has the story. 4th. [Journalism]

FROMMER, Sara Hoskinson. *Murder In C Major.* 1986 St. Martin/ Worldwide 1988. Widowed, Joan Spencer returns to Oliver, Indiana. She takes her viola and joins the local symphony. At rehearsal, oboe player George Petris collapses and dies. It's not long before there's another body, and Joan has Lt. Fred Lundquist in her kitchen.

GILPATRICK, Noreen. *The Piano Man.* 1991 St. Martin. Retired concert pianist Paul Whitman was hired to restore some once fine pianos on an island in Puget Sound. Before long, there is a series of murders. The local sheriff is gunning for the Piano Man and looking to connect him to the disappearance of Ilsa twenty years ago. Paul has to save himself. [Old Crime]

GOLDSBOROUGH, Robert. *Murder In E Minor.* 1986 Bantam/ Bantam 1987. Milan Stevens, conductor of the New York Symphony, is found stabbed in his apartment by his niece, Maria. Her boyfriend, Gerald, is the accused. But Nero Wolfe and Archie, convinced he's innocent, are checking a lot of other motives. 1st. [Revenge]

GOLIN, James. *The Philomel Foundation.* 1980 St. Martin/ International Polygonics 1986. They were five Americans, the Antigua Players, making a tour of Europe, playing their lutes and krummhorns. As they performed behind the Iron Curtain, a man died, a man they hoped to rescue. Now they have to get across the border. 1st. [Intrigue]

GOLIN, James. *Eliza's Galiardo.* 1983 St. Martin/ International Polygonics 1986. Father Valentine Gilmary has a manuscript he claims to be music written by Queen Bess. He's willing to sell it to benefit his religious order. Alan French, leader of the Antigua Players, jumps at the performance rights. But someone wants to steal it. 2nd. [Manuscripts]

GOLIN, James. *The Verona Passamezzo.* 1985 Doubleday. Count Emilio invites the Antigua Players, five American musicians, to Verona for a music festival. But before their final performance, they are embroiled in murder and mischief. 3rd.

HAUSER, Thomas. *The Beethoven Conspiracy.* 1984 Macmillan/ Tor 1985. Violist Judith Darr is given $10,000 and told to learn a piece of music. She is to be prepared to travel to a European city for four days in November. At the same time, Richard Marrett, NYPD, is investigating the deaths of several fine musicians, and follows Judith to Europe. [Manuscripts]

HAYMON, S. T. *Death Of A God.* [Mother]

HIGGINS, Joan. *A Little Death Music.* 1987 Dodd, Mead/ Charter 1988. At the last minute, concert pianist John Field was asked to fill in at the Yera Music Festival. He flew off to Fun City, Florida. On the night of the performance, music critic Sherril Thorne is killed, and Field is forced to recreate the murder scene. 1st. [Imposter]

LEWIS, William. *Gala.* 1987 Dutton/ Paperjacks 1989. In order to raise money to help support the Metropolitan Opera, Peter Camden, the manager, has planned a gala, featuring the world's five greatest tenors. Suddenly, the tenors are being killed, one by one. [Revenge]

PAUL, Barbara. *Prima Donna At Large.* [Famous People]

PAUL, Barbara. *A Chorus Of Detectives.* [Famous People]

PETERSON, Audrey. *The Nocturne Murder.* 1987 Arbor House/ Pocket 1988. Jane Winfield is in London looking up an obscure composer when she meets music critic Max Fordham. When Max is found dead in her bed-sitter, she's accused of the murder. Dr. Quentin, her dissertation director, searches the list of suspects. 1st. [Drugs]

RESNICOW, Herbert. *The Gold Curse.* 1986 St. Martin. Alexander Gold and his wife Norma paid $1,000 a seat for a benefit performance of *Rigoletto.* Their friend Julia had a premonition during the intermission that someone was about to die. Sure enough, in the final scene, the diva doesn't sing. 4th.

ROBERTS, Nora. *Public Secrets.* Bantam 1990/ PBO. Emma was almost three the first time she met her father, the rock star Brian McAvoy. The brutal treatment from her mother is over and she settles into her new life. Then when she's seven her baby half-brother dies in a failed kidnapping attempt. She's haunted by that night until . . . . [Mother]

SCHUTZ, Benjamin M. *The Things We Do For Love.* 1989 Scribner/ Bantam 1990. PI Leo Haggerty takes a bodyguard job protecting Jane Doe, a rock singer. There have been several threats against her life. Someone wants her to sign with a record company or die. Either way they'll get her music. 4th.

SLAVO, Gillian. *Death Comes Staccato.* 1988 Doubleday. Someone from the audience watches fixedly every time Alicia Weatherby performs. Alicia's mother hires Kate Baeier to find out who the man is, and if he's a threat to Alicia. Two murders later, Kate is rummaging in the past for answers. 3rd. [Drugs]

MYSTERY GAMES

The mystery tour or weekend has become a popular setting for the crime of murder. In some ways, it is like the Stately Home Murder: a motley group of people is thrown together for a week or a weekend. Most often the participants are unknown to one another, or so it seems. As the personalities of the members emerge, the murderer acts.

BABSON, Marian. *Murder On A Mystery Tour.* [Americans In England]

BOROWITZ, Albert. *The Jack The Ripper Walking Tour Murder* [Americans In England]

CHRISTIE, Agatha. *Dead Man's Folly.* 1956 Dodd, Mead/Pocket 1961. Mystery writer Mrs. Ariadne Oliver has written a Murder Hunt as part of the annual fete. Sensing something wrong, she summons Poirot. Next day, the "victim" ends up dead and a new murder hunt is on. 27th.

COLLINS, Max Allan. *Nice Weekend For A Murder.* 1986 Walker. At Mohonk Mountain House in upstate New York, Mallory and his lover, Jill, are at a Mystery Weekend. Mallory saw what he thought was a murder being committed outside his window. But the snow is clean and there's no body. As the snowstorm continues to rage, a body is found. 5th. [Revenge]

DeANDREA, William. *Killed In Paradise.* 1988 Mysterious/Mysterious 1989. Matt Cobb, network troubleshooter has the assignment: escort the mystery contest winner and her friend on an eight-day Caribbean cruise. And, oh yes, there are some mystery writers on board. Pretty soon real-life people turn up missing. [At Sea]

GIROUX, E. X. *Death For A Dietitian.* [Revenge]

GRAHAM, Caroline. *Murder At Madingly Grange.* 1991 Morrow. Simon and Laurie Hannaford, hard up for money, have turned Madingly Grange into a setting for a mystery weekend. Before long, there's a body in the conservatory and there's a totally new game to be played. 3rd.

GRAY, Malcolm. *A Matter Of Record.* 1987 Doubleday. It was to be a mystery junket on the Orient Express. But Mary Thornton died, leaving a suicide note. Back in England, PI Alan Craig is hired to find out why Mrs. Renton is upset. Then there's another murder.

HARRIS, Charlaine. *Real Murder.* [Library]

HART, Carolyn. *Design For Murder.* [Bookstore]

HESS, Joan. *Murder At The Murder At The Mimosa Inn.* 1986 St. Martin/Ballantine 1987. It was going to be a fun weekend for Claire Malloy and her daughter Caron, a weekend at an inn outside town with a murder to solve. But the man who holds the script turns into an unexpected corpse. 2nd.

MARSH, Ngaio. *A Man Lay Dead.* 1934 Little, Brown/ Jove 1978. They've all gathered at Frantock, Sir Hubert's country house, for the weekend. There's to be a game of Murders . . . but the corpse is real. Chief Inspector Roderick Alleyn sifts through the suspects to find the murderer. 1st.

MORICE, Anne. *Treble Exposure.* 1987 St. Martin. Tessa Crichton got a visit from her American friend Lorraine. Lorraine is on a Mystery Reader's Tour of England and one of her companions is Beverly, recently discharged from a mental hospital. Almost before the tour starts, a woman is dead, and evidence against Beverly piles up. Tessa takes charge. 21st.

OCORK, Shannon. *The Murder Of Muriel Lake.* Worldwide 1990/ PBO. Cecelia Burnett was attending her first Writers of Mystery Convention. But when the Queen of Mysteries, Muriel Lake, is crushed to death under a load of her own books, Cecelia turns sleuth.

MYSTERY WRITERS

Like Jessica Fletcher of "Murder, She Wrote," mystery writers—in fiction—get called in on all manner of crimes or always find the body. The added danger is that they might end up as the victims of the very genre they write about. Either situation spells entertainment for the reader.

BARNARD, Robert. *Death Of A Mystery Writer.* 1978 Scribner/ Dell 1988. Sir Oliver Farleigh-Stubbs entertained the family on his sixty-fifth birthday. It was his last, for he sipped his special liqueur and died. Fitting for a mystery writer, some thought. His last manuscript is missing. [Father]

BAXT, George. *The Affair At Royalties.* 1972 Scribner/ International Polygonics 1988. Successful mystery writer Laura Denning regained consciousness in a London nursing home. She had no recollection of the bloody kitchen at her cottage, Royalties. There was no corpse, but she had been holding a carving knife. [Jealousy]

BREEN, Jon. *Touch Of The Past.* 1988 Walker. Los Angeles bookstore owner Rachel Henning heard about a collection of vintage mysteries coming on the market.

William DeMarco, mystery writer, lived as a recluse surrounded by 1937 artifacts. The day before his garage sale, he was murdered. 2nd. [Bookstore]

BRILL, Toni. *Date With A Dead Doctor.* 1991 St. Martin. Children's mystery writer Midge Cohen suffered from her mother's continual "I've got just the man for you." But all the urologist wanted was for Midge to translate a letter from a Russian relative. But he's murdered and she's stuck with his widow. [Art]

CHRISTIE, Agatha. *Elephants Can Remember.* 1972 Dodd, Mead/ Berkley 1986. Celia Ravenscraft, the goddaughter of mystery writer Ariadne Oliver, is about to be married. Her future mother-in-law wants to know about the double murder years ago. Did Celia's mother kill her father and then herself, or was it the other way around? Poirot will help. 32nd. [Old Crime]

CLARINS, Dana. *The Woman Who Knew Too Much.* 1986 Bantam/ PBO. Celia Blandings is about to write her first mystery. As she flips through a stack of galleys, she comes across a piece of paper: In re the murder of the Director . . . . With the aid of the one-eyed ex-cop she follows a winding trail to danger.

CLARKE, Anna. *Cabin 3033.* [At Sea]

CLARKE, Anna. *Murder In Writing.* 1988 Doubleday/ Charter 1990. When Frances Coles fell and hurt her ankle, she called on Paula Glenning to take over her writing class at Merle House. The students' assignment had been a short story dealing with murder in a domestic setting. But someone took their homework too seriously. 5th. [Where There's A Will]

COLLINS, Max Allan. *No Cure For Death.* 1983 Walker/Tor 1987. Mallory, mystery writer, saved Janet from being attacked by a thug at the bus station. She caught the next bus. What, then, was she doing dead in a car at the bottom of a ravine? Her mother was beaten to death and her house set on fire before Mallory could find out what was going on. 2nd.

COLLINS, Max Allan. *Kill Your Darlings.* 1984 Walker/Tor 1988. Mallory went to Bouchercon, the mystery convention, hoping to spend some time with his hero, Roscoe Kane. Kane was found dead in his bath, and Mallory suspects murder. Then he found out about a recently discovered manuscript, by Hammett. 3rd. [Manuscript]

COLLINS, Max Allan. *A Shroud For Aquarius.* [Drugs]

CUTTER, Leela. *Death Of The Party.* [Medical]

FENSTER, Bob. *The Last Page.* Perseverance 1989/ PBO. For the second time, a mystery editor has been found slumped over her desk, a bullet hole in her heart and a rejection note pinned to a sleeve. Detective Brian Skiles and editor Anne Baker set a trap to catch a killer. [Revenge]

GILL, B. M. *Seminar For Murder.* 1986 Scribner/ Ballantine 1987. Sir Godfrey Grant, founder of the Golden Guillotine Club for mystery writers, is hosting the annual awards meeting. Detective Tom Maybridge is a guest speaker. The tension among the guests mounts until there is a real murder to solve.

GRAY, Malcolm. *Stab In The Back.* 1986 Doubleday. TV personality Logan Chester invited a few people to the country for the weekend. When obnoxious Tommy Boston is found dead in the locked study, Detective Neil Lambert, part-time mystery writer, has to separate fact from fiction. [Television]

HAGEN, Lorinda. *Winter Roses.* [Witches]

HART, Carolyn. *Death On Demand.* [Bookstore]

JORDAN, Jennifer. *A Good Weekend For Murder.* 1987 St. Martin. Thriller writer Charles Wild invited some people for his birthday celebration. The guests all have one thing in common—their dislike of Charles. His death sparks Dee Vaughn into bullying her writer husband, Barry, into playing Nick Charles to her Nora. 1st.

LORENS, M. K. *Ropedancer's Fall.* [Television]

LORENS, M. K. *Deception Island.* Bantam 1990/ PBO. Artist Frances Woodville has been a recluse on Deception Island for over twenty-five years. And now it seems there are some fakes of her work. Then there's a body in Lake Tamarack, and Winston Marlowe Sherman, professor and mystery writer, gets the call. 3rd. [Art]

LOUIS, Joseph. *Madelaine.* 1987 Bantam/ PBO. Mystery writer Evan Paris is recuperating from the death of his wife when someone intrudes. Arla is dying of cancer, and she wants Evan to find the father of her great-granddaughter. The search takes him into the middle of confused relationships. 1st.

MOFFAT, Gwen. *Snare.* [Blackmail]

MOODY, Susan. *Penny Dreadful.* [Black Detective]

MOYES, Patricia. *A Six-Letter Word For Death.* [Crossword Puzzles]

MURPHY, Warren. *Leonardo's Law.* [Locked Room]

PAPAZOGLOU, Orania. *Once And Always Murder.* 1990 Doubleday. True crime writer Patience McKenna has come home to Waverly, Connecticut, to prepare for her wedding. What she finds is a corpse in the living room and a houseful of relatives. Patience has a murder to solve before she heads for the altar. 5th. [Real Estate]

PHILBRICK, W. R. *Walk On Water.* 1990 St. Martin. Jack Hawkins' wife Megan, editor at a Boston publishing house, discovered Fiona Darling, crime writer. But Howard Halton's widow is accusing Fiona of plagiarism from her late husband's works. Jack may be wheelchair bound, but he's about to take off to help Megan. 4th. [Missing Person]

PRONZINI, Bill. *Bones.* 1985 St. Martin/ Paperjacks 1986. Michael Kiskadon had just spent a month in the hospital, where he'd almost died. That made him decide to hire Nameless to find out about his father, pulp witer Harmon Crane. Thirty-five years ago, Crane had committed suicide. Michael wants to know why. 14th. [Old Crime]

ROBERTS, Les. *An Infinite Number Of Monkeys.* 1987 St. Martin/ St. Martin 1988. Saxon, actor and part-time PI, got a call from his assistant one evening: someone had taken a shot at her husband. Quickly Saxon found that the target was really wealthy mystery writer Buck Weldon. But why does someone want him dead? 1st. [Jealousy]

ROBERTS, Nora. *Brazen Virtue.* [Serial Killer]

SCHORR, Mark. *Red Diamond, Private Eye.* 1983 St. Martin/ St. Martin 1987. Simon Jaffe drove a cab in New York City every day. At night, he returned to Long Island and another world: his stacks of pulps. One day, his wife sold his whole collection and kicked him out. In a daze he became his favorite character, Red Diamond, PI. 1st.

SHUBIN, Seymour. *Never Quite Dead Enough.* 1988 St. Martin. Twenty years ago, a young boy was found dead in a vacant lot in Boston. Joseph Kyle, columnist, had become obsessed with finding out who the child was. He died just after he returned from Philadelphia, following a lead. His son David picks up the quest. [Children]

SMITH, Julie. *True-Life Adventures.* [Kidnapping]

SPENCER, Ross H. *Monastery Nightmare.* 1986 Mysterious/ Mysterious 1987. Writer Carl Garvey disappeared from his sailboat in Lake Michigan. Garvey's agent hired PI Luke Lassiter to ghost-write the final book in the series. Luke has to return to detecting when a rash of murders starts. [Missing Person]

O . . . IS FOR

OLD CRIMES AND MURDERS

A POPULAR TOPIC for the mystery writer is the resolution of an old crime. Something in the present touches off the hidden secret: an old skeleton surfaces while the house is being renovated, or a casual statement sets off a chain of long-forgotten memories. Once propelled into the puzzle, our detective feels compelled to take it to its conclusion.

ADAMS, Harold. *The Barbed Wire Noose.* [Revenge]

ANTHONY, Evelyn. *The House Of Vandekar.* 1988 Putnam/ Harper & Row 1990. Nancy Percival had finally returned to England. One weekend David, her fiancé, took her to stay at Ashdown House, a hotel in the country. Nancy comes face to face with her past and the secrets it held.

BARNES, Linda. *Cities Of The Dead.* [Cooks]

BERRY, Carol. *The Letter Of The Law.* 1987 St. Martin/ Dell 1990. Attorney Albert Janowski was found shot to death in a seedy New York City hotel, sans trousers and shorts. As liaison between the law firm and the police, Bonnie Indermill starts poking around until she's confronted with danger . . . and death. 1st. [Lawyer]

BIGGERS, Earl Derr. *Behind The Curtain.* [Oriental]

BOYER, Rick. *The Penny Ferry.* 1984 Houghton Mifflin/ Warner 1986. John never made the last delivery of the false teeth for Doc Adams. Instead, Doc and his brother-in-law find John dead in his Lowell apartment. Soon another body is found in the chimney of an abandoned factory. 2nd.

BRANDT, Charles. *The Right To Remain Silent.* 1988 St. Martin/ St. Martin 1989. Lou Razzi had been an up-and-coming cop until he was framed and sent to jail. Fifteen years later, he's been exonerated and is serving one day on the police force to claim his honorary pension. But things have changed, or have they?

BURLEY, W. J. *Wycliffe And The Quiet Virgin.* [Christmas]

BYRD, Max. *Target Of Opportunity.* [Intrigue]

CARR, John Dickson, w/a Carter Dickson. *My Late Wives.* 1946 Morrow/ Zebra 1988. Bruce Ransom, British stage star, received the script about the multiple-wife murderer Roger Bewlay. When a murder occurs, he is faced with two conclusions. Either Bewlay is still alive or someone is imitating him. Sir Henry Merrivale gets into the act. 17th.

CASE, Peg, and John Migliore. *Death Blade.* [Journalism]

CHRISTIE, Agatha. *Elephants Can Remember.* [Mystery Writer]

CLARK, Mary Higgins. *Stillwatch.* 1984 Simon & Schuster/ Dell 1986. Pat Traymore went to Washington, D.C., to do a TV special on Senator Abigail Jennings, who may be the first woman vice president. Pat is also determined to uncover the horrible deaths of her parents when she was just a child. Someone is out to frighten her away from the answers. [Television]

CLARK, Mary Higgins. *While My Pretty One Sleeps.* [Fashion]

CLARKE, Anna. *The Deathless And The Dead.* [Writer]

CORRINGTON, John William, and Joyce H. Corrington. *So Small A Carnival.* [Journalism]

CRIDER, Bill. *Evil At The Root.* [Getting Away With Murder]

DAWSON, Janet. *Kindred Crimes.* 1990 St. Martin. Oakland PI Jeri Howard thinks her ex-husband threw a case her way, to see her fail. Philip Foster wants Jeri to find his wife. Renee left her young son with her mother-in-law and vanished. 1st. [Mother]

DEAN, S. F. X. *Death And The Mad Heroine.* [Academic]

DEAVER, Jeffrey Wilds. *Manhattan Is My Beat.* [Witness Protection Program]

DISNEY, Doris Miles. *Here Lies . . .* 1963 Doubleday/ Zebra 1988. Phoebe Upton Clarke, age seventy-two, died quietly, and her son made plans to bury her in the family plot. There is only one problem: someone is already in the grave, a man with a bullet in his skull.

DOUGLAS, John. *The Shawnee Alley Fire.* 1987 St. Martin/ St. Martin 1988. Down on his luck, photographer Jack Reese returned to Shawnee to live in his rent-free house. A woman hired him for a series of strange photo sessions. The next thing Jack knows is that policeman Edward Harter is looking at him as the woman's murderer.

DOYLE, James T. *Deadly Resurrection.* 1987 Walker. PI Dan Cronyn was hired by Paula Devlin to buy back some letters from Murray Atwood. At the payoff, Dan found Atwood dead and no letters. Dan was digging into the past when he was warned off the case. 1st. [Drugs]

DRAKE, Alison. *Black Moon.* [Witches]

DUNNE, Dominick. *The Two Mrs. Grenvilles.* 1985 Crown/ Bantam 1986. Basil Plant is the kind of man who lingers on the fringe of society, the man that other people talk to. Sure enough, Ann Grenville tells him her story, the story of how her husband died that night so many years ago.

EBERHART, Mignon G. *A Fighting Chance.* 1986 Random House/ Warner 1987. It was the eve of Julie's wedding. Her fiancé, Jim, was found with a man dead at his feet. Jim ran. Now five years later, Jim's back. Julie knows he's innocent. Before they can gather any proof, someone else has to die.

ELKINS, Aaron J. *Curses!* [Anthropology]

EMERSON, Earl W. *Fat Tuesday.* [Pornography]

ESTLEMAN, Loren D. *Sugartown.* [Missing Person]

FINK, John. *The Leaf Boats.* 1991 St. Martin. Seventeen years ago, Dutch Gillespie's second wife, Natalie, was murdered, her body buried under a pile of leaves in the park across the street. Now his daughter Hope has been raped and murdered, in the same park. [Mother]

FRASER, Anthea. *The Nine Bright Shiners.* [Jewels]

FULTON, Eileen. *Fatal Flashback.* [Television]

GILMAN, Dorothy. *The Tightrope Walker.* [Antiques]

GILPATRICK, Noreen. *The Piano Man.* [Music]

GORMAN, Edward. *The Night Remembers.* 1991 St. Martin. Lisa Pennyfeather's husband George has just been released from prison. Twelve years ago, Jack Walsh, still with the sheriff's office, had sent George to prison for murder. Now a PI, Lisa wants Jack to clear her husband of the charge. [Pornography]

GRADY, James. *Hard Bargains.* 1985 Macmillan/ Pocket 1987. Cora McGregor just wanted PI Rankin to find out if anything was happening on the unsolved murder of Parvis Naderi. There wasn't. But then, Cora wasn't who she said she was. Rankin pushes, until both their lives are on the line.

GREENLEAF, Stephen. *Grave Error.* [Blackmail]

GUTHRIE, Al. *Grave Murder.* [Economics]

HAMMOND, Gerald. *A Brace Of Skeet.* 1990 St. Martin. Deborah Calders has been left in charge while her parents are on vacation. Her first call is from Inspector Munroe. The Pentland Gun Club steward has been found dead beside a skeet trap. Deborah becomes the forensic expert and a curious investigator.

HEALY, Jeremiah. *Blunt Darts.* [Psychological]

HEBDEN, Mark. *Pel And The Party Spirit.* 1990 St. Martin. Ellen and George Bridden moved to the small town of Puyceldome in the South of France. When they went to have their tower repaired, half of it crumbled, disgorging a body left there thirty years before. Chief Inspector Pel is sent for, just in time, for there have been two murders and a kidnapping in the neighborhood. 14th. [Kidnapping]

HELGERSON, Joel. *Slow Burn.* [Arson]

HILL, Reginald. *An Advancement Of Learning.* [Academic]

HILL, Reginald. *Underworld.* 1988 Scribner/ Warner 1989. Three years ago, a young girl vanished and the crime was blamed on a self-confessed child killer who committed suicide. The folks in Burrthorpe had other thoughts. When Colin Farr starts poking into the old abandoned mine, Dalziel and Pascoe are quickly involved. 10th. [Journalism]

HUEBNER, Frederick D. *The Joshua Sequence.* [Social Issues]

HULLAND, J. R. *An Educated Murder.* [Academic]

JOHNSTON, Velda. *The Girl On The Beach.* 1987 Dodd, Mead. Kate Kiligrew chooses a small island off the coast of North Carolina, a place to lick her wounds. She discovers that twelve years earlier a murder had occurred in the house, and Martin Donnerly has just been paroled. After meeting him, she works with Martin to find out who really killed his wife. [Blackmail]

KAMINSKY, Stuart. *Think Fast, Mr. Peters.* [Famous People]

KAMINSKY, Stuart. *Lieberman's Folly.* 1991 St. Martin. In Corpus Christi, ten years ago, Juan Hernandez De Barcelona, owner of a bar and whore house, was gunned down. Now a police informant sets a trap with Hanrahan, Chicago Police Department, to catch a john who might get nasty. Hanrahan is shot and his partner Lieberman has to track down what went wrong. [Blackmail]

KELLEY, Patrick A. *Sleightly Deceived.* [Psychic]

KELMAN, Judith. *While Angels Sleep.* 1988 Berkley/ PBO. Emily had to return to Thornwood, the home of her childhood, to say goodbye: to the tragic death of her mother and her father's madness. Soon it would be part of an art colony, out of her hands. But the sins of the past are still there. [Revenge]

LAMB, Margaret. *Chains Of Gold.* 1985 St. Martin/ Ballantine 1986. Victoria Wentworth is ninety-four and she wants Penny Miller to write the family history. The fee tempts Penny. Soon she is crawling around attics, caught up in an old murder and romance. [Journalism]

LATHEN, Emma. *Something In The Air.* [Economics]

LESLIE, John. *Killer In Paradise.* Pocket 1990/ PBO. In Key West to recuperate from a gunshot wound, Chicago homicide detective Patrick Bowman doesn't get a chance to rest. Someone is murdering runaway girls on the beach and Bowman suspects the police can't handle it. [Serial Killer]

LOVESEY, Peter. *Rough Cider.* 1986 Mysterious/ Mysterious 1988. Alice Ashenfelter came to England and managed to locate history professor Theo Sinclair. At the age of nine, Theo had testified at the murder trial of Alice's father. Alice wants to know what happened. She doesn't expect a fresh murder.

MacGREGOR, T. J. *Kill Flash.* [Revenge]

MARON, Margaret. *The Right Jack.* [Imposter]

MARSHALL, William. *Manila Bay.* 1986 Viking/ Penguin 1988. They found the body in the middle of a cockfight pit. The death is tied into Battling Mendez, the best cockfighter of them all. Lt. Felix Elizalde quickly discovers something else is at stake. 1st.

MARTIN, James E. *The Mercy Trap.* [Mother]

McCONNER, Vincent. *The Man Who Knew Hammett.* [Hollywood]

McGOWN, Jill. *The Stalking Horse.* 1988 St. Martin. Bill Holt is out on parole. Sixteen years ago, he'd gone to prison for the murder of two people: his lover Alison and a private detective. He's back in town and he's going to find the real killer. [Fraud]

McSHEA, Susanna Hofmann. *Hometown Heroes.* 1990 St. Martin. Mildred Bennett returned to Raven's Wing, Connecticut, to settle her mother's estate. Within days, she, the ex-police chief and two other senior citizens are knee-deep in the investigation of missing women over the last forty years. [Missing Persons]

MEEK, M. R. D. *A Loose Connection.* [Suicide]

MICHAELS, Barbara. *Be Buried In The Rain.* [Witches]

MICHAELS, Barbara. *Shattered Silk.* [Antiques]

MICHAELS, Barbara. *Into The Darkness.* [Jewels]

MILLER, J. M. T. *Weatherby: On A Dead Man's Chest.* [At Sea]

MULLER, Marcia. *The Cheshire Cat's Eye.* 1983 St. Martin/ Mysterious 1990. Jake Kaufman asked Sharon McCone to stop by the Victorian house he was working on; he had something urgent to tell her. Sharon arrived to find Jake dead in a pool of red paint. She has just one clue, a Tiffany lamp. 3rd. [Antiques]

MULLER, Marcia. *The Legend Of The Slain Soldiers.* [Writer]

MULLER, Marcia, and Bill Pronzini. *Beyond The Grave.* [Art]

MURRAY, Stephen. *Fetch Out No Shroud.* 1990 St. Martin. Chief Inspector Alec Stainton was called out to Hartfield Park, an old RAF airfield. Andrew Hunter, war historian, had just been found shot to death. Had he uncovered a secret someone would kill for? 4th. [Writer]

NABB, Magdalen. *The Marshal And The Murderer.* [Missing Person]

NEGGERS, Carla w/a Anne Harrell. *Betrayals.* [Jewels]

ORMEROD, Roger. *An Alibi Too Soon.* [On Vacation]

PALMER, Stuart. *The Puzzle Of The Happy Hooligan.* [Hollywood]

PARKER, T. Jefferson. *Laguna Heat.* [Revenge]

PETERS, Ellis. *The Potter's Field.* [Medieval]

PETERSON, Keith. *There Fell A Shadow.* [Journalism]

PETERSON, Keith. *The Scarred Man.* 1990 Doubleday/ Bantam 1990. Reporter Michael North went to spend Christmas at the home of his boss. He met for the first time Susannah, the daughter home from college. One evening, he makes up a ghost story about a scarred man. Susannah has been dreaming of the same man for years. [Christmas]

PHILLIPS, Stella. *Death In Sheep's Clothing.* 1983 Walker/ Walker 1985. When Grace Roach, retired antique dealer, was found dead in her sitting room, a number of people fell suspect. Chief Detective Inspector Furnival follows some blind leads. 5th.

PICKARD, Nancy. *Say No To Murder.* 1985 Avon/ PBO. Jenny Cain is keeping her eye on the foundation's investment in the development of Liberty Harbor. One angry man threatened to stop the project. He's dead, but the sabotage continues. How can Jenny put an end to it? 2nd.

PICKARD, Nancy. *I. O. U.* [Mother]

PRONZINI, Bill. *Bones.* [Mystery Writer]

PULVER, Mary Monica. *The Unforgiving Minutes.* 1988 St. Martin. The town had a reputation for being the "cocaine capital of Indiana," and Detective Sgt. Peter Brichter is on this case. As they close in, Peter meets Kari Price, a lady almost secluded on the Tretower Ranch. The case takes a sudden turn. 2nd. [Drugs]

PULVER, Mary Monica. *Original Sin.* [Christmas]

PUMPHREY, Janet Kay. *A House Full Of Love.* [Intrigue]

RENDELL, Ruth, w/a Barbara Vine. *A Fatal Inversion.* 1987 Bantam/ Bantam 1988. Alex Chipstead had just bought the manor house. As he inspects the grounds, he finds a pet cemetery—the perfect place for their beloved dog Fred, who's just died. But the grave is already occupied, by a woman and a child.

RIGGS, John R. *Let Sleeping Dogs Lie.* 1986 Dembner/ St. Martin 1988. Out grouse hunting, newspaper owner Garth Ryland stumbles across a 1936 Cadillac covered with hay in an old barn. He wants to restore it but discovers that no one in town wants to touch it or talk about it. 2nd.

RINEHART, Mary Roberts. *The Album.* 1933 Farrar & Rinehart/ Zebra 1988. The five families had lived forever on exclusive Crescent Place. In and out of each other's homes, they knew each other well. At least that's what they thought until the day old Mrs. Lancaster was found in her bed, hacked to death with an axe.

ROSEN, Richard. *Fadeaway.* [Ball Games]

SATTERTHWAIT, Walter. *At Ease With The Dead.* [Indians]

SAUTER, Eric. *Skeletons.* [Serial Killer]

SIMPSON, Pamela. *Partners In Time.* Bantam 1990/ PBO. Los Angeles PI C. J. Grant felt the first rumbles of the earthquake and saw a runaway car bearing down on a young child. The next thing she knew, she was pushed to safety by Sam Hackett, a Federal marshal from 1882. And they were both working on the same case. [Real Estate]

SKLEPOWICH, Edward. *Death In A Serene City.* 1990 Morrow. In tiny San Gabriele Church in a corner of Venice, the 1,100 year-old body of Santa Teodora was stolen and a washerwoman was killed. The woman's hunchback son is a suspect, but American writer Urbino Mcintyre and his friend Barbara, a countess, think otherwise. 1st. [Art]

SMITH, Charles Merrill. *Reverend Randollph And The Splendid Samaritan.* [Revenge]

SMITH, Joan. *Why Aren't They Screaming?* [Getting Away With Murder]

SMOLENS, John. *Winter By Degrees.* 1988 Dutton/ Avon 1990. It's a dreary January in Newburyport and unemployed Nelson Rideout is salvaging windows from the old shoe factory. When the black sheep son of an old family vanishes into the Merrimack River, Nelson has to stop work and prove his brother's not a murderer.

STEVENSON, Richard. *Ice Blues.* 1986 St. Martin/ Penguin 1986. Don Strachey's car was towed away during a winter storm in Albany. When he retrieved it, something had been added: a dead body in the backseat. The body was followed by a letter, and a lot of money. 2nd. [Gay]

TAYLOR, Andrew. *Our Father's Lies.* [Father]

TAYLOR, Andrew. *An Old School Tie.* [Imposter]

TAYLOR, Matt & Bonnie. *Neon Flamingo.* [Journalism]

TELUSHKIN, Joseph. *The Unorthodox Murder Of Rabbi Wahl.* 1987 Bantam/ PBO. Rabbi Daniel Winter expected his Sunday night radio program to stir up emotions. What he didn't expect was that Rabbi Myra Wahl would jog to her death an hour later. 1st. [Clergy]

THOMAS, Ross. *Twilight At Mac's Place.* 1990 Mysterious. Steady Haynes died in a $185 room at the Hay-Adams Hotel. Isabelle, the woman he lived with, made a phone call and arranged for Steady to be buried at Arlington National Cemetery. His son, Granville, an ex-Los Angeles homicide cop, has just been offered $100,000 for Steady's memoirs. [Political]

TOGAWA, Masako. *The Master Key.* [Oriental]

TRENCH, Jason. *Typescript.* [Getting Away With Murder]

TRUMAN, Margaret. *Murder In The White House.* 1980 Arbor House/ Warner 1984. When Lansard Blaine, secretary of state, was found dead in the Lincoln Sitting Room, there was a scramble to find his murderer. Ron Fairbanks, special counsel to the President, is given carte blanche to investigate.

VALIN, Jonathan. *Second Chance.* [Missing Person]

WAKEFIELD, Hannah. *The Price You Pay.* 1990 St. Martin. Dee Street is an American attorney working for a London law firm. In the process of drawing up wills for Amanda Finch and her husband David Blake, Amanda is murdered. David is a suspect and Dee has to probe Amanda's life for clues to her death. [Political]

WALTCH, Lilla M. *The Third Victim.* [Academic]

WELLS, Tobias. *Of Graves, Worms, And Epitaphs.* 1988 Doubleday. In Wellesley, at Shangri-La Retirement

Village, people are dying faster than they should, and not from natural causes. Police Chief Knute Severson is praying for some kind of connection between the victims. They were all taking a writing class. [Writer]

WENTWORTH, Patricia. *Nothing Venture.* [Where There's A Will]

WENTWORTH, Patricia. *The Benevent Treasure.* 1953 Lippincott/ Perennial 1990. After the death of her grandmother, Candida Sayle was invited to come and live with her two great-aunts. They tell her of the Benevent treasure that brings death to anyone who touches it. Miss Silver is already on the scene, investigating the three-year-old disappearance of a young man. 25th. [Where There's A Will]

WESTLAKE, Donald E. *Trust Me On This.* [Journalism]

WHALLEY, Peter. *Robbers.* [Blackmail]

WHITNEY, Phyllis A. *Silversword.* 1987 Doubleday/ Fawcett 1988. Caroline's paternal grandmother had removed her from Maui when she was six, just after her parents died. Now her grandmother Joanna wants her to return. Caroline is eager to find out more about how her parents died and to see David, her childhood love. [Mother]

WILCOX, Stephen F. *The St. Lawrence Run.* 1990 St. Martin. T. S. W. Sheridan is in Washington, DC, as guest speaker at the Crime Historians Association of North America when professor Stefan Janezek is murdered. The professor had contacted Sheridan about an old tragedy at Castle House on one of the Thousand Islands. 2nd. [Smuggling]

WILHELM, Kate. *The Hamlet Trap.* [Theater]

WINGFIELD, R. D. *Frost At Christmas.* [Christmas]

WOODS, Sara. *Malice Domestic.* 1986 Avon/ PBO. After years of living out of the country, Uncle William Cassell returns to the family home in Wimbledon. There's a reunion at teatime and a bullet in the back after dinner. Antony Maitland is convinced Paul, the great-nephew, is innocent. 2nd. [Lawyer]

WREN, M. K. *Seasons Of Death.* 1981 Doubleday/ Ballantine 1990. Forty years ago, Leland Langtry took $10,000 in company funds and ran off with his secretary. Last week Langtry's body was found in a sealed mine tunnel, a knife still stuck between his ribs. His dead partner is blamed for the murder, but Delia says it's not so. She hires Conan Flagg to prove him innocent. 5th. [Infidelity]

ORIENT

The Orient is a made-for-murder setting for most of us. It has the charm of being exotic and relatively unfamiliar in its language and culture. The taint of Dr. Fu Manchu and the Yellow Peril may still be with us, from those Saturday afternoons at the movies, to add the mystery and horror.

BALL, John. *Singapore.* 1986 Dodd, Mead/ Paperjacks 1987. Virgil Tibbs rushes to Singapore to help Madame Motamboru out of a jam. She's been accused of murdering a visitor to her hotel suite. As long as Tibbs is there, he might as well help the local police solve another murder. 7th. [Black Detective]

BIGGERS, Earl Derr. *The Chinese Parrot.* 1926 Bobbs-Merrill/Mysterious 1987. Charlie Chan took his first trip to the mainland. As bodyguards for an expensive string of pearls, Chan and Bob Eden, the jeweler's son, went to Madden's ranch. There's been a murder, but no corpse. The only witness is a parrot that speaks Chinese. 2nd. [Jewels]

BIGGERS, Earl Derr. *Behind That Curtain.* 1928 Bobbs-Merrill/Mysterious 1987. Sixteen years ago, Hilary Gault was shot in his London office. Now Scotland Yard's Sir Frederic Bruce is killed in a San Francisco penthouse. He'd discussed his presence with Charlie Chan. Chan has to solve the first murder to know who killed Bruce. 3rd. [Old Crime]

BIGGERS, Earl Derr. *The Black Camel.* 1929 Bobbs-Merrill/Mysterious 1987. Hollywood star Shelah Fane had just arrived in Hawaii to stay for a while. At a party, she was stabbed to death with a knife. Charlie Chan was so misdirected that he almost didn't solve the case. 4th. [Revenge]

CUNNINGHAM, E. V. *The Case Of The Russian Diplomat.* 1978 Holt/ Owl 1982. A man is found floating in the pool at the Beverly Glen Hotel. Masao Masuto wants to know what happened to his clothes, his glasses, and his watch. What's more, who was the woman who reported his death? 3rd.

GASH, Jonathan. *Jade Woman.* [Antiques]

HANSEN, Joseph. *Obedience.* 1988 Mysterious/ Mysterious 1989. Le Van Nimh, importer and wealthy marina owner, is found dead on his dock. Andy, a man with a grudge, is arrested for the murder. Dave Brandstetter is hired to clear him, and he barges right into a clash of cultures. 10th. [Drugs]

JANCE, J. A. *Dismissed With Prejudice.* [Computer]

MARSHALL, William. *Far Away Man.* 1984 Holt/ Mysterious 1988. The Far Away Man delivers a single shot, and death follows. The only connection between the victims is a torn, yellow cholera vaccination certificate. Inspector Harry Feiffer is working as fast as he can. 9th. [Serial Killer]

MARSHALL, William. *Road Show.* 1985 Holt/ Mysterious 1988. Hong Kong Inspector Harry Feiffer can't figure out why bombs are exploding in his district and creating huge traffic jams. There seems to be a pattern to the destruction. Feiffer has his crew working overtime to find the last bomb. 10th.

MARSHALL, William. *Head First.* [Art]

MARSHALL, William. *Out Of Nowhere.* 1988 Mysterious/ Mysterious 1989. A van carrying four people accidently crashes into a big truck, killing the four passengers. What puzzled Inspector Harry Feiffer was that one of them had been shot dead before the crash. 14th.

MELVILLE, James. *The Wages Of Zen.* 1985 Fawcett/PBO. A group of foreigners came to live at the Chiso-ji Zen Study Center. One of them, an Irish Catholic priest, was found dead in the snow. Someone at the sacred Buddhist temple had killed him. Superintendent Otani had to find out which one was guilty. 1st. [Intrigue]

MELVILLE, James. *A Sort Of Samurai.* 1982 St. Martin/ Fawcett 1985. In the aftermath of an earthquake, Superintendent Otani found a body in the offices of an export company. Inspector Kimura seems smitten with Ilse, the secretary, and Otani's old friend, the baron, is involved. 3rd. [Smuggling]

MELVILLE, James. *Death Of A Daimyo.* [On Vacation]

MELVILLE, James. *The Reluctant Ronin.* 1988 Scribner/ Fawcett 1989. A Dutch woman is found dead in a burned-out warehouse. In her pocket is a picture of Otani and his family. Then Otani's wife reveals that she'd seen the woman kissing their daughter's husband. Otani has a real conflict. 9th. [Jealousy]

MELVILLE, James. *Kimono For A Corpse.* [Fashion]

MELVILLE, James. *The Bogus Buddha.* 1991 Scribner. At a summer school for foreigners, being held at the temple of Anraku-in, several accidents happened that could have been fatal to Professor Kido. One of the faculty is Otani's sister-in-law, and she's upset enough to confide her fears to him. The next accident is fatal. 11th. [Anthropology]

NATSUKI, Shizuko. *Murder At Mt. Fuji.* 1984 St. Martin/ Ballantine 1987. In Tokyo, Jane Prescott is tutoring Chiyo Wada in English. Chiyo invites Jane to celebrate the New Year with her family. But suddenly Chiyo is confessing to the murder of her grandfather. Jane doesn't want her to be guilty. [Where There's A Will]

NATSUKI, Shizuko. *The Third Lady.* 1987 Ballantine/PBO. Outside Paris, on a stormy night, Kohei Daigo met a fellow traveler from Japan, a beautiful woman full of allure. They made a pact: each had someone the world would be better off without. Home in Japan, the wishes of the other would be carried out. But Daigo would soon be in for a shock. [Getting Away With Murder]

NATSUKI, Shizuko. *The Obituary Arrives At Two O'Clock.* 1988 Ballantine/ PBO. The owner of the Tokyo Country Club was bashed over the head with a golf club. The owner of the golf club, Kosuke Okita, was trying to collect a lot of money from the dead man. Kosuke's alibi was that he was at a phone booth looking for the blind woman who'd phoned him by mistake. [Infidelity]

TOGAWA, Masako. *The Master Key.* 1984 Dodd, Mead/ Penguin 1985. In 1951 the four-year-old child of George Kraft was kidnapped. Now, seven years later, the K Apartments for Ladies is about to be moved, to make way for a new road. There's a child's body buried in the basement bathhouse. [Old Crime]

TOGAWA, Masako. *The Lady Killer.* [Revenge]

VAN DE WETERING, Janwillem. *The Japanese Corpse.* 1977 Houghton Mifflin/ Ballantine 1987. The young Japanese woman reported to Grijpstra and de Gier that her boyfriend was missing. She also admitted they were both part of a Japanese crime syndicate that smuggled art and drugs. Grijpstra and de Gier travel to Japan to work undercover. 5th. [Smuggling]

VAN DE WETERING, Janwillem. *Inspector Saito's Small Satori.* 1985 Putnam/ Ballantine 1987. A collection of ten short stories featuring Inspector Saito, Kyoto Police, and his remarkable talents for crime solving.

P . . . IS FOR

PATHOLOGIST

*H*AVING ATTENDED *New Mexico's Office of Medical Investigation's Death Seminar, I can fully appreciate the role of the pathologist at the murder scene. It is a bit of a surprise that the pathologist is not a more formidable character in murder fiction. This is a category that could grow.*

CORNWELL, Patricia. *Postmortem.* 1990 Scribner/ Avon 1991. She was the third young woman to die by the same method in Richmond, Virginia. Chief Medical Examiner Kay Scarpetta took the call. She has to use all her skills to catch the killer before he comes for her. 1st. [Serial Killer]

CORNWELL, Patricia. *Body Of Evidence.* 1991 Scribner. When the police ignore the calls that threaten her, historical writer Berly Madison runs away to Florida for a few weeks. The night she returns to Richmond, she's brutally murdered and Chief Medical Examiner Kay Scarpetta has a puzzle to solve. 2nd. [Writer]

DONALDSON, D. J. *Cajun Nights.* 1988 St. Martin/ St. Martin 1990. Chief Medical Examiner Andy Broussard was using all his skills to figure out why upright families in New Orleans were killing one another. Psychologist Kit Franklyn has picked up one clue already. [Revenge]

DONALDSON, D. J. *Blood On The Bayou.* [Medical]

HOROVITZ, Leslie Alan. *Causes Unknown.* Lynx 1989/PBO. Michael Friedlander returned to New York City when his brother died. The Medical Examiner, Dr. Magnus, has issued a verdict of suicide. Michael, unable to accept the decision, starts his own investigation that leads right to the medical examiner's office. [Serial Killer]

KELLERMAN, Faye. *Sacred And Profane.* [Pornography]

KEMP, Sarah. *No Escape.* 1984 Doubleday/ Signet 1985. Two people have been knifed to death and a man is blinded. Tina May, pathologist, is working to put together the picture of the Green-Eyed-Girl, the murderer. As John Kettle, her mentor, is dying, he tries to give her a new lead. 1st. [Serial Killer]

KEMP, Sarah. *The Lure Of Sweet Death.* 1986 Doubleday. Tina May discovers that a supposed murder was really a suicide. But what happened to the money the victim had withdrawn from the bank? Clues lead to a path of extortion and murder, and Tina's right in the middle. 2nd. [Serial Killer]

KEMP, Sarah. *What Dread Hand.* 1986 Doubleday/ Worldwide 1988. Tina May borrowed a cottage in Cornwall for a rest. Someone has left a box on the kitchen table ... a head without a body. When the head disappears, someone tries to scare her to death. 3rd. [Witches]

POLITICAL

After every presidential election, I expect that the readers have had it up to their eyebrows with politics. But the political arena has all the right elements for the carefully constructed murder mystery. You might call it vicarious voting . . .

BARNARD, Robert. *Political Suicide.* [Getting Away With Murder]

POLITICAL 307

BARNES, Linda. *Dead Heat.* [Insurance]

BELFORTE, Sophie. *The Lace Curtain Murders.* [Revenge]

BOWEN, Michael. *Washington Deceased.* [Locked Room]

BOYER, Rick. *The Penny Ferry.* [Old Crime]

BROWN, R. D. *Villa Head.* 1987 Bantam/ PBO. Cheney Hazzard is hired by a wealthy businessman for a strange quest: to locate the head of Pancho Villa. Others are head-hunting, too, for this head possesses an abundance of political power for the Mexican masses. 2nd. [Famous People]

CAMPBELL, Robert. *The Six Hundred Pound Gorilla.* 1987 Signet/PBO. The boiler blew at the Lincoln Park Zoo, and Jimmy Flannery has to find shelter for Baby, the gorilla, Chicago's sweetheart. Just after Baby is housed at a gay bathhouse, two men are found beaten to death. Jimmy sets out to prove murder, not Baby, caused the deaths. 2nd.

CAMPBELL, Robert. *The Gift Horse's Mouth.* 1990 Pocket/ Pocket 1991. Boss Carrigan asks Jimmy Flannery to find out who murdered Goldie Hanrahan, his right-hand woman for over thirty years, and stole her bridge-work. Flannery's investigation takes him to a secret hidden for forty years. 6th. [Mother]

CORRIS, Peter. *The January Zone.* [Australian]

DAVIS, Dorothy Salisbury. *Death Of An Old Sinner.* 1957 Scribner/ Ballantine 1987. Jimmie Jarvis, candidate for governor, and his housekeeper, Mrs. Norris, are turning over the rocks to find out who murdered Mr. Jarvis, Sr. 1st. [Holiday]

DOOLITTLE, Jerome. *Body Scissors.* 1990 Pocket. Boston's Tom Bethany has been hired to check out J. Alden

Kellicott, a potential candidate for Secretary of State. Kellicott's record seems to be flawless, but there's the murder of his elder daughter two years earlier that catches Bethany's attention. 1st. [Father]

ESTLEMAN, Loren D. *Motor City Blues.* 1980 Houghton Mifflin/ Fawcett 1986. Ben Morningstar, semiretired gangster, wants PI Amos Walker to locate his ward. Ben's just found a pornographic photo, and Marla's in it. She'd left her fancy school with a black labor leader eighteen months ago. 1st. [Blackmail]

ESTLEMAN, Loren D. *Peeper.* [Clergy]

EVERSON, David. *Recount.* 1987 Ivy/ PBO. Jam Johnson was dead and someone was out to ruin the senate chances of Doug Stone. Troubleshooter Robert Miles found the body and is out to find a killer. 1st.

EVERSON, David. *Rebound.* 1988 Ivy/ PBO. PI Robert Miles is wanted by the Illinois speaker of the house. He wants Miles to head up a commission to investigate corruption in basketball. It smells as though the corruption goes much deeper, even to murder. 2nd.

HANSEN, Joseph. *The Little Dog Laughed.* 1986 Holt/ Owl 1987. Adam Streeter, foreign correspondent, was writing the story of the decade, or so he told his blind daughter before he committed suicide. Dave Brandstetter, insurance agent, isn't too clear on the death. 8th. [Gay]

HARRISON, Ray. *Death Of An Honourable Member.* [Victorian]

HESS, Joan. *A Really Cute Corpse.* [Blackmail]

JAMES, P. D. *Devices And Desires.* 1990 Knopf/ Warner 1991. Adam Dalgleish vacationed to Larksoken where his aunt had willed him her cottage on the headlands.

A serial killer, the Whistler, had just found his fourth victim. Then Dalgleish stumbles over a body on the beach. 9th. [Serial Killer]

JANCE, J. A. *Injustice For All.* 1986 Avon/ PBO. J. P. Beaumont, Seattle PD, is on vacation at Rosario Resort. Hearing a woman scream, he finds Ginger Watkins on the beach beside a dead man. When Ginger dies in an auto accident, Beaumont is determined to find out what's going on. His first stop: Ginger's husband who is running for office. 2nd. [On Vacation]

JERINA, Carol. *Flirting With Danger.* [Journalism]

KAMINSKY, Stuart. *Buried Caesars.* [Famous People]

KERR, Philip. *March Violets.* 1989 Viking/ Penguin 1990. Berlin 1936: Bernie Gunther was escorted to the estate of a wealthy man. Herr Schemm wants Bernie to find out who murdered his daughter and her husband and emptied the diamonds from the safe. His toughest job is to locate the safecracker. 1st. [Jewels]

LATHEN, Emma, w/a R. B. Dominic. *Murder, Sunny Side Up.* 1968 Abelard/ Paperjacks 1985. Congressman Ben Safford is attending a committee hearing on the safety of Ova-Cote, a process that keeps eggs fresh indefinitely. One of the men involved in the invention is shot in the Library of Congress. And that's just the first. 1st. [Library]

MacLEOD, Charlotte. *Something The Cat Dragged In.* 1983 Doubleday/ Avon 1984. Landlady Betsy Lomax was aghast when the cat dragged Herbert Ungley's toupee into the kitchen. The man wouldn't be caught dead without it. Sure enough, he was found behind the Balaclava Society Clubhouse. Professor Shandy gets the call. He wants to know what Ungley was buying with all that money. 4th. [Fraud]

MURPHY, Haughton. *Murder Keeps A Secret.* 1989 Simon & Schuster/Fawcett 1990. Historian David Rowan was working on the biography of the late Supreme Court Justice Garrett Ainslee when he went out his Manhattan office window. Shocked, his godfather Reuben Frost dives into the murder investigation. 4th.

O'DONNELL, Lillian. *Wicked Designs.* [Where There's A Will]

ORENSTEIN, Frank. *A Candidate For Murder.* [Advertising]

PARKER, Robert B. *The Widening Gyre.* 1983 Delacorte/ Dell 1987. Spenser is handling the security for senate candidate Meade Alexander. Alexander's wife is having a few problems with sex and drugs, and someone has it on tape. A little blackmail seems in order. 10th. [Blackmail]

PEDNEAU, Dave. *Dead Witness.* [Corruption]

ROBB, T. N. *Private Eye.* 1988 Ivy/ PBO. Los Angles PD officer Jack Cleary has been dumped from the force, accused of bribery. As he surfaces from a bender, his PI brother Nick dies in a suspicious auto crash. Out to find his brother's killer, he finds rot all around him. 1st. [Corruption]

ROBERTS, John Maddox. *SPQR.* [Historical]

SALE, Medora. *Murder In Focus.* [Canadian]

SERAFIN, David. *Port Of Light.* [Intrigue]

SERRIAN, Michael. *Fatal Exit.* [Hollywood]

SHUMAN, M. K. *The Caesar Clue.* [Prostitution]

SINGER, Shelley. *Suicide King.* 1988 St. Martin/ Worldwide 1990. Rosie dragged Jake Samson off to a VIVO political party ecological benefit. When their candidate, Joe Richmond, was found hanging naked in an acacia tree, his campaign manager, Pam, called Jake. 5th.

SPICER, Michael. *Cotswold Murders.* [Clergy]

THOMAS, Ross. *Briar Patch.* 1984 Simon & Schuster/ Penguin 1985. Detective Felicity Dill is blown up by a car bomb as she heads out one morning. Her brother Benjamin flies in from Washington, D.C., to find out who murdered his sister, and why.

THOMAS, Ross. *Twilight At Mac's Place.* [Old Crime]

TRUMAN, Margaret. *Murder On Embassy Row.* [Getting Away With Murder]

TRUMAN, Margaret. *Murder In Georgetown.* [Journalism]

TRUMAN, Margaret. *Murder In The Kennedy Center.* 1989 Random House/ Fawcett 1990. Andrea Feldman's body was found across from the Kennedy Center, the same night Senator Ewald held his gala presidential fund raiser at the center. And Andrea worked for the senator. Law professor Mac Smith joins the team when the senator's son is suspected. [Intrigue]

WAKEFIELD, Hannah. *The Price You Pay.* [Old Crime]

WALLACE, Marilyn. *Primary Target.* 1988 Bantam/ PBO. Oakland PD cops Cruz and Goldstein are trying to find out who's sending threatening letters to presidential candidate Jean Talbot. One man is already dead, and Goldstein's father has disappeared. 2nd. [Revenge]

WALLACE, Robert. *An Axe To Grind.* 1990 St. Martin. Basking at Cap Ferrat, Essington Holt allows himself to be drawn into intrigue by his friend Gerald Sparrow. It seems an old woman was brutally murdered in Australia, her Dufy has been secreted away. 2nd. [Art]

WESTBROOK, Robert. *Lady Left.* [Hollywood]

WINSLOW, Don. *A Cool Breeze On The Underground.* [Missing Person]

WOLK, Michael. *The Big Picture.* 1985 Signet/ PBO. Literary agent Max Popper was the prime suspect when the PI next door was killed over a piece of film that had political implications. Several people had their hands out for this gem. To clear himself, Max has to find the film. [Corruption]

ZELMAN, Anita. *The Right Moves.* [Journalism]

PORNOGRAPHY

Whether we like it or not, pornography has become part of our lives and big business, to boot. So, of course, pornography has crept into the mystery story as a minor or even a major theme. Runaway youngsters are the most frequent victims, but others are not immune. Hard-hitting cops and tough PIs are the heroes. Parents and friends share the burden of grief.

BARNARD, Robert. *Bodies.* [Revenge]

BOWERS, Elizabeth. *Ladies' Night.* [Missing Person]

CAMPBELL, Robert. *In La-La Land We Trust.* 1986 Mysterious/ Mysterious 1987. A head surfaced in a lake in New Orleans. Then a body rolled out of a station wagon in Los Angeles, but the cops aren't paying too much attention to it. PI Whistler got involved when a lady was in distress. 1st.

CONSTANTINE, K. C. *The Man Who Liked To Look At Himself.* 1973 Saturday Review/ Godine 1987. Out hunting with a friend, Police Chief Mario Balzic is on the spot when the dog starts romping around with a bone in its mouth. It was a human femur, and it had saw marks on it. A challenging case for Balzic. 2nd.

CREWS, Lary. *Kill Cue.* 1988 Lynx/ PBO. Radio talk show host Veronica Slade was saddened when her former lover and fellow broadcaster was murdered at his radio station. She's searching for the killer. Someone's out to stop her. 1st. [Children]

CUNNINGHAM, E. V. *The Wabash Factor.* 1986 Delacorte/ Dell 1986. A bright light in the political arena had a stroke over dinner at a posh New York City restaurant. Then there was another death. Lt. Harry Golding's wife and a medical student are convinced it's murder. Golding and his family are led into a tunnel of terror. [Intrigue]

DAVIS, Dorothy Salisbury. *Lullaby Of Murder.* 1984 Scribner/ Worldwide 1989. Gossip columnist Tony Alexander sends Julie Hayes out to do a story on the Garden of Roses, where there's to be a dance marathon. Julie's story takes a different slant, and Tony kills it. Then someone kills Tony. 3rd. [Journalism]

DEAVER, Jeffrey Wilds. *Death Of a Blue Movie Star.* Bantam 1990/ PBO. Rune was working diligently on a film, a documentary about Shelly Lowe and her life making "blue movies." As Rune waited, Shelly went to take a phone call and the building blew up. 2nd. [Theater]

DOBYNS, Stephen. *Saratoga Bestiary.* [Art]

DUNDEE, Wayne D. *The Skintight Shroud.* 1989 St. Martin/ Dell 1991. The midwestern town of Rockport, Illinois, has just had a murder; Jason Hobbs was found in a ditch. Then Valerie Pine was murdered in her apartment. PI Joe Hannibal was hired by the porn movie company to find out who was killing the star actors. 2nd. [Incest]

EMERSON, Earl W. *Fat Tuesday.* 1988 Ballantine/ PBO. Attorney Kathy Birchfield gets a strange call from her client Fred: someone has sent him a rattlesnake. Kathy enlists the help of PI Thomas Black. They arrive at Fred's house, only to find him dead and his wife holding the murder weapon. Everything points to an old criminal action—almost. 4th. [Old Crime]

GORMAN, Edward. *The Night Remembers.* [Old Crime]

KANTNER, Rob. *The Harder They Hit.* 1987 Bantam/ PBO. Headless and handless corpses are turning up all over Detroit. PI Ben Perkins is right in the middle of the mystery. He's seen a lot, but he's not prepared for what he finds in the empty building. 2nd. [Serial Killer]

KELLERMAN, Faye. *Sacred And Profane.* 1987 Arbor House/ Fawcett 1988. Los Angeles PD detective Peter Decker takes Rina's two boys camping, and the boys find the charred skeletons of two young women. Using forensic dentistry, Decker traces the women right to the heart of a pornography setup. 2nd. [Pathologist]

KIKER, Douglas. *Death At The Cut.* 1988 Random House/ Ballantine 1990. Mac McFarland is doing a profile on Senator Bridges, presidential candidate. Early one morning, Mac spots a submerged car with a young woman strapped in by her seat belt. The car is across from the senator's cottage. Mac is being discouraged from investigating. 2nd. [Journalism]

MacGREGOR, T. J. *Death Sweet.* [Serial Killer]

McBAIN, Ed. *Puss In Boots.* 1987 Holt/ Mysterious 1988. Prudence Ann Markham packed up the film, left the studio, headed for her car, and died. Her husband ended up in jail, accused of her murder. Attorney Matt Hope agreed to defend him, and slipped quietly into seamy city life. 7th. [Lawyer]

RAY, Robert. *Bloody Murdock.* [Hollywood]

SANTINI, Rosemarie. *The Disenchanted Diva.* [Revenge]

SAWYER, Corinne Holt. *The J. Alfred Prufrock Murders.* [Blackmail]

STANLEY, William. *The Flying Club.* 1988 Walker. Ex–Scotland Yard Inspector Charles Beresford is at Theyby Rigg, a small flying field, when Josiah Howsald comes to him. His son Jake was killed when his herd of cows stampeded. Josiah insists it was murder.

STINSON, Jim. *Double Exposure.* [Hollywood]

WOOD, Ted. *Corkscrew.* 1987 Scribner/ Worldwide 1989. A group of bikers roared into quiet Murphey's Harbor just before a boy was found murdered in the lake. Police Chief Reid Bennett has his work cut out for him when there's involvement with a rival biker's group. 5th. [Canadian]

PROSTITUTION

Long referred to as the world's "oldest profession," prostitution is, in fact, only the second *oldest: pimping ranks as the first. Be that as it may, prostitution is the situation in which any number of murders are committed, in fact as well as in fiction.*

BLOCK, Lawrence. *A Ticket To The Boneyard.* [Revenge]

CHRISTOPHER, Constance. *Dead Man's Flower.* [Witches]

GOUGH, Laurence. *Silent Knives.* 1988 St. Martin/ Penguin 1990. Vancouver PD officer Jack Willows, on a fishing trip, snags the body of a young girl who has a tattoo. Back in the city his partner stumbles over the body of a young boy. He also has a tattoo. Now, together, they're on the trail of a deadly killer. 2nd.

LOGUE, Mary. *Red Lake Of The Heart.* 1987 Dell/ PBO. Amy Curtis put a lot of energy into protecting her younger sister, Tricia, from herself. To no avail. One morning Amy finds Tricia murdered, and she vows to find the killer . . . at whatever cost to herself.

LUTZ, John. *Dancer's Debt.* 1988 St. Martin. While on a private case, Alo Nudger doesn't pay much attention to the female corpses being pulled from the Mississippi by the police. He's been hired by Helen to find out why her boyfriend, Dancer, is acting so strangely. On a whim, he decides to follow Helen. 4th.

McDONALD, Gregory. *Fletch Won.* [Journalism]

PARKER, Robert B. *Mortal Stakes.* [Ball Game]

PARKER, Robert B. *Ceremony.* 1982 Delacorte/ Dell 1987. Her father threw her out, but her mother wanted her back home. Teenager April Kyle has disappeared into Boston's "Combat Zone." Spenser has to find her. 9th.

PARKER, Robert B. *Taming A Sea-Horse.* 1986 Delacorte/ Dell 1987. April Kyle was missing again, and Spenser flew to New York City to locate her. She's decided to go to work for a pimp. Spenser is looking for a man named Warren, and a lot of people are trying to stop him. 13th.

PAUL, Raymond. *The Thomas Street Horror.* [Historical]

PERRY, Anne. *Resurrection Row.* [Victorian]

PERRY, Anne. *Death In The Devil's Acre.* [Victorian]

SHANNON, Dell. *Chaos Of Crime.* [Serial Killer]

SHUMAN, M. K. *The Caesar Clue.* 1990 St. Martin. PI Mica Dunn heard Julia's voice on his message machine. He didn't know her, but Julia wanted him to meet her at the New Orleans Airport. The plane crashed on approach, into the bayou. Suddenly there's a suspicion of a bomb. 2nd. [Political]

SMITH, Julie. *Death Turns A Trick.* 1982 Walker/ Pinnacle 1985. Rebecca Schwartz, Jewish feminist San Francisco lawyer, is at a party at a client's, at a bordello. When there's a raid, Rebecca ends up in the police station, Kandi is dead on Rebecca's living room floor, and her uncle is about to be pegged by the cops. 1st. [Lawyer]

STORY, William L. *Final Thesis.* 1989 St. Martin. One of his students asked English professor Nick Toland to find her friend. Now Darlene has been stabbed in Boston's "combat zone," and Nick's doing a quiet investigation. [Children]

VAN DE WETERING, Janwillem. *Tumbleweed.* 1976 Houghton Mifflin/ Ballantine 1987. She drove a white Mercedes and lived on an expensive houseboat. Her neighbor called the police; he hadn't seen her for several days. Grijpstra and de Gier found her on her living room floor, a knife in her back. They started with a list of her lovers. 2nd. [Witches]

YORKE, Margaret. *Speak For The Dead.* 1988 Viking/ Penguin 1989. Corrie Foster, married for a few years to an older man, is about to repeat a pattern she learned in her school days. She's making secret trips to the West End of London. One day she turns up dead. [Psychological]

PSYCHICS, WITH A TOUCH OF MAGIC

Every now and then there appears a person who seems to have powers that escape most of us—psychic powers that can boggle the mind. While it is against the "rules" of the mystery story to have the solution to the murder or other crime come from psychic powers, the use of the psychic does emerge. Also added is a touch of magic.

CHRISTOPHER, Paula. *The Dreaming Pool.* [Horses]

GREEN, Kate. *Shattered Moon.* 1986 Dell/ PBO. Bonnie Humphrey disappeared, and her parents asked psychic Teresa Fortuna to help find her. There Bonnie was, in the shallow grave. Soon after, Teresa had a vision, another death, the ultimate blow. She foresaw her own demise.

JANESCHUTZ, Trish, aka T. J. MacGregor. *Hidden Lake.* 1987 Ballantine/ PBO. Gary Lucas, a psychic, "sees" a murder being committed. The victim is Anna, another psychic, a neighbor of Homicide Detective Deirdre O'Malley. Two more deaths lead Deirdre to an evil plot and a crooked cop.

KELLEY, Patrick A. *Sleightly Murder.* 1985 Avon/ PBO. Magician Harry Colderwood was hired to find out who was haunting Mr. Morrow with poltergeists. But Morrow falls from the top of a parking building, and Colderwood has to conjure up the magic on his own. 1st. [Manuscripts]

KELLEY, Patrick A. *Sleightly Lethal.* 1986 Avon/ PBO. Quimp, the clown, announced on TV that he'd never check out of the Finch Hotel alive. Harry Colderwood, hearing it, checked in. Then a clown was dead, stuffed into the hotel safe. Something didn't fit, and Harry was caught in a puzzle. 2nd. [Blackmail]

KELLEY, Patrick A. *Sleightly Invisible.* 1986 Avon/ PBO. Psychic Birch Osborne went to great lengths to get magician Harry Colderwood to help him. A graduate student is missing from the college library, and Osborne has been accused by another psychic of masterminding her disappearance. 3rd.

KELLEY, Patrick A. *Sleightly Deceived.* 1987 Avon/ PBO. Harry Colderwood visited the aging illusionist Arlen Roth to learn Roth's famous card-and-knife trick. But Roth was dead, and Harry became the suspect of choice. He had to clear himself. 4th. [Old Crime]

KELLEY, Patrick A. *Sleightly Guilty.* 1988 Avon/ PBO. Harry Colderwood got a phone call from his assistant Cate. Someone had kidnapped her. Harry was to get into a poker game and win big. The kidnapper would contact him later. It was going to be magic pitted against magic. 5th. [Fraud]

MATTESON, Stephanie. *Murder At The Spa.* Diamond 1990/ PBO. When actress Charlotte Graham received a phone call from her friend Pauline Langenberg, she packed up and headed for High Rock Springs. Someone was out to sabotage Pauline's spa. But suddenly Charlotte has two murders on her hands. 1st. [Where There's a Will]

McSHANE, Mark. *Seance On A Wet Afternoon.* 1961 Doubleday/ Carroll & Graf 1990. Myra Savage was a medium, giving seances three times a week. Her husband Bill was asthmatic and worked little. Myra had a plan, just a simple kidnapping and she could use her paranormal skills to help the police. [Kidnapping]

SMITH, Terrence Lore. *Yours Truly, From Hell.* 1987 St. Martin/ St. Martin 1988. General James Lee, Ret., dreams his dreams in Colorado. But as the descendant of a Victorian psychic, the dreams are of Jack the Ripper. He's compelled to go to London, even if it means facing a horrible truth. [Famous People]

VAN GIESON, Judith. *The Other Side Of Death.* [Lawyer]

VARDEMAN, Robert E. *The Screaming Knife.* Avon 1990/ PBO. Detective Worthing, San Francisco PD, put in a call for Peter Thorne. A woman had been brutally murdered, and Worthing wants Peter to use his psychic powers to tell him something about the killer. As Peter picks up the murder weapon, a crystal knife, his head fills with screams. 1st. [Gay]

WHITNEY, Phyllis A. *Rainbow In The Mist.* 1989 Doubleday/ Fawcett 1990. Unlike her psychic mother, Christy Loren is fearful of her ability to sense things and see visions. Seeking refuge with her Aunt Nona in the Blue Ridge Mountains, Christy comes face to face with the disappearance of her cousin Dierdre. [Psychological]

PSYCHOLOGICAL

There is often a thin line between the horror novel and the psychological mystery story. While the tension is building, we have left some of the macabre to the other genre, and maintained the focus on murder and mayhem.

BALLARD, Mignon F. *Raven Rock.* [Mother]

BANKS, Carolyn. *Patchwork.* [Mother]

BEATON, M. C. *Death Of A Perfect Wife.* 1989 St. Martin/ Ivy 1990. Paul and Trixie Thomas moved to a Scottish village where Trixie was the perfect wife, and so helpful to her neighbors, correcting all the wrongs in town. It was a surprise, then, when she was found dead. To everyone, that is, but Constable Hamish Macbeth. 4th.

BECK, K. K. *The Body In The Volvo.* [Fraud]

BECK, K. K. *Unwanted Attentions.* 1988 Walker/ Ivy 1990. He was obsessed with her: Benjamin Knapp had been stalking Rebecca Kendall for fifteen years. She hires PI Caruso to help her get his address; she's about to turn the tables. At his house, there's lots of blood, but no body. As Rebecca stands trial, she suddenly vanishes. Caruso now has to find her.

BOYLE, Thomas. *Post-Mortem Effects.* [Holiday]

BRANDON, Ruth. *Out Of Body, Out Of Mind.* 1988 St. Martin. Parapsychologist Dr. Jasper Hodgkins left his academic post in England to do pure research in southern California. When he disappears, his assistant, Dr. Becky Ryan, teams up with journalist Andrew Taggart to find him. [Intrigue]

CHASE, Samantha. *Postmark.* [Children]

CHASE, Samantha. *Needlepoint.* [Revenge]

CHEHAK, Susan Taylor. *The Story Of Annie D.* [Mother]

CLARKE, Anna. *One Of Us Must Die.* 1980 Doubleday/ Charter 1988. Dr. Dorothy Laver was a psychiatrist, but that didn't make it any easier for her to live with a brilliant and insane husband. She became convinced that Gerry was about to commit a very clever crime: either he would kill her or she'd be accused of murdering him.

CONNERS, Bernard F. *The Hampton Sisters.* 1987 Fine/Dell 1988. Sisters Lydia and Emily Morrow were very different. Lydia preferred her bird sanctuary and the bird books she wrote. Emily liked the social life and writing about the secrets of the wealthy. Dark forces will engulf them both.

DIBDIN, Michael. *Tryst.* Pocket 1990/ PBO. Psychologist Aileen Macklin has a new patient at London's Adolescent Psychiatric Unit. The young man insists he is schizophrenic and that someone is trying to kill him. Struggling with her own problems, Aileen has to spend time finding out who the patient really is. [Children]

ELLROY, James. *Because Of The Night.* [Missing Person]

FULTON, Eileen. *A Setting For Murder.* [Television]

GILL, B. M. *Nursery Crimes.* [Children]

GREENLEAF, Stephen. *Beyond Blame.* 1986 Villard/ Ballantine 1987. Dianne Renzel had been dead for a month, and the police still didn't know why she was murdered. Her parents hired John Tanner Marsh, lawyer turned PI, to find the killer. The path Marsh follows is a strange one, leading to a point of law. 5th.

HARRIS, Thomas. *The Silence Of The Lambs.* [Serial Killer]

HARVEY, John. *Lonely Hearts.* [Serial Killer]

HEALY, Jeremiah. *Blunt Darts.* 1984 Walker/ Popular 1986. Boston PI John Francis Cuddy was hired to find Stephen Kingston, the fourteen-year-old son of a prominent judge. Stephen had packed his survival gear and left home. When Stephen was ten, his mother had killed herself, and he might still be upset about her death. 1st. [Old Crime]

HEALY, Jeremiah. *So Like Sleep.* 1987 Harper & Row/ Pocket 1988. PI John Cuddy was doing a favor for a cop friend. William Daniels, a young black man, confessed to his therapy group that he'd just killed his white girlfriend Jennifer. But Cuddy's path takes him back into a murderer's past. 2nd.

HENDERSON, M. R. *If I Should Die.* 1985 Doubleday/ Avon 1986. Eleven years ago, Kay's teenage romance had deteriorated into a deadly nightmare. Now Matt Briggs has escaped from his prison, and it's happening all over again.

HENDERSON, M. R. *By Reason Of . . .* 1986 Doubleday/ Avon 1987. Eve Foxx and her daughter were alone at the California ranch when a storm came up. As the electricity died and the roads became choked with mud slides, Eve is in terror when someone slips into the house—a crazed killer.

JANESCHUTZ, Trish, aka T. J. MacGregor. *In Shadow.* 1985 Ballantine/ PBO. Research chemist Denise Markham was working on a new drug, one to replace cocaine. As she crossed campus to the parking lot, she was murdered. Detective John Conway was questioning her friends, students, lovers . . . and the killer. [Drugs]

JOSHUA, Benjamin, MD. *A Drop Of Blood.* [Medical]

KELLERMAN, Jonathan. *Over The Edge.* 1987 Atheneum/ Signet 1988. The call came in the middle of the night from Jamey Cadmus. He'd been hospitalized and wanted Alex Delaware, his psychologist, to help him. Before Alex can get to the hospital, Jamey escaped, and Alex was drawn deeper and deeper into murder and terror. 3rd. [Serial Killer]

KELLERMAN, Jonathan. *Silent Partner.* 1989 Bantam/ Bantam 1990. Psychologist Alex Delaware met her again at a party. Sharon wanted his help . . . again. Then she was dead, a suicide. He has to explore her psyche and his own before he can find a resolution. 4th. [Suicide]

LAIKEN, Deirdre S. *Death Among Strangers.* [Children]

LEWIN, Elsa. *I, Anna.* 1984 Mysterious/ Mysterious 1987. Anna went to a singles party and ended up back at the man's apartment. At fifty, and recently divorced, Anna should have known better. Her nightmare had just started. Where would it end?

LINDSEY, David L. *Heat From Another Sun.* [Blackmail]

LYSAGHT, Brian. *Sweet Deals.* [Missing Person]

MARTIN, Lee. *Death Warmed Over.* 1988 St. Martin/ Worldwide 1991. A postman is found dead next to a burned 1957 Chevy. The next thing Detective Deb Ralston knows, she's deep into a kidnapping and murder. She sits down with a psychiatrist to figure out what kind of a person the murderer is. 4th.

MARTIN, Lee. *Hal's Own Murder Case.* 1989 St. Martin. Fort Worth homicide detective Deb Ralston, due to deliver any day, takes off to find her teenage son, off on spring break. Before she catches up with him, he's been charged with murder and is in the Las Vegas, N.V., jail. 5th. [Father]

MARTIN, Lee. *The Mensa Murders.* [Serial Killer]

MATHIS, Edward. *Little Man Blues.* [Serial Killer]

MATHIS, Edward. *Only When She Cries.* Berkley 1989/ PBO. Lt. Ben Cloud was just finishing a narcotics stakeout when the call came in—a double homicide. The crime had all the earmarks of the serial killer Julian Arrowstone, last heard from in Chicago. It looked like he'd moved to Texas, although some of the evidence didn't fit. [Serial Killer]

McBAIN, Ed. *Snow White and Rose Red.* [Mother]

McINERNY, Ralph. *Body And Soil.* 1989 Atheneum/ Worldwide 1991. The Stanfields wanted a divorce and they both wanted Andrew Broom as their lawyer. Before Andrew could file papers, Hal Stanfield was dead on his kitchen floor and Pauline was suspected of his murder. Andrew thinks the evidence is too pat, just before Pauline disappears. 2nd. [Lawyer]

MEEK, M. R. D. *The Split Second.* [Lawyer]

MILLER, Judi. *Phantom Of The Soap Opera.* [Television]

MILLS, D. F. *Dark Room.* [Serial Killer]

NABB, Magdalen. *The Marshal's Own Case.* [Gay]

NAGY, Gloria. *Radio Blues.* 1988 St. Martin. On her fortieth birthday, Aroma Sweet was delivered her twin sister's head and the *New York Times.* Aroma was a potential suspect or she might be the next victim. Soon she's discovering lots about her twin. [Television]

PARKER, Robert B. *Crimson Joy.* [Mother]

PEARSON, Ridley. *Undercurrents.* [Serial Killer]

PETERS, Elizabeth. *The Love Talkers.* 1980 Dodd, Mead/ Tor 1990. Laurie's invitation came from Great Aunt Ida: Come to Idlewood and finish your dissertation. Uncle Ned was well but Aunt Lizzie thought there were faeries in the woods. Her half-brother, Doug, whom she hasn't seen for years, will also be there. As soon as Laurie arrives, strange things start to happen. [Mother]

PRICE, Nancy. *Sleeping With The Enemy.* 1987 Simon & Schuster/ Jove 1988. Sara Burney was married to a man obsessed with her. She lied and cheated and then made her move; she faked her own death and vanished. Happy in her new life, she suddenly discovers that he's found her. [Suicide]

RADLEY, Sheila. *Death In The Morning.* 1979 Scribner/ Bantam 1987. The body of Mary Gedge was found floating face down in the shallow river. It was readily agreed that she'd been held under the water. Inspector Quantrill finds a very strange motive for Mary's death. 1st.

RENDELL, Ruth. *One Across, Two Down.* [Crossword]

RENDELL, Ruth. *An Unkindness Of Ravens.* [Incest]

RENDELL, Ruth. *Talking To Strange Men.* 1987 Pantheon/ Ballantine 1988. The battle was between London Central and Moscow Centre: purloined code books, agents and moles, double-crosses and defections. They were merely children at play until a lonely, inquisitive clerk thinks he's decoding messages from a real spy ring. [Children]

RENDELL, Ruth. *The Bridesmaid.* 1989 Mysterious/ Mysterious 1990. Philip Wardman was a quiet young man. At his sister's wedding, he met Senta Phelan, a young actress who looked remarkably like the statue in his garden. Senta insists that he prove his love for her.

RENDELL, Ruth. *Going Wrong.* 1990 Mysterious. Guy Curran is obsessed by his love for his childhood sweetheart Leonora Chisolm. He fears that someone in her family is trying to drive a wedge between them. He's going to do something about it.

RITCHIE, Simon. *The Hollow Woman.* [Canadian]

ROBERTS, Nora. *Sacred Sins.* [Serial Killer]

RYP, Ellen. *Deadly Bonds.* Warner 1989/ PBO. Carla Temple taught English at a fine school in Fernstaad, Switzerland. Suddenly, young women are being killed and they all attend the Marlowe School. As terror mounts, Carla struggles to protect her students, and herself. [Revenge]

SERAFIN, David. *The Angel Of Torremolinos.* [Missing Person]

SIMMONS, John. *Midnight Walking.* [Theater]

SIMONSON, Sheila. *Larkspur.* [Bookstores]

SMOKE, Stephen. *Voices In The Night.* [Revenge]

TRIPP, Miles. *Video Vengeance.* 1991 St. Martin. Two years ago, Mary Coomber's husband died in a car accident. Since then, she's inherited a fair fortune from her aunt and is considering marriage. Suddenly, her husband appears, claiming he had amnesia. Mary's fiancé hires PI John Samson to prove the man is a liar. 9th. [Where There's a Will]

UPFIELD, Arthur W. *The Bachelors Of Broken Hill.* [Australian]

WHITNEY, Phyllis A. *Rainbow In the Mist.* [Psychic]

WILHELM, Kate. *Sweet, Sweet Poison.* [Bees]

YORK, Rebecca. *Life Line.* [Medical]

YORKE, Margaret. *Speak For The Dead.* [Prostitution]

R . . . IS FOR

RAPE

*R*APE IS ANOTHER OF THOSE THEMES *that are particularly disturbing, especially to women. Yet, as part of our lives, rape occurs in the mystery story also.*

CARLSON, P. M. *Murder Is Academic.* [Academic]

GORMAN, Edward. *The Autumn Dead.* 1987 St. Martin/ Ballantine 1989. Jack Dwyer's old girlfriend is willing to pay $1,000 for his help. Janet needs a suitcase that is still in the condo where she was living. She's a bit afraid of her ex-lover. Janet dies, and someone else wants the suitcase. 4th. [Blackmail]

HARRIS, Charlaine. *Secret Rage.* [Academic]

KELLERMAN, Faye. *The Ritual Bath.* 1986 Arbor House/ Fawcett 1987. Rina Lazarus was at the *mikvah* when she heard a noise. One of the women had been beaten and raped. Peter Decker, Los Angeles PD, had to spend a lot of time with Rina before he could put the pieces together. 1st.

LANSBURY, Coral. *Felicity.* [Academic]

LaPIERRE, Janet. *Unquiet Graves.* 1987 St. Martin. Ilona Beiggren was last seen at Joe Mancuso's dinner party. Her body was found beaten, and Joe, professor of computer science, was the main suspect. There had been a rash of murders and rapes in the Port Silva area. Joe had to clear himself.

LEONARD, Elmore. *Freaky Deaky.* 1988 Arbor House/ Warner 1989. Greta Wyatt walked into Detroit Police Headquarters and claimed she'd been raped by Woody Ricks, one of the city's richest citizens. Chris Mankowski, Sex Crimes, is looking into it. Then he discovers Robin Abbott and Skip Gibbs and what they are up to. [Fraud]

MINAHAN, John. *The Face Behind The Mask.* 1986 Norton/ Signet 1986. He was almost too good-looking. He was a rapist with robbery and murder thrown in. And he was loose in New York City. Detective "Little John" Rawlings is out to get him locked up. 3rd. [Serial Killer]

PHILBIN, Tom. *Death Sentence.* [Clergy]

REYNOLDS, John Lawrence. *The Man Who Murdered God.* [Clergy]

REAL ESTATE

One of our favorite industries lending itself to murder is the real estate business. Quietly buying up properties that will soon be valuable and forcing others to sell so-called worthless building sites are issues to kill for.

ADAMSON, M. J. *A February Face.* [Witches]

BARTH, Richard. *The Condo Kill.* 1985 Scribner/ Fawcett 1991. Thelma Winters has lived for thirty-two years in the same apartment. Now she and Angelo are the only two tenants left. When she can't keep her mind on her Bingo game, she tells Margaret Binton that the owners want to drive her out. 3rd.

BEATON, M. C. *Death Of An Outsider.* [Witches]

BLOCK, Lawrence. *Out On The Cutting Edge.* [Missing Person]

BOWMAN, Robert J. *The House Of Blue Lights.* 1987 St. Martin. Michael Sloane was the champion of the poor, running a shelter. A development group wants the area. Lawyer Cassandra Thorpe agrees to help find the man who owns a tiny piece of the land. She finds more than she bargained for. [Lawyer]

BROD, D. C. *Murder In The Store.* [Economics]

BURNS, Rex. *Suicide Season.* 1987 Viking/ Penguin 1988. Two multi-million dollar real estate deals have gone sour in the past few months. Denver PI Devlin Kirk is hired to find out who the inside person is who is handing out secret information. Suddenly, the prime suspect is dead. 1st. [Espionage]

CAMPBELL, Robert. *The Cat's Meow.* [Clergy]

CHRISTMAS, Joyce. *A Fête Worse Than Death.* [Where There's a Will]

CLEEVES, Ann. *Come Death And High Water.* [Birdwatching]

COLBERT, James. *Skinny Man.* [Arson]

CORK, Barry. *Laid Dead.* [Ball Games]

DENTINGER, Jane. *Death Mask.* [Theater]

DOUGLAS, John. *Blind Spring Rambler.* 1988 St. Martin. Bill Edmonson headed for Blind Spring, West Virginia, in 1923, to prove that an Italian coal miner was innocent of the murder of a prospector five years earlier. Bill's partner, Frank Grant, was killed, and he now has two murders to solve.

DUNLAP, Susan. *Too Close To The Edge.* [Fraud]

ENGER, L. L. *Comeback.* Pocket 1990/ PBO. After the death of his wife, ex-Detroit Tigers' hitter Gun Pederson headed for the Minnesota woods. He wanted quiet and time with Mazy, his daughter. But a real estate deal threatend to divide the town and now Mazy is missing. 1st. [Father]

FENNELLY, Tony. *The Closet Hanging.* [Gay]

FLYNN, Don. *Ordinary Murder.* 1987 Walker. *Daily Press* reporter "Fitz" Fitzgerald had an assignment he hated: the Romance of Buildings. Then his friend Timmy asked him to find out who killed his son. Going in two directions, he runs into a real heartbreak. 3rd.

GREENWOOD, John. *Mists Over Mosley.* [Witches]

GRIFFITHS, John. *Snake Charmer.* [Academic]

HESS, Joan. *Madness In Maggody.* 1991 St. Martin. Jim Bob and his partner are having a Grand Opening for their new supermarket. Some of the other store owners in Maggody are concerned they'll be put out of business. But when twenty-three people end up in the hospital, police chief Arly Hanks suspects someone put something in the food. 3rd. [Children]

HILARY, Richard. *Pieces Of Cream.* [Black Detective]

HOLT, Hazel. *Mrs. Malory Investigates.* 1990 St. Martin. Charles Richardson had left the small village and gone to America, where he'd made a lot of money. He's planning to return and marry Lee Montgomery, a local estate agent. When Lee goes missing, Charles asks his old friend Sheila Malory to investigate. 1st. [Infidelity]

KALLEN, Lucille. *C. B. Greenfield: The Piano Bird.* 1984 Random House/ Ballantine 1985. While Maggie Rome is on the Gulf Coast, she helps a woman who's locked her keys in her car. When the woman, part of a musical cast, is found dead, Maggie wonders which one of the crew wanted to get rid of her. 4th. [Journalism]

KELLERMAN, Faye. *Milk And Honey.* [Infidelity]

KIJEWSKI, Karen. *Katwalk.* [Fraud]

KITTREDGE, Mary. *Rigor Mortis.* [Medical]

LANGTON, Jane. *Dark Nantucket Noon.* 1975 Harper & Row/ Penguin 1986. At a noontime total eclipse, Helen Green was shot to death on Nantucket Island. Homer and Mary Kelly are on the island, where Homer is doing some research. They are immediately drawn into the crime where love and greed abound. 2nd.

LANGTON, Jane. *Natural Enemy.* [Bees]

LEWIS, Roy. *A Trout In The Milk.* 1986 St. Martin. Arnold Landon, from the Planning Office, was sent up to Northumbria to settle a land dispute. Miss Sauvage-Brown was against any development. Landon walked in and found her body, only it turned out to be her housemate. Was she dead by mistake? 3rd. [Manuscript]

LUTZ, John. *Tropical Heat.* 1986 Holt/ Avon 1987. PI Fred Carver was hired by Edwina to find her lover, Willis Davis. The police were convinced he'd committed suicide by walking into the sea. But as Carver digs into the man's past, he gets derailed. 1st. [Suicide]

McCALL, Wendell aka Ridley Pearson. *Aim For The Heart.* 1990 St. Martin. Chris Klick watched as the small plane crash-landed at the regional airport in Butte Peak, Idaho. But the crash is suspicious. Now a young woman is missing from the county records office. 2nd. [Missing Person]

McMULLEN, Mary. *The Other Shoe.* 1981 Doubleday/ Jove 1987. Four years ago Clare Herne was acquitted of her aunt's murder. Now her past is haunting her. She teams with Justin Channon to clear her name. Under the guise of writing a family history, Justin asks a few questions too many.

MORGAN, Kate. *A Slay At The Races.* [Horses]

MURPHY, Dallas. *Apparent Wind.* 1991 Pocket. Doom Loomis has returned to the Florida Keys to inherit his father's 42-foot sloop. But it turns out that dad also owned Omnium Settlement, the whole town. And two rival developers want to acquire it, even if it is half under water.

O'BRIEN, Meg. *The Daphne Decisions.* [Journalism]

ORENSTEIN, Frank. *A Killing In Real Estate.* 1988 St. Martin. Appleboro, in upstate New York, was divided. Some of the old families needed money and were interested in Van Houten's real estate development. Others were against it. When there was a death, Hugh Morrison took over with a little help from Harriet.

PAPAZOGLOU, Orania. *Once And Always Murder.* [Mystery Writer]

PIESMAN, Marissa. *Unorthodox Practices.* Pocket 1989/ PBO. Nina Fischman, lawyer for NYC Housing Court, has two elderly women suddenly dead in rent-controlled apartments. She has to do a lot of digging to uncover a real estate scam. [Lawyer]

POLLOCK, Richard. *The Episode.* [Journalism]

RHOADS, J. W. *The Contract.* 1986 Holt/ Avon 1988. Apartments are scarce in Paris. Monsieur Bavdoin has signed a *viager*, a contract to pay an annuity to the old lady who owns the apartment. The longer she lives, the more the apartment will cost him. Then she disappears.

RIDER, J. W. *Jersey Tomatoes.* 1986 Arbor House/ Pocket 1987. The Jersey City waterfront would be a billion-dollar deal for the developer who got his hands on it. Cooper Jarrett had the connection and won the deal. Then he made a bad mistake: he hired Malone.

SHERMAN, Steve. *The Maple Sugar Murders.* 1987 Walker. Lyme, New Hampshire, is in a stew. A New Jersey real estate operator wants to develop the valley. When a real estate agent dies, Hugh Quint, ex–Boston cop, is dragged into the investigation. The killing goes on. 1st.

SIMPSON, Pamela. *Partners In Time.* [Old Crime]

STEVENSON, Richard. *On The Other Hand, Death.* [Gay]

STOREY, Alice. *First Kill All The Lawyers.* [Journalism]

THACKERY, Ted, Jr. *Preacher.* 1988 Jove/ PBO. The Preacher came to Farewell, New Mexico, to help his old classmate. Reverend Spence suspected a friend had been murdered in a helicopter crash. He wants the Preacher to play poker for the truth. [Father]

VAN GIESON, Judith. *North Of The Border.* 1988 Walker. Attorney Neil Hamel's ex-lover, Carl Roberts, is running for Congress, and someone's sending notes threatening his adopted son. He wants Neil to look into it. After two trips to Mexico, she looks for answers much closer to home. 1st. [Lawyer]

WARD, E. C. *A Nice Little Beach Town.* 1989 St. Martin/ St. Martin 1990. Old Sven wanted Chandler Cairns to go out on the boat with him that night. He should have gone, because they found Sven drifting in the boat, dead. What first looks like suicide turns to murder and Cairns is arrested. He has to clear himself. 1st. [Father]

WEBSTER, Noah. *A Flight From Paris.* [Economics]

WEINMAN, Irving. *Hampton Heat.* 1987 Atheneum/Fawcett 1989. Lenny Schwartz and his wife, Karen, don't quite get their Hampton vacation. A historian is found dead, buried in the sand, and an old Indian deed to a choice piece of land is missing. 2nd. [On Vacation]

WILLIAMS, David. *Treasure Preserved.* [Fraud]

WUAMETT, Victor. *Deeds Of Trust.* 1991 St. Martin. Frank Baker, retired school teacher, has his money tied up in a crooked condo deal. He wants realtor Chase Randel to get him out of the mess. But Baker has just fallen from an eighth-floor window. Chase has to protect Baker's widow and his own payday. 2nd. [Insurance]

YAFFE, James. *Mom Meets Her Maker.* [Mother]

REVENGE

Judging by the size of this category, revenge is the most popular motivation for murder. For old or young, rural or urban, revenge is an emotion that festers. It gets beneath the skin, irritates, and finally erupts in an explosion of murder.

ADAMS, Harold. *The Barbed Wire Noose.* 1987 Mysterious/ Mysterious 1988. They found Albert Foote hanged by a barbed wire noose. In the middle of a blizzard, Carl Wilcox has to sort out suspects and motives, old crimes and passions. 7th. [Old Crime]

ADAMS, Harold. *The Man Who Missed The Party.* 1989 Mysterious/ Mysterious 1990. Carl Wilcox is at the family hotel in Corden, S.D., just in time for the tenth reunion of the high school's Class of 1924. When the star quarterback and class Casanova is found murdered in the hotel shower, Carl has to find the killer. 8th.

ALLEN, Steve. *Murder On The Glitter Box.* [Television]

ANDERSON, James. *Additional Evidence.* [Infidelity]

BABBIN, Jacqueline. *Bloody Special.* [Television]

BABSON, Marian. *Death In Fashion.* [Fashion]

BALL, John. *The Cool Cottontail.* [Black Detective]

BARNARD, Robert. *Bodies.* 1986 Scribner/ Dell 1988. Four people were shot to death at *Bodies* studio, where they were photographing for the body-builders magazine. Superintendent Percy Trethowan plows through London's Soho until he discovers that the studio was used for filming soft porn. 4th. [Pornography]

BAXT, George. *The Tallulah Bankhead Murder Case.* [Famous People]

BEATON, M. C. *Death Of A Hussy.* [Manuscript]

BELFORTE, Sophie. *The Lace Curtain Murders.* 1986 Atheneum. The congressional seat is vacant, and there's a scramble by contenders. One of them, Mary Agnes O'Pake, is murdered in the midst of the battle for votes. Molly Rafferty, history professor, and Boston PD Detective Nick Hannibal join more than hands to locate the murderer. 1st. [Political]

BIGGERS, Earl Derr. *The Black Camel.* [Oriental]

BIRKETT, John. *The Queen's Mare.* [Horses]

BLOCK, Lawrence. *A Ticket To The Boneyard.* 1990 Morrow. Matt Scudder gets a phone call from his old hooker friend Elaine. Twelve years ago, she was abused and threatened by a very violent man. Matt arranged to have the man jailed. Now he's out, vowing to leave Matt and all his women dead. [Prostitution]

BOROWITZ, Albert. *This Club Frowns On Murder.* [Infidelity]

BRADDON, Russell. *Funnelweb.* [Serial Killer]

BRAND, Christianna. *Heads You Lose.* 1942 Dodd, Mead/ Bantam 1988. A young woman is found beheaded in the ditch behind Squire Pendock's mansion. Before Inspector Cockrill can solve the crime, another woman is murdered. Now they all suspect each other. 1st.

BURKE, James Lee. *A Morning For Flamingos.* [Drugs]

BURLEY, W. J. *Wycliffe And The Scapegoat.* [Holiday]

BURLEY, W. J. *Wycliffe And The Four Jacks.* 1985 Doubleday/ Avon 1987. Novelist David Cleeve was receiving threats, a Jack of Diamonds mailed to him. Before the vacationing Superintendent Wycliffe can solve the problem, Cleeve is dead. 12th. [On Vacation]

CAMPBELL, Robert. *Alice In La-La Land.* [Television]

CANDY, Edward. *Words For Murder Perhaps.* [Academic]

CANNELL, Dorothy. *The Widow's Club.* 1988 Bantam/ Bantam 1989. Primrose and Hyacinth, of Flowers Detection, are poking around in Chitterton Fells. They've been hired by an insurance company to find out why so many errant husbands are dying in the quiet village. They enlist Ellie Simon Haskell to infiltrate the Widow's Club. 2nd. [Insurance]

CARLSON, P. M. *Audition For Murder.* [Theater]

CHASE, Elaine Raco. *Dark Corners.* [Journalism]

CHASE, Samantha. *Needlepoint.* Tudor 1989/ PBO. Ted Chandler was found dead in his car at the bottom of the Chaptank River, a piece of needlepoint in the glove compartment. Sara hadn't even had a chance to tell him she was pregnant. As she tries to put her life together, her sister Ginny takes a cruise, never to return. [Psychological]

CLARK, Dick. *Murder On Tour.* [Music]

COHEN, Anthea. *Guardian Angel.* [Medical]

COLLINS, Max Allan. *Nice Weekend For A Murder.* [Mystery Games]

CORK, Barry. *Unnatural Hazard.* [Ball Games]

CORRINGTON, John William, and Joyce H. Corrington. *A Civil Death.* 1987 Viking/ Fawcett 1989. Denise Lemoyne, assistant DA, stopped to visit her godmother and found her dead. A diary on the desk leads the police to suspect Madeline's husband of the murder. Denise uses all her resources to prove him innocent. 3rd.

CRESPI, Trella. *The Trouble With A Small Raise.* [Advertising]

DAVEY, Jocelyn. *A Dangerous Liaison.* 1987 Walker. Vickie McKenzie had a contract to write the biography of British tycoon Lord Cranford. As she delves into his past, she discovers a dark secret. Now he's being threatened from several directions. She calls Oxford don Ambrose Usher. 7th. [Writer]

DeANDREA, William. *Killed On The Ice.* 1984 Doubleday/ Mysterious 1987. The network planned to film a Christmas ice show, only the ice was bloodied by the body of psychiatrist Paul Dinkover. The young skating star, Wendy, hated him. But Matt Cobb, network troubleshooter, has to look more closely. 4th. [Christmas]

DEXTER, Colin. *The Riddle Of The Third Mile.* [Academic]

DONALDSON, D. J. *Cajun Nights.* [Pathologist]

DORNER, Marjorie. *Nightmare.* [Children]

DUNCAN, W. Glen. *Rafferty's Rules.* 1987 Ballantine/ PBO. Vivian Mollison was doing a thesis on hierarchy in modern tribes, picking motorcycle gangs to study. For ten months, the gang had her. At home she's in bad shape. Her father wants Rafferty, Dallas PI, to find them . . . and kill them. 1st. [Drugs]

DUNLAP, Susan. *An Equal Opportunity Employer.* 1984 St. Martin/ Paperjacks 1985. Meter reader Vejay Haskell stopped to visit a friend. They argued and she left. When he was found dead, she became the most likely suspect. On her own, Vejay starts uncovering secrets while trying to stay hidden. 1st. [Antiques]

DUNLAP, Susan. *Not Exactly A Brahmin* [Fraud]

DUNLAP, Susan. *The Last Annual Slugfest.* 1986 St. Martin. At the opening night of the annual Slugfest, Edwina Henderson falls dead after sampling some of the dishes. Everyone who has ever had a run-in with Edwina is suspected. But it takes meter reader Vejay Haskell to drop down on the culprit. 3rd. [Cooks]

DUNLAP, Susan. *Diamond In The Buff.* 1990 St. Martin/ Dell 1991. Detective Jill Smith answers a felony assault call. Hasbrouck Diamond had been assaulted by a eucalyptus branch. While Jill sorts out Diamond's feud with the lady next door, a young man staying at Diamond's house is murdered. 6th.

EARLY, Jack. *Razzamatazz.* [Arson]

ECCLES, Marjorie. *Cast A Cold Eye.* 1988 Doubleday. As architect Clive Lethbridge sipped tea in his study, someone used a Victorian lead crystal inkwell to end his days. Detective Inspector Gil Mayo discovers that any number of people hated Clive. 3rd.

ELBERT, Joyce. *Murder At A. A.* 1988 Signet/ PBO. As they gathered round the coffeepot at the A.A. meeting, Daniel took a sip, gagged, and dropped dead. His last word was "Jean," and she was standing at his side. It's a mad scramble for Jean to find the murderer before she's arrested. [Gay]

ESTLEMAN, Loren D. *The Midnight Man.* 1982 Houghton, Mifflin/ Fawcett 1987. Black militants gunned down three cops, and only one of them lived. Amos Walker, as a favor, offers his services to the victim's wife. It's not long before he discovers that someone besides the police is on a parallel path. 3rd.

ESTLEMAN, Loren D. *Roses Are Dead.* 1985 Mysterious/ Mysterious 1987. Ex–hit man Peter Macklin is in the middle of a divorce. His attorney wants a favor: protect a woman from a homicidal ex-lover. Suddenly Peter discovers that there's a contract out on him. He hopes it's not his own son. 2nd.

FENSTER, Bob. *The Last Page.* [Mystery Writer]

FRIEDMAN, Mickey. *Paper Phoenix.* 1986 Dutton/ Ballantine 1987. Maggie Longstreet came out of her depression when she heard that the editor of a radical newspaper had died in a fall. In her mind, Maggie's ex-husband was implicated, and she's out to discover the connection. [Journalism]

FULTON, Eileen. *Death Of A Golden Girl.* [Television]

GIRDNER, Jaqueline. *Adjusted To Death.* Diamond 1990/ PBO. Kate Jasper kept her appointment with her chiropractor, only to find Scott Younger dead on the examining room table. Dr. Maggie Lambrecht, fearful of what the murder will do to her practice, begs Kate to find out who the killer is. 1st. [Father]

GIROUX, E. X. *A Death For Adonis.* 1984 St. Martin/ Ballantine 1986. Sculptor Sebastian Calvert was found catatonic, holding the dead body of his young lover, David. Twenty-four years later, Sebastian's daughter wants barrister Robert Forsythe to find out the truth. 1st. [Lawyer]

GIROUX, E. X. *A Death For A Doctor.* 1986 St. Martin/ Ballantine 1987. Dr. Foster, his wife, and two sons are murdered in their cottage. Only the baby is left alive. Abigail Sanderson, Forsythe's secretary, poses as a relative. Someone is coming back for the baby . . . and Abigail. 4th. [Lawyer]

GIROUX, E. X. *Death For A Dietitian.* 1988 St. Martin/ Ballantine 1989. Abigail Sanderson is at the Jester, a country inn owned by a friend's daughter. There's to be a Mystery Party. The script is written, the guests have arrived, and Abigail is to be the detective and solve the murder. But the lines have been rewritten. 6th. [Mystery Games]

GOLDSBOROUGH, Robert. *Murder In E Minor.* [Music]

GOSLING, Paula. *Hoodwink.* 1988 Doubleday. Fred Norris is writing a book about the ten-year-old death of socialite Ariadne Finch. Norris dies, and the manuscript is stolen from his editor. Lt. Jake Chase is running in circles, unraveling a feud, and finding a diary. [Writer]

GRAFTON, Sue. *"D" Is For Deadbeat.* 1987 Holt/ Bantam 1988. Alvin Daggett hires PI Kinsey Millhone to deliver a check for $25,000 to a fifteen-year-old boy. The check for her fee bounces, Alvin washes up on the beach, and she is having a tough time finding the boy. 4th.

GRANGER, Bill, w/a Joe Gash. *Priestly Murders.* [Clergy]

GRANT-ADAMSON, Lesley. *Wild Justice.* [Journalism]

GRAYSON, Richard. *Death On The Cards.* [Historical]

GRIMES, Martha. *I'm The Only Running Footman.* 1986 Little, Brown/ Dell 1987. In London, a shop girl dies on the cobbles. Far away in Devon, a young woman is murdered. Scotland Yard's Richard Jury notices that they were both strangled with their own scarfs. He'll travel far to find this killer. 8th.

GRIMES, Martha. *The Five Bells And Bladebone.* 1987 Little, Brown/ Dell 1988. Antiques dealer Trueblood found a body stuffed in the desk that had just been delivered. Who would want Simon Lear dead? Then Richard Jury has to find out why the dead woman in London looks like Simon's widow. 9th.

GUTHRIE, Al. *Private Murder.* Bantam 1989/ PBO. Mac MacKenzie was on his way to market when Henrietta Novack asked him to pick her up a coffee cake. By the time he returned, Henrietta was dead. Now her sister Abby is accused of the crime and the bearer bonds are missing. 1st. [Mother]

HALL, Robert Lee. *Murder At San Simeon.* [Famous People]

HANSEN, Joseph. *Early Graves.* [Gay]

HARDWICK, Mollie. *Perish In July.* [Theater]

HAVILL, Steven F. *Heartshot.* [Drugs]

HAYES, Helen & Thomas Chastain. *Where The Truth Lies.* [Hollywood]

HILL, Reginald. *Ruling Passion.* 1977 Harper & Row/ Dell 1985. Peter Pascoe took his girl Ellie to Thornton Lacey for a reunion with college friends. But the thatched cottage had three bodies, blasted by a shotgun, and Colin is missing. Pascoe finds it hard to be objective. 8th. [On Vacation]

JANCE, J. A. *Until Proven Guilty.* 1985 Avon/ PBO. The little girl had been murdered. At the funeral, J. P. Beaumont, Seattle PD, saw a beautiful woman carrying a single red rose. As Beaumont works to solve the crime, his relationship with the lady named Anne deepens. 1st.

JANCE, J. A. *Trial By Fury.* 1986 Avon/ PBO. Darwin's body was found behind the dumpster at Bailey's Food Store. Homicide detectives J. P. Beaumont and his partner Ron Peters follow a tough trail and find revenge. 3rd.

KAISER, Ronn. *Made In Beverly Hills.* 1986 Avon/ PBO. Movie producer Helene Daniels was shot in her Bel Air house in the middle of the night. Inspector Quintin Wing, Los Angeles PD, has a long list of suspects. He thought he had the case all solved. [Hollywood]

KANTNER, Rob. *Made In Detroit.* [Drugs]

KELLEY, Patrick A. *Sleightly Invisible.* [Psychic]

KELLY, Susan. *The Summertime Soldiers.* 1986 Walker. When a man is found murdered behind a Cambridge bar, the People's Revolutionary Cadre claims that more deaths will follow. Liz Conners, free-lance writer, is doing an article on the group. She gets in almost too deep to get out alive. 2nd.

KELLY, Susan. *Until Proven Innocent.* [Corruption]

KELMAN, Judith. *While Angels Sleep.* [Old Crime]

KENYON, Michael. *A Healthy Way To Die.* 1986 Doubleday/ Avon 1987. It was an expensive spa and had a select clientele. During an aerobics class, Mr. Kettle keeled over, dead. Attempted murder and another death strain the competence of Inspector Peckover and his assistant, Twitty. 1st. [Black Detective]

KERRIGAN, Philip. *Dead Ground.* [Christmas]

KNIGHT, Alanna. *Deadly Beloved.* [Victorian]

KRENTZ, Jayne Ann. *Gift Of Gold.* [Art]

LARSEN, Gaylord. *Dorothy And Agatha.* [Famous People]

LEE, Elsie. *Satan's Coast.* 1987 Zebra/ PBO. Suddenly widowed, Nell Valentine took her young stepson to Portugal, to the castle of his ancestors. But things aren't what they seem, and she and Chris are soon in danger. [Smuggling]

LEMARCHAND, Elizabeth. *The Wheel Turns.* 1983 Walker/ Walker 1986. Laura Raymond's body was found in the garage, the car motor still running—a terrible accident. But as Inspector Tom Pollard and his assistant Gregory Toye ask questions and listen to the local gossip, it seems that something else might have happened. 15th. [Accident]

LEWIS, Roy. *Men Of Subtle Craft.* 1988 St. Martin. The local magistrate, Patrick Yates, was involved in a dispute over the title of Kilgour Estates. One of the villagers ended Yates's life with a medieval crossbow bolt. Arnold London, interested in ancient buildings, is on the spot. 4th.

LEWIS, William. *Gala.* [Music]

LINDSEY, David L. *In The Lake Of The Moon.* [Father]

LIVINGSTON, Jayson. *Point Blank.* 1990 St. Martin. First an aerobics instructor was brutally murdered, a French coin left on her back. Then there was another, and another. Homicide detective Stu Redlam must find some connection between the women before there are any more corpses. [Serial Killer]

LOGAN, Margaret. *Deathhampton Summer.* 1988 Walker/ Fawcett 1989. Center Hampton has its "days" for making the party rounds. But the very first "day" of the social season ends in death. Tainted lobster is the suspect. Tersh Trowbridge and son are in the middle of the fray when another death occurs.

LUCE, Carol Davis. *Night Stalker.* [Father]

LUPICA, Mike. *Extra Credits.* [Academic]

LUTZ, John. *Scorcher.* 1987 Holt/ Avon 1988. A serial killer is on the loose in Miami. One of his victims is PI Fred Carver's son. He's out for blood. At one of Carver's stops, he's behind the scenes of a wealthy family with a disturbed son. 2nd. [Serial Killer]

MacDONALD, Patricia. *No Way Home.* [Gay]

MacGREGOR, T. J. *Kill Flash.* 1987 Ballantine/ PBO. Now married, Quin St. James and Mike McCleary are running the detective agency. Mike's old friend, movie producer Gill Kranish, hired them to find out who's trying to shut down his film. A little digging turns up an old murder. 2nd. [Old Crime]

MacGREGOR, T. J., w/a Alison Drake. *Fevered.* 1988 Ballantine/ PBO. Judge Henry Michael and his family were brutally murdered during the night. Homicide Detective Aline Scott and her PI friend Ryan Kincaid are going through his cases, looking for a suspect, when someone else dies. 2nd.

MacLEOD, Charlotte. *The Convivial Codfish.* [Christmas]

MATERA, Lia. *Hidden Agenda.* [Lawyer]

MATHIS, Edward. *From A High Place.* [Getting Away With Murder]

MATHIS, Edward. *Dark Streets And Empty Places.* 1986 Scribner/ Ballantine 1988. PI Dan Roman was hired by a wealthy Texan to find his granddaughter. Her husband said she was visiting friends. Dan set out to check and found himself in the middle of a gigantic puzzle. 2nd.

MATHIS, Edward. *Another Path, Another Dragon.* [Drugs]

MATHIS, Edward. *September Song.* 1991 Scribner. PI Dan Roman's ex-wife Susie needs him. Seven years ago, she and Betty testified against the Wagermans—father and son. The two men have been released from prison, and Betty turned up dead. Everywhere Susie goes, the men follow her. 7th. [Fraud]

MAXWELL, Thomas. *The Saberdene Variations.* 1987 Mysterious/ Mysterious 1989. Anna Thorne was brutally murdered, and Victor Saberdene was determined to put the killer, Carl Varada, away. Victor fell in love with and married Anna's sister Caro. Now, eight years later, another man confesses to Anna's killing. Varada is free, and he's coming for Caro. [Getting Away With Murder]

MAYOR, Archer. *Open Season.* 1988 Putnam/ Avon 1989. Lt. Joe Gunther, Brattleboro, Vermont, had a rash of strange crimes. They all seemed to have been set up by a ski-masked killer. And they all had to do with the three-year-old Kimberly Harris murder trial.

McCLINTICK, Malcolm. *The Key.* 1987 Doubleday/ Avon 1990. Mrs. Boller was murdered while walking her dog. A key was left on her back, and there were no footprints in the new snow. Clairmont City detectives Kelso and Smith are investigating the murder when a young woman is killed. Judge Boller has answers. 2nd. [Infidelity]

McMULLEN, Mary. *The Doom Campaign.* 1974 Doubleday/ Jove 1988. Things are at a peak for Letty Garth. Her ad agency has landed a great account and she's met someone special. Suddenly, things start to fall apart, and she knows she is being stalked. If she doesn't track him down . . . she'll be dead.

McMULLEN, Mary. *Until Death Do Us Part.* 1982 Doubleday/ Jove 1987. Jane Frame, executive headhunter, was bitter. In her New York City brownstone, she plotted to bring down her ex-husband. Her loyal staff watched her get in deeper and deeper, until the tables turned.

MELVILLE, Jennie. *Windsor Red.* [Medical]

MEREDITH, D. R. *Murder By Impulse.* 1988 Ballantine/ PBO. Amy Steele died in a fiery crash. Eight months later, just as the police find a charred thermos laced with sleeping pills, Amy returns. Lawyer John Lloyd Branson and his new assistant are handling the messy divorce when, this time, Amy really dies. 1st. [Lawyer]

MILNE, A. A. *The Red House Mystery.* [Locked Room]

MONTGOMERY, Yvonne. *Scavengers.* [Manuscript]

MOODY, Susan. *Penny Post.* [Black Detective]

MORTIMER, John. *Summer's Lease.* [On Vacation]

MULLER, Marcia. *Eye Of The Storm.* 1988 Mysterious/ Mysterious 1989. Sharon McCone's sister has joined with a few others to restore an old house for a "boatel," a B and B for boaters. Right from the start, things go wrong, including a ghost in the orchard. Sharon comes to help and walks into murder. 8th.

MULLER, Marcia. *There Hangs The Knife.* [Art]

MULLER, Marcia. *Trophies And Dead Things.* [Where There's A Will]

MURPHY, Dallas. *Lover Man.* 1987 Scribner/ Pocket 1988. Artie Deemer lives off the paychecks of his dog Jellyroll's acting. When Artie's ex-girlfriend is murdered, the police come calling. She's left Artie a packet of photographs. He and Jellyroll gnaw on the bones of this mystery. 1st. [Smuggling]

MURRAY, William. *When The Fat Man Sings.* 1987 Bantam/ Bantam 1988. Fulvio was a great tenor but a terrible gambler. With a little help from Shifty Anderson, he recoups his losses. Fulvio pursuades Shifty to fly to the New York racetracks as a well-paid personal handicapper. Then the trouble starts. 3rd. [Horses]

NEVINS, Francis M., Jr. *The 120-Hour Clock.* [Where There's a Will]

O'DONNELL, Lillian. *Casual Affairs.* [Medical]

O'DONNELL, Lillian. *The Other Side Of The Door.* [Children]

O'HARA, Kenneth. *Death Of A Moffy.* [Kidnapping]

ORENSTEIN, Frank. *Paradise Of Death.* [Advertising]

OSTER, Jerry. *California Dead.* 1986 Harper & Row/ Charter 1988. Rancho Maria is a quiet and wealthy seaside resort until the murders start. Lt. Sam Branch is about to chip away at the glittering facade and find a killer.

PALEN, Adeline. *Death Among The Lilacs.* 1986 Blue Spruce/ PBO. Moira St. Clair wanted revenge on the man who had cost her her job. She moved to the East Coast where he'd relocated, and started writing her book. She'll murder him . . . fictionally. She never dreams she will be the murder victim.

PALMER, Stuart. *The Penguin Pool Murder.* [Economics]

PALMER, Stuart. *The Puzzle Of The Silver Persian.* 1934 Doubleday/ Bantam 1986. They'd all met on the transatlantic crossing, where Rosemary had vanished overboard. In London, another of Hildegarde Withers's table companions died. Then, as the remaining voyagers gather in Cornwall, Hildegarde is quite unable to prevent another death. 5th. [Missing Person]

PALMER, Stuart. *The Puzzle Of The Red Stallion.* [Horses]

PARKER, T. Jefferson. *Laguna Heat.* 1985 St. Martin/ St. Martin 1986. Laguna Beach Homicide Detective Tom Shephard investigates a vicious murder. Soon there is another. As each clue appears, Tom's whole past history is about to disintegrate around him. [Old Crime]

PAUL, Barbara. *In-Laws And Outlaws.* 1990 Scribner. Gillian Clifford sat in her Chicago office and read about the death of her brother-in-law, a man she hadn't seen since her husband died. When she calls Connie, the widow, she discovers that Raymond's the fourth death in four months for the Decker family. Connie begs Gillian to come to Boston at once.

PAUL, Raymond. *The Tragedy At Tiverton.* [Historical]

PAYNE, Laurence. *Vienna Blood.* 1985 Doubleday. PI Mark Savage answered the call from Vienna. His Aunt Alice, aging opera star, needs him. A man in Vienna is claiming to be her son, the son who vanished in the war when he was only nine. She wants Mark to find him. 3rd. [Missing Person]

PENTECOST, Hugh. *Murder In Luxury.* [Infidelity]

PERRY, Anne. *Bethlehem Road.* [Victorian]

PHILBIN, Tom. *Precinct: Siberia.* 1985 Fawcett/ PBO. She may have looked older, but Mary Baumann was only thirteen. She was dead, brutally left to die. Detective Joe Lawless, from Precinct Siberia, the toughest beat in town, wondered if he'd ever find her killer. Then he got an idea. 1st. [Mother]

PICKARD, Nancy. *Marriage Is Murder.* 1987 Scribner/ Pocket 1988. Just as Jenny Cain and Geof Bushfield set the date for their wedding, there is a rash of domestic violence in Port Frederick—the deadly kind. Geof is investigating the deaths of the husbands when Jenny discovers that her brother-in-law might be next. 4th.

PRONZINI, Bill, and Marcia Muller. *The Lighthouse.* 1987 St. Martin/ St. Martin 1987. Jan Ryerson and his wife, Alix, moved to the lighthouse in Oregon and, from the first, they were on a wrong footing with their neighbors. When a young woman is found strangled, Jan is suspected. That's only the beginning of their nightmare.

QUEST, Erica. *Death Walk.* [Where There's A Will]

RADLEY, Sheila. *The Chief Inspector's Daughter.* 1980 Scribner/ Bantam 1988. Jasmine Wood's house was broken into, just as a magazine article appeared showing some of her valuables. She's fearful of another robbery, but she doesn't expect to die. Inspector Quantrill's daughter is involved. 2nd.

RADLEY, Sheila. *Who Saw Him Die?* 1988 Scribner/ Bantam 1988. Jack Goodrum and his new wife move to Tower House and a new life. Then Jack runs down and kills the town drunk in a terrible accident. Tower House is broken into, Jack is killed with his own gun, and Quantrill is forced to leave much of the sleuthing to Hilary Lloyd. 7th.

REED, J. D., and Christine Reed. *Exposure.* [Ball Games]

REYNOLDS, William J. *The Nebraska Quotient.* [Blackmail]

RHODE, John, and Carter Dickson. *Fatal Descent.* [Locked Room]

RICE, Craig. *The Lucky Stiff.* 1945 Simon & Schuster/ Bantam 1987. Just before she was to die in the electric chair, Anna Marie St. Clair was freed. She arranges for the authorities to announce her death. Anna Marie has plans of her own . . . revenge. 7th.

RIGGS, John R. *The Last Laugh.* [Holiday]

ROBERTS, Nora. *Sweet Revenge.* [Jewels]

RUSSELL, Alan. *No Sign Of Murder.* [Artist]

RYP, Ellen. *Deadly Bonds.* [Psychological]

SANTINI, Rosemarie. *A Swell Style Of Murder.* 1985 St. Martin. Rick Ramsey, the WASP with a trust fund, was jogging in Soho when he tripped, and there before his eyes was a hand with no body. When he told his novelist-wife, she wanted to do a book about it. And the trouble began. 1st.

SANTINI, Rosemarie. *The Disenchanted Diva.* 1987 St. Martin. Rick Ramsey was keeping an eye on his Aunt Amanda's two dozen tiger cats when he found the body of a young girl in his aunt's basement. He and his wife Rosie, the writer, start out to investigate and end up on the wrong side of town. 2nd. [Pornography]

SIMPSON, Dorothy. *The Night She Died.* 1981 Scribner/ Bantam 1985. Julie Holmes had lived in the neighborhood for only six weeks. As her husband returned from night school, he found her stabbed body inside the front door. Inspector Luke Thanet has to find the person who wanted her dead. 1st.

SIMS, L. V. *To Sleep, Perchance To Kill.* 1988 Charter/ PBO. San Jose Homicide has another case, and Sgt. Dixie Struthers is on it. Victor Peters died in a locked room at his computer company. Dixie finds out that hate has a very long arm. 3rd. [Locked Room]

SMITH, Alison. *Someone Else's Grave.* [Holiday]

SMITH, Alison. *Rising.* 1987 St. Martin. Police Chief Judd Springfield is investigating the death of an engineer working on the Collidge Corners dam. When another death occurs, there is a suspicion that the dam is not being properly built. Judd springs into action. 2nd.

SMITH, Charles Merrill. *Reverend Randollph And The Splendid Samaritan.* 1986 Putnam/ Ivy 1987. James Trent, the Splendid Samaritan, was found dead with his hands wired in prayer and clasping a bloody $100 bill. Suddenly, there seem to be copycat killers in other parts of the country as well. 6th. [Old Crime]

SMITH, Janet L. *Sea Of Troubles.* Perseverance 1990/ PBO. Attorney Annie MacPherson has to take the ferry to the San Juan Islands to check out a potential sale of Windsor Resort for a client. Little does she know that a kidnapping is being planned. [Kidnapping]

SMITH, Joan. *A Masculine Ending.* 1988 Scribner/ Fawcett 1989. Loretta Lawson borrowed a friend's flat in Paris for a meeting. But there's a man sleeping in the other bedroom. The next day the man is gone, leaving behind bloody sheets. The only clue Loretta has is a review copy of an academic text soon to be published. 1st. [Manuscript]

SMITH, Julie. *Tourist Trap.* [Social Issues]

SMOKE, Stephen. *Voices In The Night.* 1988 Berkley/ PBO. Erin Holiday is a very popular radio talk-show psychologist. Then one night a woman phones in, telling Erin Erin's own childhood. Erin's bedroom is demolished. Someone's out to get her, and she doesn't know why. [Psychological]

SPILLANE, Mickey. *The Killing Man.* 1989 Dutton/ Signet 1990. Mike Hammer enters his office one Saturday morning to find Velma beaten unconscious on the floor and a man brutally murdered in his office chair. Had someone mistaken the stranger for Mike? 12th. [Intrigue]

STEED, Neville. *Die-Cast.* 1988 St. Martin/ St. Martin 1988. Peter Marklin, antique toy collector, planned to reproduce the Flamingo model plane. He's interrupted by the death of Ben Maxwell and the disappearance of Maxwell's young daughter. Maxwell's past had returned to haunt him. 2nd. [Antiques]

STINSON, Jim. *Low Angles.* [Hollywood]

SWIGART, Rob. *Toxin.* [Intrigue]

THOMSON, June. *The Dark Stream.* 1986 Doubleday. Stella Reeve had come back to Wynford—a bad penny. She seemed to have some sort of relationship with newcomer Alex Larson. When Stella is found drowned in a shallow ford, Inspector Rudd suspects something a bit more than an accident. 12th.

TOGAWA, Masako. *The Lady Killer.* 1985 Dodd, Mead/ Ballantine 1987. Mr. Honda, Japanese engineer, while on his travels, seduced young women. Suddenly, he discovers that each of the women is turning up dead. His lawyers are following a cold trail, looking to set him free. [Oriental]

UNDERWOOD, Michael. *The Uninvited Corpse.* 1987 St. Martin. Solicitor Rosa Epton was coerced into drawing up a will for wealthy Vernon Gray. She was also supposed to find him a housekeeper. A few days later, both Gray and the housekeeper have vanished. 3rd.

WALLACE, Marilyn. *Primary Target.* [Political]

WASHBURN, L. J. *Wild Night.* 1987 Tor/ PBO. PI Lucas Hallan is checking out the ghost town of Chuckwalla as a possible site for making silent films. Then someone starts blasting with a rifle. Lucas loads up for the final showdown. 1st.

WEISS, Mike. *No Go On Jackson Street.* [Journalism]

WERNER, Patricia. *The Will.* [Where There's A Will]

WILCOX, Stephen F. *The Dry White Tear.* 1989 St. Martin. Uncle Charlie Dugan was the black sheep of the family, and now he's dead. Stabbed with a fishing knife. His nephew, free-lance journalist T. S. W. Sheridan inherited his cottage on the Finger Lakes and the job of finding the murderer. 1st. [Father]

WITTEN, Barbara Yager. *The Isle Of Fire Murder.* [Infidelity]

WRIGHT, L. R. *The Suspect.* 1985 Viking/ Penguin 1987. Carlyle Burke phoned his brother-in-law coaxing him to visit. Only minutes into the encounter, George bashed Carlyle over the head and killed him. Sgt. Karl Alberg, RCMP, thinks the case is closed. But the motive bothers him. 1st. [Canadian]

YORKE, Margaret. *Evidence To Destroy.* 1987 Viking/ Penguin 1988. When Lydia Cunningham picked her daughter Thelma up at the Milton St. Gabriel Station, she had no notion her life would be changed forever. As Thelma flitted about, men clinging to her, one of them would make the difference. [Incest]

YORKE, Margaret. *Death On Account.* Penguin 1988/ PBO. Robbie Robinson was one of those people who are easily ignored. He'd been passed over for promotion at the bank and was a mere fixture in his own home. He plots: rob the bank, kill his wife, have an affair. He knows he'll never carry out his fantasies. But then one day he does . . .

RICHARD III

Next to the crimes of Jack the Ripper, no murders in history have drawn so much attention and energy as the murders of Richard III. There is a Richard III Society with international chapters throughout the world. The debate continues to be heated: Did he or did he not kill the Princes in the Tower? There are numerous scholarly books on the subject and a few murder mysteries.

DOHERTY, Paul C. *The Fate Of Princes.* [Historical]

PETERS, Elizabeth. *The Murders Of Richard III.* 1974 Dodd, Mead/ Mysterious 1986. Jacqueline Kirby joins a group of dedicated scholars of Richard III as they gather at a country mansion to prove, once again, that someone else had offed the Princes in the Tower.

History starts to repeat itself, so Jacqueline jumps in to stop a practical joker. 2nd. [Where There's A Will]

TEY, Josephine. *The Daughter Of Time.* 1952 Macmillan/ Pocket 1987. Alan Grant of Scotland Yard was flat on his back in hospital when his actress friend brought him a stack of portraits to think about. Intrigued with one of them, he investigates the case of Richard III. 3rd. [Historical]

TOWNSEND, Guy M. *To Prove A Villain.* 1985 Perseverance/ PBO. Dr. John Forest was teaching a course on British history. Right in the middle of the semester, his colleague, Dr. Marian James-Tyrell, was smothered by an intruder. At least that's what her husband said. Forest discovers a connection between Marian's death and the murders of Richard III. [Academic]

RUSSIA

A recent addition which adds to the variety of settings for the murder mystery is Russia. Stuart Kaminsky has a popular series featuring Inspector Porfiry Rostnikov. It would be worthwhile tracking down the earliest books in the series.

KAMINSKY, Stuart M. *Death Of A Dissident.* Ivy 1989/PBO. Dissident Aleksander Garnovsky was due to stand trial the next day, an enemy of the state. But tonight someone would kill him. Soon there's a trail of bodies for Inspector Rostnikov to follow. 1st. [Intrigue]

KAMINSKY, Stuart M. *Red Chameleon.* 1985 Scribner/ Charter 1986. A man broke into the Savitskaya apartment and shot the elderly Jew in the bathtub. Rostnikov is assigned the dreary case. As he tracks down a killer, he's suddenly ordered to stop. He figures out how to keep going. 3rd. [Imposter]

KAMINSKY, Stuart M. *A Fine Red Rain.* 1987 Scribner/ Ivy 1988. In disfavor, Inspector Rostnikov has been demoted to the pickpocket squad. In Arbat Square, he sees a man on top of Gogol's head jump to his death. More curious is the death of the man's partner on a faulty trapeze the same day. 4th. [Smuggling]

KAMINSKY, Stuart M. *A Cold Red Sunrise.* 1988 Scribner/ Ivy 1989. Inspector Rostnikov is on assignment in Siberia. Commissar Rutkin was murdered while he was looking into the death of Samsonov's daughter. Samsonov was a dissident about to be released to the West. Who doesn't want him released? 5th.

S . . . IS FOR

AT SEA

IT MUST BE THE HEADINESS of being a small speck on the vast ocean that is conducive to murder at sea. A collection of strangers, with no local police to institute an intensive investigation, gives the killer a modicum of security. Alas, it will not last.

BABSON, Marian. *The Cruise Of A Deathtime.* 1984 Walker/ Warner 1991. In a cabin on A Deck, a couple lay dead on the second day out of Miami. Next day, three natives were found at the bottom of an elevator shaft, and four guests are shot dead in their deck chairs. Tomorrow there will be five.

BECK, K. K. *Death In A Deck Chair.* 1984 Walker/ Ivy 1987. Iris Cooper and her Aunt Hermione are on the last lap of their 1927 world tour. The first day out, a young male secretary is found stabbed in his deck chair. Iris puts her head together with reporter Jack Clancy to find the murderer. 1st.

BORTHWICK, J. S. *Bodies Of Water.* 1990 St. Martin/ St. Martin 1991. Sarah Deane's brother Tony is working as a deckhand on the *Pilgrim,* sailing the coast of Maine. His boss, David Mallory, invites Sarah and Alex McKenzie to come aboard for two weeks. As Mallory delivers bibles to the remote churches, Sarah finds a body washed up on shore. 4th. [Smuggling]

CHARLES, Hampton. *Miss Seeton At The Helm.* Berkley 1990/ PBO. Miss Emily Seeton was invited on a Heron

Halcyon Holiday Cruise through the Greek Islands. Some of her fellow passengers are London's greatest art dealers. In the middle of a bitter dispute, one of them is murdered and Miss Seeton has to step in. 7th. [Art]

CLARK, Mary Higgins, et al. *Caribbean Blues.* 1988 Paperjacks/ PBO. Lady Hannah is aboard the cruise ship *Countess,* wearing the Caribbean Blues, matched sapphires. The stones have a curse and Lady Hannah dies. Seven PI's are on board, and they undertake to solve the crime.

CLARKE, Anna. *Cabin 3033.* 1986 Doubleday/ Charter 1989. Paula Glenning is returning to England aboard the *Gloriana.* Soon she's inserted herself into the lives of mystery writer Louis Hillman and his agent wife. Feeling seasick, Josephine falls and cracks her head on the tub. But was it an accident? 2nd. [Mystery Writer]

DeANDREA, William. *Killed In Paradise.* [Mystery Games]

EBERHART, Mignon G. *The Patient In Cabin C.* 1983 Random House/ Warner 1985. Monty Montgomery invited a group of people aboard his fancy yacht. Monty went overboard—he said he was pushed. Then the steward, Juan, ended up dead, and the accusations started to fly. Sue Gates and Stan Brooke wanted the puzzle solved while they were still alive. [Blackmail]

GIBBS, Tony. *Dead Run.* 1988 Random House/ Ivy 1989. Uncle Dennis sold Gillian Verdean *Glory* for next to nothing to keep his creditors from claiming it. When Uncle Dennis is beaten to death, Gillian discovers that something is hidden on board.

GORMAN, Edward. *Several Deaths Later.* 1988 St. Martin. Tobin accepted a week's work on a cruise ship filming the game show *Celebrity Circle.* The show's host, Ken Norris, ended up with a knife in his back. Before

Tobin has time to react, there are more bodies. [Mother]

LLEWELLYN, Sam. *Dead Reckoning.* 1987 Summit/ Pocket 1989. Charlie Agutter designed a new rudder. When the yacht was wrecked, his brother was on board and died. Everyone blamed Charlie's new rudder. But he knew it was sabotage and set out to prove it. 1st. [Jealousy]

LLEWELLYN, Sam. *Blood Orange.* 1989 Summit/ Pocket 1990. James Dixon is awash in money troubles. The catamaran he and Charlie Agutter designed is grossly in the red. Only winning the Round the Isles race will bail him out. To enter, he needs a sponsor. Orange Cars agrees to sponsorship. Then Dixon's racing friends start turning up dead. 2nd. [Economics]

MARSH, Ngaio. *Clutch Of Constables.* 1969 Little, Brown/ Jove 1986. On impulse, Troy Alleyn took the relaxing river cruise from Norminster to Longminster and back. On board were seven passengers, all strangers. One of the guests is found drowned in the river and Inspector Alleyn is called to insure his wife's safety. 25th. [Art]

MILLER, J. M. T. *Weatherby: On A Dead Man's Chest.* Ballantine 1989/ PBO. Captain Zachary Frye barged into PI Weatherby's office. Twenty years ago, he and John Crowe had searched out the sunken Spanish tribute ship *Santa Fabula.* Frye wants Weatherby to find it again. 2nd. [Old Crime]

SERIAL KILLERS

One mystery editor has noted that while 1987 was the year of drugs, 1988 would go down in the history of the mystery as the year of the serial killer . . . and the trend continues. While in actuality, the serial killer is in the minority, as killers go, the subject does make for the dramatic story.

ABSHIRE, Richard K., and William R. Clair. *Gants.* 1985 SOS/ Dell 1987. The Dallas Police Department had their hands full with the Slasher, who was leaving bodies all over the city. They had almost no time to deal with their captain, who was dead of a bullet to his head in a dingy hotel room. But something suggests a connection to the Slasher for Charlie Gants. [Suicide]

ADAMSON, M. J. *Not Till A Hot January.* 1987 Bantam/ PBO. NYPD Lt. Balthazar Marten was on assignment in San Juan, Puerto Rico, looking for laundered money. Before he even got a sunburn, three women were strangled, and the killer was still at large. 1st.

BARNES, Linda. *Coyote.* [Smuggling]

BATTIN, B. W. *The Creep.* 1987 Fawcett/ PBO. There was a note left with each of the victims in the sedate community of Maple Grove, Pennsylvania. It read: "Creep." Detective Kelsey McNeil, told to keep out of it, was looking for the wife of the school principal when she found herself in the middle of the bloody case.

BAYER, William. *Pattern Crimes.* 1987 Villard/ Signet 1988. It looked as though Jerusalem had a serial killer on its hands. First a young prostitute, then a nun. Now an Arab transvestite is dead. Detective David Barley has the case, and he's looking for a pattern to the crimes. [Intrigue]

BRADBURY, Ray. *Death Is A Lonely Business.* 1985 Knopf/ Bantam 1987. It is the early 1950s and a struggling writer is haunted by a series of deaths in Venice, California. With Lt. Elmo Crumly, he wanders the dilapidated streets until he confronts the killer ... and himself. [Writer]

BRADDON, Russell. *Funnelweb.* 1991 St. Martin. Christopher Westbury is a virtuoso violinist and a psychopathic genius. Using the deadly funnelweb spider, he's just murdered Michael Saxon, the world's greatest dancer. As the number of victims mounts, Scotland Yard's Chief Inspector Cheadle struggles to find the pattern to the killings. [Revenge]

BROWN, Frederic. *The Screaming Mimi.* [Journalism]

BROWN, Frederic. *The Lenient Beast.* 1956 Dutton/ Carroll & Graf 1988. John Medley woke one morning and found a dead man in his backyard. Tucson police officers Frank Ramos and Fern Cahan are working to identify the victim. Something bothers Frank, and he gnaws at it almost too long.

CAMPBELL, R. Wright. *Malloy's Subway.* 1981 Atheneum/ Tor 1988. Malloy was forced to retire from the NYPD after he took four bullets. Now he's a Transit Authority officer. Someone is killing people on the subway and leaving a Monopoly card. There's no way Malloy can let the killer ride away free.

CORNWELL, Patricia Daniels. *Post Mortem.* [Pathologist]

DeFELITTA, Frank. *Funeral March.* [Hollywood]

DeNOUX, O'Neil. *The Big Kiss.* Zebra 1990/ PBO. The first body was pulled out of the river after three days and it looked like a mob vendetta killing. Homicide Detective Dino La Stanza has two more bodies on his hands, and he's looking for a serial killer. [Corruption]

DOWNEY, Timothy. *A Special Executioner.* [Journalism]

ELLROY, James. *Silent Terror.* 1986 Avon/ PBO. Plunkett, a serial killer, is traveling the country, seemingly murdering at will. FBI Inspector Dusenberry, of the Serial Killer Task Force, is obsessed with finding him. Plunkett meets someone very much like himself.

SERIAL KILLERS

FORREST, Richard. *Lark.* 1986 Signet/ PBO. Lt. Tommy Lark's first homicide was the sexually mutilated corpse of a young girl. Then there was another, and another. Tommy's checking a cult leader, a talk show host, and a man who drives a camper.

GERSON, Jack. *Deathwatch.* [Intrigue]

GILL, B. M. *Suspect.* 1981 Scribner/ Ballantine 1985. A nurse from the local hospital is found murdered. Then there is another death that fits the same pattern. Emotions are running high as the police try to ferret out this vicious killer.

GOSLING, Paula. *The Wychford Murders.* [Where There's A Will]

GOUGH, Laurence. *The Goldfish Bowl.* [Canadian]

GRANGER, Bill. *Public Murders.* 1987 Warner/ PBO. She was a schoolteacher from Sweden, on holiday. She left the sweltering streets of Chicago for the coolness of Grant Park, where she was found dead. Special Squad members Terry Flynn and Karen Kovac have the case. 1st.

HARRIS, Thomas. *The Silence Of The Lambs.* 1988 St. Martin/ St. Martin 1989. Clarice Starling was recruited from her FBI classes to interview Hannibal Lecter, a famed psychiatrist, who was incarcerated for murder. Dr. Lecter knows all about serial killers, and Clarice has to get him to talk. 2nd. [Psychological]

HARVEY, John. *Lonely Hearts.* 1989 Holt/ Avon 1990. Shirley Peters was strangled in her own flat in the Midlands, and police picked up her common-law husband. He was still in jail when the second body turned up. Now Detective Inspector Charlie Resnick is looking for the connection between the two women. 1st. [Psychological]

HAUSER, Thomas. *Dear Hannah.* 1987 Tor/ Tor 1988. Richard Marrett, NYPD, doesn't like the pattern in the series of killings of young women. Hannah Wade is trying to ignore the dead roses sent through the mail. But when she hears from an old classmate, she decides it couldn't hurt to have dinner with him.

HENDERSON, M. R. *The Killing Game.* [Hollywood]

HENTOFF, Nat. *The Man From Internal Affairs.* 1985 Mysterious/ Mysterious 1986. Someone is leaving body parts in trash cans all over the Lower East Side. Detective Noah Green prowls the streets trying to talk to people who vanish at the sight of a cop.

HORNSBY, Wendy. *Half A Mind.* 1990 NAL/ Onyx 1991. Recovering from a blow to the head which has left him with partial amnesia, Lt. Roger Tejeda is jogging on the beach. And there's a box holding a severed head. It looks like the work of a man awaiting his sentence. Is the wrong man in jail? 2nd.

HOROWITZ, Leslie Alan. *Causes Unknown.* [Pathologist]

ISRAEL, Peter. *If I Should Die Before I Die.* 1989 Mysterious/ Mysterious 1990. A killer is murdering young women in New York City by smothering them with a pillow. Nora, noted TV sex therapist, enlists the help of Phil Revere, assistant to her lawyer husband. Nora's suspicious that the killer is one of her clients. 2nd. [Lawyer]

JAMES, P. D. *Devices And Desires.* [Political]

KANTNER, Rob. *The Harder They Hit.* [Pornography]

KANTNER, Rob. *Dirty Work.* 1988 Bantam/ Bantam 1988. Alex Farr, the DJ who's the darling of the airways, is the main link to a series of rapes and stranglings. PI Ben Perkins has been hired to clear Alex of the crimes. 3rd. [Television]

KELLERMAN, Jonathan. *Over The Edge.* [Psychological]

KELLY, Susan. *The Gemini Man.* 1985 Walker/ Ballantine 1986. Writer Liz Conners found the woman across the hall murdered. Jack Lingerman, Cambridge PD, answered the call. Liz can't help herself: she starts playing detective and almost ends up a corpse. 1st.

KEMP, Sarah. *No Escape.* [Pathologist]

KEMP, Sarah. *The Lure Of Sweet Death.* [Pathologist]

KENDALL, Jack. *Playing For Keeps.* [Children]

KOENIG, Joseph. *Floater.* 1986 Mysterious/ Mysterious 1987. Buck White's wife was found floating in the Everglades. As county sheriff, he was on a cold trail to find her killer. Meantime, bodies keep turning up in the area, and a serial killer is on the loose.

LANGTON, Jane. *Good And Dead.* 1986 St. Martin/ Penguin 1987. A lot of people seem to be dying in Nashoba, Massachusetts; dying of things they aren't ill with. Homer Kelly and his wife, Mary, are busy sorting the natural deaths from the unnatural ones. 6th.

LESLIE, John. *Killer In Paradise.* [Old Crime]

LEWIN, Michael Z. *Late Payments.* 1986 Morrow/ Penguin 1987. It looks as though someone is systematically murdering the handicapped in Indianapolis. Lt. Leroy Powder, between his other cases, is following every lead that comes his way. 3rd.

LINDSEY, David L. *A Cold Mind.* 1983 Harper & Row/ Pocket 1985. Three prostitutes have been found dead in the past few months in Houston, Texas. Not sure it's murder, Homicide Detective Stuart Haydon is examining the lives of the women. An unexpected virus leads to a more unexpected killer. 1st. [Medical]

LIVINGSTON, Jayson. *Point Blank.* [Revenge]

LUTZ, John. *Scorcher.* [Revenge]

MacGREGOR, T. J. *Dark Fields.* [Smuggling]

MacGREGOR, T. J. *Death Sweet.* 1988 Ballantine/ PBO. Ross Young hires Quin St. James and Mike McCleary to find out who has murdered his stepsister. It looks like the series of crimes is following the signs of the zodiac. The case drives a wedge between Quin and Mike, and their marriage may not survive the solution. 3rd. [Pornography]

MARSHALL, William. *Far Away Man.* [Oriental]

MARTIN, Lee. *The Mensa Murders.* 1990 St. Martin. Beverly Hart wants Detective Deb Ralston to look into her sister's death. Bev thinks she's been murdered. A second killing, and Deb is fearful that Ft. Worth has a serial killer. 7th. [Psychological]

MATHIS, Edward. *Little Man Blues.* 1988 Tor. Detective Hamilton Pope returned from vacation to Merriweather, Texas, and faced several murders. As violence escalates, Pope stacks up his clues, shuffles them, and sets a startling trap. [Psychological]

MATHIS, Edward. *Only When She Cries.* [Psychological]

MATHIS, Edward. *See No Evil.* [Blackmail]

MILLS, D. F. *Dark Room.* Diamond 1990/ PBO. Slowly recovering from her husband's fatal accident, Skye Meredith opened her business photographing children. One day she received a roll of film in the mail—pictures of a young woman in death. Then there was more film, and suddenly Skye is a suspect. [Psychological]

MINAHAN, John. *The Face Behind The Mask.* [Rape]

MITCHELL, Gladys. *The Rising Of The Moon.* 1984 St. Martin/ Paperjacks 1986. When the circus came to town, the young tightrope walker was found murdered. Then another woman died. Simon and Keith, two young boys, team up with Dame Beatrice to unravel the case. 19th.

NAHA, Ed. *On The Edge.* Pocket 1989/ PBO. The murder of the young co-ed had been brutal. As Lt. Kevin Broskey investigates, he discovers two other young women from Bay City College have died in a similar manner. Broskey's old friend, crime reporter Jake Mayer, is at his side, digging out clues. [Journalism]

O'DONNELL, Lillian. *Lady Killer.* [Mother]

PEARSON, Ridley. *Undercurrents.* 1988 St. Martins/ St. Martins 1989. Lou Boldt, Seattle Homicide, heads a special task force. He's on the trail of the Cross Killer who has eluded the police for over six months. With the help of Daphne Matthews, police psychologist, Boldt's picture of the killer becomes clear. [Psychological]

PEDNEAU, Dave. *A.P.B.* 1987 Ballantine/ PBO. The small West Virginia town is plagued by a serial killer, and all the victims are the wives of cops. Whit Pynchon, special investigator, is running down clues as fast as he can. Anna Tyson-Tyree, police reporter, is close on his heels. Suddenly, Whit's daughter is being held hostage. 1st.

ROBERTS, Nora. *Sacred Sins.* 1987 Bantam/ PBO. Ben Paris, Washington, D.C., Police Department, is in charge of a case full of terror. Young women are being killed by the "Priest." To add to the problem, he's working closely with psychiatrist Tess Court. Will they get close enough to stop the killings? 1st. [Psychological]

ROBERTS, Nora. *Brazen Virtue.* 1988 Bantam/ PBO. Grace McCabe, mystery writer, went to Washington, D.C., to see her sister. Grace discovered that Kathy was moonlighting for Fantasy, Inc., high-class sex by phone. Kathy is murdered, and then there's another. The only lead is the telephone. 2nd. [Mystery Writer]

SAUTER, Eric. *Skeletons.* 1990 Dutton. It was the third break-in in a little over a month, and each was more destructive. Philadelphia police detective Patrick Paige, at the next one, finds his recent lover brutally murdered. His past is haunting him: years ago, his wife died in a similar manner. [Old Crime]

SCHUTZ, Benjamin M. *Embrace The Wolf.* 1986 Bantam/ PBO. Five years ago, twin girls were snatched from a suburban Washington, D.C., home. Now, out of the blue, there's a phone call. Mrs. Saunders wants PI Leo Haggerty to find her husband, who took off almost as soon as he put down the receiver. It's a race against time for Leo. 1st.

SHANKMAN, Sarah aka Alice Storey. *Impersonal Attractions.* [Writer]

SHANNON, Dell. *Mark Of Murder.* 1964 Morrow/ Mysterious 1986. Lt. Luis Mendoza, Los Angeles PD, is called back from his vacation when his friend Sgt. Art Hackett is forced off a mountain road—an attempted murder. Even though Mendoza gets involved in the rampage of a serial killer, he won't let go of the chance to find Art's attacker. 8th. [Blackmail]

SHANNON, Dell. *Chaos Of Crime.* 1985 Morrow/ Worldwide 1989. There is a killer roaming Los Angeles. He picks up hookers, murders them, carves crosses on their chests, and vanishes in the dark. He's being called the Werewolf, and his victims are numbering in the forties. Luis Mendoza is waiting for a break in the case. 36th. [Prostitution]

SMITH, J. C. S. *Jacoby's First Case.* [Infidelity]

STUART, Anne. *Seen And Not Heard.* 1988 Pocket/ PBO. Claire McIntyre, caught up in a nightmare, fled to Paris and Marc Bonnard. She tried to ignore the murders of old women in the city and lose herself in Marc's love. But her fears grew stronger, till suddenly she's in a flight for her life.

TRENCH, Jason. *The Hammer.* [Blackmail]

WILCOX, Collin. *The Pariah.* 1988 Mysterious/ Mysterious 1989. They are the people who don't count, the nameless and faceless of the city. And someone is killing them. Lt. Frank Hastings has only two clues: a pimp who's a witness, and a computer printout. But someone is following the killer. 15th. [Clergy]

WILLEFORD, Charles. *Sideswipe.* 1987 St. Martin/ Ballantine 1988. Hoke Mosley, Miami PD, has a lot on his mind: two teenage daughters, and his partner who's eight months pregnant. He's also on the trail of a killer, a man who robs and murders his victims. 3rd.

SHERLOCK HOLMES

It's been over a hundred years now since the first Sherlock Holmes mystery story appeared, and a goodly number of years since the last one... by Sir Arthur Conan Doyle. But somehow the Master lives on. Periodically, another author surfaces and delights us with the continuing adventures of Sherlock Holmes.

ARNOLD, Alan. *Young Sherlock Holmes.* 1985 Pocket/ PBO. It's Sherlock Holmes's first murder case. Away at school, his favorite professor dies mysteriously, and Holmes insists the death is related to several others. Taking young Watson in tow, he toils to the solution.

BIGGLE, Lloyd, Jr. *The Quallsford Inheritance.* 1986 St. Martin/ Penguin 1987. Sherlock Holmes and his apprentice, nineteen-year-old Parker, are on the Isle of Graesney. Edmund Quallsford has recently killed himself. Amid a crumbled fortune and hints of smuggling, Holmes discovers murder. [Smuggling]

BOUCHER, Anthony. *The Case Of The Baker Street Irregular.* 1940 Simon & Schuster/ Carroll & Graf 1986. When word got out that a Hollywood movie studio was about to film a Doyle classic, some Sherlock Holmes followers were upset. Suddenly a whole cast of characters is caught up in a dramatic scenario. [Intrigue]

BROWN, Russell A. *Sherlock Holmes And The Mysterious Friend Of Oscar Wilde.* 1988 St. Martin. In London in 1895, Holmes, out of necessity, accepts the help of Oscar Wilde. Two predicaments have presented themselves to Holmes. The first involves the blackmailing of a prominent man. The second is a threat against Holmes's very life.

ESTLEMAN, Loren D. *Sherlock Holmes Vs. Dracula.* 1978 Doubleday/ Penguin 1979. Journalist Thomas C. Parker is authorized by his paper to hire Sherlock Holmes to investigate the strange happenings at Whitby Harbor. A ship had run aground. The captain was lashed to the wheel and drained of blood. And the cargo was fifty boxes of dirt and a black dog.

GREENBERG, Martin Harry, and Carol-Lynn Rossel Waugh, eds. *The **New** Adventures Of Sherlock Holmes.* 1987 Carroll & Graf/ Carroll & Graf 1988. A collection of sixteen short stories written for the centennial of the first Sherlock Holmes mystery.

GREENWOOD, L. B. *Sherlock Holmes And The Case Of The Raleigh Legacy.* 1986 Atheneum/ St. Martin 1987. Holmes has a most unusual case, one that goes back to the time of Sir Walter Raleigh. A cryptic letter alludes to hidden treasure. The last remnant of the family is Aleck, and the treasure must lie at the estate of Nightsead. 1st.

HARDWICK, Michael. *The Revenge Of The Hound.* 1987 Villard/ Pinnacle 1989. London is agog with the prospect of Edward VII's coronation. Then a derelict is killed by a huge hound, and Oliver Cromwell's skeleton is stolen. Holmes and Watson are looking into the attempts to blackmail the king.

VAN ASH, Cay. *Ten Years Beyond Baker Street.* 1984 Harper & Row/ Perennial 1988. Dr. Petrie pries Sherlock Holmes, retired for ten years, away from his bees in Sussex to help rescue Nayland Smith from the grasp of Dr. Fu Manchu.

SMUGGLING

If it's movable, valuable, scarce, or illegal, it will be smuggled into or out of a country. Leaving drugs aside, the objects to be smuggled are almost infinite.

ALLINGHAM, Margery. *More Work For The Undertaker.* 1949 Doubleday/ Avon 1989. Within a few months, two of the Palinode siblings are dead under strange circumstances. Shunned as eccentric by their neighbors, the three remaining children are left alone. On the same street, someone is placing advance orders for coffins. Albert Campion is asked to investigate. 13th. [Where There's A Will]

BAILEY, Hilary. *Hannie Richards.* 1985 Random House/ Ballantine 1987. Hannie was a housewife and mother. She was also a smuggler. There was lots of excitement in her life, and she traveled a lot. On this particular trip, someone is following her. Will this be her last mission?

BANNISTER, Jo. *The Mason Codex.* [Anthropology]

BARNES, Linda. *Coyote.* 1990 Delacorte. A young Hispanic woman showed up at Carlotta's office. Manuela Estefan wants Carlotta to get back her green card. But the green card is at the police department; it was found with the body of another Hispanic woman. When another woman dies, does Boston have a serial killer on the streets? 3rd. [Serial Killer]

BAXT, George. *Satan Is A Woman.* [Witches]

BIGGLE, Lloyd, Jr. *The Quallsford Inheritance.* [Sherlock Holmes]

BORTHWICK, J. S. *Bodies Of Water.* [At Sea]

BOYER, Rick. *Billingsgate Shoal.* 1982 Houghton Mifflin/ Warner 1985. Sitting on his deck at Cape Cod, depressed Doc Adams watched a trawler that had gone aground on the shoal. He suggested that a friend take a look at it. The friend was found dead. To cure his depression, Doc decided to take on the mystery. 1st.

BRAUN, Lilian Jackson. *The Cat Who Played Brahms.* [Cats]

CHANCE, Lisbeth. *Baja Run.* 1986 Walker/ Tor 1988. On an island in the Sea of Cortez, mourning the death of her grandfather, Anna Michelotti overheard a conversation not meant for her ears. Her grandfather's business partner had decided that if she became a problem, she'd be dealt with. Now Anna only wants to survive.

EBERHART, Mignon G. *Three Days For Emeralds.* [Where There's A Will]

ESTLEMAN, Loren D. *Silent Thunder.* 1989 Houghton Mifflin/Fawcett 1990. Constance Thayer took an automatic pistol from her husband's collection and emptied it into his naked body. Amos Walker has been hired to collect any dirt he can on Doyle Thayer, Jr., to make his wife look clean by comparison. 10th. [Intrigue]

FROST, Joan Van Every. *Silvershine.* [Fashion]

HARRISON, Ray. *Death Of A Dancing Lady.* [Victorian]

HEALD, Tim. *Brought To Book.* 1988 Doubleday. Publisher Vernon Hemlock was closeted with his rare collection of erotica when he died. Simon Bogner, visiting at the country estate, became the target of suspicion. He has to clear himself. 9th. [Manuscripts]

JERINA, Carol. *Sweet Jeopardy.* 1988 Charter/ PBO. The three men were playing golf when they became sick and quickly died. Mercedes Underwood was the first suspect. She called her granddaughter Jillian Fletcher to get PI Jackson Fury on the case. 2nd. [Fraud]

KAMINSKY, Stuart M. *A Fine Red Rain.* [Russian]

LEE, Elsie. *Satan's Coast.* [Revenge]

MacGREGOR, T. J. *Dark Fields.* 1987 Ballantine/ PBO. PI Quin St. James stopped at the house of her fiancé and found him brutally murdered. Mike McCleary, Miami PD, has the assignment. In the middle of a hurricane, the murderer is after Quin. 1st. [Serial Killer]

MacLEOD, Charlotte. *The Luck Runs Out.* [Academic]

MacLEOD, Charlotte, w/a Alisa Craig. *A Dismal Thing To Do.* 1986 Doubleday/ Avon 1988. Janet Rhys was hunting for an antique when there was a truck accident and her car was stolen. The truck burned to a crisp and two men died. Janet has to clue in her husband Madoc, RCMP, as to the nuances of the crime. 3rd. [Canadian]

McBRIARTY, Douglas. *Whitewater VI.* 1987 Walker. J. J. Jaynes died in a boating accident on the Chattooga River. When Sheriff McPhee starts asking questions, he's badly injured. It's up to Cherokee Deputy Billy Birdsong to put all the pieces together. 1st. [Indian]

McMULLEN, Mary. *Something Of The Night.* 1980 Doubleday/ Jove 1986. Kells Cavanaugh received a distress letter from his young son. He immediately flew to London to check out the man his ex-wife was about to marry. Things were worse than even he could have imagined.

MELVILLE, James. *A Sort Of Samurai.* [Oriental]

MITTERMEYER, Helen. *Brief Encounter.* 1988 Dell/ PBO. After the bitter blow Luna McAfee had suffered during her brief affair with Dray Lodge in Germany, she wasn't too happy to encounter the young senator in Washington, D.C. Then the horror began: break-ins, surveillance, and threats. [Lawyer]

MURPHY, Dallas. *Lover Man.* [Revenge]

O'DONNELL, Lillian. *Cop Without A Shield.* 1983 Putnam/ Fawcett 1985. Distraught over the death of her husband, Norah Mulcahaney left her badge and her gun and went to York County, Pennsylvania. But the abduction and death of a young woman draws Norah back to work. She discovers that the whole town is involved in a secret. 8th. [Infidelity]

PARIS, Ann. *Graven Image.* 1987 Pocket/ PBO. The trip was to be a lark. Just deliver some things to her boss at his new house on a Greek island off Rhodes. His marriage was about to take place. She bumped into Jim Border, and strange things began to happen during the night.

PAYNE, Laurence. *Dead For A Ducat.* [Missing Person]

PHILLIPS, R. A. *Gun Play.* 1987 Foul Play. As Elton Dancey investigated what seemed to be a petty blackmail scheme involving beautiful Sabrina, he was led deeper and deeper into a rash of violence. Then he uncovered an international arms deal. 1st. [Blackmail]

PRONZINI, Bill. *Labyrinth.* 1980 St. Martin/ Paperjacks 1987. A young woman was found dead on the beach. She had a business card from Nameless, but he'd never met her. Then Nameless is hired to protect Martin Talbot from the man who blames him for his wife's death. What's the connection? 6th. [Gay]

PRONZINI, Bill. *Breakdown.* 1991 Delacorte. Nameless was hired to prove that Thomas Lujack hadn't run down his partner with his Cadillac Seville on a dark San Francisco street, despite the testimony of three witnesses. Then one of the men scheduled to testify swears that Lujack tried to run him down. 19th.

SHUMAN, M. K. *The Maya Stone Murders.* [Archeology]

STERN, Richard Martin. *You Don't Need An Enemy.* [Indian]

TAYLOR, Andrew. *Waiting For The End Of The World.* 1984 Dodd, Mead/ Penguin 1985. William Dougal got blackmailed into keeping an eye on Dr. Vertag, leader of a survivalist group. Suddenly from Dougal's past beautiful Zelda shows up. When she's kidnapped, he's off on the chase leading right to the old castle. 2nd. [Kidnapping]

THOMPSON, Estelle. *A Toast To Cousin Julian.* [Australia]

VAN DE WETERING, Janwillem. *The Japanese Corpse.* [Oriental]

WILCOX, Stephen F. *The St. Lawrence Run.* [Old Crime]

WOOD, Ted. *When The Killing Starts.* 1989 Scribner. Although Police Chief Reid Bennett was on vacation, Mrs. Michaels wanted him to find her son. Jason had gone off with a group of mercenaries. Several bodies turn up, and Reid is at risk. 6th. [Canadian]

WOOD, Ted. *On The Inside.* [Canadian]

ZANNOS, Susan. *Trust The Liar.* [Anthropology]

SOCIAL ISSUES

Although someone once said that if you want to send a message try Western Union, social issues do turn up from time to time in the murder mystery. Whatever is popular in society can find a voice intertwined with mayhem and the mystery puzzle.

DUNCAN, W. Glen. *Rafferty: Poor Dead Cricket.* 1988 Fawcett/ PBO. Cricket Dawes, a secretary at the plutonium processing plant, died in a parking lot after someone shot her. Missing was the collection of files she'd stolen from her office. PI Rafferty was hired to find the killer . . . and the files. 3rd.

GRETH, Roma. . . . *And Now You Don't.* [Missing Person]

HANSEN, Joseph. *Nightwork.* [Gay]

SOCIAL ISSUES

HIAASEN, Carl. *Tourist Season.* 1986 Putnam/ Warner 1987. Strange things are happening in Miami, including several weird deaths that are having a deadly impact on the tourist trade. PI Brian Keyes was hired to clear a client and ends up saving Miami. [Journalism]

HUEBNER, Frederick D. *The Joshua Sequence.* 1986 Fawcett/ PBO. Stephen Turner, software specialist, was gunned down on a Seattle street. Kate Warden, his sister, hired Matt Riordan to find out who killed her brother. Matt's path goes back years to Turner's antinuclear activities. Matt trips over corpses, and the case brings him to the brink of madness. 1st. [Old Crime]

HUEBNER, Frederick D. *The Black Rose.* 1987 Fawcett/ PBO. Bernie hired Matt Riordan, Seattle lawyer, to find environmental specialist Larry Kramer. He was working on the development of a ski resort. Two days later Bernie's dead. Matt is bound to find his killer; he finds much more. 2nd. [Lawyer]

KALLEN, Lucille. *C. B. Greenfield: A Little Madness* [Journalism]

PARETSKY, Sara. *Blood Shot.* 1988 Delacorte/ Dell 1989. Caroline, a friend of V.I. Warshawski, wants her to find out who her father is. When another of her friends is found dead, V.I. is drawn into problems involving an old chemical plant and a man who kept a secret notebook. 5th.

PICKARD, Nancy. *Dead Crazy.* 1988 Scribner/ Pocket 1989. Jenny Cain, director of the Port Frederick Foundation, is working to develop a recreation center for the mentally ill. The perfect spot just happened to have a body in it. Suspected is a disturbed young man. Before Jenny solves this one, another will die. 5th. [Blackmail]

SMITH, Evelyn. *Miss Melville Regrets.* 1986 Fine/ Fawcett 1987. Miss Susan Melville was New York City upper crust, but with little income. She decided to crash a very posh party, and end it all . . . go out with a bang. Instead, she shot the guest speaker who was about to turn her apartment building into condos. Thus begins her new career. 1st.

SMITH, Julie. *Tourist Trap.* 1986 Mysterious/ Mysterious 1987. It was going to be a unique experience for Jewish feminist lawyer Rebecca Schwartz. She and Rob Burns were going to an Easter sunrise service. What they hadn't expected was a real person on the cross, there for all the tourists to see. There's a mad killer on the loose. 3rd. [Revenge]

TAPPLY, William G. *The Marine Corpse.* 1986 Scribner/ Ballantine 1987. Stu Carver was living on the streets of Boston, studying the homeless. He's found dead in an alley, murdered. Brady Coyne, retained by the family, follows a strange route to find the killer. 4th. [Intrigue]

TRIPP, Miles. *Death Of A Man-Tamer.* 1987 St. Martin. Paul Phelan, trapper of wild animals for the zoo, awoke naked and locked in a cage. His captors were dressed in black leather. The next time he woke up, Paul was in a wooded area next to a dead woman. He hired John Samson to prove he didn't kill her. 6th.

SUICIDE OR MURDER?

One of the perfect solutions for the plotting of murder is to make the victim appear to have taken his or her own life. And, for the ultimate in revenge, the plan is for the supposed victim to commit suicide and have it appear to be murder, with clues deftly planted and a killer spelled out.

ABSHIRE, Richard K., and William R. Clair. *Gants.* [Serial Killer]

BRAUN, Lilian Jackson. *The Cat Who Played Post Office.* [Cats]

BRYANT, Dorothy. *Killing Wonder.* 1981 ATA/ Popular 1985. The celebrated author India Wonder was having a get-together of women writers at her home. Jessamy Posey, beginning writer, was invited. As India rose to propose a toast, she keeled over dead. Has one of the guests poisoned her? [Writers]

CARLSON, P. M. *Murder Misread.* [Children]

COOPER, Susan Rogers. *Other People's Houses.* [Witness Protection Program]

CROSS, Amanda. *Death In A Tenured Position.* [Academic]

CROSS, Amanda. *Sweet Death, Kind Death.* [Academic]

DELMAN, David. *Dead Faces Laughing.* 1987 Doubleday. The comedian Charley the Elf died. His car blew up with him in it. Lt. Jacob Horowitz, NYPD, recognizes it as a contract job. But which one of Charlie's relatives or friends would do that to him? 8th.

ENGEL, Howard. *The Suicide Murders.* 1984 St. Martin/ Penguin 1985. Mrs. Yorke wanted PI Benny Cooperman to check up on her husband. She thought Chester might be seeing another woman. Then Chester committed suicide. As Benny probes the case, he discovers that things aren't what they seem. 1st. [Canadian]

GARDNER, Erle Stanley w/a A. A. Fair. *Bedrooms Have Windows.* 1949 Morrow/ Avon 1990. While tailing a hustler, Donald Lam was sidetracked to the Kozy Dell Slumber Court. A few doors down, a suicide pact was taking place. Suddenly, there are too many bodies, and Donald is on the run from sure arrest. 12th. [Blackmail]

GOLDSBOROUGH, Robert. *Death On Deadline.* [Journalism]

GREENWOOD, John. *The Mind Of Mr. Mosley.* 1987 Walker/ Bantam 1988. Inspector Mosley was sent down to Upper Crudshaw to verify a suicide. The quiet village seems to be bursting with crime. The widow Tunnicliffe reported that £500 had been stolen from her, and the vicar is accused of running a brothel. 4th.

GRINDAL, Richard. *Over The Sea To Die.* 1990 St. Martin. Physician Charles Mackinnon is on the island of Skye, filling in for the local doctor. As he walks along a cliff, he sees a woman thrown onto the rocks below. The police are skeptical, calling it suicide. Charles can't keep himself from becoming involved. [Drugs]

HAMMOND, Gerald. *The Worried Widow.* 1988 St. Martin. Jenny Hendrickson is convinced her husband did not kill himself. She asks Keith Calder to find out the truth. Sam had been a hard-boiled union boss, but had become very ill. Keith has to dodge Inspector Munro for solid answers. 10th. [Insurance]

HANNA, David. *The Opera House Murders.* [Theater]

HART, Roy. *A Pretty Place For A Murder.* 1988 St. Martin. Vera worked at the pub, and in her spare time she was at the Suttons, a big house reduced to an arts and crafts center. Superintendent Roper was called to Cort Abbas when Vera's body was found in a ditch. Then there's a suicide and a note admitting to Vera's murder. 2nd.

HART, Roy. *Breach Of Promise.* 1991 St. Martin. For fifty years, Enid Kingsley had cared for her brother who had been injured in the war. He was confined to a wheelchair, and she even had to cut up his food. On a walk one morning, Enid found the body of their dear friend shot to death in his caravan. Superintendent Roper starts his questioning. 5th. [Imposter]

HILL, Reginald. *Bones And Silence.* 1990 Delacorte/ Dell 1991. Dalziel received an anonymous letter and then another from someone planning on suicide. As the town prepares for Corpus Christi, and the series of pageants that make up the *Mysteries,* the letters become more frequent and more determined. 16th. [Theater]

JEFFRIES, Roderic. *Too Close By Half.* [Art]

KELLERMAN, Jonathan. *Silent Partner.* [Psychological]

KELMAN, Judith. *Where Shadows Fall.* [Academic]

LARSEN, Gaylord. *The 180-Degree Murder.* [Academic]

LeCLAIRE, Anne D. *Every Mother's Son.* [Academic]

LIVINGSTON, Jack. *Die Again, Macready.* [Arson]

LUTZ, John. *Tropical Heat.* [Real Estate]

LYONS, Arthur. *At The Hands Of Another.* 1983 Holt/ Owl 1986. An old love shows up in Jacob Asch's life. She wants him to investigate her husband's death. The insurance company is refusing to pay. They say that Sharon's husband killed himself. 7th. [Insurance]

MEEK, M. R. D. *A Loose Connection.* 1989 Scribner/ Worldwide 1991. On a trip to the Cotswolds, Amanda Edgerton had a shock. There was Queenie, a woman who had died in a fire twenty years ago. She couldn't wait to tell her friend Dorothea. Then Amanda was found drowned in the river, a suicide. Now solicitor Lennox Kemp gets involved. 6th. [Old Crime]

PETERSON, Audrey. *Death In Wessex.* Pocket 1989/ PBO. Jane Winfield is researching some music in a small English village. Her professor, Andrew Quentin, is visiting a friend at Braden Beck. Just before the annual festival, a man is found dead on the estate. The police call it suicide. Quickly following is the murder of a young woman. 2nd. [Where There's A Will]

PRICE, Nancy. *Sleeping With The Enemy.* [Psychological]

PRONZINI, Bill. *Jackpot.* 1990 Delacorte/ Dell 1991. David Burnett won $200,000 at the Reno slot machines and then killed himself with an overdose of sleeping pills. At least, that's the story the police gave his sister Allyn. She doesn't believe it and hires Nameless to discover the truth. 18th. [Corruption]

RINEHART, Mary Roberts. *Miss Pinkerton.* [Insurance]

SCHUTZ, Benjamin M. *A Tax In Blood.* [Intrigue]

SPRINKLE, Patricia Houck. *Murder On Peachtree Street.* 1991 St. Martin. Prominent TV personality Dean Anderson was found dead in his office, the gun on the floor. The police are calling it suicide. But his old friend Sheila Travis thinks it's murder. Together with her Aunt Mary, they traipse up and down Peachtree Street looking for answers. 3rd. [Television]

TAPPLY, William G. *Death At Charity's Point.* 1984 Scribner/ Ballantine 1985. Brady Coyne, Boston lawyer, is summoned to Florence Gresham's North Shore home to prove that her son's death wasn't suicide. At quiet Ruggles School, where George taught, Brady finds romance . . . and murder. 1st. [Lawyer]

THOMPSON, Monroe. *The Blue Room.* Bantam 1990/PBO. Jim Henry heard over lunch that his old school friend Morris Patterson had killed himself. Jim doesn't believe it and drives down to Jackson, Mississippi, where Morris lived, and died, to find out the truth. [Gay]

UPTON, Robert. *Fade Out.* [Hollywood]

VAN DE WETERING, Janwillem. *Outsider In Amsterdam.* 1975 Houghton Mifflin/ Ballantine 1986. The man was still hanging, bare toes pointed toward the floor and wearing a very expensive watch. It looked like suicide to Grijpstra and de Gier. In life, Piet Verboom had run the restaurant. In death, there was a scramble for the rest of his business. 1st. [Drugs]

VAN DE WETERING, Janwillem. *Hard Rain.* 1986 Pantheon/ Ballantine 1988. Martin IJsbreker was found shot, the gun in his hand. He'd been the banker for the Society for Help Abroad, a front for an international vice ring. Unfortunately, the head of the ring was Fernandus Willem, boyhood friend of the Commissaris. 11th. [Corruption]

T . . . IS FOR

TELEVISION AND RADIO

THE MEDIA, especially television and radio, takes its own place as a setting for murder. The part of the media that we see and hear is only a fraction of what goes on in studios throughout the world. Our murder tales take us behind the scenes and into complex relationships.

ALLEN, Steve. *Murder On The Glitter Box.* 1989 Zebra/ Zebra 1990. When TV talk show host Terry Cole went off on vacation, Steve Allen agreed to take his place. His first night was a disaster. Movie star Hal Hoaglund downed some of Terry's vodka and died . . . on camera. 2nd. [Revenge]

BABBIN, Jacqueline. *Bloody Special.* 1972 Curtis/ International Polygonics 1988. Irma came out of the shower and found TV producer Bruce Berman sprawled in the middle of her bed, a kitchen knife sticking out of his chest. Clovis Kelley, NYPD, has the unlucky job of questioning friends and co-workers. [Revenge]

BABSON, Marian. *Cover-Up Story.* 1988 St. Martin. Struggling public relations firm Perkins & Tate landed a plum. They were to represent a musical act, Black Bart and His Hillbillies, on their British TV filming. From the beginning, it began to turn sour—then it turned to murder. 1st. [Getting Away With Murder]

BABSON, Marian. *Encore Murder.* 1990 St. Martin. With Trixie Dolan's help, Evangeline Sinclair is working on her memoirs. But rival Griselda van Kirstenburg plans her own expose. Then a strange murder occurs and the household is thrown into a turmoil. 2nd. [Manuscript]

BIEDERMAN, Marcia. *Post No Bonds.* 1988 Scribner/ Penguin 1989. The local bondsman isn't doing very well, so Grace Stark takes over the business from her husband. When she makes $50,000 bail on a drug dealer at the TV station, he skips. Grace won't be cheated. With Darcy, the dealer's girlfriend, they track him down. 1st. [Drugs]

BRETT, Simon. *Dead Giveaway.* 1986 Scribner/ Dell 1987. Charlie Paris was doing a bit appearance on the pilot of a game show, *If the Cap Fits.* The host took a sip of water and died. Even with someone in custody, Charlie still prowls the set. When they reshoot the pilot, Charlie makes his move. 10th.

CAMPBELL, Robert. *Alice In La-La Land.* 1988 Pocket/ PBO. Nell Twelvetrees is convinced that her TV-talk-show host husband wants her dead before the divorce settlement is made. She wants PI Whistler to protect her. But the problems in this family go way below the surface. 2nd. [Revenge]

CLARK, Mary Higgins. *Stillwatch.* [Old Crime]

CREWS, Lary. *Extreme Close-Up.* Lynx 1989/ PBO. Radio talk-show hostess Veronica Slate has a personal problem. Angela Mastry is coming to Tampa to star in a film, and Angela is her lover's ex-wife. When Angela is murdered, David is framed for her death. Veronica has to save him. 2nd. [Drugs]

DEAN, S. F. X. *Nantucket Soap Opera.* 1987 Atheneum. Professor Neil Kelly, on Nantucket Island, meets all of the Hollywood crew filming a historical soap opera.

Before long, the bodies pile up and dark secrets are exposed. 6th. [Father]

DeANDREA, William. *Killed In The Ratings.* [Fraud]

DeANDREA, William. *Killed In The Act.* [Fraud]

DeANDREA, William. *Killed With A Passion.* 1983 Doubleday/ Mysterious 1987. TV troubleshooter Matt Cobb is in upstate New York looking into rumors of corruption in cable TV. Then he gets caught up in the murder of his friend's fiancé. Matt will feel guilty about his part in the outcome. 3rd. [Jealousy]

DeANDREA, William L. *Killed On The Rocks.* 1990 Mysterious. G. B. Dost is out to take over the Network. But someone is writing crank letters about him, trying to quash the deal. As a group of lawyers and stockholders meet in a remote house in upstate New York, Matt Cobb has to prevent treachery. 6th. [Fraud]

FRASER, Antonia. *The Cavalier Case.* 1991 Bantam. Researching a TV project, *Ghosts And Ourselves,* Jemima Shore falls in love, with 17th century Cavalier poet Decimus Meredith, 1st Viscount Lackland. But when murder strikes, Jemima plots to ring the final curtain at the Cavalier Celebration. 7th. [Witches]

FULTON, Eileen. *Take One For Murder.* 1988 Ivy/ PBO. High above the Hudson, at Mortimer Meyer's estate, the cast of *The Turning Seasons* is being wined and dined. Then their host is murdered, just after the toast. Nina McFall dives in to find the killer, and finds herself scripted to die. 1st. [Blackmail]

FULTON, Eileen. *Death Of A Golden Girl.* 1988 Ivy/ PBO. May Minton, aging actress, had just landed a role in a soap opera. Several others wanted the same part. Nina McFall found May dead in her bathtub. She calls Dino

Rossi, NYPD, for help. But now she's got information she won't share with him. 2nd. [Revenge]

FULTON, Eileen. *Dying For Stardom.* 1988 Ivy/ PBO. At the lavish Tavern on the Green, the winner of a talent show for a part in a soap opera keels over just before her acceptance speech. When the runner-up also dies, actress Nina McFall and NYPD's Dino Rossi race to catch the killer. 3rd. [Blackmail]

FULTON, Eileen. *Lights, Camera, Death.* 1988 Ivy/ PBO. Every star likes fans, but the one writing to Nina McFall calls himself her "secret lover." When an actor playing her lover in the soap opera dies, Nina has to take her admirer seriously. But what will he do when he finds out about Dino? 4th. [Jealousy]

FULTON, Eileen. *A Setting For Murder.* 1988 Ivy/ PBO. Angela Dolan, co-star to Nina McFall, is in trouble. Angela had borrowed a brooch that Nina has bad feelings about. Now Angela's boyfriend is dead, and she's the major suspect. Where is the rest of the jewelry? 5th. [Psychological]

FULTON, Eileen. *Fatal Flashback.* Ivy 1989/ PBO. Nina McFall rented an old farm house in upstate New York. She arrives to find that a young woman was murdered at the farm ten years earlier. The killer is still free. Nina and Dino are dragged into a hunt for a murderer. 6th. [Old Crime]

GIELGUD, Val. *Through A Glass Darkly.* [Blackmail]

GORMAN, Edward. *Murder Straight Up.* 1986 St. Martin/ Ballantine 1987. Jack Dwyer is working as a security guard at Channel 3. Watching the monitor, he sees the 10 p.m. anchorman keel over, dead on prime time. One chase leads to another until Jack has a pile of facts. 2nd.

GRANGER, Ann. *Say It With Poison.* 1991 St. Martin. Meredith returned to England for the wedding of her godchild Sara, daughter of her much-married movie star cousin Eve Owens. Someone is playing tricks on Sara, and then a former lover turns up dead. Inspector Alan Markby and Meredith are thrown together in murder. 1st. [Blackmail]

GRAY, Malcolm. *Stab In The Back.* [Mystery Writer]

JEFFERS, H. Paul. *Murder On The Mike.* 1984 St. Martin/ Ballantine 1988. The producer of the radio show *Detective Fitzroy's Casebook* has been shot to death. It had to be someone at the studio. The only person without an alibi was David Reed. His girlfriend Maggie tearfully begs PI Harry MacNeil to prove David innocent. 2nd. [Getting Away With Murder]

JONES, Cleo. *The Case Of The Fragmented Woman.* 1986 St. Martin/ Worldwide 1988. Mary and Jill are close friends. Jill finds out her husband is having an affair with soap opera star Hermione. Hermione disappears. Then her head shows up as a prize on a local quiz show, and Mary has to keep Jill from housewife heaven. [Infidelity]

KANTNER, Rob. *Dirty Work.* [Serial Killer]

LORENS, M. K. *Ropedancer's Fall.* Bantam 1990/ PBO. Winston Marlowe Sherman's feuding partner, PBS talk-show host John Falkner, has been brutally murdered. Then Falkner's son disappears, and Winston has to find him, at any cost. That's not all he finds. 2nd. [Mystery Writer]

LUPICA, Mike. *Dead Air.* 1986 Villard/ Ballantine 1987. TV reporter Peter Finley's ex-girlfriend, Peggy Lynn, vanished. Everyone thought she was dead, and each had a different idea as to who had killed her. It takes Peter, his ex-cop father, and part of his TV crew to get the whole thing on video for the six o'clock news. 1st. [Missing Person]

LUTZ, John. *Shadowtown.* [Vampire]

MILLER, Judi. *Phantom Of The Soap Opera.* 1988 Dell/PBO. NYPD Detective Terry Morrison is on a tough case. Soap opera star Kristi is dead in her dressing room. Within days, another member of the soap opera is killed in the same way. Terry is beside herself with this serial murderer. [Psychological]

NAGY, Gloria. *Radio Blues.* [Psychological]

PARKER, Robert B. *Stardust.* 1990 Putnam. Jill Joyce, prima donna star of TV series *Fifty Minutes,* is being harassed by phone calls and letters. Spenser is hired to protect her and find out who's behind the harassments. But when Jill's stunt double is shot and killed, Spenser's job turns deadly. 17th. [Father]

ROBERTS, Les. *Not Enough Horses.* [Gay]

SHERWOOD, John. *A Shot In The Arm: Death At The BBC.* [Where There's A Will]

SPRINKLE, Patricia Houck. *Murder On Peachtree Street.* [Suicide]

TUCKER, John Bartholomew. *He's Dead, She's Dead: Details At Eleven.* 1990 St. Martin. Jim Sasser, former network commentator and successful thriller writer, is asked to do some investigating. Northern Industries has just taken over the Republic Broadcasting System, and already a young woman is dead. [Drugs]

THEATER

The play's the thing, and the players often have a different script than the one they've been handed. Old hurts surface, and petty jealousies abound. There is as much drama backstage as there is when the curtains goes up. Sometimes theater people die outside the theater—a complicating factor for the ardent detective.

BARNES, Linda. *Blood Will Have Blood.* 1986 Fawcett/ PBO. Director Arthur Darien is putting on a production of *Dracula*. When someone puts blood in an actor's Bloody Mary, the actor quits. Darien wants Michael Spraggue to find out who is in the dirty-tricks business. 2nd. [Drugs]

BELL, Josephine. *Curtain Call For A Corpse.* 1965 Macmillan/ Perennial 1988. The Shakespeare Players Ltd. were playing *Twelfth Night* at an English prep school. Mr. Fenton never made the curtain call. Inspector Mitchell stages his own performance to flush out a confession. 4th.

BLOCK, Lawrence. *Burglars Can't Be Choosers.* [Blackmail]

BRETT, Simon. *What Bloody Man Is That?.* 1987 Scribner/ Dell 1989. Charlie Paris is in Warminster playing in *Macbeth* for a repertory company. Warnock Belvedere, one of the actors, is found dead in the drinks storeroom. The man wasn't liked—anyone could be his killer. 12th. [Children]

CARLSON, P. M. *Audition For Murder.* 1985 Avon/ PBO. Actor Nick O'Conner and his wife, Lisette, are at an upstate New York college, teaching and acting. Things start happening to Lisette—practical jokes and then some—till one of them proves fatal. Maggie Ryan can't help snooping into motive and opportunity. 1st. [Revenge]

CARLSON, P. M. *Rehearsal For Murder.* 1988 Bantam/ PBO. Nick O'Conner is hoping for a long run of his musical when Ramona, the lead actress and backer, is shot just outside the theater. Nick and his wife Maggie

Ryan have to hurry to find the murderer, the kidnapped child, and the ransom. 5th. [Getting Away With Murder]

DEAVER, Jeffrey Wilds. *Death Of A Blue Movie Star.* [Pornography]

DENTINGER, Jane. *Murder On Cue.* 1983 Doubleday/ Dell 1984. For Josh O'Roarke, actress, it would be steady work, even if it is as understudy for the lead, the impossible Harriett Weldon. Between rehearsals, Harriett dies from a nasty fall. The cast is just one mass of suspects. 1st.

DENTINGER, Jane. *First Hit Of The Season.* 1984 Doubleday/ Dell 1985. Theater critic Jason Saylin and actress Irene Ingersall are feuding. At a party after the opening, Jason stumbles out of his study and falls over dead. Josh O'Roarke wonders who else wanted him dead. 2nd.

DENTINGER, Jane. *Death Mask.* 1988 Scribner. Actress/ writer Jocelyn O'Roarke agrees to help save the old theater from adventurous real estate interests. At the preview performance, Burton Evans takes his final curtain call. To keep the show afloat, Josh has to find the killer. 3rd. [Real Estate]

FLETCHER, Lucille. *Mirror Image.* [Missing Person]

FRASER, Antonia. *Cool Repentance.* 1982 Norton/ Norton 1985. Actress Christabel Cartwright has returned to her family, and they seem prepared to forgive her. Then during the Larminster Festival a young woman dies, dressed in Christabel's clothes. Jemima Shore is looking for the truth. 4th. [Jealousy]

GORMAN, Edward. *Murder In The Wings.* 1986 St. Martin/ Ballantine 1987. Jack Dwyer lands a part in a play, only to find himself investigating the murder of the director. How else can he clear his friend of the crime and get back to work? 3rd.

GRAHAM, Caroline. *Death Of A Hollow Man.* 1989 Morrow/ Avon 1990. At opening night, the leading man in *Amadeus* cuts his throat on stage . . . for real! It's up to Chief Inspector Tom Barnaby to find out who removed the safety tape from the straight razor. 2nd. [Blackmail]

HANNA, David. *The Opera House Murders.* 1985 Leisure/ PBO. Diva Maria Viscardi's husband, a petty loan shark, was found dead outside the stage door of the opera house. The police called it suicide. Maria calls in lawyer Tammy Drake to get the facts. Tammy gets taken for a long ride. [Suicide]

HARDWICK, Mollie. *Perish In July.* 1990 St. Martin. A Gilbert and Sullivan fundraiser is just what Doran Fairweather and her husband Rodney Chelmarsh need in their time of grief. Then the prima donna disappears, only to be found dead in a prop chest. And Rodney has a mid-life crisis. 5th. [Revenge]

HART, Carolyn. *Something Wicked.* [Bookstore]

HILL, Reginald. *Bones And Silence.* [Suicide]

LITTLEPAGE, Layne. *Murder-By-The-Sea.* 1987 Doubleday/ Worldwide 1989. Vivienne Montrose, retired actress, agreed to take part in the Carmel theater production of *A Classic Case of Murder.* Then one of the cast died . . . for real. Matt Ross, a young writer, and Vivienne sleuth out the intricacies of some close relationships. [Where There's a Will]

LORENS, M. K. *Sweet Narcissus.* [Manuscript]

MacLEOD, Charlotte. *The Plain Old Man.* [Art]

MacLEOD, Charlotte, w/a Alisa Craig. *The Grub-And-Stakers Pinch A Poke.* [Canadian]

MARON, Margaret. *Baby Doll Games.* 1988 Bantam/ PBO. It was a Halloween performance for the children and their parents. As the little ghost danced, then floated down from a tree limb, she was impaled on a fence. Lt. Sigrid Harald, NYPD, was in the audience and stepped right in. 5th. [Children]

MORICE, Anne. *Murder In Outline.* 1979 St. Martin/ Bantam 1986. Actress Tessa Crichton was invited to judge a performance at her alma mater. She was surprised to find the school rife with gossip and petty crime. She was even more surprised to find murder. 13th.

O'DONNELL, Lillian. *Falling Star.* 1979 Putnam/ Ballantine 1987. Julia Schuyler, daughter of a famous actor, and once a great actress herself, is at the bottom of the heap. Wanting help from Mici, it comes too late. Julia was stabbed to death. Why would anyone kill a down-and-out drunk? 2nd. [Manuscript]

PALMER, William J. *The Detective And Mr. Dickens.* [Victorian]

PAUL, Barbara. *The Fourth Wall.* 1979 Doubleday/ Bantam 1987. Abigail James arrives in New York City to do a rewrite of part of her second act. She soon learns that things are happening to the cast. Who is out to close her play? And why is the whole cast at risk?

PAYNE, Laurence. *Knight Fall.* 1987 Doubleday. Sir Gerald Grantley gives his greatest performance in *King Lear*—then in the early hours of the morning he's impaled on a churchyard fence. PI Mark Savage has to decide if it's an accident, suicide, or murder. 10th. [Blackmail]

QUOGAN, Anthony. *The Fine Art Of Murder.* [Canadian]

RESNICOW, Herbert. *The Gold Gamble.* 1988 St. Martin. Alexander Gold and Burton Hanslik have invested $2.5 million in a revival of *Guys And Dolls.* Norma and Pearl are co-producing. Three days before the critic's preview, the understudy is murdered in her dressing room, and the star has first place on the billing as murderer. 5th. [Infidelity]

SIMMONS, John. *Midnight Walking.* 1986 Fawcett/ PBO. Five years ago playwright Jennifer Wilde died in a fall from her hotel window. Her last play, *Claims Past Due,* is set to open, with her sister Elene playing the lead. Elene is behaving strangely, struggling to remember who killed her sister. [Psychological]

SMITH, Kay Nolte. *Catching Fire.* 1982 Coward McCann/ Paperjacks 1986. There's trouble at the off-Broadway performance of Maeve Jerrold's play *Firestorm.* During the picketing of the theater, a man is shot. Actor Erik Dante is the suspect. He has to devise his own script to clear himself and find the killer. [Journalism]

WILHELM, Kate. *The Hamlet Trap.* 1987 St. Martin/ St. Martin 1988. The Harley Theater in Oregon was about to start a new season. When the director's niece Ginny is suspected of murdering her fiancé, PIs Charlie Meiklejohn and his wife start an intensive search that leads straight to the theater company's heart. 1st. [Old Crime]

ZILINSKY, Ursula. *A Happy English Child.* 1988 Doubleday. At a Yorkshire production of *Hamlet,* Algernon Jagat, as his final act, died. Detective Inspector Winterkill is sorting through the cast brought in for the production, knowing that the killer is still in the wings. [Mother]

V . . . IS FOR

ON VACATION

*V*ACATIONS ARE FOR REST *and relaxation, for travel, for seeing the sights, and for experiencing the taste of different foods and climates. That's what vacations are for. But not for your favorite sleuth. Travel means only a new setting for the old topic of crime and murder.*

BABSON, Marian. *Unfair Exchange.* [Kidnapping]

BARNARD, Robert. *The Case Of The Missing Brontë.* [Manuscript]

BARNARD, Robert. *The Cherry Blossom Corpse.* [Writers]

BARTH, Richard. *Deadly Climate.* 1988 St. Martin/ Ballantine 1989. Margaret Binton took a chance and won a sleek RV. She and three of her friends took off for Florida, where they came upon rows of efficiency apartments peopled with oldsters who seemed more prisoners than guests. 4th. [Drugs]

BOND, Michael. *Monsieur Pamplemousse On The Spot.* [Cooks]

BRAHMS, Caryl, and S. J. Simon. *Murder À La Stroganoff.* [Dance]

BRAND, Christianna. *Tour De Force.* 1955 Scribner/ Carroll & Graf 1988. On vacation on the Italian island of San Juan el Pirata, Inspector Cockrill can't get away from work. A fellow tourist has been stabbed to death in her hotel room. They'd only known her a short time, but her countrymen want to help find her killer. 6th. [Jealousy]

BURLEY, W. J. *Wycliffe And The Four Jacks.* [Revenge]

DILLON, Eilís. *Sent To His Account.* 1961 British Book Centre/ Perennial 1986. Miles de Cogan had inherited a large estate, Dangan House, from a cousin. As he began to settle into his new position, he found the body of Mr. Reid on his library couch. Fortunately, his ex-landlady's son, Inspector Hensley, is vacationing nearby. [Fraud]

DOBSON, Margaret. *Nightcap.* [Art]

DUNCAN, W. Glen. *Rafferty: Last Seen Alive.* [Drugs]

GILMAN, Dorothy. *Mrs. Pollifax And The Golden Triangle.* [Intrigue]

GIROUX, E. X. *A Death For A Darling.* 1985 St. Martin/ Ballantine 1986. Abigail Sanderson was making a duty visit, spending a few days with Honoria Farquson. Abigail calls her boss Robert Forsythe when she discovers that his favorite movie star is also a guest at the country house. Then a woman dies, and they have to go to work. 2nd. [Blackmail]

HILL, Reginald. *An April Shroud.* [Insurance]

HILL, Reginald. *Ruling Passion.* [Revenge]

JANCE, J. A. *Injustice For All.* [Politics]

KAYE, M. M. *Death In Berlin.* [Jewels]

KENYON, Michael. *A Free-Range Wife.* [Infidelity]

LEMARCHAND, Elizabeth. *Who Goes Home?* 1986 Walker. On vacation in the country, Superintendent Tom

Pollard and his wife see a man circling a deserted house. A few days later the house burns. Then they discover the skeleton bricked up in the chimney. [Imposter]

LINSCOTT, Gillian. *A Whiff Of Sulphur.* 1988 St. Martin. Ex-cop Birdie Linnet led the Tooth & Claw Adventure Holiday to a Caribbean island. Justin wandered off with Birdie's daughter, and there was a body in the sulphur pool. The Adventure Holiday turns into a real survival game. 3rd. [Father]

LIVINGSTON, Nancy. *Incident At Parga.* 1988 St. Martin. His nephew Matthew wanted Mr. Pringle to join a group for two weeks' sailing in the Aegean Sea. Matthew's fiancée, Liz, is surprised that he's invited the Fairchilds and their two beautiful daughters. Then Liz dies, and Mr. Pringle won't accept it as an accident. 3rd. [Getting Away With Murder]

McMULLEN, Mary. *A Grave Without Flowers.* 1983 Doubleday/ Jove 1987. Emily Devon and a friend are on vacation in England to "do" the National Trust Gardens. With a hired driver and their dog Leo, they set out for the countryside, only to land in the middle of robbery and murder.

MELVILLE, James. *Death Of A Daimyo.* [Oriental]

MORTIMER, John. *Summer's Lease.* 1988 Viking. Molly Pargeter was excited about the Italian villa she'd rented for the family for the summer. At La Felicita, Molly becomes obsessed with Mr. Kettering, owner of the villa. She stumbles on a strange "wish list." [Revenge]

MOYES, Patricia. *Down Among The Dead Men.* 1961 Holt/ Owl 1986. Emmy and Henry Tibbett are vacationing in Merrybridge Haven. Pete Rawnsley had recently drowned and there are some suspicions about his death. Now there's another mishap. Henry has to work in the dark. 2nd. [Insurance]

MURRAY, Stephen. *Salty Water.* 1989 St. Martin. Tracy Ashford wanted out of the seaside resort town; they stripped her of her beauty queen title when she stripped for a newspaper photo. Inspector Alec Stainton, on vacation, is drawn into the case when Tracy's nude body is washed up on the beach. 2nd.

NEEL, Janet. *Death On Site.* 1989 St. Martin. Inspector John McLeish and Francesca Wilson met Alan Fraser on vacation in Scotland, where Alan had a near-fatal fall. Back in London, at a construction site, Alan's next fall, from a scaffold, killed him. Only this time it was no accident. 2nd. [Fraud]

ORMEROD, Roger. *An Alibi Too Soon.* 1988 Scribner. On vacation with his wife in Wales, Inspector Richard Patton gave his old friend Llew a call. Llew begged him to drive right over. When they arrive, Llew's house is burning and he's dead. The only clue is a reference to an old crime. 3rd. [Old Crime]

PAGE, Katherine Hall. *The Body In The Kelp.* 1991 St. Martin. Vacationing on Sanpere Island, Faith Fairchild is left to her own resources when her husband is called away. To while away the time, she tries to unravel the clues embroidered into a quilt that lead to a treasure . . . and murder. 2nd. [Drugs]

WEINMAN, Irving. *Hampton Heat.* [Real Estate]

WRIGHT, Eric. *Death In The Old Country.* 1985 Scribner/Signet 1986. Inspector Charlie Salter and his wife Annie are vacationing in England. The owner of Boomewood Hotel is murdered, and Charlie is dragged into the case. It's one of those situations where no one is who he says he is. 3rd. [Imposter]

WRIGHT, Eric. *A Body Surrounded By Water.* 1987 Scribner/ Signet 1989. Charlie Salter and his family are vacationing on Prince Edward Island. His father-in-law, Montagu, is excited about the possibility of the Great Seal returning to the island. But two murders stand in the way. 5th. [Canadian]

VAMPIRES

This category may be a tiny one but it is one that has a long history and a fatal fascination. Long removed from Transylvania, the vampire may surface most anywhere and at any time. And the vampire can be quick to vanish, only to return, perhaps, in your neighborhood.

DANIELS, Philip. *The Dracula Murders.* 1986 Critic's Choice/ PBO. It was the club's annual affair, and instead of the traditional Halloween party, they decided on a Horror Ball. Then a stranger entered the festivities and all hell broke loose. [Holiday]

GREENBERG, Martin H., and Charles G. Waugh, eds. *Vamps.* 1987 DAW/ PBO. A collection of short stories featuring lady vampires. They work all night and sleep by day—from some of the leading horror story authors.

HAMBLEY, Barbara. *Those Who Hunt The Night.* 1988 Del Rey/ Del Rey 1989. The vampires of Edwardian London are being eliminated. As they lie sleeping in their coffins, the covers are being lifted, exposing them to the sun. In order to save his wife, Lydia, a vampire victim, James Asher, Oxford don, has to find clues to the killer. [Historical]

LUTZ, John. *Shadowtown.* 1988 Mysterious/ Mysterious 1989. The security guard on the set of the TV soap opera *Shadowtown* was murdered. The only witness insists the crime was committed by a "vampire." NYPD's Oxman and Tobin want the script of terror to stop. 2nd. [Television]

POPESCU, Petru. *In Hot Blood.* 1989 Fawcett/ PBO. Laura Walker, looking for a fresh start, settles in New Orleans. Meeting the Lecouveurs, she feels caught up in their powers. Even Alain, the nephew, is struggling against five centuries of unholy family tradition.

SKIPP, John, and Craig Spector. *The Light At The End.* 1986 Bantam/ PBO. Terrible things were happening on the subways beneath the streets of Manhattan. People were dying most horrible deaths. One man is on the run. He won't stop, till the light at the end.

VICTORIAN

What began as a trickle is becoming a nice little brook. There is a growing array of mystery stories set during the reign of Victoria. A few of these are based on actual crimes or historical events. Others contribute the ambience and the customs of the times for our added enjoyment. The crimes are the same, only the settings are different. [See also "Historical" and "Medieval"]

BLOCH, Robert & Andre Norton. *The Jekyll Legacy.* [Famous People]

CARR, John Dickson. *Scandal At High Chimneys.* 1959 Harper & Row/ Carroll & Graf 1988. Matthew Damon had a secret, a secret he vowed to divulge only when one of his children planned to marry. The time has come, but before he can speak, he's murdered. Private detective Jonathan Whicher had delivered the letter that started the mystery—now he's determined to end it. [Father]

FREEBORN, Richard. *The Russian Crucifix.* 1987 St. Martin. The summer of 1860 was memorable for Guy Seddenham. At the seaside resort of Ventnor, he fell in love with two women. One was later found drowned, and her crucifix was discovered in the other's bedroom. Guy must know the truth.

HARRISON, Ray. *Why Kill Arthur Potter?* 1983 Scribner/ Popular 1985. Not only does Sgt. Bragg of the City of London Police have a new constable, but he also has a new case: a simple clerk has been found dead in an alley. Bragg and Morton end up in Monaco to find the killer. 1st.

HARRISON, Ray. *Death Of An Honourable Member.* 1985 Scribner/ Berkley 1988. Sir Walter Greville, House of Commons, was dead from a typical household accident, a fall down the stairs. But a note to the coroner suggests otherwise. Sgt. Bragg and Constable Morton find themselves unraveling scandals. 3rd. [Political]

HARRISON, Ray. *Death Of A Dancing Lady.* 1986 Scribner/ Berkley 1988. Lloyds of London is worried. There are too many claims for ships that sink under mysterious conditions. Since Constable Morton is visiting Galveston, Texas, he checks out the latest missing ship. The clues, pieced together, lead straight to the Foreign Office. 4th. [Smuggling]

HARRISON, Ray. *A Season For Death.* 1987 St. Martin/ Berkley 1989. It looked like an accident: Dean Hadley at St. Paul's had become entangled in the bell rope and strangled. But as Sgt. Bragg and Constable Morton look more closely at the case, they discover a clever blackmailer who's setting his sights on royalty. 6th. [Blackmail]

HARRISON, Ray. *Harvest Of Death.* 1988 St. Martin/ Berkley 1990. Recuperating from a wound, Sgt. Bragg is with a cousin in a Dorset village. When Mr. Ollerton is found shot, Bragg cannot help but get involved. There will be another death before he discovers the "golden goose." 7th. [Blackmail]

JACKSON, Marion J. A. *The Punjat's Ruby.* [Jewels]

KEATING, H. R. F., w/a Evelyn Hervey. *The Governess.* 1983 Doubleday/ Berkley 1988. Harriet Unwin came to the Thackerton household as governess. When Mr. Thackerton is stabbed in the library, she's accused. She makes a desperate attempt to prove her innocence. Mary Vilkins has to come out of the kitchen. 1st.

KEATING, H. R. F., w/a Evelyn Hervey. *The Man Of Gold.* [Accident]

KEATING, H. R. F., w/a Evelyn Hervey. *Into The Valley Of Death.* 1986 Doubleday/ Berkley 1989. Governess Harriet Unwin got an urgent call for help from her friend Mary Vilkins. At a pub where Mary worked, the landlord has been convicted of murder. Mary knows he's innocent. Harriet puts her own life in jeopardy to cheat the hangman. 3rd. [Blackmail]

KNIGHT, Alanna. *Deadly Beloved.* 1990 St. Martin. Mabel Kellar set out by train to visit her sister, but she never arrived. Instead, her torn and blood-stained cloak, together with a butcher knife, was found along the tracks. Inspector Faro is questioning her husband, the police surgeon. 3rd. [Revenge]

LINSCOTT, Gillian. *Murder, I Presume.* 1990 St. Martin. Rivalry abounds in the excitement of exploring Africa. Peter Pentland lost a leg on the last expedition. Colonel Hardy Strethan and Philip Bright are planning rival journeys when Sebastian Ewart, out to sabotage them, is killed by a rare African poison. Peter becomes the sleuth. [Getting Away With Murder]

VICTORIAN

PALMER, William J. *The Detective And Mr. Dickens.* 1990 St. Martin. When there's a brutal murder that has its roots in the world of the London theater, Charles Dickens and Wilkie Collins join forces with Inspector William Field of the Metropolitan Protectives of London to ferret out the killer. [Theater]

PERRY, Anne. *The Cater Street Hangman.* 1979 St. Martin/ Fawcett 1985. A maid in the Ellison household was strangled. Inspector Pitt was admitted to the home to investigate the murder. His visit seems to cause a great deal of discomfort. The attraction between the Inspector and Charlotte will have to wait until the killer is contained. 1st.

PERRY, Anne. *Callander Square.* 1980 St. Martin/ Fawcett 1988. Charlotte Ellison Pitt can hardly restrain her curiosity when there are two murders in Callander Square. She has access to places where her husband could not go, and it pleases her to find him information. 2nd. [Blackmail]

PERRY, Anne. *Paragon Walk.* 1981 St. Martin/ Fawcett 1986. In sedate Paragon Walk, a young woman was brutally raped and murdered. While Inspector Pitt investigates, Charlotte manages to get inside the houses on the Walk and do her own questioning. The confrontation at the cemetery almost ends her life. 3rd. [Jealousy]

PERRY, Anne. *Resurrection Row.* 1981 St. Martin/ Fawcett 1986. Someone exhumed Lord Agustus Fitzroy-Hammond and left him sitting in a hansom cab. They reburied him, but he showed up again in a church pew. Inspector Pitt follows his leads while Charlotte pursues hers. 4th. [Prostitution]

PERRY, Anne. *Rutland Place.* 1983 St. Martin/ Fawcett 1986. It all started when Charlotte's mother lost a locket with a picture best not revealed. Now Rutland

Place is in a turmoil that ends in sudden death. Inspector Pitt is assigned the case, but he still needs Charlotte. 5th. [Incest]

PERRY, Anne. *Bluegate Fields.* 1984 St. Martin/ Fawcett 1986. The boy's body was found in the sewer at Bluegate Fields, not the best part of town. It was obvious to Inspector Pitt that the young man was from a good family. Charlotte is listening to anyone who will talk to her. 6th. [Gay]

PERRY, Anne. *Death In The Devil's Acre.* 1985 St. Martin/ Fawcett 1988. A doctor was found in Devil's Acre, a London slum. He'd been stabbed in the back and mutilated. As Inspector Pitt is looking into the case, three more bodies are discovered. Charlotte has to pretend to be divorced to gather her valuable information. 7th. [Prostitution]

PERRY, Anne. *Cardington Crescent.* 1987 St. Martins/ Fawcett 1988. Death strikes very close to home for Charlotte. Her brother-in-law George March was found dead at his morning coffee. His wife Emily is suspected. Charlotte will do almost anything to save her sister. And one of the things she does best is nose out scandals and secrets. 8th. [Father]

PERRY, Anne. *Silence In Hanover Close.* 1988 St. Martin/ Fawcett 1989. Robert Yorke's widow is about to marry someone in the Foreign Office. Inspector Pitt is asked to look very quietly into the unsolved murder of Yorke a few years earlier. Charlotte locates invaluable evidence to clear the inspector of another murder case. 9th. [Getting Away With Murder]

PERRY, Anne. *Bethlehem Road.* 1990 St. Martin. The elderly gentleman was found on Westminster Bridge, tied to a lamppost with his own scarf. This was only the first of several Members of Parliament to die. As

Inspector Pitt leads the investigation, Charlotte follows her own paths. 10th. [Revenge]

PETERS, Elizabeth. *The Crocodile On The Sandbank.* [Anthropology]

PETERS, Elizabeth. *The Curse Of The Pharaohs.* [Anthropology]

PETERS, Elizabeth. *The Mummy Case.* [Anthropology]

PETERS, Elizabeth. *Lion In The Valley.* [Anthropology]

PETERS, Elizabeth. *The Deeds Of The Disturber.* [Anthropology]

W ... IS FOR

WHERE THERE'S A WILL

THE ISSUE OF INHERITANCE shows up on a regular basis in the crime novel. After all, it lends itself nicely to being the main motive for murder. But the twists and turns of new wills or unsuspected heirs adds to the mischief of the mystery. And what if there really is no will?

ALLINGHAM, Margery. *More Work For The Undertaker.* [Smuggling]

BARNARD, Robert. *At Death's Door.* [Writer]

BARNARD, Robert. *Corpse In The Gilded Cage.* 1984 Scribner/ Dell 1988. Perce and Elsie Spender woke one morning and found they'd inherited titles and a country estate. But after a few weeks of a cold house and a long walk to the kitchen, they decided to sell it. Then Perce took a tumble over the bannister. Now there's a murder to solve.

BRAND, Christianna. *Suddenly In His Residence.* 1946 Dodd, Mead/ Bantam 1988. The family had gathered at Swanswater for the anniversary of their grandmother's death. Sir Richard decides to change his will ... again. When he's found dead, the accusations start to fly. As Inspector Cockrill homes in on the killer, a bomb falls on Swanswater. 3rd.

BREAN, Herbert. *Wilders Walk Away.* 1948 Morrow/ International Polygonics 1987. Reynold Frame, photo-journalist, went to Wilders Lane, Vermont, on an assignment for *Life*. The Wilders have a habit of not dying, they just walk away. Frame finds a fresh grave and starts digging for more. 1st. [Journalism]

BRETT, Simon. *A Nice Class Of Corpse.* 1987 Scribner/ Dell 1988. After the death of her husband, Melita Pargeter moves into a seaside home for retirees, Devereux House. She may not be as genteel as the other residents, but she knows a murder when there is one ... and then another. 1st.

CARR, John Dickson. *The Problem Of The Wire Cage.* [Ball Games]

CAVANDISH, Faith. *Silent Portrait.* 1988 Lynx/ PBO. Until a few days ago Claire Norton hadn't known she was adopted. In San Francisco she's about to meet her mother and twin sister and hear the reading of her great-grandmother's will. As soon as she arrives, the trouble starts. [Art]

CHRISTMAS, Joyce. *Suddenly In Her Sorbet.* 1988 Fawcett/ PBO. At the exclusive charity ball Helen Harpennis collapsed and died after a taste of her sorbet. Lady Margaret Priam is determined to catch the killer before NYPD Detective Sam de Vere can catch his breath. Margaret enlists Prince Paul of Italy as her Watson. 1st. [Mother]

CHRISTMAS, Joyce. *A Fête Worse Than Death.* Fawcett 1990/ PBO. Lady Margaret Priam arrived at the party at six-thirty, just in time for the screams. For her hostess, Emma, Lady Ross, lies strangled on the bathroom floor. Despite admonishers from her friend Inspector Sam de Vere, Margaret starts her own investigation. 3rd. [Real Estate]

CLARKE, Anna. *The Poisoned Web.* [Mother]

CLARKE, Anna. *Soon She Must Die.* 1983 Doubleday/ Charter 1988. Jane Bates is nursing a young heiress who has only a few months to live. She plots to match up her patient and her lover, hoping Robert can get written into Rosamund's will. But someone is trying to hurry Rosamund to the grave.

CLARKE, Anna. *Murder In Writing.* [Mystery Writer]

DeANDREA, William, w/a Philip Degrave. *Keep The Baby, Faith.* 1986 Doubleday/ Paperjacks 1988. Harry Ross has been reduced to doing the TV listing for a newspaper. Then out of the blue, Faith, his sister's friend, shows up. She's scared and pregnant. Someone from her husband's family has made several attempts on her life and that of her unborn child.

DILLON, Eilís. *Death At Crane's Court.* [Medical]

DISNEY, Doris Miles. *The Day Miss Bessie Lewis Disappeared.* 1972 Doubleday/ Zebra 1987. Henry Fletcher remembered something his ex-wife had told him about an old deed. He's about to turn the information into a lot of money. But Miss Bessie has the last word.

DRUMMOND, John Keith. *Thy Sting, Oh Death.* [Bees]

DRUMMOND, John Keith. *'Tis The Season To Be Dying.* [Christmas]

DUNLAP, Susan. *Pious Deception.* [Clergy]

EBERHART, Mignon G. *The Bayou Road.* [Historical]

EBERHART, Mignon G. *Three Days For Emeralds.* 1988 Random House/ Warner 1989. Lacy Wales had a desperate letter from her old friend Rose. She drove to the country and, as Lacy served her a soothing whiskey, Rose dropped dead. But up in Rose's bedroom is a lovingly inscribed photo of Lacy's fiancé. [Smuggling]

EMERSON, Earl W. *Poverty Bay.* 1985 Avon/ PBO. Lance Tyner has just inherited $15 million, and the rest of the family is furious. His girl, Lucy, with only $55 in her pocket, contacts PI Thomas Black: Lance is missing and she wants him found. 2nd.

FISH, Robert L. *Always Kill A Stranger.* [Intrigue]

FLINN, Denny Martin. *San Francisco Kills.* Bantam 1991/ PBO. As The priest solemnized the marriage, a shot rang out and the groom fell dead at the white satin-shod feet of his bride. Called upon by the father of the bride, Spence Holmes, possessing the same logic and deductive powers of his grandfather, unravels a complicated murder plot. [Father]

FRANKEL, Valerie. *A Deadline For Murder.* Pocket 1991/ PBO. Belle Beatrice, beautiful publisher of *Midnight*, a woman's soft-porn magazine, was strangled. According to her prophetic will PI Wanda Mallory had a week to catch the killer and inherit a half million dollars. 1st. [Medical]

GOSLING, Paula. *The Wychford Murders.* 1986 Doubleday/ Worldwide 1988. Three women have died on the Wychford towpath. Inspector Luke Abbott tries to find a connection. The link is Dr. Jennifer Eames, an old love of Luke's. As he tries to protect her, she drifts deeper into danger. [Serial Killers]

HALLERAN, Tucker. *Sudden Death Finish.* 1985 St. Martin/ St. Martin 1986. Attorney Dick Ellis has another case for PI Cam MacCardle. The youngest lawyer in the firm, Tom Horton, has been murdered in front of his own house. Cam starts examining Horton's last cases for a clue. Then Cam finds Horton's diary. 2nd.

HANSEN, Joseph. *Steps Going Down.* 1985 Foul Play/ Penguin 1986. Darryl Cutter was biding his time. The old man had promised him the business and his money. Enter Chick, young, pretty, and seductive. The old man dies that night, and Darryl spirals toward destruction. [Gay]

HENSLEY, Joe L. *Fort's Law.* 1987 Doubleday. When rich old Aunt Ruth died, her nephew Jesse was arrested. Lawyer Jack Fort defends him. Things get complicated because Jack is in love with Jesse's wife. 1st.

HILL, Reginald. *Child's Play.* 1987 Macmillan/ Warner 1988. Old Gwendoline Huby caused more trouble dead than alive. Her will stated that her missing son was to get her healthy fortune . . . if he could be found before 2015. Otherwise, three charities were to inherit. 10th.

HORNSBY, Wendy. *No Harm.* 1987 Dodd, Mead/ Worldwide 1989. Kate Teague's mother is dead—a mugging, said the police. But as Kate grieves over her loss, several attempts are made on her life. Lt. Roger Tejeda is working to keep her alive. 1st.

IRVINE, Robert. *Gone To Glory.* [Ball Games]

JOHNSTON, Jane. *Paint Her Face Dead.* [Journalism]

KAHN, Michael A. *The Canaan Legacy.* 1988 Lynx. Graham Anderson Marshall III, from a prestigious Chicago law firm, died of passion with an expensive call girl. A codicil to his will left $50,000 to care for a pet's grave. Graham never had a pet. Rachael Gold is hired by the law firm to check it out. [Lawyer]

KIJEWSKI, Karen. *Katapult.* 1990 St. Martin. Alma, Kat Colorado's adopted grandmother, called in the middle of the night. Johnny had just been found in his car, stabbed to death. As Kat digs into her gentle cousin's life, she keeps turning up things that don't fit her image of him. 2nd. [Father]

LAURENCE, Janet. *A Tasty Way To Die.* [Cooks And Cooking]

LITTLEPAGE, Layne. *Murder-By-The-Sea.* [Theater]

MacLEOD, Charlotte. *The Withdrawing Room.* [Imposter]

MARTIN, Lee. *Too Sane A Murder.* 1984 St. Martin/ Dell 1986. Just a few hours into the New Year, Ft. Worth PD Detective Deb Ralston arrives at a house where four people are dead and two children unaccounted for. Wandering around the house is twenty-eight-year-old Orlead, recently released from a mental hospital. Deb is convinced he's innocent. 1st.

MARTIN, Lee. *Murder At The Blue Owl.* 1988 St. Martin/ Worldwide 1990. Deb Ralston is visiting her friend's mother, Margali, an aging movie star. As they watch some of her old films, Margali keels over. Someone has put an ice pick in her brain. It's not too long before old crimes surface and present murder attempts abound. 3rd.

MATERA, Lia. *The Smart Money.* 1988 Bantam/ PBO. Attorney Laura DiPalma, after completing an unpopular case, returned to the town of her childhood. She had just one purpose: to get revenge on her ex-husband. Instead, she finds trouble, danger, and love. 1st. [Lawyer]

MATTESON, Stefanie. *Murder At The Spa.* [Psychic]

McCAHERY, James R. *Grave Undertaking.* Knightsbridge 1990/ PBO. Retired radio actress Lavina London agreed to accompany her friend Winnie to the funeral home to make final arrangements for her father. When the funeral director was found murdered in his best casket, Lavina can hardly wait to follow up on the mystery. 1st. [Blackmail]

McCRUMB, Sharyn. *Sick Of Shadows.* Ballantine 1990/ PBO. Elizabeth MacPherson accepts an invitation to her cousin Eileen's wedding. In her family, the first cousin to marry inherits the great-aunt's fortune, and Eileen is all ready to walk down the aisle. She doesn't make it. 1st.

McINERNY, Ralph. *Abracadaver.* 1989 St. Martin. The ring that turned up at the church magic show had the initials FG. And Frances Grice had been missing for months. Although her husband had posted a reward, he was a suspect in her disappearance. Father Dowling wants to know why Aggie Miller had the ring. 12th. [Clergy]

McMULLEN, Mary. *A Dangerous Funeral.* 1977 Doubleday/ Jove 1988. The Converse family had converged on Cape Cod to mourn the death of Uncle Philip and to hear the reading of his will. Then an old botanist was found dead on the beach. Kate Converse and her journalist cousin Jack suspect he was murdered. [Journalism]

McMULLEN, Mary . *The Gift Horse.* 1985 Doubleday/ Jove 1986. Darrell Hyde is the black sheep of the family. He knew his old aunt in Albuquerque has named him her heir. He heads for the Southwest, perhaps to hurry her along. But is someone else out to get Aunt Lally, too?

MEEK, M. R. D. *This Blessed Plot.* [Lawyer]

MEREDITH, D. R. *The Sheriff And The Branding Iron Murders.* 1985 Walker/ Avon 1986. Aging Western artist Willie Russell is bushwhacked during a tornado in the Panhandle. The person suspected is Johnny, brother of the sheriff's girlfriend. Charles has to clear his name as he stumbles around in a hundred-year-old massacre. 2nd.

MICHAELS, Barbara. *The Grey Beginnings.* [Accident]

MILLER, J. M. T. *Weatherby.* 1987 Ballantine/ PBO. Jill Thaddeus hires PI Weatherby to find her brother: Jill's afraid her father is about to disinherit both his children. Weatherby finds schemes within schemes and they all point to one person. 1st.

MORICE, Anne. *Design For Murder.* 1988 St. Martin. For twenty years Martha had cared for Aunt Dolly while her cousin Christine married and went out to Africa. Then Christine writes to say she was coming home. She wants Martha to find her a suitable house. And home she comes . . . with two husbands.

MULLER, Marcia. *Trophies And Dead Things.* 1990 Mysterious. Jerry Hilderly was shot down on the street. As Sharon McCone and her boss Hank clear out his apartment they discover a holographic will just three months old. The will disinherits his two sons and leaves his money to four strangers. Sharon has to find them. 11th. [Revenge]

NATSUKI, Shizuko. *Murder At Mt. Fuji.* [Oriental]

NEILSON, Andrew. *Dead Straight.* 1986 Fawcett/ PBO. Angelica Hofer, top race driver, watched as her lover died in a mysterious crack-up. She persuades his brother, Jonty Church, to drive in one more race to get the truth about the accident. Will it be a deadly race?

NEVINS, Francis M., Jr. *The 120-Hour Clock.* 1986 Walker/ Penguin 1987. Con man Milo Turner just had a shock. Ann Haskell, the only woman he's ever loved, is dead. It wasn't an accident. Looking into Ann's background, he finds a strange law of probate. 1st. [Revenge]

NEVINS, Francis M., Jr. *The Ninety Million Dollar Mouse.* 1987 Walker. Con man Milo Turner was hired at gunpoint to examine some handwriting samples. Is the holographic will a fake? The will leaves a $90 million company to a powerful cult, the Drakean Union. 2nd.

O'DONNELL, Lillian. *Wicked Designs.* 1980 Putnam/ Fawcett 1988. Norman was insisting that his aunt had been murdered, and he wanted Mici Anhalt from the Crime Victim's Board to find the killer. Aunt Blanche had influential friends, including a lady being gossiped about. Mici finally finds a trail to follow. 3rd. [Political]

PENN, John. *An Ad For Murder.* 1982 Scribner/ Bantam 1985. Major Tom Cheryl didn't think the book ad was so funny: "Coming soon—THE DEATH OF MAJOR CHERYL." It wasn't too long before he started having a series of accidents. Then his wife Aileen struggled to open a package and was killed.

PENN, John. *A Deadly Sickness.* 1985 Scribner/ Bantam 1986. Alan Poston and his wife, Diana, like living the good life, but Alan's father is taking much too long to die. Someone helps the old man over the edge. Then there are other deaths, and Superintendent Thorne is called in. 3rd. [Imposter]

PENN, John. *Unto The Grave.* 1987 Bantam/ PBO. Superintendent Thorne and his wife are visiting friends who run Wychwood House Hotel. An unwelcome guest ends up in the swimming pool, his head bashed in. As Thorne examines the evidence, there is another death. 4th.

PETERS, Elizabeth. *The Murders Of Richard III.* [Richard III]

PETERSON, Audrey. *Death In Wessex.* [Suicide]

PHILIPS, Edward. *Death Is Relative.* 1985 Avon/ PBO. He may be seventy, but Frank Clarke is still driven by money. His mother, ninety-three, has decided to leave half her fortune to the old-age home. Frank sets out to liquidate as many of her assets as possible before she dies. Then cousin Estelle comes to visit . . . . [Gay]

PICKARD, Nancy. *Generous Death.* 1987 Pocket/ PBO. Eccentric Arnie Culverson promised the Port Frederick Civic Foundation all his millions. When he died in his antique bed in the museum, he'd changed his will. Then Jenny Cain, director, becomes suspicious when another benefactor dies. 1st.

PICKARD, Nancy. *Bum Steer.* 1990 Pocket/ Pocket 1990. Cat Benet IV is dying and is leaving the Port Frederick Civic Foundation his 4 million dollar Crossbones Ranch. Jenny Cain flies out to Kansas just as Cat is murdered in his hospital bed. There are some things about his will that need looking into. 6th. [Imposter]

PRATHER, Richard S. *The Amber Effect.* 1986 Tor/ Tor 1987. Shell Scott answered the door to find a naked woman standing in the hall. The lady had a dead man in her apartment, and she says he tried to kill her. Shell dives into the puzzle and dodges killers. 31st.

QUEST, Erica. *Death Walk.* 1988 Walker. Kate Maddox has just been appointed detective chief inspector, the first woman to hold the post. Belle Latimer, victim of a hit-and-run, is murdered. Then her accountant is poisoned. The Cotswold murder case is a challenge, and Kate's out to prove herself. [Revenge]

RADLEY, Sheila. *A Quiet Road To Death.* 1984 Scribner/ Penguin 1985. Angela's cat was beheaded and a note left for her: "Your turn next." Inspector Quantrill had been investigating the beheading of a young woman, so the note particularly interested him. But Angela ended up being run over. 5th.

RHODE, John. *The Cloverton Affair.* 1933 Dodd, Mead/ Perennial 1988. John Cloverton died suddenly. His old friend Dr. Priestly was convinced he'd been murdered, but the autopsy report said otherwise. Priestly decided on a séance and a trap to get the killer. 14th. [Witches]

ROBINSON, Peter. *A Dedicated Man.* [Infidelity]

SANDERS, George. *Crime On My Hands.* [Hollywood]

SHANNON, Dell. *Blood Count.* 1986 Morrow/ Worldwide 1988. Mrs. Canaday was found in a car wreck, but something else had caused the bash behind her ear. Her family had no idea why she'd planned a few days in Los Angeles. Between his other cases, Mendoza must find out why she was killed. 37th.

SHAW, Patricia. *Never Paint A Stranger.* [Art]

SHERWOOD, John. *A Shot In The Arm: Death At The BBC.* 1983 Scribner/ International Polygonics 1985. 1937, London: Angela Chatham is about to destroy her husband Tony's career at the BBC—she wants a divorce. Soon accusations are flying as fast as the bullets. The police have their suspicions but no evidence. [Television]

SPRINKLE, Patricia Houch. *Murder In The Charleston Manner.* [Accident]

TAYLOR, Elizabeth Atwood. *The Cable Car Murder.* 1981 St. Martin/ Ivy 1988. Maggie Elliott had never been close to her half-sister, but she was saddened when Celia died, run down by a cable car. Now, two years later, her brother-in-law is about to remarry, and Maggie doesn't like the new bride one bit. 1st. [Christmas]

TAYLOR, Elizabeth Atwood. *Murder At Vassar.* [Academic]

THOMPSON, Gene. *Nobody Cared For Kate.* [Hollywood]

TRAVIS, Elizabeth. *Deadlines.* 1987 Scribner/ St. Martin 1989. Sally Templeton was shocked when she arrived at her grandmother's Connecticut estate to find her drugged and bedridden. There are a lot of people in and out of her grandmother's house, and Sally looks at each one carefully. Does one of them want her dead?

TRIPP, Miles. *Video Vengeance.* [Psychological]

WENTWORTH, Patricia. *Wicked Uncle.* [Blackmail]

WENTWORTH, Patricia. *Nothing Venture.* 1932 Lippincott/ Warner 1990. Ambroase Weare's will is very clear. Jervis has three months to marry after his grandfather's death to inherit a fortune. Just two days before the wedding, Jervis is jilted. His ex-fiancée will inherit unless he finds a wife. [Old Crime]

WENTWORTH, Patricia. *The Brading Collection.* [Jewels]

WENTWORTH, Patricia. *Through the Wall.* 1950 Lippincott/ Perennial 1989. Hard-working Marion Brand inherited a large fortune from an unknown uncle and soon moved down to Cove House. There lived the closer relatives that were passed over in her favor. Soon there's a murder and the police request the help of Miss Silver. 19th. [Blackmail]

WENTWORTH, Patricia. *The Watersplash.* 1951 Lippincott/ Warner 1987. One Friday night William Jackson drowned in the watersplash near the church. A week later Clarice Dean drowned in the same way. Maud Silver and Frank Abbott are finding jealousy, blackmail, and greed in quiet Greenings. 20th. [Blackmail]

WENTWORTH, Patricia. *The Benevent Treasure.* [Old Crime]

WENTWORTH, Patricia. *The Alington Inheritance.* 1958 Lippincott/ Perennial 1990. When her guardian was dying she told Jenny Hill that the Alington estate really belonged to her and there was a letter to prove it. The relatives at Alington will do anything to prevent Jenny from taking over the estate. Miss Silver steps in to assist her. 31st. [Father]

WERNER, Patricia. *The Will.* 1988 Paperjacks/ PBO. Leigh Castle returned to Culver City for her mother's funeral. The shock came at the reading of the will. Hania, the eldest, inherited everything. Then, at the old copper mine, Anastasia was found dead. Leigh and the lawyer Broden Lancaster sort through the past for answers. [Revenge]

WILCOX, Collin. *Silent Witness.* 1990 Tor. Constance Hale Price was murdered in her wine-country home while her husband and son slept. At least that's what her husband told the sheriff. But her sister Janice can't quite believe the story. She hires Alan Berkhardt to find the truth. 2nd. [Father]

WOODS, Sara. *Bloody Instructions.* 1962 Harper & Row/ Avon 1986. Elderly solicitor James Winter died at teatime in his chambers, a dagger in his back. Antony Maitland is defending a visitor to the office that afternoon, actor Joseph Dowling, who had the bloody dagger. 2nd. [Lawyer]

WOODS, Sara. *They Stay For Death.* [Medical]

WITCHES, CURSES, AND A LITTLE VOODOO

The "dark on the other side" often makes for an added element in the mystery story. Ghosts wander in and out of rooms, and spirits hint of hidden secrets. Folklore and a curse or two take their places beside witchcraft, voodoo, and the occult.

ADAMSON, M. J. *A February Face.* Bantam 1987/ PBO. Balthazar Marten was handed a strange case in Puerto Rico. On a remote beach five bodies have washed up, all embalmed but shot in the head. The word is out that it's voodoo. With Sixto Cardenas he heads for Lozia and danger. 2nd. [Real Estate]

BAXT, George. *Satan Is A Woman.* 1987 International Polygonics/ PBO. Visiting London, Max Van Larsen, NYPD, attends a witches' sabbath. He promptly loses his mind and returns to New York City in a straightjacket. After the usual chicken soup doesn't work, Sylvia flies to London for the answers. 3rd. [Smuggling]

BEATON, M. C. *Death Of An Outsider.* 1988 St. Martin/ Ivy 1990. Moved to the village of Cnothan, Constable Hamish Macbeth gets a chilly reception. Mainwaring, another newcomer to Cnothan, complains of witchcraft. Macbeth is skeptical until a body turns up. 3rd. [Real Estate]

CAMPBELL, Robert. *The Cat's Meow.* 1988 NAL/ Signet 1990. Something is happening around sewer inspector Jimmy Flannery's parish church. There's a suspicion of a black mass just before Father Damen is found dead. Someone wrote "CAT'S MEOW" on the street. 5th.

CARVIC, Heron. *Witch Miss Seeton.* 1971 Harper & Row/Berkley 1988. A cow was found dead in Plummergen, and it looked like some kind of ritual. Probably Nuscience. And all those people are handing over their money in the name of religion. If the police could just get Miss Seeton to infiltrate this group . . . . 3rd. [Fraud]

CHESBRO, George C. *An Affair Of Sorcerers.* 1979 Simon & Schuster/ Dell 1988. A psychic healer is in jail, accused of murder. A friend wants Mongo to clear him. The path leads to more bodies and a scientific experiment that goes very wrong. 3rd.

CHRISTOPHER, Constance. *Dead Man's Flower.* 1988 Paperjacks/ PBO. PI August Lee found the body of a young woman in a park in Manhattan. As a former undercover cop, she puts her experience to work, first at a modeling agency and then with Dr. Hugh Boulanger, Haiti's master of voodoo. [Prostitution]

CRAMER, Kathryn, and David G. Hartwell. *Christmas Ghosts* [Christmas]

DRAKE, Alison. *Black Moon.* Ballantine 1989/ PBO. The dancer's body was found in a dumpster on Tango Key. For Homicide Detective Aline Scott, her investigation takes her back to a series of murders that happened over fifty years ago and the dark world of Santería, a mystic Cuban religion. 3rd. [Old Crime]

FRASER, Antonia. *The Cavalier Case.* [Television]

GREELEY, Andrew M. *Happy Are The Meek.* 1985 Warner/ PBO. Father Blackie had a strange problem to solve: Mrs. Quinlin was insisting that her husband's ghost was haunting her house, just because he didn't have a Christian burial. It looked like an exorcism was in order. 2nd. [Clergy]

GREENWOOD, John. *Mists Over Mosley.* 1986 Walker/ Bantam 1987. Strange things are happening in Upper Marldale. The church clock winds itself, and cats refuse to go out after dark. Inspector Jack Mosley is sent to investigate and finds a coven of witches. Then an artist friend is found hanged. 4th. [Real Estate]

HAGAN, Lorinda. *Winter Roses.* 1985 Leisure/ PBO. Calling off her marriage the day before the ceremony, Leslie flees to her aunt's house in Virginia City, Nevada. There are stories about Aunt Rose's house; it's supposed to be haunted. When Leslie disappears, Rose has to use her wits as a mystery writer to solve a real puzzle. [Mystery Writer]

KEMP, Sarah. *What Dread Hand.* [Pathologist]

LEMARCHAND, Elizabeth. *Troubled Waters.* 1982 Walker/ Walker 1985. American Edward Tuke came to Woodcombe to see a genealogist about tracing his family. That afternoon he was found face down in a brook—a dreadful accident. In a short time letters arrive at the police station screaming "cover-up." Pollard and Toye get the assignment. 13th.

LEWIS, Roy. *The Devil Is Dead.* 1990 St. Martin. Planning officer Arnold Landon is examining the abandoned St. Michael's Church at Kentside. It was supposed to be the site of the ancient Raging Wolf Cult. There under the rose hedge he discovered the body of a dog. But the next body would be that of a man. 5th. [Manuscript]

MacLEOD, Charlotte. *Wrack And Rune.* [Antiques]

MacLEOD, Charlotte. *The Curse Of The Giant Hogweed.* 1985 Doubleday/ Avon 1986. Professor Peter Shandy and two of his colleagues from Balaclava Agricultural College went to Wales where there's a problem with oversized hogweed. Helping to eradicate the giant pest, Shandy falls under a spell. 5th.

McCLINTICK, Malcolm. *Mary's Grave.* [Holiday]

MICHAELS, Barbara. *Ammie, Come Home.* 1968 Meredith/ Berkley 1987. Sara was staying at her Aunt Ruth's house in Georgetown while attending the university.

But there was a disturbed spirit living at the house and it attached itself to Sara. Only a search into the history of the house will quiet the ghost.

MICHAELS, Barbara. *The Dark On The Other Side.* 1970 Dodd, Mead/ Berkley 1988. Linda Randolph felt stranger and stranger: the house talked to her. Then Michael came to do a series of articles about her husband, Gordon. Michael watches as Linda seems to deteriorate, and a witch comes to dinner.

MICHAELS, Barbara. *Wait For What Will Come.* 1978 Dodd, Mead/ Berkley 1990. Carla Tregallas was the last surviving relative to bear the family name and that's why Cousin Walter left her the old family mansion on the Cornish coast. But with the house came an ancient curse about to be reawakened. [Americans In England]

MICHAELS, Barbara. *Here I Stay.* 1983 Congdon & Weed/Tor 1985. Andrea is trying to make a living running a country inn, while she makes a home for her convalescent brother Jim. A ghost intrudes.

MICHAELS, Barbara. *Be Buried In The Rain.* 1985 Atheneum/ Berkley 1986. Julie Newcomb was all but forced to travel to the old family home in Virginia to care for her ailing grandmother. On the road she discovers the skeletons of a woman and a baby. She also is beginning to feel a presence in the house. [Old Crime]

MITCHELL, Gladys. *Here Lies Gloria Mundy.* 1982 St. Martin/ Paperjacks 1986. Anthony Wotton hadn't seen Gloria Mundy for years, until she showed up at his country estate and stayed for lunch. When a small house on the estate burned, Gloria died in the fire. So how come she was seen in London a week later? Has Gloria returned as a witch? 61st.

PAINE, Michael. *Cities Of The Dead.* [Archeology]

RHODE, John. *The Cloverton Affair.* [Where There's A Will]

SIMS, L. V. *Death In The Family.* 1987 Charter/ PBO. Pete's niece is missing; her mother says she's run away. Her mutilated body is found in a closet at Winchester House. Detective Dixie Struther, Pete's partner, tries to keep him boxed in while she follows a satanic trail. 2nd. [Incest]

STEWART, Mary. *Thornyhold.* 1988 Morrow/ Fawcett 1989. When cousin Geillis died, she remembered her namesake fondly and left her the house Thornyhold. It wasn't till she moved into the home that Gilly discovered that her cousin had been a witch, and some of her powers are encroaching on Gilly.

THAYER, Nancy. *Spirit Lost.* 1988 Scribner/ Avon 1989. John Constable wanted to paint, so he and his wife Willy bought a centuries-old house on Nantucket Island. Safe in his attic with his paints and canvases, John encounters a ghost, a young woman who becomes his obsession. Can Willy save her husband? [Holiday For Murder]

THOREAU, David. *The Book Of Numbers.* [Intrigue]

VAN DE WETERING, Janwillem. *Tumbleweed.* [Prostitution]

WALLACE, Marilyn. *A Case Of Loyalties.* 1986 St. Martin/ Ballantine 1987. Tricia Rayborn stole a car and went for a joyride. Soon she was in the Oakland Police Station. The car had been used in the killing of Cliff Hawkins, and she's the prime suspect. It takes patient digging for homicide detectives Carlos Cruz and Jay Goldstein to find the real murderer. 1st.

WILHELM, Kate. *The Dark Door.* 1988 St. Martin/ Tudor 1990. Someone has been setting fires to old abandoned hotels or other empty buildings throughout the country. The insurance companies want Charlie Meiklejohn to head up an independent investigation. Somehow, madness is involved. 3rd. [Arson]

WOODS, Sara. *Naked Villainy.* 1987 St. Martin/ Avon 1988. Emile has been arrested for the murder of his father. His fingerprints were on the poker. Antony Maitland, QC, is to try the case. In examining what happened that night, Antony discovers that in addition to the murder there was a black mass. 48th. [Father]

WITNESS PROTECTION PROGRAM

The witness protection program was devised to give a person a new identity and a new life, a protection from retaliation. Finding someone so protected is supposed to be impossible. But, as with any puzzle, this one can also be solved with persistence.

BABSON, Marian. *Death Swap.* 1984 Walker/ Walker 1987. Nancy Harper was reluctant to swap her house in New Hampshire for a place outside London so her husband could do some research. Then Arnold had an accident in the car and someone tried to push him in front of a bus. Why is someone out to kill him? [Americans In England]

BRANDON, Jay. *Tripwire.* 1987 Bantam/ PBO. Elizabeth Truett stopped by the office late one night and saw her boss murdered. Next thing she knew, she and her husband had been hidden away. There's a contract out on her, and she's terrified that her son Bryan holds the paper.

CODY, Liza. *Stalker.* 1984 Scribner/ Warner 1986. The simple case had gone foul for PI Anna Lee. Mr.

Thurman was looking for a man who had taken money from him under false pretenses. The culprit was found dead, and Thurman vanished, leaving Brierly Security with an unsolved mystery. 3rd.

COOPER, Susan Rogers. *Other People's Houses.* 1990 St. Martin. Lois Bell was a teller at the Longbranch Bank. But when Sheriff Milton Kovak arrived at her house she was sitting in the car in the garage and her husband and three children were dead, carbon monoxide poisoning. That wasn't the only thing wrong at the house. 3rd. [Suicide]

DEAVER, Jeffrey Wilds. *Manhattan Is My Beat.* Bantam 1989/ PBO. The old man was dead, shot to death in his seedy apartment. Rune had come to pick up the video movie he'd rented eighteen times in the past month. The movie is *Manhattan Is My Beat* based on a true crime with a million dollars still missing. 1st. [Old Crime]

DELINSKY, Barbara. *Fingerprints.* 1988 Worldwide/ PBO. Carly Quinn had been the chief witness at an arson trial. The man she sent to prison had vengeful friends. Even though she's in the witness protection program, she's finding it hard to relax. She's also very alone, until she meets Ryan Cornell.

HILLERMAN, Tony. *The Ghostway.* [Indians]

PATTI, Paul. *Silhouettes.* 1990 St. Martin. An aging mobster was found dead in his Palm Beach mansion, a failure of the Witness Protection Program. As Andy Amato and his wife Gabrielle investigate for the police department, there's a rash of mobster murders. Someone has penetrated the secret witness list. 1st. [Corruption]

STUART, Anne. *Escape Out Of Darkness.* 1987 Dell/ PBO. Maggie Bennett, lawyer for Third World Causes, is always off on some jaunt or another. This time she's assigned to transport Mack Pulaski, recording producer, from his hideout in Utah to Houston. Mack had seen something he shouldn't have. Someone wants him dead. 1st. [Drugs]

WRITERS AND THEIR CONVENTIONS

Writers are either the inquisitive detective or the deserving victim in the current crop of mystery stories. They may also play the benign role of conduit for the murder. Whatever role the writer plays, the world of publishing makes a delightful setting for murder.

ABERCROMBIE, Barbara. *Run For Your Life.* 1984 Morrow/ Fawcett 1986. Training for the marathon, Sara Hoyt decided to write a book about a woman training for the marathon. Her book has a lot of suspense. Then her life starts to mirror her writing.

BARNARD, Robert. *Death Of A Literary Widow.* 1979 Scribner/ Dell 1988. Oswaldston was a grimy town; its only claim to fame was the late Walter Machin, writer. He'd left behind two manuscripts and two wives. Now there's a revival of his work, and his first wife, Hilda, is dead. An accident? Or was the fire supposed to cover up a murder? [Imposter]

BARNARD, Robert. *The Cherry Blossom Corpse.* 1987 Scribner/ Dell 1988. Perry Trethowan of Scotland Yard had been persuaded by his sister to join her at the Romantic Novelist's Association meeting in Bergen, Norway. And when best-selling writer Amanda Fairchild is found floating in a fjord, someone had more than romance on his or her mind. 3rd. [On Vacation]

BARNARD, Robert. *At Death's Door.* 1988 Scribner/ Dell 1989. Cordelia Mason had come to the Sussex village to gather information for a book about her actress mother, Dame Myra. She was to interview the famous writer Benedict Cotterell, the father she didn't know. Then Dame Myra was found dead in a room over the local pub. [Where There's A Will]

BRADBURY, Ray. *Death Is A Lonely Business.* [Serial Killer]

BRYANT, Dorothy. *Killing Wonder.* [Suicide]

CLARKE, Anna. *The Mystery Lady.* 1986 Doubleday/ Charter 1989. Paula Glenning's publisher wants her to do a biography of Rosie O'Grady, the romance writer and mystery lady. With James at her side, Paula starts the research. As she reads through the novelist's publications, something doesn't fit. 3rd. [Imposter]

CLARKE, Anna. *The Deathless And The Dead.* Charter 1989/PBO. John Broome has come over from Oxford to talk to Lord Heron about Emily Wetherington, a Victorian poetess. While he gathers material for his book, John senses that things are not quite right between the lord and his lady. [Old Crime]

CLARKE, Anna. *The Lady In Black.* Charter 1990/ PBO. Reader George Meredith at Chapman & Hall was handed a manuscript to evaluate. It had been left at the office by a young woman dressed in black and closely veiled. Meredith has the strong suspicion that the novel is really a confession to murder. [Victorian]

CLINE, Edward. *First Prize.* [Missing Person]

COOPER, Natasha. *A Common Death.* 1990 Crown. Willow King, part-time civil servant, has kept the other part of her life secret for years. Under the name Cressida Woodruffe, she writes romantic novels. When her boss is murdered, Willow lies about her whereabouts to protect her secret and she becomes a suspect. [Fraud]

CORNWELL, Patricia D. *Body Of Evidence.* [Pathologist]

COYNE, P. J. *Manuscript For Murder.* 1987 Dodd, Mead. Hardy West, author, told his agent Ned Spearbroke that he was writing a political exposé using tapes from a man named McKendrick. The next day McKendrick is dead and West is missing. More murders occur. 1st. [Blackmail]

DAVEY, Jocelyn. *A Dangerous Liaison.* [Revenge]

DUFFY, Margaret. *A Murder Of Crows.* [Intrigue]

DUFFY, Margaret. *Death Of A Raven.* [Intrigue]

ECCLES, Marjorie. *Death Of A Good Woman.* 1989 Doubleday. When the snow finally melted in Lavenstock, it gave up the body of Fleur Saville, historical romance writer, missing since three days before Christmas. At first Chief Inspector Mayo thought she'd been just another run-away wife. But now it's murder. 2nd. [Blackmail]

FRIEDMAN, Mickey. *A Temporary Ghost.* 1989 Viking/ Penguin 1990. Georgia Lee Maxwell was hired to ghostwrite a book for Vivien Howard, whose husband had been murdered in their New York City apartment two years before. A dark cloud still hangs over Vivien as it does on Mas Rose, the farm house in Provence where they are staying. 2nd. [Infidelity]

GOSLING, Paula. *Hoodwink.* [Revenge]

HANDLER, David. *The Man Who Died Laughing.* 1988 Bantam/ PBO. Ghost-writer Hoagy Hoag was in Hollywood with his dog Lulu. He's working on Sonny Day's memoirs. Someone wants to kill the book, and Sonny is shot to death. To stay alive, Hoagy has to find the killer. 1st. [Children]

HANDLER, David. *The Man Who Would Be F. Scott Fitzgerald.* 1990 Bantam/ PBO. Hoagy was hired to ghostwrite the life of novelist Cameron Noyes. They had barely started the project when his editor died in a fall. But when Cam's girlfriend was found murdered with his bowie knife and Cam disappears, Hoagy was on the trail. 3rd. [Fraud]

KITTREDGE, Mary. *Murder In Mendocino.* 1987 Walker/ Worldwide 1990. Charlotte Kent is in Pelican Rock, California, working on a history of Stanley Hardwick, physician in the early days of the town. Someone else wants to write the same book, but she's found murdered. Is there a plot to stop the history from being published? 1st.

LIVINGSTON, Jack. *Hell-Bent For Election.* 1988 St. Martin/ Signet 1991. Joe Binney was called to West Virginia to take on a case. When a woman was killed in an explosion, it seems unrelated. He stumbles into a web of power unlike anything he knows and uncovers a lot of old crime. 4th. [Getting Away With Murder]

McCRUMB, Sharyn. *Bimbos Of The Death Sun.* TSR 1987/ PBO. The featured writer at the Rubicon was none other than Appin Dungannon, a most popular and most detested cult author. He is killed by a bullet to his heart, and it takes mild-mannered Dr. James Owens Mega, author of the *Bimbos of the Death Sun*, to play detective.

McIVER, N. J. *Come Back, Alice Smythereene!.* 1985 St. Martin/ Paperjacks 1986. Poet and critic Arnold Simon leads a double life. He's also Alice Smythereene, steamy romance writer. Sherry Windsor, who poses as Alice, has vanished, and Arnold is trying to locate her. Now he's cast as a victim. [Imposter]

MOFFAT, Gwen. *Rage.* 1990 St. Martin. Travel writer Timothy Argent is missing in the California wilderness. His publisher wants Miss Melinda Pink, gothic writer, to follow his trail and find out what happened to him. She quickly learns that Argent wasn't traveling alone. 13th. [Jealousy]

MULLER, Marcia. *The Legend Of The Slain Soldiers.* 1985 Walker/ Signet 1987. Elena Oliverez got an emergency call from her mother. Ciro Cisneros, retired history professor, had been found dead at the pool, and her mother is yelling murder. What was the book Ciro was working on? And who didn't want it finished? 2nd. [Old Crime]

MURRAY, Stephen. *Fetch Out No Shroud.* [Old Crime]

PAPAZOGLOU, Orania. *Sweet, Savage Death.* 1984 Doubleday/ Penguin 1985. Patience McKenna wrote romance novels to finance her serious writing. At the third annual Conference of American Writers of Romance, a murderer is hiding out. Patience has to find the killer to save herself. 1st. [Cats]

PAPAZOGLOU, Orania. *Wicked, Loving Murder.* 1985 Doubleday/ Penguin 1986. Patience McKenna is working for *Writing* magazine when a man falls out of a closet and into her arms, dead. When the second corpse turns up, her new friend Ivy Tree is arrested. Patience starts her own investigation. 2nd.

PAPAZOGLOU, Orania. *Death's Savage Passion.* 1986 Doubleday/ Penguin 1987. This time Patience McKenna is in the middle of a battle between the Mystery Writers of America and Writers of Romantic Suspense. But the bodies start to pile up, and she has to go back to investigating murder. 3rd.

PAPAZOGLOU, Orania. *Rich, Radiant Slaughter.* 1988 Doubleday. True-crime writer Patience McKenna is on her first book tour, and her last. At a book signing in Baltimore, Pay finds an avid mystery reader under the table, dead. She can't help but get involved. 4th.

PETERS, Elizabeth. *Die For Love.* 1984 Congdon & Weed/ Tor 1987. Attending the Historical Romance Writers of the World Conference—tax deductible—is librarian Jacqueline Kirby. Dubretta Duberstein, scandal columnist, dies. Then Valerie Valentine, mortally threatened, asks Jacqueline for her help. 3rd. [Imposter]

SHANKMAN, Sarah aka Alice Storey. *Impersonal Attraction.* 1985 St. Martin/ Paperjacks 1987. Annie Tannenbaum is teaching a course on writing at San Francisco State while her best friend Samantha is the reporter on the serial killer stalking Mt. Diablo. [Serial Killer]

SMITH, Joan. *The Polka Dot Nude.* Jove 1989/ PBO. Biographer Audrey Dane was writing up the memoirs of Hollywood star Rosalie Hart. She had the personal diaries and papers and a portrait of the actress. Suddenly all her materials, her manuscript and the painting are stolen. [Art]

STEPHAN, Leslie. *Reprise.* 1988 St. Martin. Hampford, Massachusetts, wasn't too pleased with Orianna Soule's script for the town's tricentennial pageant—some of the history was better forgotten. Upset, Orianna threatened to publish it in a book. Then they found her dead. 3rd.

TAYLOR, Phoebe Atwood. *The Mystery Of The Cape Cod Tavern.* 1934 Norton/ Foul Play 1985. Writer Eve Prence turned the two-hundred-year-old house into an inn again. She surrounded herself with other writers as much as she could. Now Eve is found dead, in a room with a blind boy. Asey Mayo arrives to find the killer. 4th.

UPFIELD, Arthur W. *An Author Bites The Dust.* [Australian]

WALLACE, Carol McD. *Walking Dream.* 1987 St. Martin/ Berkley 1989. Sarah Llewellyn was researching American heiresses and their British husbands when she was invited to Saltire to examine the papers of Lauretta Wright. But it wasn't until Sarah went to Neville Park, where the rest of Lauretta's papers were, that the trouble started. [Drugs]

WELLS, Tobias. *Of Graves, Worms And Epitaphs.* [Old Crimes]

WESLEY, Carolyn. *King's Castle.* 1987 Walker. Elena Stevens, writer, found out by accident that her father was munitions magnate Rainey King. She finagles a writing assignment at his home. There is a house full of secrets, and someone wants her to return to New York City . . . very soon. [Father]

BRITISH WOMEN MYSTERY WRITERS

*I*NCLUDED FOR YOUR ENJOYMENT *is the following list of British women mystery writers. Some of the authors have been around for a long while, and others are recent additions to the field. Only those who have had a publication since 1985 are annotated in the preceding pages. A few of the women might be considered gothic writers, but are included nevertheless. The list is not meant to be inclusive, just convenient.*

Joan Aiken
Catherine Aird
Stella Allan
Margery Allingham
Evelyn Anthony

Marian Babson
M. C. Beaton
Josephine Bell
Evelyn Berckman
Charity Blackstock
Christianna Brand
Gwendoline Butler

Dorothy Cannell
Sarah Caudwell
Agatha Christie
Anna Clarke
Ann Cleeves
Liza Cody

Anthea Cohen
Leela Cutler

Elizabeth Daly
June Drummond
Margaret Duffy
Dorothy Dunnett

Margaret Erskine

Ann C. Fallon
E. X. Ferrars
Joan Fleming
Anthea Fraser
Antonia Fraser
Celia Fremlin
Frances Fyfield

B. M. Gill
E. X. Giroux

Paula Gosling
Lesley Grant-Adamson

Palma Harcourt
Mollie Hardwick
S. T. Haymon
Evelyn Hervey
Georgette Heyer
Patricia Highsmith
Jane Aiken Hodge
Charlotte Hunt
Elspeth Huxley

P. D. James

M. M. Kaye
Mary Kelly
Sarah Kemp

Elizabeth Lemarchand
Gillian Linscott

Jessica Mann
Laurie Mantell
Minette Marrin
Ngaio Marsh
M. R. D. Meek
Jennie Melville
Gladys Mitchell
Gwen Moffat
Susan Moody
Anne Morice
Patricia Moyes

Magdalen Nabb

Anne Perry
Ellis Peters
Stella Phillips
Joyce Porter

Erica Quest

Sheila Radley
Ruth Rendell

Dorothy L. Sayers
Dorothy Simpson
Joan Smith
Shelly Smith
Jean Stubbs

Josephine Tey
Estelle Thompson
June Thomson

Barbara Vine

Mignon Warner
Patricia Wentworth
Ethel Lina White
Pauline Glen Winslow
Sara Woods

Margaret Yorke

FEMALE DETECTIVES

*O*NE OF THE MOST FREQUENT *requests has been for mysteries about women detectives. This is a listing of women detectives who are series characters. The women may be professional or amateur, and are accompanied by their partners or spouses. Their professions have been added. Again, because of their popularity, the notation has been made if the author is British. The vast majority of the authors listed are also humorous.*

AMES, Delano: Jane, mystery writer, and Dagobert Brown, lawyer. British.
ANDERSON, James: Jessica Fletcher, mystery writer.
ARNOLD, Margot: Penny Spring, anthropologist, and Toby Glendower, archaeologist. British.

BARNES, Linda: Carlotta Carlyle, former Boston cop, private investigator.
BARTH, Richard: Margaret Binton, widow.
BEATON, M. C.: Constable Hamish Macbeth and Priscilla Halburton-Smythe. Scotland.
BECK, K. K.: Iris Cooper, Stanford student, and Jack Clancy, reporter.
BELFORTE, Sophie: Molly Rafferty, history professor.
BERNE, Karin: Ellie Gordon, manager for law office.
BERRY, Carole: Bonnie Indermill, free-lance secretary.
BIEDERMAN, Marcia: Grace Stark, bail-bondswoman.
BLACK, Lionel: Kate, journalist, and Henry Theobald, barrister. British.
BORTHWICK, J. S.: Sarah Deane, English professor, and Dr. Alex McKenzie.
BRETT, Simon: Mrs. Pargeter, widow.

CANNELL, Dorothy: Ellie Simon, interior designer. British.
CARL, Lillian Stewart: Rebecca Reed, historian.
CARLSON, P. M.: Maggie Ryan, statistician, and Nick O'Connor, actor.
CARVIC, Heron: Miss Emily Seeton, retired art teacher. British.
CAUDWELL, Sarah: Julia Larwood, lawyer. British.
CHASE, Elaine Raco: Nikki Holden, journalist, and Roman Cantrell, private investigator.
CHRISTIE, Agatha: Miss Jane Marple, spinster. British.
CHRISTIE, Agatha: Mrs. Ariadne Oliver, mystery writer. British.
CHRISTIE, Agatha: Tuppence and Tommy Beresford, private investigators. British.
CHRISTMAS, Joyce: Lady Margaret Priam, a lady of leisure.
CLARKE, Anna: Paula Glenning, English professor. British.
CLEEVES, Ann: Molly and George Palmer-Jones, birdwatchers. British.
CODY, Liza: Anna Lee, private investigator. British.
COKER, Carolyn: Andrea Perkins, art restorer.
CONANT, Susan: Holly Winter, journalist.
CORNWELL, Patricia: Kay Scarpetta, Chief Medical Examiner.
CORRINGTON, John William and Joyce H. Corrington: Denise Lemoyne, assistant district attorney; Wes Colwin, reporter; and "Rat" Trapp, New Orleans Police Department.
CRESPI, Trella: Simona Griffo, advertising.
CREWS, Lary: Veronica Slade, radio talk-show host.
CROSS, Amanda: Kate Fansler, English professor.
CUTLER, Leela: Lettie Winterbottom, mystery writer, and her niece Julia. British.

D'AMATO, Barbara: Cat Marsala, free-lance journalist.
DAVIS, Dorothy Salisbury: Julie Hayes, journalist.
DELMAN, David: Sgt. Helen Horowitz and Lt. Jacob Horowitz, Nassau Police Department.
DENTINGER, Jane: Jocelyn O'Roarke, actress.

FEMALE DETECTIVES 437

DEVON, D. G.: Temple Kent, fashion model.
DRAKE, Alison aka T. J. MacGregor: Aline Scott, homicide detective.
DRUMMOND, John Keith: Matilda Worthing, retired court reporter, and her housemate Martha Shaw.
DUFFY, Margaret: Ingrid Langley, novelist, and her husband Patrick Gillard, MI5. British.
DUNLAP, Susan: Vejay Haskell, meter reader.
DUNLAP, Susan: Jill Smith, homicide detective.
DUNLAP, Susan: Kiernan O'Shaughnessy, MD, PI.

FERRARS, E. X.: Virginia Freer and her ex-husband Felix. British.
FRANKEL, Valerie: Wanda Mallory, Do It Right Detective Agency.
FRASER, Antonia: Jemima Shore, television reporter. British.
FREELING, Nicholas: Arlette, widow of Inspector Van der Valk. Dutch.
FRIEDMAN, Mickey: Georgia Lee Maxwell, journalist.
FYFIELD, Frances: Helen West, Crown Prosecutor, and Detective Superintendent Geoffrey Bailey. British.

GEORGE, Elizabeth: Detective Thomas Lynley and his partner Sergeant Barbara Havers.
GILMAN, Dorothy: Mrs. Pollifax, widow, part-time CIA.
GIRDNER, Jaqueline: Kate Jasper, PI.
GIROUX, E. X.: Abigail Sanderson, legal secretary, and Robert Forsythe, barrister. British.
GORDON, Alison: Kate Henry, baseball writer.
GRAFTON, Sue: Kinsey Millhone, PI.
GRANT-ADAMSON, Lesley: Rain Morgan, gossip columnist. British.

HARDWICK, Mollie: Doran Fairweather, antique dealer. British.
HART, Carolyn: Annie Laurance, owner of a mystery bookstore.
HERVEY, Evelyn aka H. R. F. Keating: Harriet Unwin, governess. British.

HESS, Joan: Claire Malloy, bookstore owner.
HESS, Joan: Arley Hanks, sheriff of Maggody, Arkansas.
HOLLAND, Isabelle: Reverend Claire Aldington, minister.
HORNSBY, Wendy: Kate Teague, teacher, and Lt. Roger Tejeda.
HOWE, Melodie Johnson: Maggie Hill, "temp," and Claire Conrad, PI.

JACKSON, Marian J. A.: Miss Danforth, PI.
JAMES, P. D.: Cordelia Gray, private investigator. British.

KALLEN, Lucille: Maggie Rome, reporter, and C. B. Greenfield, newspaper owner.
KELLERMAN, Faye: Rina Lazarus, widow, and Peter Decker, LAPD.
KELLY, Susan: Liz Conners, free-lance writer, and Jack Lingerman, Cambridge Police Department.
KEMP, Sarah: Dr. Tina May, pathologist. British.
KENNEY, Susan: Roz Howard, English professor.
KIJEWSKI, Karen: Cat Colorado, PI.
KITTREDGE, Mary: Charlotte Kent, free-lance writer.
KITTREDGE, Mary: Edwina Crusoe, RN.
KNIGHT, Kathryn Lasky: Calista Jacobs, author of children's books.

LAKE, M. D.: Peggy O'Neill, campus police.
LaPIERRE, Janet: Meg Halloran, teacher, and police chief Vince Gutierrez.
LINSCOTT, Gillian: Nimue Hawthorne, travel agent, and ex-cop Birdie Linnet. British.
LLEWELLYN, Carolyn: Kate Roy, art restorer.
LOCKRIDGE, Richard and Frances: Pamela and Jerry North.

MacGREGOR, T. J.: Quin St. James, private investigator, and Mike McCleary, ex-cop.
MacLEOD, Charlotte: Helen and Peter Shandy, professor.
MacLEOD, Charlotte: Sarah Kelling and Max Bittersohn, art historian.

FEMALE DETECTIVES 439

MacLEOD, Charlotte, w/a Alisa Craig: Dittany Henbit, secretarial service. Canadian.
MacLEOD, Charlotte, w/a Alisa Craig: Janet Wadman and Inspector Madoc Rhys, RCMP. Canadian.
MANN, Jessica: Tamara Hoyland, undercover agent.
MARON, Margaret: Lieutenant Sigrid Harald, NYPD.
MARSH, Ngaio: Troy, artist, and Inspector Roderic Alleyn. British.
MARTIN, Lee: Detective Deb Ralston, Fort Worth Police Department.
MATERA, Lia: Willa Jansson, lawyer.
MATERA, Lia: Laura DiPalma, lawyer.
MATHEWSON, Joseph: Alicia von Helsing, artist.
MATTESON, Stefanie: Charlotte Graham, actress.
McCONNELL, Frank: Bridget O'Toole, ex-nun, and Harry Garnish, private investigator.
McCRUMB, Sharyn: Elizabeth MacPherson, studying forensic pathology.
MELVILLE, Jennie: Charmian Daniels, police inspector. British.
MEREDITH, D. R.: John Lloyd Branson, lawyer, and his assistant Lydia Fairchild.
MEYERS, Annette: Xenia Smith and Leslie Wetzon, headhunters.
MITCHELL, Gladys: Dame Beatrice Lestrange Bradley, psychiatrist. British.
MONTGOMERY, Yvonne: Finny Aletter, ex-stockbroker.
MOODY, Susan: Penny Wanawake, photographer. British.
MORGAN, D. Miller: Daisy Marlow, private investigator.
MORGAN, Kate: Dewey James, librarian.
MORICE, Anne: Tessa Crichton, actress. British.
MOYES, Patricia: Emmy and Inspector Henry Tibbett. British.
MULLER, Marcia: Sharon McCone, private investigator.
MULLER, Marcia: Elena Oliverez, museum curator.
MULLER, Marcia: Joanna Stark, security specialist.

NEEL, Janet: Francesca Wilson, civil servant, and Detective Inspector John McLeish.

O'BRIEN, Meg: Jessica James, journalist.
O'DONNELL, Lillian: Mici Anhalt, Victim's Assistance Program.
O'DONNELL, Lillian: Lieutenant Norah Mulcahaney, NYPD.
O'DONNELL, Peter: Modesty Blaise, retired. British.
OLIPHANT, B. J.: Shirley McClintock, rancher.
OLIVER, Anthony: Lizzie Thomas, widow, and John Webber, retired policeman. British.
O'MARIE, Sister Carol Anne: Sister Mary Helen, nun.

PALMER, Stuart: Hildegarde Withers, schoolteacher.
PAPAZOGLOU, Orania: Patience McKenna, writer.
PARETSKY, Sara: V. I. Warshawski, private investigator.
PERRY, Anne: Charlotte and Inspector Thomas Pitt. British.
PETERS, Elizabeth: Amelia Peabody and Radcliffe Emerson, archaeologists. British.
PETERS, Elizabeth: Jacqueline Kirby, librarian.
PETERS, Elizabeth: Victoria Bliss, art historian.
PETERSON, Audrey: Jane Winfield, writer, and Andrew Quentin, muscian. British.
PICKARD, Nancy: Jennifer Cain, civic foundation.
PIESMAN, Marissa: Nina Fischman, lawyer.
POWERS, Elizabeth: Viera Kolarova, private investigator.

QUEST, Erica: Detective Chief Inspector Kate Maddox. British.

RESNICOW, Herbert: Norma and Alexander Gold, retired.
RESNICOW, Herbert: Isabel Macintosh, dean of faculty, and Giles Sullivan, retired criminal lawyer.
RICH, Virginia: Mrs. Eugenia Potter, cook.
RINEHART, Mary Roberts: Nurse Hilda Adams, Miss Pinkerton, private investigator.
ROBERTS, Gillian: Amanda Pepper, schoolteacher.
ROOSEVELT, Elliott: Eleanor Roosevelt, First Lady.

SHAH, Diane K.: Paris Chandler, journalist.
SHERWOOD, John: Celia Grant, horticulturist. British.

FEMALE DETECTIVES

SILVER, Victoria: Lauren Adler, graduate student.
SIMS, L. V.: Dixie T. Struthers, San Jose PD.
SMITH, Evelyn E.: Susan Melville, free-lance assassin, retired.
SMITH, Joan: Loretta Lawson, scholar. British.
SMITH, Julie: Rebecca Schwartz, lawyer.
SMITH, Julie: Skip Langdon, policewoman.
STEVENS, Reed: Ginny Fistoulari and Nick Axbrewder, private investigators.
STOREY, Alice: Samantha Adams, journalist.

TAYLOR, Elizabeth Atwood: Maggie Elliott, PI.
TELUSHKIN, Joseph: Rabbi Daniel Winter and Brenda Goldstein, police psychologist.
TONE, Teona: Kyra Keaton, lady detective.
TRAVIS, Elizabeth: Carrie and Ben Potter, publishers.

VAN GIESON, Judith: Neil Hamel, lawyer.

WATSON, Clarissa: Persis Willum, artist.
WENDER, Theodora: Glad Gold, English professor, and Alden Chase, policeman.
WENTWORTH, Patricia: Miss Maud Silver, retired. British.
WHEAT, Carolyn: Cassandra Jameson, lawyer.
WILHELM, Kate: Charlie Miklejohn, private investigator, and his wife Constance Liedle, psychologist.
WOLZIEN, Valerie: Susan Henshaw, housewife.
WOODS, Sara: Jenny and Antony Maitland, lawyer. British.

YAFFE, James: Mom and her son Dave, Public Defender's Office.

AWARD WINNERS

THE EDGAR WINNERS, MYSTERY WRITERS OF AMERICA

*E*ACH MAY, *the Mystery Writers of America present Edgar Awards for the best works of the previous year. It has been quite easy to locate the Edgar winners for any particular year, but not so easy to identify the rest of the writers who were nominated. All the nominees for a category are listed; the winner of the Edgar is listed first. In addition, the Grand Master for each year is included. The Grand Master Award is given to a mystery writer for his or her lifetime achievement.*

GRAND MASTER FOR 1985

Ed McBain (Evan Hunter)

BEST NOVEL OF 1985

L. R. Wright: *The Suspect* (Viking/Penguin)
Paul Auster: *City of Glass: The New York Trilogy, Part 1* (Sun & Moon Press)
Simon Brett: *A Shock To The System* (Scribner)
Ruth Rendell: *The Tree Of Hands* (Pantheon)
Ruth Rendell: *An Unkindness Of Ravens* (Pantheon)

BEST FIRST NOVEL OF 1985

Jonathan Kellerman: *When The Bough Breaks* (Atheneum)
Daniel Stashower: *The Adventure Of The Ectoplasmic Man* (Morrow)

Tony Fennelly: *The Glory Hole Murders* (Carroll & Graf)
Dick Lochte: *Sleeping Dog* (Arbor House)

BEST PAPERBACK ORIGINAL OF 1985

Warren Murphy: *Pigs Get Fat* (Signet)
Conall Ryan: *Black Gravity* (Ballantine)
Philip Ross: *Blue Heron* (Tor)
Sean Flannery: *Broken Idols* (Charter)
Earl W. Emerson: *Poverty Bay* (Avon)

GRAND MASTER FOR 1986

Michael Gilbert

BEST NOVEL OF 1986

Barbara Vine, aka Ruth Rendell: *A Dark-Adapted Eye* (Bantam)
Brian Freemantle: *The Blind Run* (Bantam)
Joe Gores: *Come Morning* (Mysterious)
Roger L. Simon: *The Straight Man* (Villard)
P. D. James: *A Taste For Death* (Knopf)

BEST FIRST NOVEL OF 1986

Larry Beinhart: *No One Rides For Free* (Morrow)
Mike Lupica: *Dead Air* (Villard)
Joseph Koenig: *Floater* (Mysterious)
Gary Devon: *Lost* (Knopf)
Richard Hyer: *Riceburner* (Scribner)

BEST PAPERBACK ORIGINAL OF 1986

Robert Campbell: *The Junkyard Dog* (Signet)
Lilian Jackson Braun: *The Cat Who Saw Red* (Jove)
R. D. Brown: *Hazzard* (Bantam)

Nick Christian: *Ronin* (Tor)
Kate Green: *Shattered Moon* (Dell)

GRAND MASTER FOR 1987

Phyllis A. Whitney

BEST NOVEL OF 1987

Aaron Elkins: *Old Bones* (Mysterious)
Linda Barnes: *A Trouble Of Fools* (St. Martin)
B. M. Gill: *Nursery Crimes* (Scribner)
Peter Lovesey: *Rough Cider* (Mysterious)
Charlotte MacLeod: *The Corpse In Oozak's Pond* (Mysterious)

BEST FIRST NOVEL OF 1987

Deirdre S. Laiken: *Death Among Strangers* (Macmillan)
Parnell Hall: *Detective* (Donald I. Fine)
John Lantigua: *Heat Lightning* (Putnam)
Dallas Murphy: *Lover Man* (Scribner)
Domenic Stansberry: *The Spoiler* (Atlantic Monthly)

BEST PAPERBACK ORIGINAL OF 1987

Sharyn McCrumb: *Bimbos Of The Death Sun* (TSR, Inc.)
Robert Crais: *The Monkey's Raincoat* (Bantam)
Walter Dillon: *Deadly Intrusions* (Bantam)
James N. Frey: *The Long Way To Die* (Bantam)
Gabrielle Kraft: *Bullshot* (Pocket)

GRAND MASTER FOR 1988

Hillary Waugh

BEST NOVEL OF 1988

Stuart M. Kaminsky: *A Cold Red Sunrise* (Scribner)
Thomas H. Cook: *Sacrificial Ground* (Putman)

K. C. Constantine: *Joey's Case* (Mysterious)
Tony Hillerman: *A Thief Of Time* (Harper & Row)
David L. Lindsey: *In The Lake Of the Moon* (Atheneum)

BEST FIRST NOVEL OF 1988

David Stout: *Carolina Skeletons* (Mysterious)
Mary Lou Bennett: *Murder Once Done* (Perseverance)
J. Madison Davis: *The Murder Of Frau Schutz* (Walker)
Elizabeth George: *A Great Deliverance* (Bantam)
Shelly Reuben: *Julian Solo* (Dodd)

BEST PAPERBACK ORIGINAL OF 1988

Timothy Findley: *The Telling Of Lies* (Dell)
Frederick D. Huebner: *Judgment By Fire* (Fawcett)
Lia Matera: *A Radical Departure* (Bantam)
Keith Peterson: *The Trapdoor* (Bantam)
Ted Thackery: *Preacher* (Jove)

GRAND MASTER FOR 1989

Helen McCloy

BEST NOVEL OF 1989

James Lee Burke: *Black Cherry Blues* (Little, Brown)
Andrew Coburn: *Goldilocks* (Scribner)
Frances Fyfield: *A Question Of Guilt* (Pocket)
Bartholomew Gill: *Death Of a James Joyce Scholar* (Morrow)
Eugene Izzi: *The Booster* (St. Martin)

BEST FIRST NOVEL OF 1989

Susan Wolfe: *The Last Billable Hour* (St. Martin)
Barry Berg: *Hide And Seek* (St. Martin)
Susan Taylor Chehak: *The Story Of Annie D.* (Houghton)
Melodie Johnson Howe: *The Mother Shadow* (Viking)
Bruce Zimmerman: *Blood Under The Bridge* (Harper & Row)

BEST PAPERBACK ORIGINAL OF 1989

Keith Peterson: *The Rain* (Bantam)
Jeffery Wilds Deaver: *Manhattan Is My Beat* (Bantam)
Eugeen Izzi: *King Of The Hustlers* (Bantam)
Randy Russell: *Hot Wire* (Bantam)
Deborah Valentine: *A Collection Of Photographs* (Bantam)

THE ANTHONY AWARDS

The Anthony Awards started in 1986 at Bouchercon XVII. A large percentage of those attending the Bouchercon are mystery readers and, as fans, wanted a say in honoring their favorite authors. Thus, anyone who registered for the convention could participate in the voting.

BEST NOVEL OF 1985

Sue Grafton: *"B" Is For Burglar* (Holt)
Sarah Caudwell: *The Shortest Way To Hades* (Scribner)
Charlotte MacLeod: *The Plain Old Man* (Doubleday)
John D. MacDonald: *The Lonely Silver Rain* (Knopf)
Sara Paretsky: *Killing Orders* (Morrow)

BEST FIRST NOVEL OF 1985

Jonathan Kellerman: *When The Bough Breaks* (Atheneum)
Susan Kelly: *The Gemini Man* (Walker)
Dick Lochte: *Sleeping Dog* (Arbor House)
Robert Reeves: *Doubting Thomas* (Crown)
Andrew Vachss: *Flood* (Donald I. Fine)

BEST PAPERBACK ORIGINAL OF 1985

Nancy Pickard: *Say No To Murder* (Avon)
P. M. Carlson: *Murder Is Academic* (Avon)

THE ANTHONY AWARDS

Earl Emerson: *Poverty Bay* (Avon)
Kate Green: *Shattered Moon* (Dell)
Patrick A. Kelley: *Sleightly Murder* (Avon)

BEST NOVEL OF 1986

Sue Grafton: *"C" Is For Corpse* (Holt)
Lawrence Block: *When The Sacred Ginmill Closes* (Arbor House)
John Lutz: *Tropical Heat* (Holt)
Nancy Pickard: *No Body* (Scribner)
Jonathan Valin: *Life's Work* (Delacorte)

BEST FIRST NOVEL OF 1986

Bill Crider: *Too Late To Die* (Walker)
Joan Hess: *Strangled Prose* (St. Martin)
Faye Kellerman: *The Ritual Bath* (Arbor House)
Joseph Koenig: *Floater* (Mysterious)
Mike Lupica: *Dead Air* (Villard)

BEST PAPERBACK ORIGINAL OF 1986

Robert Campbell: *The Junkyard Dog* (Signet)
Lilian Jackson Braun: *The Cat Who Saw Red* (Jove).
J. A. Jance: *Trial By Fury* (Avon)
Rob Kantner: *Back-Door Man* (Bantam)
Warren Murphy: *Trace: Too Old A Cat* (Signet)

BEST NOVEL OF 1987

Tony Hillerman: *Skinwalkers* (Harper & Row)
Linda Barnes: *A Trouble Of Fools* (St. Martin)
Aaron Elkins: *Old Bones* (Mysterious)
Elizabeth Peters: *Trojan Gold* (Atheneum)
Nancy Pickard: *Marriage Is Murder* (Scribner)

BEST FIRST NOVEL OF 1987

Gillian Roberts: *Caught Dead In Philadelphia* (Scribner)
Michael Allegretto: *Death On The Rocks* (Scribner)
Robert J. Bowman: *House Of Blue Lights* (St. Martin)
Mary Monica Pulver: *Murder At The War* (St. Martin)
Les Roberts: *An Infinite Number Of Monkeys* (St. Martin)

BEST PAPERBACK ORIGINAL OF 1987

Robert Crais: *The Monkey's Raincoat* (Bantam)
Lilian Jackson Braun: *The Cat Who Played Brahms* (Jove)
Carolyn G. Hart: *Death On Demand* (Bantam)
Conrad Haynes: *Bishop's Gambit Declined* (Bantam)
Lia Matera: *Where Lawyers Fear To Tread* (Bantam)
Sharyn McCrumb: *Bimbos Of The Death Sun* (TSR, Inc.)

BEST NOVEL OF 1988

Thomas Harris: *The Silence Of The Lambs* (St. Martin)
Dorothy Cannell: *The Widows Club* (Bantam)
Sue Grafton: *"E" Is for Evidence* (Holt)
Tony Hillerman: *A Thief Of Time* (Harper & Row)
Sara Paretsky: *Blood Shot* (Delacorte)
Nancy Pickard: *Dead Crazy* (Scribner)
Bill Pronzini: *Shackles* (St. Martin)
Les Roberts: *Pepper Pike* (St. Martin)

BEST FIRST NOVEL OF 1988

Elizabeth George: *A Great Deliverance* (Bantam)
Mary Lou Bennett: *Murder Once Done* (Perseverance)
Caroline Graham: *The Killings At Badger's Drift* (Adler & Adler)
Linda Grant: *Random Access Murder* (Avon)
Gar Anthony Haywood: *Fear Of The Dark* (St. Martin)
David Stout: *Carolina Skeletons* (Mysterious)

BEST NOVEL OF 1989

Sarah Caudwell: *The Sirens Sang Of Murder* (Delacorte)
Susan Dunlap: *Pious Deception* (St. Martin)
Carolyn G. Hart: *A Little Class On Murder* (Doubleday)
Margaret Maron: *Corpus Christmas* (Doubleday)

BEST FIRST NOVEL OF 1989

Karen Kijewski: *Katwalk* (St. Martin)
Jill Churchill: *Grime And Punishment* (Bantam)
Melodie Johnson Howe: *The Mother Shadow* (Viking)
Edith Skom: *The Mark Twain Murders* (Council Oak)

BEST PAPERBACK ORIGINAL OF 1989

Carolyn G. Hart: *Honeymoon With Murder* (Bantam)
Malachai Black aka Barbara D'Amato: *On My Honor* (Zebra)
D. R. Meredith: *Murder By Deception* (Ballantine)

SHAMUS AWARDS

The Shamus Awards are also given out at the annual Bouchercon Convention. However, the voting is limited to membership in the Private Eye Writers of America, and not open to the general participants of the convention.

BEST HARDCOVER PI NOVEL OF 1985

Sue Grafton: *"B" Is For Burglar* (Holt)
Harold Adams: *The Naked Liar* (Mysterious)
Doug Hornig: *Hardball* (Scribner)
Robert B. Parker: *A Catskill Eagle* (Delacorte)
Bill Pronzini: *Bones* (St. Martin)

Best First PI Novel of 1985

Wayne Warga: *Hardcover* (Scribner)
Edward Gorman: *New, Improved Murder* (St. Martin)
Dick Lochte: *Sleeping Dog* (Arbor House)
Andrew Vachss: *Flood* (Donald I. Fine)
Ben Schutz: *Embrace The Wolf* (Bluejay)

Best Paperback PI Novel of 1985

Earl Emerson: *Poverty Bay* (Avon)
Douglas Heyes: *The Rainy City* (Ballantine)
Warren Murphy: *Trace: Pigs Get Fat* (Signet)
Philip Ross: *Blue Heron* (Tor)

Best PI Novel of 1986

Jeremiah Healy: *The Staked Goat* (Harper & Row)
Lawrence Block: *When The Sacred Ginmill Closes* (Arbor House)
Robert Campbell: *In La-La Land We Trust* (Mysterious)
Max Allan Collins: *The Million Dollar Wound* (St. Martin)
Sue Grafton: *"C" Is For Corpse* (Holt)

Best First PI Novel of 1986

J. W. Rider: *Jersey Tomatoes* (Arbor House)
Larry Beinhart: *No One Rides For Free* (Morrow)
Carl Hiassen: *Tourist Season* (Putnam)

Best Paperback PI Novel of 1986

Rob Kantner: *The Back-Door Man* (Bantam)
Kenn Davis: *Melting Point* (Fawcett)
Earl Emerson: *Nervous Laughter* (Avon)
T. J. MacGregor: *Dark Fields* (Ballantine)
Warren Murphy: *Trace: Too Old A Cat* (Signet)

BEST PI NOVEL OF 1987

Michael Allegretto: *Death On the Rocks* (Scribner)
Robert J. Bowman: *The House Of Blue Lights* (St. Martin)
John Douglas: *Shawnee Alley Fire* (St. Martin)
Parnell Hall: *Detective* (Donald I. Fine)
Les Roberts: *An Infinite Number Of Monkeys* (St. Martin)

BEST FIRST PI NOVEL OF 1987

Benjamin Schutz: *A Tax In Blood* (Tor)
Linda Barnes: *A Trouble Of Fools* (St. Martin)
Loren D. Estleman: *Lady Yesterday* (Houghton)
Edward Gorman: *Autumn Dead* (St. Martin)
John Lutz: *Ride The Lightning* (St. Martin)

BEST PAPERBACK PI NOVEL OF 1987

L. J. Washburn: *Wild Night* (Tor)
Robert Crais: *Monkey's Raincoat* (Bantam)
Gaylord Dold: *Snake Eyes* (Ivy)
David Everson: *Recount* (Ivy)
Joseph Louis: *Madelaine* (Bantam)

BEST PI NOVEL OF 1988

John Lutz: *Kiss* (Holt)
Max Allan Collins: *Neon Mirage* (St. Martin)
Earl Emerson: *Deviant Behavior* (Morrow)
Jeremiah Healy: *Swan Dive* (Harper & Row)
Sara Paretsky: *Blood Shot* (Delacorte)

BEST FIRST PI NOVEL OF 1988

Gar Anthony Haywood: *Fear Of The Dark* (St. Martin)
Michael Cormany: *Lost Daughter* (Lyle Stuart)
Wayne D. Dundee: *The Burning Season* (St. Martin)

Walter Satterthwait: *Wall Of Glass* (St. Martin)
Philip Lee Williams: *Slow Dance In Autumn* (Peachtree)

BEST PAPERBACK PI NOVEL OF 1988

Rob Kantner: *Dirty Work* (Bantam)
John Birkett: *The Last Private Eye* (Avon)
Gaylord Dold: *Bonepile* (Ballantine)
David Everson: *Rebound* (Ivy)
W. R. Philbrock: *The Crystal Blue Persuasion* (Onyx)

REFERENCE BOOKS

BARGAINNIER, Earl, ed. *Comic Crime* 1987 Bowling Green State University Popular Press.
BOURGEAU, Art *The Mystery Lover's Companion* 1986 Crown. Four categories of crime fiction, annotated.
BREEN, Jon L. *What About Murder? A Guide To Books About Mystery And Detective Fiction* 1981 Scarecrow Press.
BREEN, Jon L. *Hair Of The Sleuthhound: Parodies Of Mystery Fiction* 1982 Scarecrow Press.
BREEN, Jon L. *Novel Verdicts: A Guide To Courtroom Fiction* 1984 Scarecrow Press.
BREEN, Jon L. & Martin Harry Greenberg, eds. *Murder Off The Rack: Critical Studies Of Ten Paperback Masters* 1989 Scarecrow Press.
HORNING, Jane *The Mystery Lover's Book Of Quotations: The Wit And Wisdom Of The World's Great Crime Writers* 1988 Mysterious.
HUBIN, Allen J. *The Bibliography Of Crime Fiction 1749–1975* 1979 Publishers, Inc.
HUBIN, Allen J. *Crime Fiction, 1749–1980: A Comprehensive Bibliography* 1984 Garland.
HUBIN, Allen J. *1981–1985 Supplement To Crime Fiction, 1749–1980: A Comprehensive Bibliography* 1988 Garland.
KEATING, H. R. F. *Crime & Mystery: The 100 Best Books* 1987 Carroll & Graf/ Carroll & Graf 1987. Covers titles from 1845 (Poe) to 1986 (P. D. James).
MENENDEZ, Albert J. *The Subject Is Murder: A Selective Subject Guide To Mystery Fiction* 1986 Garland. Not annotated.
MENENDEZ, Albert J. *The Subject Is Murder: A Selective Subject Guide To Mystery Fiction, Volume 2* 1990 Garland. An update from Volume 1, Not annotated.
NICHOLS, Victoria and Susan Thompson *Silk Stalkings: When Women Write Of Murder* 1988 Black Lizard Books. A survey of series characters created by women authors in crime and mystery fiction.

PANEK, LeRoy Lad *An Introduction To The Mystery Story* 1987 Bowling Green State University Popular Press.

PENZLER, Otto, Chris Steinbrunner & Marvin Lachman, eds. *Detectionary: A Bibliographical Dictionary Of Leading Characters In Mystery Fiction* 1977 Overlook Press/ Ballantine 1980.

REILLY, John M., ed. *Twentieth-Century Crime And Mystery Writers* 2nd. ed. 1985 St. Martin.

RILEY, Dick & Pam McAllister *The Bedside, Bathtub & Armchair Companion To Agatha Christie* 1983 Frederick Ungar.

STEINBRUNNER, Chris & Otto Penzler, Eds. *Encyclopedia Of Mystery & Detection* 1986 McGraw/ Harcourt 1984.

SYMONS, Julian *Bloody Murder: From The Detective Story To The Crime Novel: A History* rev. ed. Penguin 1985.

WINN, Dilys, ed. *Murder Ink: The Mystery Readers Companion* 1977 Workman.

WINN, Dilys, ed. *Murderess Ink: The Better Half* 1979 Workman.

WINN, Dilys, ed. *Murder Ink* rev. ed. Workman 1984.

AUTHOR INDEX

Abercrombie, Barbara   426
Abshire, Richard K.   361, 379
Adams, Harold   188, 211, 287, 335, 336
Adamson, Lydia   84, 172
Adamson, M. J.   329, 361, 419
Aird, Catherine   96
Albert, Marvin   34, 62, 112, 132, 133, 215, 232, 262
Aldyne, Nathan   62, 112, 149, 150, 166
Alexander, Gary   34, 112, 166
Alexander, Lawrence   127, 162
Allegretto, Michael   12, 62
Allen, Steve   127, 336, 384
Allingham, Margery   105, 133, 177, 371, 406
Anderson, James   188, 336
Anderson, Virginia   172
Anthony, Evelyn   287
Arnold, Alan   370
Arnold, Margot   19, 198
Ashford, Jane   132
Ashford, Jeffrey   154
Asimov, Isaac   1, 90

Babbin, Jacqueline   336, 384
Babson, Marian   12, 18, 25, 31, 90, 122, 132, 139, 154, 169, 188, 198, 211, 215, 232, 248, 253, 279, 336, 358, 384, 395, 424
Bailey, Hilary   372
Ball, John   59, 300, 336
Ballard, Mignon F.   271, 320
Bandy, Franklin   198
Bank, Lawrence Henry   112
Banks, Carolyn   271, 320
Banks, Joan   13, 195
Banks, Oliver   34
Bannister, Jo   19, 372
Barnard, Robert   1, 13, 31, 48, 86, 111, 133, 154, 177, 248, 271, 281, 306, 312, 336, 395, 406, 426
Barnes, Linda   62, 102, 112, 124, 182, 196, 262, 287, 307, 361, 372, 390
Barth, Richard   86, 113, 140, 329, 395
Barthelme, Peter   15, 113
Bass, Milton   199
Battin, B. W.   361
Baxt, George   59, 113, 128, 150, 154, 199, 211, 262, 281, 336, 372, 419
Bayer, William   63, 199, 221, 361
Beaton, M. C.   63, 140, 221, 248, 320, 330, 336, 419

Beck, K. K. 63, 140, 199, 221, 222, 262, 321, 358
Becklund, Jack 154, 263
Beechcroft, William 199
Beinhart, Larry 122, 140
Belforte, Sophie 307, 336
Bell, Josephine 390
Belsky, Dick 222
Bernard, Robert L. 1
Berry, Carole 122, 236, 287
Biederman, Marcia 113, 385
Biggers, Earl Derr 216, 287, 300, 301, 336
Biggle, Lloyd, Jr. 370, 372
Birkett, John 173, 337
Bishop, Paul 105, 113
Black, Lionel 76, 222
Blackstock, Charity 20, 90, 113, 244
Blake, Nicholas 125
Bloch, Robert 128, 400
Block, Lawrence 13, 34, 63, 74, 75, 96, 140, 150, 166, 216, 248, 263, 316, 330, 337, 390
Bohjalion, Christopher A. 211
Bond, Michael 102, 103, 111, 196, 395
Borgenicht, Miriam 63, 236, 271
Borowitz, Albert 18, 188, 279, 337
Borthwick, J. S. 1, 34, 58, 113, 358, 372
Boucher, Anthony 96, 199, 245, 370
Bowen, Michael 245, 307
Bowers, Elizabeth 263, 312
Bowman, Robert J. 236, 330

Boyer, Rick 34, 113, 287, 307, 372
Boyle, Thomas 166, 321
Bradbury, Ray 361, 427
Braddon, Russell 337, 361
Brahms, Caryl 110, 395
Brand, Christianna 211, 337, 395, 406
Brandon, Ruth 199, 321, 424
Brandt, Charles 288
Braun, Lilian Jackson 35, 84, 85, 90, 177, 196, 222, 372, 379
Brean, Herbert 63, 222, 406
Breen, Jon L. 75, 281
Brett, John 35, 113
Brett, Simon 86, 154, 155, 385, 390, 407
Brill, Toni 35, 282
Bringle, Mary 86, 199
Brod, D. C. 122, 330
Brown, Frederic 222, 362
Brown, R. D. 2, 128, 307
Brown, Russell A. 370
Bryant, Dorothy 379, 427
Buckley, William F., Jr. 200
Bunn, Thomas 86, 232
Burke, James Lee 114, 140, 184, 337
Burkey, Dave 173
Burley, W. J. 35, 91, 128, 166, 288, 337, 396
Burns, Rex 114, 125, 133, 253, 263, 330
Byrd, Max 200, 288

Cairns, Alison 155
Camp, John 100
Campbell, Robert Wright 96, 125, 271, 307, 312, 330, 337, 362, 385, 419

AUTHOR INDEX

Candy, Edward 2, 140, 253, 337
Cannell, Dorothy 103, 177, 196, 337
Carlson, P. M. 2, 63, 86, 155, 253, 328, 337, 379, 390
Carr, John Dickson 52, 133, 177, 211, 245, 288, 400, 407
Carvic, Heron 140, 141, 419
Case, Peg 222, 288
Caudwell, Sarah 13, 35, 188, 236
Cavandish, Faith 35, 407
Chance, Lisbeth 372
Chandler, Raymond 63, 133
Charles, Hampton 35, 52, 200, 216, 232, 358
Chase, Elaine Raco 64, 223, 338
Chase, Samantha 87, 321, 338
Chastain, Thomas 177, 237
Chehak, Susan Taylor 271, 321
Chesbro, George C. 200, 420
Christie, Agatha 52, 91, 177, 244, 245, 279, 282, 288
Christmas, Joyce 272, 330, 407
Christopher, Constance 316, 420
Christopher, Paula 173, 318
Chudley, Ron 79, 114
Clarins, Dana 282
Clark, Dick 275, 338
Clark, Mary Higgins 132, 212, 288, 359, 385
Clarke, Anna 2, 19, 134, 155, 162, 177, 272, 282, 289, 321, 359, 407, 408, 427
Clarke, T. E. B. 64
Cleeves, Ann 58, 330
Clemeau, Carol 2
Clift, A. Denis 200
Cline, Edward 263, 427
Clothier, Peter 35
Cockrell, Amanda 25
Cody, Liza 276, 424
Cohen, Anthea 155, 253, 254, 338
Cohen, Charles 91, 188
Coker, Carolyn 36, 188
Colbert, James 31, 330
Collins, Eliza G. C. 36
Collins, Max Allan 26, 114, 232, 248, 279, 282, 283, 338
Collins, Michael 105, 114
Conant, Susan 64, 111
Conners, Bernard F. 322
Constantine, K. C. 91, 134, 141, 155, 313
Cook, Bruce 114, 134
Cooper, Natasha 141, 427
Cooper, Susan Rogers 379, 425
Cork, Barry 52, 53, 330, 338
Cormany, Michael 188, 263
Cornwell, Patricia Daniels 305, 362, 428
Corrington, John William 134, 178, 223, 289, 338
Corris, Peter 48, 49, 50, 182, 263, 307
Coyne, P. J. 64, 428
Craig, M. S. 32, 141

Craig, Philip R.   3, 20
Crais, Robert   233, 249
Cramer, Kathryn   91, 420
Crespi, Trella   15, 338
Crews, Lary   87, 114, 313, 385
Crider, Bill   3, 64, 156, 189, 216, 289
Cross, Amanda   3, 264, 379
Cunningham, E. V.   201, 301, 313
Curran, Terrie   244, 249
Cutter, Leela   254, 283

Dale, Celia   141
Dalton, Martina   178
D'Amato, Barbara   114, 223
Daniels, Philip   166, 399
Davey, Jocelyn   338, 428
Davidson, Diane Mott   103, 254
Davis, Dorothy Salisbury   166, 201, 264, 307, 313
Davis, Kenn   36, 59, 60, 150
Davis, Maggie   114
Dawson, David Laing   79, 254
Dawson, Janet   272, 289
Dean, S. F. X.   4, 101, 134, 166, 189, 244, 249, 289, 385
DeAndrea, William L.   37, 91, 141, 142, 201, 212, 279, 339, 359, 386, 408
Deaver, Jeffery Wilds   37, 289, 313, 391, 425
DeBrosse, Jim   32, 223
DeFelitta, Frank   169, 362
Deford, Frank   53, 201
Delinsky, Barbara   425
Delman, David   4, 201, 223, 379
Denham, Bertie   64, 202

DeNoux, O'Neil   105, 362
Dentinger, Jane   330, 391
Dewhurst, Eileen   64, 156, 202
Dexter, Colin   5, 64, 142, 166, 178, 189, 212, 339
Dibdin, Michael   87, 322
Dillon, Eilís   142, 254, 396, 408
Disney, Doris Miles   142, 156, 178, 189, 289, 408
Dobson, Margaret   13, 37, 75, 216, 264, 396
Dobyns, Stephen   37, 115, 189, 313
Doherty, P. C.   162, 258, 355
Dold, Gaylord   115, 142, 264
Doolittle, Jerome   134, 307
Donaldson, D. J.   254, 305, 339
Dorner, Marjorie   87, 339
Douglas, John   289, 330
Dowling, Gregory   202
Downey, Timothy   223, 362
Downing, Warwick   13, 237
Doyle, James T.   105, 115, 142, 289
Dozois, Gardner   128
Drake, Alison   290, 420
Drummond, John Keith   57, 91, 408
Duffy, Margaret   202, 203, 233, 428
Duncan, W. Glen   115, 339, 376, 396
Dundee, Wayne D.   182, 314
Dunlap, Susan   26, 97, 103, 115, 142, 143, 178, 264, 331, 339, 408
Dunne, Dominick   290

AUTHOR INDEX

Early, Jack   32, 105, 115, 340
Eberhart, Mignon G.   65, 162, 290, 359, 373, 408
Eccles, Marjorie   65, 143, 190, 272, 340, 428
Elbert, Joyce   150, 340
Elkins, Aaron J.   20, 37, 53, 178, 290
Elkins, Charlotte   143
Ellroy, James   264, 322, 362
Emerson, Earl W.   290, 314, 409
Engel, Howard   37, 65, 79, 80, 143, 379
Enger, L. L.   134, 331
Engleman, Paul   53, 65, 264
Estleman, Loren D.   65, 97, 134, 135, 143, 203, 224, 265, 290, 308, 340, 370, 373
Everson, David   53, 272, 308
Eversy, Robert   122

Farrell, Maud   150, 254
Feld, Bernard   224, 272
Fennelly, Tony   150, 331
Fenster, Bob   283, 340
Ferrars, E. X.   50, 115, 212, 272
Fink, John   272, 290
Fish, Robert L.   21, 26, 143, 178, 203, 409
Fiske, Dorsey   5, 249
Fletcher, Lucille   265, 391
Fliegel, Richard   169
Flinn, Denny Martin   135, 409
Flynn, Don   224, 233, 276, 331
Flynn, Lucine Hansz   26
Follett, Ken   38
Footman, Robert   203

Forrest, Richard   363
Francis, Dick   17, 38, 50, 125, 135, 143, 173, 174, 224, 233
Frankel, Valerie   255, 409
Fraser, Anthea   216, 290
Fraser, Antonia   212, 386, 391, 420
Freeborn, Richard   401
Friedman, Kinky   212
Friedman, Mickey   38, 143, 190, 224, 340, 428
Frommer, Sara Hoskinson   276
Frost, Joan Van Every   38, 65, 132, 373
Fulton, Eileen   65, 212, 290, 322, 340, 386, 387

Galbraith, Ruth   5, 80
Gardner, Erle Stanley   65, 143, 216, 237, 379
Gardner, John   203
Garve, Andrew   203
Gash, Jonathan   26, 27, 265, 301
Gault, William Campbell   65, 190, 212
Geller, Michael   54, 174
George, Elizabeth   5, 87, 135, 182
Gerson, Jack   204, 363
Gibbs, Tony   359
Gielgud, Val   65, 387
Gilbert, Michael   156
Gill, B. M.   5, 87, 150, 283, 322, 363
Gillespie, Robert R.   101, 115
Gilligan, Roy   213
Gillis, Jackson   143
Gilman, Dorothy   28, 204, 290, 396

Gilpatrick, Noreen 276, 290
Girdner, Jaqueline 135, 341
Giroux, E. X. 66, 178, 182, 237, 238, 280, 341, 396
Godfrey, Ellen 80, 246
Godfrey, Thomas 92
Goldsborough, Robert 224, 276, 341, 380
Golin, James 204, 249, 277
Goodrum, Charles A. 244, 249
Gordon, Alison 54, 224
Gores, Joe 216
Gorman, Edward 15, 66, 272, 290, 314, 328, 359, 387, 391
Gosling, Paula 5, 38, 115, 341, 363, 409, 428
Gough, Laurence 80, 115, 316, 363
Goulart, Ron 16, 66
Grady, James 291
Grafton, Sue 66, 178, 182, 196, 272, 342
Graham, Caroline 66, 182, 280, 392
Granger, Ann 66, 388
Granger, Bill 97, 224, 342, 363
Grant, Charles 92
Grant, Linda 101, 125, 144
Grant-Adamson, Lesley 21, 92, 135, 225, 342
Gray, Caroline 135
Gray, Malcolm 38, 246, 280, 283, 388
Grayson, Richard 162, 342
Greeley, Andrew M. 97, 213, 420
Green, Kate 318
Greenan, Russell H. 66, 183

Greenberg, Martin 246, 370, 399
Greenberg, Rosalind M. 166
Greene, Douglas G. 246
Greenleaf, Stephen 13, 66, 233, 238, 255, 265, 291, 322
Greenwood, John 331, 380, 420
Greenwood, L. B. 371
Greth, Roma 266, 376
Griffiths, John 6, 331
Grimes, Martha 342
Grindal, Richard 115, 380
Grissom, Ken 115, 225
Gunning, Sally 135
Guthrie, Al 123, 273, 291, 342

Haddam, Jane 97, 166
Hagen, Lorinda 283, 421
Hager, Jean 184, 273
Haiblum, Isidore 116
Hall, Adam 13, 156
Hall, Parnell 116
Hall, Robert Lee 92, 128, 129, 163, 342
Halleran, Tucker 66, 150, 409
Hambley, Barbara 163, 399
Hammond, Gerald 196, 204, 291, 380
Handler, David 87, 144, 428, 429
Hanna, David 380, 392
Hansen, Joseph 116, 150, 151, 196, 301, 308, 342, 376, 410
Hanson, Dirk 101
Hardwick, Michael 371
Hardwick, Mollie 28, 38, 116, 343, 392

AUTHOR INDEX

Harris, Charlaine   6, 244, 280, 328
Harris, Thomas   322, 363
Harrison, Harry   205
Harrison, Ray   67, 144, 308, 373, 401
Harriss, Will   244, 249
Hart, Carolyn   75, 76, 167, 190, 280, 283, 392
Hart, Jeanne   196
Hart, Roy   67, 179, 380, 381
Harvey, John   322, 363
Hauser, Thomas   249, 277, 364
Havill, Steven F.   116, 343
Hayes, Helen   169, 343
Haymon, S. T.   273, 277
Haynes, Conrad   6, 135
Haywood, Gar Anthony   60, 67, 87
Heald, Tim   249, 373
Healy, Jeremiah   67, 179, 291, 322, 323
Hebden, Mark   233, 249, 291
Helgerson, Joel   32, 291
Heller, Keith   163
Henderson, M. R.   170, 323, 364
Hendricks, Michael   67, 250
Hensley, Joe L.   190, 196, 238, 410
Hentoff, Nat   364
Hess, Joan   6, 21, 67, 76, 88, 116, 205, 213, 233, 280, 308, 331
Hiaasen, Carl   225, 377
Higgins, Joan   179, 277
Hilary, Richard   60, 116, 213, 331
Hill, Reginald   7, 28, 77, 92, 116, 144, 157, 197, 225, 291, 343, 381, 392, 396, 410

Hillerman, Tony   21, 117, 184, 185, 425
Hilton, John Buxton   88, 157, 163
Holland, Isabelle   88, 92, 98, 266
Holt, Hazel   190, 331
Holt, Samuel   117
Hooper, Kay   135, 183
Horansky, Ruby   14, 144
Hornig, Doug   157, 255
Hornsby, Wendy   364, 410
Horovitz, Leslie Alan   306, 364
Hoving, Thomas   39
Howatch, Susan   144, 266
Hoyt, Richard   185
Huebner, Frederick D.   32, 238, 292, 377
Hulland, J. R.   7, 292
Hunsburger, H. Edward   39
Huxley, Elspeth   17, 213, 217

Innes, Michael   39
Irvine, Robert   54, 410
Israel, Peter   238, 364

Jackson, Marion J. A.   217, 402
Jacobs, Nancy Baker   170, 255
James, P. D.   308, 364
Jance, J. A.   101, 117, 157, 273, 301, 309, 343, 396
Janeschutz, Trish   117, 318, 323
Jeffers, H. Paul   67, 132, 157, 167, 217, 388
Jeffries, Roderic   39, 144, 179, 381
Jerina, Carol   144, 213, 225, 309, 373

Jevons, Marshall 7, 123
Johnston, Jane 225, 410
Johnston, Velda 68, 163, 213, 292
Jones, Cleo 190, 388
Jordan, Cathleen 7, 93
Jordan, Jennifer 284
Joshua, Benjamin, MD 255, 323

Kahn, Michael A. 238, 410
Kaiser, Ronn 170, 343
Kallen, Lucille 58, 225, 226, 332, 377
Kaminsky, Stuart 68, 129, 170, 179, 205, 292, 309, 356, 357, 373
Kantner, Rob 117, 314, 343, 364, 388
Katz, Michael J. 54, 117
Kaye, M. M. 17, 205, 217, 396
Keating, H. R. F. 14, 68, 402
Kellerman, Faye 190, 306, 314, 328, 332
Kellerman, Jonathan 88, 117, 323, 365, 381
Kelley, Patrick A. 68, 144, 250, 292, 318, 319, 343
Kelly, Susan 106, 343, 344, 365
Kelman, Judith 7, 292, 344, 381
Kelvin, Ned 7
Kemelman, Harry 98, 106
Kemp, Sarah 306, 365, 421
Kendall, Jack 88, 365
Kennealy, Jerry 39, 68, 125, 135, 174
Kenney, Susan 8
Kenyon, Michael 60, 117, 190, 233, 344, 396

Kerr, Philip 217, 309
Kerrigan, Philip 93, 344
Kienzle, William X. 98, 144, 157, 255, 273
Kijewski, Karen 135, 144, 332, 410
Kiker, Douglas 226, 314
Kittredge, Mary 88, 255, 256, 332, 429
Klass, David 8, 88
Knight, Alanna 344, 402
Knight, Kathryn Lasky 21
Koenig, Joseph 365
Kohler, Vincent 117, 226
Kraft, Gabrielle 145, 217, 239
Krentz, Jayne Ann 40, 344
Krich, Rochelle Majer 191, 256
Kunetka, James W. 21, 205

Lachman, Charles 239
Laiken, Deirdre S. 88, 324
Lake, M. D. 8, 118
Lamb, Margaret 226, 292
Langton, Jane 8, 57, 332, 365
Lansbury, Coral 8, 328
LaPierre, Janet 233, 273, 328
Larsen, Gaylord 8, 9, 130, 344, 381
Lathen, Emma 123, 245, 293, 309
Latimer, Jonathan 266
Laurence, Janet 103, 411
LeClaire, Anne D. 9
Lee, Elsie 40, 179, 205, 344, 373
Lemarchand, Elizabeth 14, 179, 344, 396, 421
Leonard, Elmore 145, 329
Leslie, John 293, 365

Levi, Peter 21
Levine, Paul 239, 256
Lewin, Elsa 324
Lewin, Michael Z. 365
Lewis, Roy 145, 239, 250, 332, 344, 421
Lewis, Roy Harley 76, 226
Lewis, William 278, 345
Lindsey, David L. 68, 135, 256, 324, 345, 365
Linscott, Gillian 136, 157, 397, 402
Littlepage, Layne 392, 411
Livingston, Jack 33, 68, 157, 381, 429
Livingston, Jayson 345, 366
Livingston, Nancy 157, 397
Llewellyn, Caroline 40
Llewellyn, Sam 123, 213, 360
Lochte, Dick 68
Logan, Margaret 345
Logue, John 33, 54, 55, 226
Logue, Mary 316
Lorens, M. K. 40, 250, 284, 388, 392
Lorne, David 233
Louis, Joseph 284
Lovell, Marc 250
Lovesey, Peter 293
Luce, Carol Davis 136, 345
Lupica, Mike 9, 266, 345, 388
Lutz, John 157, 197, 217, 233, 316, 332, 345, 366, 381, 389, 399
Lyons, Arthur 69, 197, 266, 381
Lyons, Nan 103, 273
Lysaght, Brian 266, 324

MacDonald, Patricia J. 151, 345, 346
MacGregor, Rob 28
MacGregor, T. J. 293, 315, 345, 366, 373
Machin, Meredith Land 69
MacLeod, Charlotte 9, 28, 29, 40, 69, 80, 81, 93, 104, 106, 118, 145, 179, 205, 217, 309, 346, 373, 374, 392, 393, 411, 421
Malcolm, John 29, 41, 118
Mann, Jessica 22, 42, 183, 217, 256
Maron, Margaret 69, 88, 89, 179, 180, 293, 393
Marsh, Ngaio 42, 93, 280, 360
Marshall, William 42, 293, 301, 302, 366
Martin, James E. 273, 293
Martin, Lee 136, 234, 324, 366, 411
Martin, Nancy 206
Mason, Clifford 42, 60
Matera, Lia 9, 180, 239, 346, 411
Matheson, Don 218
Mathis, Edward 69, 118, 145, 158, 183, 267, 324, 346, 366
Matteson, Stefanie 319, 411
Matthews, Patricia 180
Maxwell, A. E. 69
Maxwell, Thomas 158, 346
Mayor, Archer 347
McAleer, John 245, 250
McBain, Ed 69, 94, 118, 213, 240, 273, 315, 325
McBriarty, Douglas 186, 267, 374
McCafferty, Taylor 158
McCahery, James R. 69, 411
McCall, Wendell 118, 267, 333

McClintick, Malcolm 94, 167, 191, 347, 421
McClure, James 18
McConnell, Frank 69
McConner, Vincent 170, 293
McCormick, Claire 9, 42, 186
McCrumb, Sharyn 22, 167, 180, 186, 412, 429
McDermid, Val 151, 158
McDonald, Gregory 136, 226, 267, 316
McDowell, Rider 136
McGill, E. J. 101, 180
McGivern, William P. 214, 250
McGown, Jill 70, 94, 145, 170, 191, 274, 293
McInerny, Ralph 10, 98, 191, 240, 256, 325, 412
McIver, N. J. 180, 429
McMullen, Mary 16, 70, 158, 191, 227, 333, 347, 374, 397, 412
McMurry, Sarah 158
McShane, Mark 234, 319
McShea, Susanna Hofmann 267, 294
Meek, M. R. D. 158, 191, 240, 251, 294, 325, 381, 412
Melville, James 22, 133, 206, 214, 302, 303, 374, 397
Melville, Jennie 256, 347
Meredith, D. R. 22, 159, 191, 240, 347, 412
Meyers, Annette 145
Michaels, Barbara 10, 14, 19, 22, 29, 136, 163, 167, 181, 218, 294, 413, 421, 422
Miles, Keith 55

Miller, J. M. T. 294, 360, 413
Miller, Judi 325, 389
Mills, D. F. 325, 366
Milne, A. A. 246, 347
Milne, John 197
Minahan, John 218, 329, 367
Mitchell, Gladys 110, 367, 422
Mitchell, James 174
Mitchell, Kay 98, 191
Mittermeyer, Helen 241, 374
Moffat, Gwen 70, 214, 284, 429
Montgomery, Yvonne 251, 347
Moody, Susan 22, 61, 77, 183, 284, 348
Moore, Barbara 22, 111, 112, 186
Morgan, D. Miller 70, 214
Morgan, Kate 174, 333
Morice, Anne 280, 393, 413
Morrow, J. T. 206
Mortimer, John 136, 348, 397
Moyes, Patricia 107, 197, 284, 397
Muller, Marcia 29, 42, 43, 94, 294, 348, 413, 430
Murphy, Dallas 333, 348, 374
Murphy, Haughton 110, 123, 126, 137, 310
Murphy, Warren 246, 284
Murray, Lynne 70
Murray, Stephen 192, 294, 398, 430
Murray, William 43, 145, 175, 348
Myers, M. Ruth 206

AUTHOR INDEX

Nabb, Magdalen 151, 206, 218, 234, 267, 294, 325
Nagy, Gloria 325, 389
Naha, Ed 227, 367
Natsuki, Shizuko 159, 192, 303, 413
Neel, Janet 123, 145, 267, 398
Neggers, Carla 218, 219, 227, 295
Neilson, Andrew 413
Nevins, Francis M., Jr. 348, 413, 414
Noel, Atanielle Annyn 71
Nordan, Robert 98, 274

O'Brien, Meg 118, 227, 333
O'Callaghan, Maxine 71, 219
OCork, Shannon 281
O'Donnell, Lillian 89, 192, 251, 256, 274, 310, 348, 367, 374, 393, 414
O'Hagan, Joan 43, 77, 206, 348
O'Hara, Kenneth 234
Oliphant, B. J. 29, 192
Oliver, Anthony 30, 43
O'Marie, Sister Carol Anne 99
Orde, A. J. 137, 159
Orenstein, Frank 16, 310, 333, 349
Ormerod, Roger 145, 159, 214, 219, 274, 295, 398
Oster, Jerry 349

Page, Emma 214, 268
Page, Katherine Hall 118, 398
Page, Martin 44
Paine, Michael 22, 423
Palen, Adeline 349

Palmer, Stuart 123, 170, 175, 268, 295, 349
Palmer, William J. 393, 403
Papazoglou, Orania 86, 284, 333, 430
Paretsky, Sara 146, 257, 377
Paris, Ann 94, 375
Parker, Robert B. 55, 71, 106, 118, 137, 274, 310, 316, 325, 389
Parker, T. Jefferson 206, 295, 349
Patti, Paul 106, 425
Paul, Barbara 30, 71, 130, 219, 278, 349, 393
Paul, Raymond 164, 317, 350
Payne, Laurence 71, 268, 350, 375, 393
Pearson, Ridley 325, 367
Pedneau, Dave 106, 310, 367
Penn, John 10, 71, 181, 214, 414
Pentecost, Hugh 33, 89, 181, 192, 207, 350
Perry, Anne 71, 137, 151, 159, 183, 214, 317, 350, 403, 404
Peters, Elizabeth 23, 24, 30, 181, 234, 274, 325, 355, 405, 414, 431
Peters, Ellis 94, 137, 259, 260, 261, 295
Peterson, Audrey 119, 278, 382, 414
Peterson, Keith 95, 137, 227, 295
Petievich, Gerald 106
Philbin, Tom 99, 151, 234, 274, 329, 350
Philbrick, W. R. 71, 234, 268, 285

Phillips, Edward   82, 152, 415
Phillips, Mike   61, 146
Phillips, R. A.   71, 375
Phillips, Stella   295
Pickard, Nancy   71, 146, 181, 274, 295, 350, 377, 415
Piesman, Marissa   241, 333
Pollack, Richard   227, 334
Popescu, Petru   400
Porter, Anna   181, 228
Prather, Richard S.   71, 146, 181, 268, 415
Price, Anthony   25, 30
Price, Nancy   326, 382
Pronzini, Bill   106, 152, 285, 295, 350, 375, 382
Pulver, Mary Monica   33, 71, 95, 119, 167, 295, 296
Pumphrey, Janet Kay   207, 296
Putre, John Walter   44, 146
Pyle, A. M.   126

Quest, Erica   351, 415
Quill, Monica   99
Quogan, Anthony   82, 394

Radley, Sheila   14, 268, 326, 351, 415
Randisi, Robert J.   44, 159, 251
Rathbone, Julian   77, 124
Rauch, Constance   89, 159
Ray, Robert J.   72, 89, 95, 146, 170, 197, 315
Reed, J. D.   55, 351
Rendell, Ruth   89, 108, 183, 296, 326
Resnicow, Herbert   10, 44, 72, 108, 109, 111, 146, 152, 167, 192, 197, 241, 246, 278, 394

Reynolds, John Laurence   99, 329
Reynolds, William J.   72, 137, 183, 351
Rhoads, J. W.   334
Rhode, John   247, 351, 416, 423
Rice, Craig   72, 192, 241, 351
Rich, Virginia   104, 214
Richardson, Robert   55, 152, 251
Rider, J. W.   334
Riggs, John R.   168, 296, 351
Rinehart, Mary Roberts   197, 296, 382
Risenhoover, C. C.   55, 89, 119, 152, 215, 228
Ritchie, Simon   82, 234, 326
Robb, T. N.   106, 310
Roberts, Gillian   72
Roberts, John Maddox   164, 310
Roberts, Les   16, 152, 181, 215, 268, 285, 389
Roberts, Nora   18, 219, 275, 278, 285, 327, 351, 367, 368
Robinett, Stephen   124, 269
Robinson, Peter   192, 416
Robinson, Robert   10, 251
Roosevelt, Elliott   95, 130, 131, 146, 159, 193, 219, 251
Rosen, Richard   56, 296
Ross, Jonathan   147, 193, 269
Russell, Alan   44, 351
Ryp, Ellen   327, 351

Sale, Medora   30, 82, 310
Sanders, George   171, 416

AUTHOR INDEX

Sanders, Lawrence 124, 147
Sangster, Jimmy 72, 137
Santini, Rosemarie 315, 351, 352
Satterthwait, Walter 186, 220, 296
Sauter, Eric 296, 368
Sawyer, Corinne Holt 72, 315
Sayers, Dorothy L. 16, 119
Scholefield, A. T. 89, 147
Schopen, Bernard 269
Schorr, Mark 285
Schutz, Benjamin A. 207, 278, 368, 382
Serafin, David 168, 207, 208, 269, 310, 327
Serrian, Michael 171, 310
Shah, Diane K. 193, 228
Shankman, Sarah 168, 229, 368, 431
Shannon, Dell 72, 317, 368, 416
Shaw, Patricia 44, 416
Sherburne, James 147, 164, 165, 175, 176
Sherman, Steve 334
Sherwood, John 44, 45, 77, 78, 234, 389, 416
Shubin, Seymour 89, 285
Shuman, M. K. 25, 310, 317, 375
Silver, Victoria 10
Simmons, John 327, 394
Simon, Roger 193
Simonson, Sheila 76, 327
Simpson, Dorothy 137, 183, 193, 269, 352
Simpson, Pamela 296, 334
Sims, L. V. 183, 247, 352, 423
Singer, Shelley 119, 257, 311

Skipp, John 400
Sklepowick, Edward 45, 297
Skom, Edith 11, 252
Slavo, Gillian 119, 279
Smith, Alison 168, 352
Smith, Charles Merrill 297, 352
Smith, Evelyn 45, 119, 378
Smith, J. C. S. 193, 369
Smith, Janet L. 235, 353
Smith, Joan (British) 14, 159, 215, 252, 297, 353
Smith, Joan (Canadian) 45, 82, 431
Smith, Julie 160, 168, 235, 241, 252, 286, 317, 353, 378
Smith, Kay Nolte 229, 394
Smith, Richard C. 137, 147
Smith, Terrence Lore 131, 320
Smoke, Stephen 327, 353
Smolens, John 297
Snow, C. P. 160
Spencer, Ross 269, 286
Spicer, Michael 100, 311
Spillane, Mickey 208, 353
Sprinkle, Patricia Houck 11, 14, 382, 389, 416
Squire, Elizabeth Daniels 72, 229
Stanley, William 315
Stansberry, Dominic 56, 229
Steed, Neville 31, 138, 353
Stephan, Leslie 431
Stern, Richard Martin 101, 119, 187, 375
Stevens, Christian D. 147, 229
Stevenson, Richard 152, 153, 297, 334

Stewart, Gary 100, 269
Stewart, Mary 423
Stinson, Jim 171, 315, 353
Storey, Alice 229, 334
Story, William L. 89, 317
Strunk, Frank C. 73, 147
Stuart, Anne 119, 208, 369, 425
Sucher, Dorothy 215
Swaim, Don 131, 252
Swigart, Rob 208, 353

Taibo, Paco Ignacio, III 73
Tapply, William G. 31, 56, 73, 119, 124, 138, 183, 197, 208, 241, 242, 378, 382
Taylor, Andrew 138, 181, 220, 235, 252, 297, 375
Taylor, Elizabeth Atwood 11, 95, 416
Taylor, Matt 229, 297
Taylor, Phoebe Atwood 431
Telushkin, Joseph 100, 298
Tey, Josephine 165, 356
Thackery, Ted, Jr. 138, 334
Thayer, Nancy 168, 423
Thomas, Donald 165
Thomas, Ross 106, 298, 311
Thompson, Estelle 50, 376
Thompson, Gene 45, 138, 171, 242, 417
Thompson, Monroe 153, 383
Thomson, June 45, 138, 181, 193, 275, 354
Thoreau, David 56, 168, 208, 423
Togawa, Masako 298, 303, 304, 354
Tone, Teona 119, 126, 165
Tourney, Leonard 165, 194
Townsend, Guy M. 11, 356

Travis, Elizabeth 46, 215, 275, 417
Trench, Jason 73, 160, 298, 369
Tripp, Miles 160, 194, 327, 378, 417
Truman, Margaret 73, 160, 208, 209, 230, 242, 252, 298, 311
Tucker, John Bartholomew 120, 131, 209, 389
Turnbull, Peter 33, 168
Turow, Scott 160
Tyler, Alison 31, 209

Uccillo, Linda 46
Underwood, Michael 95, 160, 354
Upfield, Arthur W. 50, 51, 327, 431
Upton, Robert 56, 172, 215, 383

Valentine, Paul W. 62, 209
Valin, Jonathan 57, 120, 270, 298
Van Ash, Cay 371
Van de Wetering, Janwillem 107, 120, 257, 304, 317, 376, 383, 423
Van Gieson, Judith 58, 242, 320, 334
Vardeman, Robert E. 153, 320
Vidal, Gore 111

Wakefield, Hannah 209, 242, 298, 311
Walker, Walter 161, 194
Wallace, Carol McD. 120, 432
Wallace, Marilyn 311, 354, 423

AUTHOR INDEX

Wallace, Patricia 11, 120
Wallace, Robert 46, 312
Waltch, Lilla M. 11, 298
Ward, Donald 120, 139, 153
Ward, E. C. 335
Warga, Wayne 76, 252
Warmbold, June 230
Washburn, L. J. 354
Watson, Clarissa 46, 73
Watson, Peter 47, 220
Waugh, Carol-Lynn 95, 104
Waugh, Hillary 18, 58
Webster, Noah 120, 124, 197, 335
Weeks, Dolores 120, 194
Weinman, Irving 47, 107, 257, 335, 398
Weiss, Mike 230, 354
Wells, Tobias 298, 432
Wender, Theodora 11, 12, 168
Wentworth, Patricia 73, 139, 181, 209, 220, 270, 299, 417, 418
Werner, Patricia 354, 418
Wesley, Carolyn 139, 432
Westbrook, Robert 172, 312
Westlake, Donald 18, 100, 210, 220, 230, 235, 299
Whalley, Peter 73, 299
Wheat, Carolyn 74, 107, 242, 243
White, Ned 102, 161
White, Terri 147, 220
Whitney, Phyllis A. 47, 78, 89, 235, 275, 299, 320, 327
Wilcox, Collin 47, 90, 100, 139, 184, 369, 418
Wilcox, Stephen F. 139, 299, 354, 376

Wilhelm, Kate 33, 57, 299, 327, 394, 424
Willeford, Charles 161, 369
Williams, David 12, 47, 147, 182, 194, 247, 253, 335
Williams, Philip Carlton 148, 243
Williams, Philip Lee 48
Williamson, Chet 153, 257
Wilson, Gahan 210
Wiltz, Chris 139, 153, 168, 253
Windner, Robert 102, 210
Wingate, Anne 270
Wingfield, R. D. 95, 194, 299
Winslow, Don 270, 312
Witten, Barbara Yager 195, 354
Wolfe, Susan 148, 243
Wolk, Michael 107, 120, 312
Wolzien, Valerie 120, 195
Wood, Ted 82, 315, 376
Woodrell, Daniel 107
Woods, Sara 139, 195, 210, 243, 257, 300, 418, 424
Woods, Sherryl 31, 104, 121, 230, 231
Woolrich, Cornell 184
Wren, M. K. 76, 182, 195, 300
Wright, Eric 12, 33, 83, 95, 182, 195, 198, 398, 399
Wright, L. R. 48, 83, 84, 355
Wuamett, Victor 198, 335

Yaffe, James 12, 275, 335
Yarbro, C. Q. 187, 258
York, Rebecca 258, 327
Yorke, Margaret 90, 184, 195, 270, 317, 327, 355

Zannos, Susan 25, 376
Zelman, Anita 231, 312
Zilinsky, Ursula 275, 394
Zimmelman, Lue 121, 221

Zollinger, Norman 195, 243
Zubro, Mark Richard 100, 139, 153